Command Conflicts in
Grant's Overland Campaign

Command Conflicts in Grant's Overland Campaign

Ambition and Animosity in the Army of the Potomac

DIANE MONROE SMITH

McFarland & Company, Inc., Publishers
Jefferson, North Carolina, and London

LIBRARY OF CONGRESS CATALOGUING-IN-PUBLICATION DATA

Smith, Diane Monroe.
Command conflicts in Grant's Overland Campaign : ambition and animosity in the Army of the Potomac / Diane Monroe Smith.
p. cm.
Includes bibliographical references and index.

ISBN 978-0-7864-6817-1
softcover : acid free paper ∞

1. Overland Campaign, Va., 1864. 2. Grant, Ulysses S. (Ulysses Simpson), 1822–1885 — Military leadership. 3. United States. Army of the Potomac. Corps, 5th (1862–1865) I. Title.
E476.52.S64 2013   973.7'36 — dc23   2012040984

BRITISH LIBRARY CATALOGUING DATA ARE AVAILABLE

© 2013 Diane Monroe Smith. All rights reserved

No part of this book may be reproduced or transmitted in any form or by any means, electronic or mechanical, including photocopying or recording, or by any information storage and retrieval system, without permission in writing from the publisher.

On the cover: "Grant and His Officers," chromolithograph, E. Boell, 1865 (Prints & Photographs Division, Library of Congress)

Manufactured in the United States of America

McFarland & Company, Inc., Publishers
Box 611, Jefferson, North Carolina 28640
www.mcfarlandpub.com

To my mother, Irene Kells Monroe, who,
back at the time of the Civil War Centennial,
when a dollar was a dollar,
gave me $1 to buy a square foot of the Gettysburg Battlefield.

Acknowledgments

First and foremost, I thank my husband, Ned, without whose support and collaboration, this work could never have been completed. I also wish to thank the staff at the Bangor Public Library, especially Bill Cook, Patrick Layne and Karen Alley. I deeply appreciate the services of the library and many other institutions around the country that made it possible for me to access the many valuable works done by historians, past and present. I also wish to thank Doug Richardson at Fort Donelson for his recommendations of resources on the war in the West.

I wish to gratefully acknowledge my indebtedness to the late Edward Steere for his exemplary account of the Wilderness. I was also fortunate enough to find William Matter's book, *If It Takes All Summer*, an admirable work on Spotsylvania. Upon corresponding with Bill, I discovered that he wrote his book on Spotsylvania with Steere's book in mind, hoping to pick up where Steere left off with the Army of the Potomac moving from the Wilderness to the coming battles at Spotsylvania. I highly recommend Matter's work for an enlightening consideration of the 5th Corps' role and its army's actions at Spotsylvania, and the responses and attitudes of the army's commanders in the terrible conflicts of May 7–21, 1864. I am very much in the debt of these, and many other scholars who have amassed such an amazing body of research and writings on Grant, Halleck, Thomas and the war and commanders in the West, on the Army of the Potomac and its commanders, and on the Overland Campaign of 1864.

Table of Contents

Acknowledgments vi
Preface 1

ONE
◆ Grant's Rise to Power 5

TWO
◆ Grant the Hero: Forts Henry and Donelson — and Then
   There Was Shiloh 19

THREE
◆ It Takes Buell and Bragg to Make Grant Look Good 54

FOUR
◆ The Army of the Potomac Carries Old Baggage into
   the Wilderness 90

FIVE
◆ The Wilderness 103

SIX
◆ On to Spotsylvania 117

SEVEN
◆ Spotsylvania: Laurel Hill, Again and Again 128

EIGHT
◆ The 5th Corps at the North Anna and the Totopotomoy 154

NINE
◆ Cold Harbor — Another Tragic Muddle 167

TEN
◆ Petersburg 192

Appendix: Federal Overland Campaign Commanders After the War 211
Chapter Notes 225
Bibliography 241
Index 245

Preface

EVERYONE WANTED A PIECE OF Ulysses S. Grant in 1864. Politicians, such as Sen. Elihu Washburne and Assistant Secretary of War Charles Dana, who had both nurtured Grant's military career, used their considerable political influence to assure Grant's advance up the military ladder. Even Abraham Lincoln, facing reelection in the fall of the year, was depending on Grant for victories as the spring campaign of the ongoing Civil War commenced. Favorable news from the Federal fronts could only improve Lincoln's sagging political standing, and all that without the risk of a military hero who would want his office. One of the prerequisites of Grant's fitness for the newly created rank of lieutenant general was his declaration that he had no political ambitions.[1]

In the meantime, Grant's military cronies — "Grant's Men," as they were known — could count on their commander and friend to carry them along with him to the dizzying heights they hoped he would attain. Grant could be counted on to overlook many of these friends' faults, and he often went out of his way to push forward their careers. His faith in them was explicit. What they told him, he believed. It was a very rocky road for anyone who contradicted or got in the way of this ambitious, and often unscrupulous, group of western officers.

Much has been written over the years about U.S. Grant, and the ever-swinging pendulum of public opinion seemingly veered from panegyric to condemnation and back again. There are, of course, more moderate considerations of Lieutenant General Grant, that neither fiercely defend nor savagely prosecute the man who commanded all the Union armies in the field during the eventful months from the spring of 1864 to the spring of 1865. It would, after all, prove to be the last year of the American Civil War, and during that year, Grant undeniably led the Federal armies that defeated the Confederacy and restored the Union. But he also was, undeniably, the guiding hand behind the Army of the Potomac's Overland Campaign in 1864, with its bloody battles and dubious "victories," for which Grant's defenders would place any questions of fault or failure on someone else — anyone else — in the Army of the Potomac.

A close consideration of the Overland Campaign and those last months of the war reveals much. In particular, a look at Grant's handling, though one might say mishandling, of the Army of the Potomac's 5th Corps is a revelation of the foibles and flaws of U.S. Grant. They are faults that, as they are seen again and again, become glaringly and unavoidably apparent. It is also essential to consider the many alliances or cabals that developed among "Grant's Men" during his rise to the pinnacle of the American military system. Just how Grant got to be lieutenant general is a feat that baffled even some of his best friends and staunchest supporters.

Grant's successes and failures in his early military and civilian careers have been minutely examined over the years. While some insist he showed the early promise of a great leader, it smacks of really having to try way too hard when Grant's admirers have to labor so mightily to make a brave but intemperate quartermaster, who had a way with horses, into a great leader of men and a military genius. One thing is, however, particularly relevant. By the time of the American Civil War, U.S. Grant had failed at everything he had undertaken. Having failed in the military, in farming and in various businesses, he was, one could easily say, a desperate man. The one bright spot in his life, his marriage to Julia Dent Grant and their children, only placed greater pressure on him, as a husband and father who seemed incapable of financially supporting his family. Grant's story is a rather twisted version of the American success story. In order for him to begin his meteoric rise to the command of the United States Army, and ultimately to become the nation's chief executive, one must look to his friends, or at least those who professed to be his friends, and his other ambitious supporters.

Many would concede that Grant was an unlikely candidate for greatness. Short of stature and careless in dress, Grant entered the U.S. Military Academy against his will, coerced by his ambitious father to take advantage of a free education. Grant suffered from both amusia (tone deafness that made all music unrecognizable) and arrhythmia (he was unable to march in time), inconvenient handicaps for a soldier. It is said that Grant had an odd gait, and walked as if he were falling forward. But regardless of these drawbacks, Ulysses S. Grant, trailed by a cloud of cronies, sycophants, and ardent advocates, would march in his own eccentric way through the war, "falling forward" into the leading role of the country's military hero and savior.

It is an odd assortment of men who rose to greatness with U.S. Grant. Most of them were westerners, but not all. Some of the others who ascended to power with Grant were like him, in that they, too, had "failed" in life, either in their own eyes or by everyone else's estimation. William T. Sherman might be

Brigadier General U.S. Grant, October 1861 (*Review of Reviews*).

offered as a case in point. He, like Grant, had failed in life, and had, like Grant, married "above himself" to a woman who he could not afford to keep in the style to which she was accustomed. "Grant's Men" were, for the most part, West Point graduates, not volunteers, and those who would rise to the top of Grant's military tree were, for the most part, *not* engineers. It seems that West Point's engineers, the elite of that institution's graduates, though they might find themselves temporarily in favor, usually were not Grant's cup of tea.[2] Sherman's attitude toward the elite members of the military profession — the engineers — is perhaps typical. After the war, Sherman observed that the engineers certainly were good scholars, "but the difficulty is they are put into these favored corps and begin directly to look down upon the rest of the army. They themselves fail to acquire that practical experience with soldiers which every officer ought to have." It is not difficult to think of a number of engineer officers — Gouverneur Warren, Washington Roebling or Robert E. Lee, for that matter — who, far from looking down on their armies, thought rather highly of their men, and the case could certainly be made that they had more experience and success in the field than Sherman did. Warren and Roebling and Lee also managed to avoid that dread of innovation, avoidance of initiative, or the tendency for excessive caution that handicapped some West Point–trained engineer generals, such as George McClellan and Henry Halleck. Then there are the intangibles to consider. Is it a coincidence that the only two major generals in the Federal army who were shorter than U.S. Grant — Philip Sheridan and John Logan — became his great favorites?[3]

The lives of all of the men who will be encountered in this book have been looked at in detail by many authors and students of the war over the years. Some of the alliances are well known, and some are not. Knowing who was actively promoting whom, or who was depending upon others to further their own careers or destroy a rival's reputation, reveals much. Let's bring the major players in this piece on stage as they appeared in Grant's meteoric rise to fame.

ONE

Grant's Rise to Power

On April 16, 1861, two days after the Rebels fired on Fort Sumter, the citizens of Galena, Illinois, held a mass meeting to discuss what action should be taken. While many citizens in the North were clamoring for a swift military response, just how that would be accomplished remained to be seen. Certainly no eyes at the meeting in Galena turned to the taciturn 39-year-old clerk in his family's tannery business, U.S. Grant, for although he was a graduate of West Point's class of 1843, he was a failed soldier, a former captain in the U.S. Army who had been forced to resign. But what sets the meeting in Galena apart from the thousands that took place all across the United States, is the attendance of three men, including young Grant, who would play such prominent parts in the upcoming strife. One was no surprise. Congressman Elihu Washburne, representing Galena's district in Washington, was part of a dynasty of overachievers from Maine, who over the years would include several congressmen, a senator, governors, a Civil War general, a secretary of state, foreign ministers and the founder of the Gold Medal Flour Company.[1] But another man who attended could be said to have been an unlikely candidate for greatness. Democrat John Rawlins's education was distinguished by its brevity, having spent 24 months in country schools and a year at a seminary. He read law with a Galena attorney and became a partner in a law firm. Rawlins's law career was successful, his intelligence and determination apparently overcoming what he lacked in formal education. Before the end of the decade, Washburne would be secretary of state to President U.S. Grant, the former lieutenant general of the U.S. Army, with Rawlins serving as his secretary of war. It is the sort of script that even the most bold and whimsical Hollywood writer would hesitate to propose.

Despite his military background, Grant, who was more than anxious to reenter the military, found it difficult to find a command. Initially without political influence, and perhaps preceded by his damaged military reputation, he finally was assigned by Illinois governor Richard Yates to command of the Illinois 7th District Regiment. The 7th was a regiment that nobody else wanted. A band of 1,250 undisciplined, untrained militiamen, who might be better described as an armed mob than a regiment, the unit had just lost their colonel, a drunken dreamer under whose command the regiment had earned the name "Governor Yates' Hellions." One of Grant's first real "victories" was turning the 7th into the semblance of a military unit, albeit a volunteer regiment. But to add to the tensions of trying to bring discipline to this rowdy regiment, Grant also had to deal with the problem that the men of the 7th, who had been mustered into the regiment as militiamen who would serve for a month, had also agreed to enter Federal service for three years if needed. Fewer than half of his men had so far agreed to keep that part of the bargain. Grant received help in promoting the men's reenlistment from two influential Illinois politicians whose fates would be joined to Grant's own, John Logan and John McClernand.[2] Many had expected prosecession Democrat John Logan to cast his lot with the Confederacy, and there would be some — Sherman and George Thomas — who never quite trusted Logan's conversion from "Negrophobe to Negrophile." Where McClernand had labored for a political compromise, Logan had openly supported the South's right to secede. But it was the persuasive exhortations of both Logan and McClernand that saw most of the 7th District Regiment sign up for three years' service in their newly created 21st Illinois with Grant as their commander. Both Logan and McClernand would serve under Grant in the war, with varying success. In August of 1861, thanks to the efforts of Elihu Washburne, Grant received one of the four brigadierships that Illinois congressmen were given to parcel out.[3] And Washburne was already working on Grant's advance to major general.[4] Washburne, who represented northwestern Illinois in the U.S. House of Representative from 1853 to 1869, was an early supporter of Lincoln. Washburne wrote Lincoln's 1860 presidential campaign biography, and was one of the few Republicans, because of threats made against Lincoln, who had dared to meet the president-elect when his train arrived in Washington.[5] It was said that Lincoln once commented to Washburne, "About all I know of Grant I have got from you."[6]

In mid–August of 1861, three other major players in the war in the West came upon the stage. Gen. Robert Anderson, who gained everlasting fame with his defense of Fort Sumter, had been misjudged by Buchanan's pro–Southern secretary of war, John B. Floyd, who had believed that the Kentucky-born Anderson would also be Southern in his sympathies. Before the first shots of the war were fired, Floyd sent Don Carlos Buell, then a major, to tell Anderson verbally that he must expect no reinforcement. Yet he wanted Anderson to defend the forts in Charleston to the last extremity. But Floyd, meanwhile, told Anderson in a letter that if he were attacked by a superior force, he need not sacrifice himself and his men. As historian John Waugh comments, having Floyd as the U.S. secretary of war was like having the wolf guarding the sheep.[7]

In May of 1861, Anderson took command of the Department of Kentucky. After Confederate generals Leonidas Polk and Gideon Pillow violated Kentucky's neutrality, Anderson was given orders to occupy that state, and he promptly set up headquarters in Louisville. Anderson also had authority to appoint four brigadier generals to serve under him in Kentucky. Three of the officers he chose for promotion were William T. Sherman, Don Carlos Buell, and George Thomas.[8] At this time, the future triumvirate of Grant, Sherman and Sheridan ruling the country's military seemed not only unlikely, but unimaginable.

To understand why Lincoln developed such an affection for and confidence in U.S. Grant, perhaps it is essential to consider the president's relationship with George McClellan, "Little Mac." McClellan was a great organizer, and when he assumed command following the debacle at Bull Run, McClellan accomplished wonders for the demoralized army that would come to be known as the Army of the Potomac. But overcome by excessive caution, McClellan, aided by misinformation from his Pinkerton operatives, wildly overestimated the enemy, and consequently overestimated the number of troops he must have before attempting to confront the Rebels. Also, anxious to get rid of any restraint from the aged commander of the armies, Gen. Winfield Scott, McClellan adopted an adversarial stance with Scott, the president and his Cabinet in Washington. When elevated to command of the country's army, McClellan avoided and snubbed the president. And when it became evident that McClellan was not going to fight, he blamed everyone but himself. When McClellan came down with typhoid at Christmas, the more radical members of Congress added to the tension by initiating a joint committee to act as watchdog on the conduct of the war. As he recovered, McClellan refused to divulge if he had plans for an advance, or what they might be. Perhaps the only ones more puzzled by McClellan's inactivity than Lincoln, were his Rebel opponents. At the end of January, an exasperated Lincoln issued General Order No. 1, calling for movement of all Union land and naval forces on February 22nd. It resulted in McClellan, on February 3rd, reluctantly coming forth with a plan, revealing it to Lincoln and his newly appointed secretary of war, Edwin M. Stanton. When the wounded Confederate general Joseph Johnston was removed from command and replaced by Robert E. Lee, McClellan described Lee as "too cautious & weak under grave responsibility," and "wanting in moral firmness when pressed by heavy responsibility & is likely to be timid & irresolute in action."[9] As the "timid and irresolute" Lee began to force McClellan back away from Richmond, McClellan had no doubt that it was Washington's lack of support that was responsible for Lee's success. At one point, when the Committee on the Conduct of the War suggested that Lincoln replace McClellan, Lincoln wanted to know with whom? When a committee member replied, "Anybody," Lincoln's quick response, which addressed the crux of the problem, was "*Anybody* will do for you, but not for me. I must have *somebody*."[10]

When Halleck was brought to Washington from the West in July to be general in chief of the armies, it had to have been a crushing blow for George McClellan. It would displace McClellan from overall command, relegating him to mere command of the Army of the Potomac. And if there was one man McClellan disdained more than Halleck, it was John Pope (USMA, 1842), so it could only have been a painful obligation when he was ordered to remove his army from the Peninsula and send them to reinforce Pope's attempt to advance on the Rapidan in Virginia. But when Pope's movement ended in a demoralizing defeat dealt by the Rebels at the Second Battle of Bull Run, McClellan, the master at reorganizing and reenergizing defeated armies, was called upon again. While the subsequent battle, Antietam, wasn't strictly another defeat for the Unionists, it was McClellan's caution that prevented it from being a turning point in the war. In the weeks after Antietam, Lincoln urged McClellan to go after the enemy, but it was not to be. In September, Lincoln relieved McClellan from command of the army and appointed Gen. Ambrose Burnside. Fires and frying pans come to mind. Burnside excelled in spending huge numbers of lives nonsensically, such as at Burnside Bridge at Antietam, and at Fredericksburg, where he commanded the army in December of 1862. But perhaps Joseph Hooker, Lincoln's next commander for the Army of the Potomac, was the greatest disappointment. A clever, aggressive and confident commander, Hooker at a vital moment came undone. The supposed combination of being stunned by a nearby explosion and an apparent loss of nerve left Hooker unable to do what it took to take advantage of the real advantages he had gained against the enemy at Chancellorsville.[11]

The second member of the future triumvirate, Sherman, in June of 1861 had accepted command of the reconstituted 13th U.S. Infantry.[12] After Bull Run, where Sherman committed his four regiments piecemeal in the futile fight for Henry's Hill, he incurred 600 killed, wounded and missing. But his performance, viewed positively by his superiors, was rewarded with a general's star that August.[13] But Sherman had not, apparently, endeared himself to his men, having become separated from his brigade in the melee after the battle. But more importantly, Sherman's disdain for volunteer soldiers clearly dates from this, his first combat command, and his contempt was seemingly observed by many of his volunteers. Sherman, while vociferous in his criticism of his troops, demonstrated his inability to maintain control of citizen soldiers, a trait that would have interesting repercussions in Sherman's future campaigns.[14] Another startling familial habit is displayed in John Sherman's memoirs, in which he declares that the outcome of Bull Run in 1861, his brother's first battle, was considered by both sides to be a draw! Such rose-colored glasses prompt one to question other observations of the Sherman brothers.[15] However, there was an interesting difference of opinion between William T. and John Sherman regarding where in August of 1861 West Point–trained officers could or should best serve. While William believed that the regular army and its officers held the country's fate in its hands, John believed that regular officers should be doled out to the new volunteer regiments, who could benefit from their education and experience. John engaged in a loud and angry argument with then commander of the army, General Scott, over the best possible use of regular officers, with John insisting they should be commanding the volunteers. John Sherman seemingly takes credit for the replacement of Scott in his statement regarding the old warrior, "I never ceased to respect the old general for the great service he had rendered his country; but his day was past." Whatever role Sherman played, he was ably aided by the ambitious Gen. George McClellan, who actively worked for Scott's retirement.[16]

In August of 1861, Sherman came to Kentucky as brigadier general of volunteers to serve as second in command to Gen. Robert Anderson. General Sherman, based in Louisville, was assigned by Anderson to protect the Louisville and Nashville Railroad, an important Federal supply line. Sherman was already exhibiting signs of stress and nervousness, when his commander, General Anderson, having asked to be relieved, named Sherman as his successor. While responsibility for part of Kentucky had made Sherman anxious, responsibility for the whole state put Sherman over the edge. Among those under Sherman's command was Gen. George Thomas, a Virginian and West Point graduate, class of 1840. A one-time roommate of Sherman, Thomas had cast his lot with the Union and, unaided by political allies in Washington, would have to defend his loyalty to the Union again and again when unscrupulous competitors for command questioned Thomas's dependability. And while Sherman would later claim in his memoirs to have been responsible for vouching to Lincoln for Thomas's loyalty, it was, in fact, Gen. Robert Anderson who stood up for Thomas, reassuring the president of Thomas's good faith.[17] Ironically, while Thomas never hesitated to throw himself behind the Union cause in the first days of the war, Sherman, serving as superintendent of a Louisiana military academy, though he notified his employers that he would resign if Louisiana seceded, was in no hurry to offer his services to his country. After the firing on Sumter, his brother John had urged Sherman to come quickly to Washington to find himself an advantageous assignment.

John Sherman, who became one of Ohio's senators, embarrassed his more conservative brother with his abolitionist stance, but John nonetheless brought power and influence to bear on General Sherman's career. Before William T. Sherman returned to the army, John Sherman wrote to William that there was interest in having him come to the War Department, where Secretary Chase suggested that William T. Sherman could be "virtually Secretary of War, and could easily step into any military position that offers."[18] But William Sherman responded that he would bide his time, for it was his belief that those who held top commands at the beginning of the war would pay for their green troops' mistakes. Sherman would

General George Thomas (Library of Congress).

wait for the opportunities that would present themselves when the earliest commanders were swept away to their ultimate ignominious fates. After his resignation and departure from Louisiana, Sherman, in early April 1861, stating that he would be unable to support his family on a military salary, took on the presidency of a railroad in St. Louis.[19]

Ironically, General Thomas took up the struggle with those same challenges that Sherman had initially avoided when Thomas was assigned to a training camp outside Lexington, Kentucky. Thomas was entrusted with turning raw recruits into soldiers. Dealing with a dearth of weapons and supplies, Thomas ended up personally signing loans to suppliers who refused to extend credit to the government. Thomas succeeded in what Sherman refused to try, turning western volunteers into the Army of the Cumberland, the army that, under Thomas, never experienced defeat.[20]

But to return to Sherman's command in Kentucky in 1861, Sherman became Thomas's commander, and as Thomas was approaching the Cumberland Gap, the key to eastern Tennessee, he was ordered by an apprehensive Sherman to withdraw. The frustrated Thomas replied that he would withdraw according to Sherman's orders, though he assured Sherman that the Rebel force that Sherman believed stood between him and Thomas did not exist. This, along with Sherman's eccentric behavior, resulted in one of Sherman's requests to be relieved of command being granted. He was replaced by Gen. Don Carlos Buell, one of McClellan's protégés, taking Sherman's place in, what historian Kenneth Noe calls, the Kentucky "hot seat." Buell's newly created Department of the Ohio covered Kentucky and Tennessee east of the Cumberland River, as well as Indiana, Michigan and Ohio.[21] Sherman was ordered to report to Gen. Henry Halleck in St. Louis, and here another major player in Grant's career came upon the scene. On November 19, 1861,

General Halleck was sent to replace Gen. John Frémont as commander of the Department of the Missouri. It wasn't a particularly popular development, and even a man like the ever-dutiful Andrew Foote, commander of the Union river fleet, was tempted to apply for a command elsewhere.[22] Under instructions from Gen. George B. McClellan, who replaced Gen. Winfield Scott as commander in chief of the Army that November, Halleck reversed Frémont's controversial attempts at slave emancipation. While Washington was still concerned that antislavery actions would alienate Border State fence-sitters, Halleck implemented McClellan's directions to prohibit fugitive slaves from Union-held territory, even returning slaves to owners sympathetic to the Union.[23]

It was a lucky thing for Sherman that Halleck took command when he did. As a Halleck biography points out, Sherman was one of Halleck's only real friends, and Halleck looked out for his young protégé, Sherman. General Buell, who had succeeded the increasingly unstable William T. Sherman on November 15, had become commander of the Department of the Ohio, while Halleck sent Sherman off on an inspection tour of nearby garrisons. But Sherman's continued behavior of seeing danger where little existed forced Halleck to recall him to St. Louis and insist that he take a 20-day leave. Halleck reported to McClellan that "Gen. S.[herman] physical and mental system is so completely broken by labor and care as to render him for the present completely unfit for duty." Newspaper reports that Sherman was insane did little to aid his recovery. It was a far cry from the fame Sherman so longed for. As Sherman wrestled with his own demons, the future team of Sherman and Grant had to wait for better days.[24]

Meanwhile, Rep. Elihu Washburne, after visiting Grant at his headquarters in Cairo, returned to Washington to lobby the government for better supplies, transportation and clothing for the favored general. Yet Grant was not without his detractors, several of whom spread stories that Grant was again suffering from intemperance, rumors that reached Washburne's, and even Lincoln's, ears. When questioned, Grant's principal staff officer, Captain John Rawlins, assured Washburne there was no basis for the accusations, and he assured the congressman that, though he loved Grant like a father, if Grant should become intemperate, Rawlins would resign and leave Grant's staff. Rawlins also suggested that Washburne consult Navy Flag-Officer Andrew Foote regarding Grant's behavior and character. An avowed teetotaler and an abolitionist, Foote was instrumental in discontinuing the grog ration in the U.S. Navy.[25]

Elihu Washburne (Library of Congress).

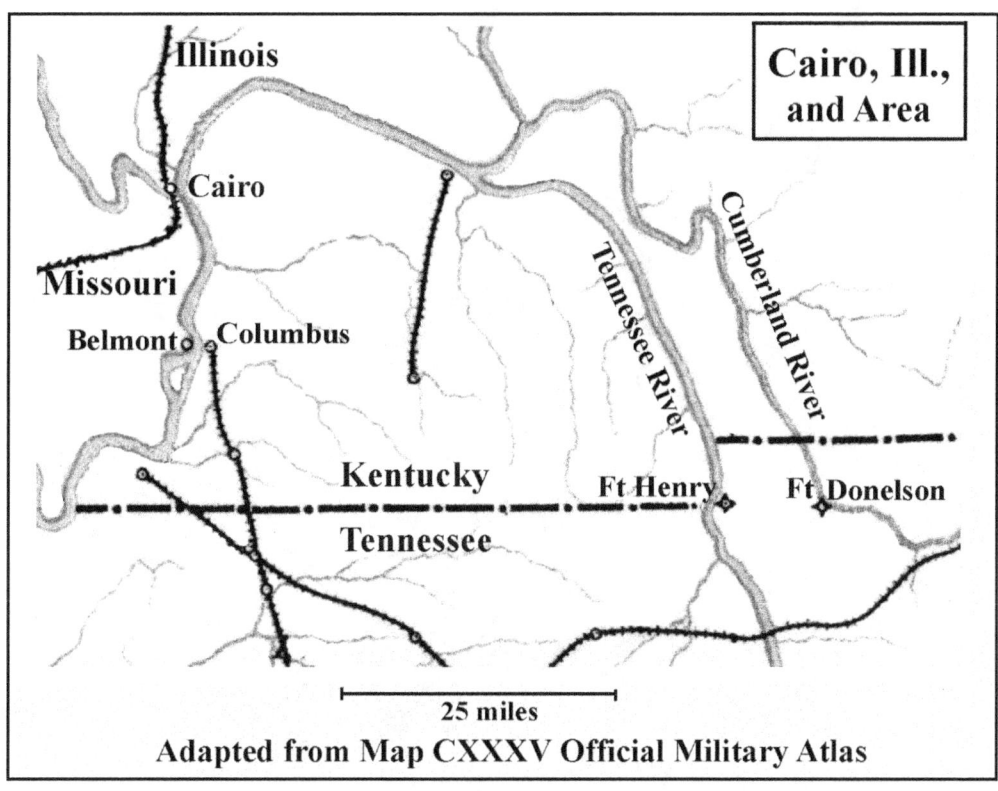

Cairo, Illinois, and area. Adapted from Map CXXV, *Official Atlas* (Ned Smith).

Many consider the real debut of Grant's Civil War military service to be the Battle of Belmont in November of 1861. Well after the war, the Spanish Republic was having a presentation sword prepared as a gift to the former lieutenant general and president of the United States when he visited them during his world tour in 1877. They requested a list of Grant's victorious battles, and he listed Belmont as his first victory.[26] However, a brief look at the fight at Belmont, with Grant's behavior before, during and after the battle, is revealing, and perhaps shows a pattern of things to come. After all, in later years Grant would insist on listing Belmont as his first victory, and even its culmination in hasty retreat did not seem to affect Grant's perception of the action, while criticism of his performance, at the time and afterward, only seemed to make him more defensive and increase the ruddy hue of his rose-colored glasses.

Grant's first demonstration of his aggressive nature began in November of 1861, while Grant had his base in Cairo, Illinois. After the Confederates seized Columbus, Kentucky, a frustrated Grant was still casting longing looks at the "Gibraltar of the West," though he accepted the impossibility of investing the town that no Federal boat could pass.[27] Columbus had along its banks 140 guns, including 10-inch Columbiads, 11-inch howitzers and one 128-pounder Whitworth rifled gun. There were also floating mines in the river and a great chain designed to prevent boats from passing.[28] But Grant wanted to test the mettle of his green troops on Belmont, Missouri, a cluster of three houses squatting on a mud flat with a boat landing just across the river from, and under the guns of, Columbus.

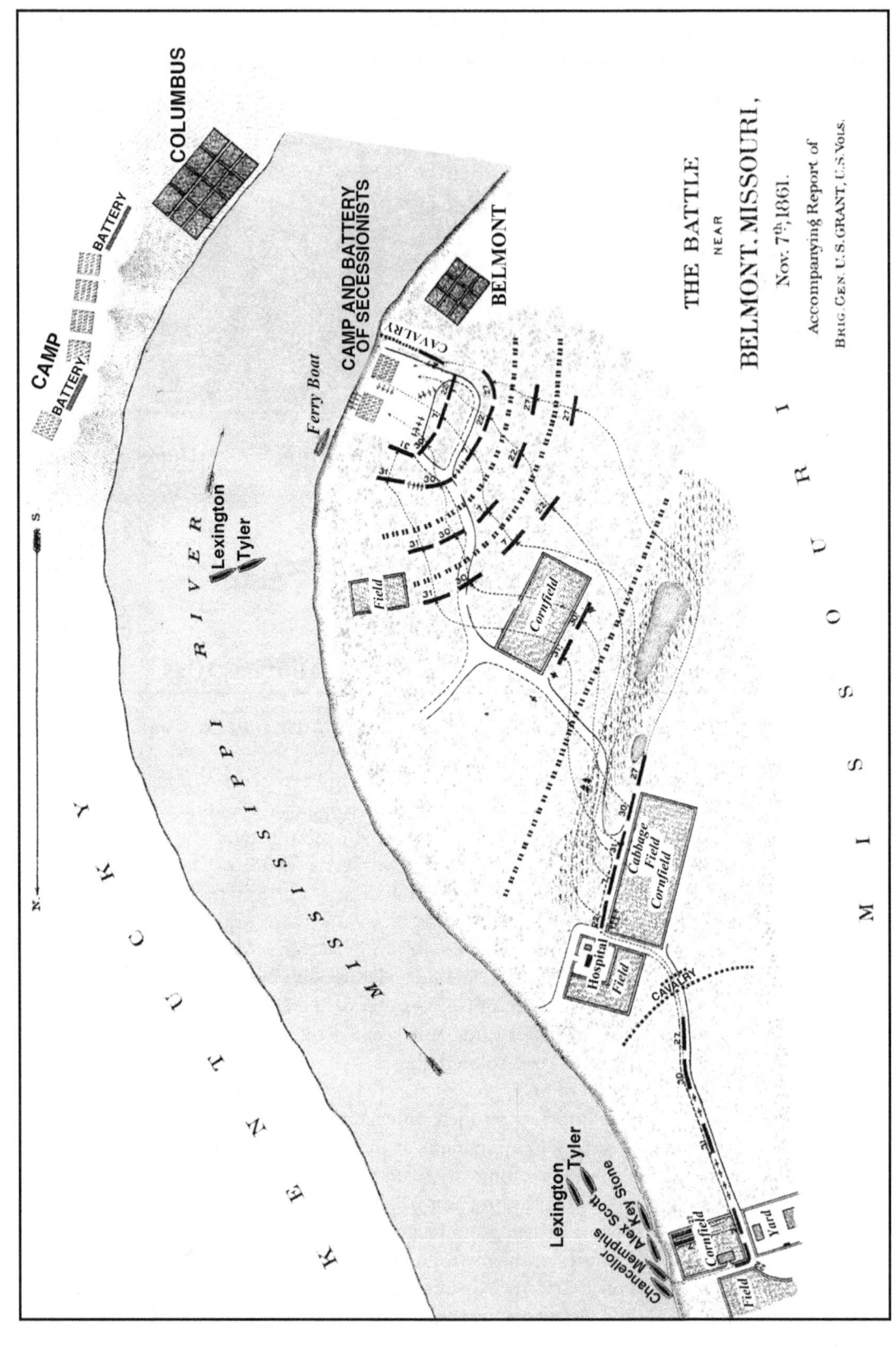

As Belmont historian Nathaniel Hughes observes, it was a town that wasn't a town and undoubtedly attracted so much attention only because of its proximity to Columbus. The capture of Columbus by Rebel general Leonidas Polk, in September of 1861, violated Kentucky's neutrality. As soon as Polk had taken the first hostile step into Kentucky, Grant, who had been taking his own steps toward seizing Columbus, was able with pleasure to point the finger at the Confederates for violating Kentucky's neutrality before he did.[29] Erroneous reports that the Rebels were preparing to move troops prompted Gen. John Frémont, Grant's soon-to-be-relieved commander, to order Grant to plan a demonstration on Belmont. Frémont, in political hot water with Washington, was relieved from command on November 2, and Gen. Henry W. Halleck was sent west to replace Frémont as commander of the Department of the Missouri on November 19, 1861. This period of transition between Frémont and Halleck gave Grant his chance to act. Armed with Frémont's order to make a demonstration to the south, Grant continued to plan and put into action what was supposed to have been merely a feint against the Confederates. But Grant would use an alleged Rebel threat to one of his columns as an opportunity to turn his demonstration into an assault.[30] From Gen. Charles F. Smith (USMA, 1825), whom Grant had known as the commandant of cadets at West Point and who was commander at nearby Paducah, Grant requested a demonstration that would convince the Rebels that Columbus was being attacked. With the cooperation of several other commanders that first week of November 1861, Grant had, in all, some 15,000 Federals on the move simultaneously, being watched by the nervous Rebels.[31]

To approach Belmont, where the three states meet on the shores of the Missouri River, Grant brought just over 3,000 soldiers down the river on four transports, guarded by two gunboats. The expedition spent the first night aboard the boats tied up on the Kentucky shore, eight miles below Cairo and 11 miles above Columbus. Spirits were high among the members of the expedition, and Grant acknowledged that he could hardly take these men back to Cairo without giving them a chance to fight. And who knew what the commander who replaced Frémont would do; such chances for action did not grow on trees.[32] The next day, Grant had his two gunboats and his transports, their decks crowded with men, steam down to the lowest point on the Missouri side of the river that would accommodate their landing, out of sight, if not out of range of the Rebel batteries. As Grant's expedition debarked, the gunboats under the command of Commodore Henry Walke sailed off to do what they could to occupy the attention of the enemy at Columbus. But when the shells from the guns at Columbus threatened Grant's transports far more than the protecting gunboats, Walke had the transports moved upstream.[33]

After leaving five companies to guard their transports, four-and-a-half Federal regiments, two companies of cavalry, and a six-gun battery under John McClernand's command invested Belmont, which had been occupied by six Confederate regiments sent over from Columbus to augment the small force at Belmont and help meet this Unionist incursion. The Rebels' reinforcements were under the command of Brigadier General Gideon

Opposite: The map accompanying General Grant's report on Belmont shows, in the lower left, the landing of his troops, their progress toward the "secessionists" camp, the series of enclosing arcs as the Union troops advanced, and the positions of the Union gunboats *Lexington* and *Tyler*. The Confederate "camp" on the opposite bank held powerful artillery batteries (*Official Records*, Ser. 1, Vol. III, 267).

Pillow, a soldier Grant held in contempt and would encounter again in the coming months.[34] Meanwhile, while McClernand advanced, Grant remained behind to position his reserve force and a battery to protect the transports. It is puzzling why Grant sent an inexperienced commander into battle against an unknown enemy, while he fiddled with rear elements. Grant would explain it away by saying that he had "no staff officer that could be trusted" with the responsibility of placing the expedition's battery and guarding the transports. McClernand and Grant did, however, confer before McClernand deployed his men for an attack, and Grant, at last, took command.[35]

After a determined struggle between the two inexperienced forces, the Rebels ran out of ammunition, and after their stubborn defense, they fell back in some disorder to their camp. Columbus attempted to shell the approaching Unionists, but with little effect. The Federals eventually drove the Rebels out, taking possession of the camp as the enemy sought shelter on the banks of the river. Though the attack upon the hapless Rebels seemingly had strengthened, it was luck rather than coordination that brought various elements of Grant's attack together. For as the Rebels sought shelter in their camp, which Belmont historian Hughes describes as more of a self-made trap than a sanctuary, the fight turned into something like a mob chasing a mob.[36] But while the Federals looted and burned the camp, Leonidas Polk, commander at Columbus, was bringing 2,500 to 3,000 Confederates across the river to a point below Belmont to cut off Grant and his men from their transports. While John McClernand made a speech to his soldiers regarding their great victory, and troops happily hunted through the Confederate camp for battlefield souvenirs, the Federals were interrupted when the expedition's surgeon drew Grant's attention to the two transports loaded with Rebels heading in their direction, a threat the Union gunboats seemed unable to deter. That, in combination with Federal officers putting the camp to the torch to stop the looting, and Columbus's biggest gun beginning to lob its enormous shells into the middle of the camp's parade ground, made it apparent that it was time to leave.[37]

Though at first Grant refused to believe that the increased traffic on the river included Rebel transports, once convinced, Grant calmly attempted to get his men to turn captured Rebel guns on their approaching enemy. But panic reigned among his troops, and they needed little encouragement to adopt an alternative, to get to and reboard their transports. As the recently arrived Rebels made an assault on both flanks of Grant's hastily formed column, the Federals had to fight their way out of a tight spot, with Grant, Logan and McClernand's steadiness going a long way to bring their faltering troops to the river. Despite Grant's assertions that there was no running away, his force's passage to the river became a rout. And once the men were boarded, still under fire from the Rebels, the flotilla lost no time in pulling away. They had unintentionally left a party behind that had not made it back to the landing, and after the departure of the Unionists, McClernand not only sent one of the gunboats back to collect the remnant, but also insisted that he himself be put ashore to go and personally search for the missing men. They were found, rescued, and then caught up with Grant's flotilla, which was heading upstream to Cairo. Though this sort of initiative might have been appreciated by some commanders, the speed with which McClernand had notified Washington about his role at Belmont, and the congratulations that Lincoln sent to McClernand, but not Grant, had rather the opposite effect. If Grant was catching Lincoln's eye as one of his fighting generals, Lincoln was not ready to acknowledge it.[38]

In the end, the Rebels and Grant lost an equal number of combatants, around 600 each, with the Federals leaving 125 of their wounded behind. While some wounded were exchanged after the battle, for some reason several of the Federals taken prisoner by the Rebels at Belmont were never exchanged. They were first kept in the makeshift prison of an old slave pen in Memphis, and eventually ended up at Andersonville, from which the survivors would not come home until April of 1865.[39] All in all, it is baffling that Grant shouted to a newspaperman, who came out in a boat at Cairo to greet the returning Federal flotilla, that he and his troops had had a great victory.[40] And in a letter to his father within days of the fight, Grant insisted that there had been "no hasty retreating or running away."[41] While it obviously mattered to Grant that his father think well of him, in the weeks ahead Grant would have to curb his father's efforts to cash in on his son's name by seeking government contracts for harnesses. Grant, when he found out, put a quick end to his father's plans.[42] In addition to contemporary criticism that questioned the purpose of his expedition, the sorry ending at Belmont followed Grant; even years later during his presidential campaign in 1868, his critics resurrected questions about the battle.[43] And yet Grant apparently cherished and defended his positive memory of Belmont for the rest of his life. He defensively dedicated more than six pages of description and consideration to Belmont in his memoirs, more than such a seemingly minor and inglorious engagement demanded.[44]

Though Grant considered Belmont a victory, many journalists and observers did not, and criticism rained down on him. As one journalist pundit commented about Belmont, jokingly paraphrasing Perry's victory message, "We have met the enemy, and he is not ours."[45] But did Grant at least learn any lessons from Belmont? Perhaps he learned how effective cooperation between land and naval forces could be, for he would take great advantage of the Federal navy in the future. From the navy's point of view, the commander of the vessels that accompanied Grant's Belmont venture was quite sure that disaster would have befallen the Federals if it hadn't been for the navy's presence.[46] Perhaps Grant also learned that you could manufacture a reason for having an unnecessary or risky battle, and get away with it. Belmont historian Nathaniel Hughes gives careful attention to Grant's impatience prior to his expedition to make an attempt on Belmont and/or Columbus, and Hughes also considers Grant's lack of information about the enemy he was going to attack. Then there's a complete lack of evidence regarding the dispatch Grant claimed to have received on the first night of his Belmont expedition relating to Richard Oglesby being in trouble and needing rescue. Grant historian extraordinaire John Simon points out that no archival evidence exists that Grant ever received such a dispatch. It seems that a number of Grant scholars have considered that Grant, impatient for a fight as well as a way to make a name for himself, not only made Belmont happen, but then insisted on describing it as the victory he so desired.[47] Or there is Grant's premise that the enemy was always just as worried about what he might do as he was worried about them, which, as historian Brooks Simpson points out, led Grant to concentrate on his own plan to the point of sometimes neglecting to consider just what his enemy might do.[48] It led to some bad surprises in the next months.

Many Federals seemed to recognize the strategic importance of the Confederates' Forts Henry and Donelson, the list of claimants includes Generals Grant, McClernand, Buell, Sherman, Flag Officer Foote, C.F. Smith and Halleck among others. However,

Halleck told McClellan that he would need 60,000 men to do it, and McClellan said it shouldn't be done at all at that time.[49] But as described in the next chapter, the taking of Henry and Donelson would force Columbus to surrender, and later render Memphis and Nashville vulnerable. Oddly, the Rebel commander charged with defending the Confederate Western Department, Gen. Albert Sidney Johnston, was unable to convince Jefferson Davis that the situation in the West, with growing Federal troop strength threatening Johnston's scattered force, was a desperate one that demanded immediate action.[50] But Davis refused to allow Johnston to pull his scattered forces together, for he was convinced that the Confederacy's ability to hold on to all its territory against the Union threat would encourage European recognition of the Richmond government. Davis chose to ignore Johnston's warnings. Historian Benjamin F. Cooling described the consequences of the Rebel indifference: "Henry-Donelson was a brilliantly missed opportunity for the Confederacy to smash an uncertain Union strategic thrust by an untested Yankee general." Cooling's description is hardly a glowing endorsement of the movements Grant would make on Forts Henry and Donelson, nor the execution of his plans, but an indictment of the Rebel leadership that allowed him to do it. While Cooling admires Grant, he gives honest testimony to the mistakes that were made by the enemy Grant faced.[51]

While Johnston held overall command of the Rebel forces in the West, there was no such arrangement for the Federals. The order that gave Halleck command of the Department of the Missouri also created the Department of the Ohio commanded by Buell, making Halleck and Buell equal in rank and expected to cooperate with one another. Both ambitious, neither Halleck nor Buell were willing to cooperate with the other, and both strove to impress McClellan that their plans for action against the strongholds were best. The lack of an overall commander in the West seemingly did not encourage action against the Confederates despite the fact that the Rebels were trying to cope with the impossible situation handed to them by their government — that of protecting a huge area with a defensive line that had both of its flanks in the air. When Buell's Army of the Ohio finally made the first advance, Grant fumed at making feints to support the movement of a column led by Gen. George Thomas that Buell had sent into Kentucky.[52]

During the struggle for dominance in Kentucky, Thomas, commander of Buell's 1st Division, advanced in the snow and sleet of January of 1862, determined to drive the Rebels out of eastern Tennessee. Forbidden by Buell to destroy private property along the marching route, Thomas modified the order not to tear down fence rails to allow removal of the top rails only, and soon Thomas's frozen soldiers had campfires burning. On January 19, 1862, Thomas met his Rebel foes at Mill Springs, also known as Logan Cross Roads, on the banks of the Cumberland. Though Thomas had been a brigadier general since the previous fall, he hadn't stopped wearing his old colonel's uniform, and it was at Mill Springs that he first donned the uniform of a brigadier.[53] Though Thomas had planned to be the aggressor, his Confederate foes, under the command of Gen. George Crittenden, had other ideas. The Rebels, 12,000 strong, attacked Thomas's 7,000 before dawn, but Thomas was not caught off guard. He had established strong picket lines and patrolling cavalry vedettes, which gave Thomas an hour's warning of the impending enemy assault. Thomas, taking his force in hand, fended off the Rebel attack and, in turn, routed the Confederates, capturing 14 pieces of Rebel artillery, 1,500 mules and horses and the enemy's entire camp equipage, including wagons, arms, ammunition and stores.

The victory was so complete that when the battle ended with darkness, though Thomas had planned to continue fighting the next day, he found that the Rebels had crossed the Cumberland, leaving even their colors and wounded behind. Crittenden's men, one by one and in groups, deserted — his army melting away. Thomas's victory at Mill Springs broke the right of the Confederates' long defensive line and was the first real victory of the war. Buell congratulated Thomas for his victory, but Lincoln inexplicably did not. Though the newly appointed secretary of war, Edwin M. Stanton, hinted at promotion, it was not forthcoming, and Thomas's victory passed unacknowledged. If he had been promoted after Mill Springs, it would have given him rank over those who would later pass him by and receive independent commands: Generals Buell and U.S. Grant. Though Thomas would eventually be given the rank of major general of volunteers, it was not until months later, on April 25, 1862, and it was not backdated to the day of his victory at Mill Springs, as was then the usual protocol. It is unknown whether Thomas, a Virginian, was still viewed with some suspicion. Most likely, however, he was overlooked because he had no political supporter in Washington.[54] Thomas's victory left Johnston's right flank uncovered, exposed the Cumberland Gap and the Confederates' east-west rail link, and left the door to invasion of partisan eastern Tennessee ajar and the road to Nashville open to the east. Although Richmond was concerned, Davis seemed paralyzed, and weeks after Johnston appealed for reinforcement, none was forthcoming, yet Thomas would be unable to take advantage of the opportunities he had created.[55]

This time period is but one of many occasions when one wonders how Thomas managed to cope with the inadequacies of those who commanded him. Perhaps the writings of journalist William Shanks offer an answer. While Shanks's sycophancy regarding Grant, Sherman and Sheridan is revolting, the savagery of his attacks on Gen. William S. Rosecrans illustrates his vindictive and partisan nature. Yet a quotation Shanks attributes to General Thomas, who was speaking to a disappointed subordinate, has the ring of truth about it. Shanks tells that Thomas told a Colonel Scribner, who felt unfairly treated and overlooked after the reorganization of the army after Chickamauga, "Colonel, I have taken a great deal of pains to educate myself not to feel." If an element of courage is the ability to continue on in one's duty when overlooked and overruled, Thomas would prove a very brave man.[56]

After Mill Springs, Thomas wanted to advance into East Tennessee, going through the Cumberland Gap and moving on Chattanooga and Knoxville. McClellan approved of Thomas's plan, but Thomas's commander, Buell, did not.[57] While Buell had turned the 23,000 poorly trained recruits into a well-drilled army of 40,000, he also emulated his mentor McClellan, refusing to take direction from Washington. Egged on by Military Governor Andrew Johnson, who wished to be formally reinstalled in Nashville, Buell ignored repeated pleas from Lincoln to rescue the Rebel-occupied homes of East Tennessee's Union sympathizers. In 1861, as he was building his army, Buell told McClellan that he had no fear of being attacked by A. Sidney Johnston, with whom he had served in antebellum Texas. Buell quipped that November, "should almost as soon expect to see the Army of the Potomac marching up the road" as General Johnston. But Buell's assessment of Johnston was, in fact, appropriate for a time, but Buell's expectations, that the enemy would cooperate by staying put while he made his preparation and executed his own battle plans, would catch up with him in the future.[58]

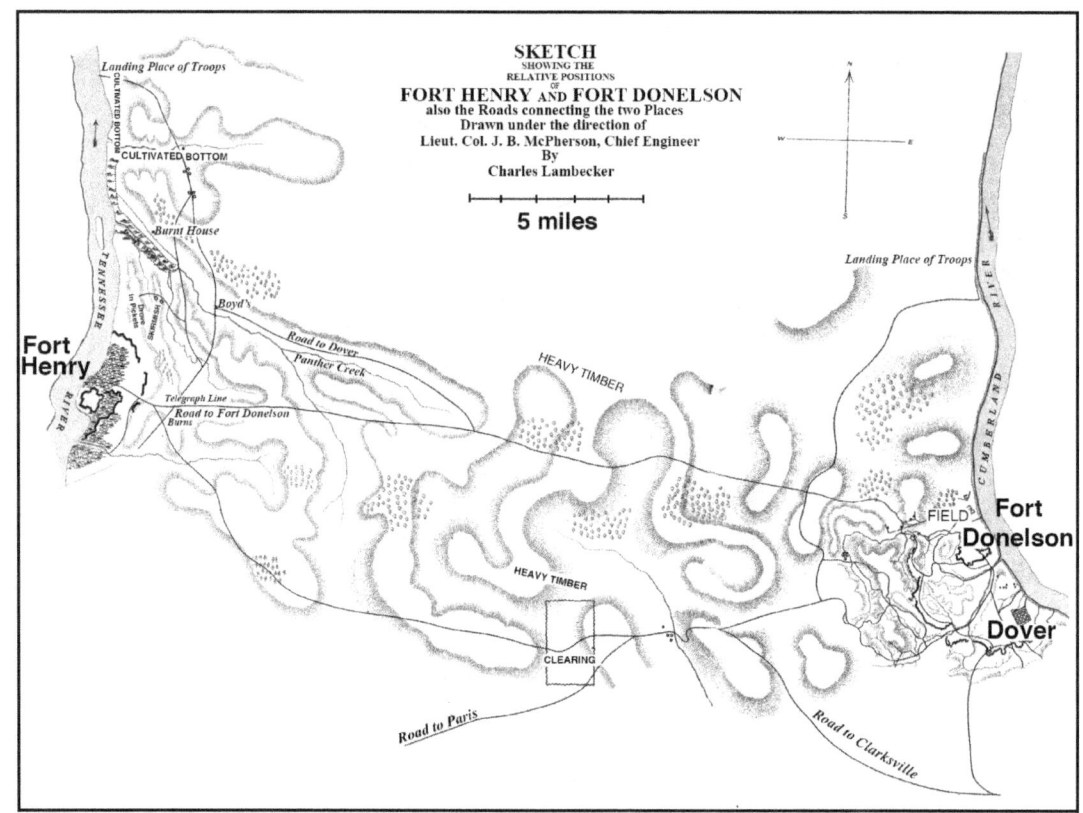

Forts Henry and Donelson. Adapted from Plate XI, #2, *Official Atlas* (Ned Smith).

Thus, the struggle over Tennessee and Kentucky over the next three years might have been avoided if Buell had allowed it to be settled by Thomas in early 1862. However, as Thomas biographer Thomas Van Horne points out, ensuing conflict for dominance in the two contested states would cost the Federals alone 100,000 casualties. The conflict between Rebels and Federals wasn't the only conflict going on. While Buell's man Thomas had scored a great victory, the other Union commander in the west, Gen. Henry Halleck, his heart set on becoming the overall commander in the West, was poised, reluctantly, to allow his man, U.S. Grant, to initiate a campaign against Forts Henry and Donelson. Though Halleck had little confidence in Grant's abilities, he also knew that if he didn't use the soldiers at his disposal, McClellan would see to it that they would be sent to his rival, Buell. So Halleck began a campaign to acquire territory and landmarks, and, most importantly, control of the rivers, as opposed to destroying the enemy's armies. It was a campaign in which Thomas and Buell would be playing minor roles. And as Confederate president Jefferson Davis finally began to abandon his insistence on maintaining a defensive line that guarded an impracticable breadth of territory in the West, it made the consolidation of previously scattered Rebel troops possible, and would make them a force to be reckoned with. It was bad timing for the ascendance of a commander like Halleck, who seemed more interested in acquiring places and power than fighting the enemy's armies. Meanwhile, Lincoln would continue, unsuccessfully, to press Buell, Halleck and McClellan to move.[59]

Two

Grant the Hero: Forts Henry and Donelson — and Then There Was Shiloh

As early as mid–January of 1862, U.S. Grant approached Halleck about a campaign for the control of the Cumberland and Tennessee Rivers, using the two rivers to then attack the Confederate interior. If nothing else, Belmont had taught Grant the importance of control of the rivers. He had almost lost his own small force to a counterattack by a swift-moving flotilla of Rebels. And ironically, Grant's fumbling attack against Belmont had so startled Polk, the commander at Columbus, that he refused to send reinforcements to Forts Henry or Donelson.[1] But Halleck initially rejected Grant's plan to attack Henry and Donelson out of hand. The erection of the two forts was an acknowledgment of the defensive significance of the Tennessee and Cumberland Rivers, for if the Federals controlled those rivers, the Rebels would be forced to give up Columbus without a fight, leaving the Mississippi available for a movement southward toward Memphis.[2] But Lincoln was hearing from all his commanders, Buell, Halleck and McClellan, that nothing could be done. While Halleck rejected McClernand's and U.S. Grant's proposals,[3] Lincoln began getting suggestions for possible advancement on the enemy directly from Gen. John McClernand, who as a political general and one of Grant's division commanders bypassed the recalcitrant Halleck and went straight to the top. McClernand was a political appointee with considerable influence in southern Illinois, and a powerful Democrat who supported the war and, therefore, had some sway with the administration in Washington. McClernand was ambitious for an independent command for himself, and didn't hesitate to go over the heads of his military superiors, but while he was keeping Lincoln in the picture regarding possible enemy weak points to attack, and Lincoln yearned for an advance on the enemy, the president may nevertheless have had doubts that the inexperienced McClernand was the man for the job. While McClernand was writing to Lincoln, Grant was corresponding with Representative Washburne, keeping him aware of the plan that Grant and McClernand had devised an operation in Tennessee using the rivers.[4]

Finally, Lincoln would wait no more. On January 27, 1862, Lincoln issued "President's General Order Number One," which ordered both land and naval forces to make a general movement on February 22nd. And gunboat commander Andrew Hull Foote added his voice to Grant's regarding the feasibility of an attack on Fort Henry,[5] finally leading Halleck to reply positively to Grant when he again petitioned to be allowed to move against the Confederate fort. Or perhaps it was, as historian B.F. Cooling relates, McClellan's warning of Beauregard's potential reinforcement of Kentucky that caused Halleck's concern. Rebel reinforcements of Kentucky.[6] Whatever the impetus, on January 30th, when Halleck telegraphed Grant to make his preparations for his proposed movement on Fort Henry, Grant's headquarters rang with cheers.[7]

The locations the Confederates had chosen for their forts had been limited by the necessity of locating them outside neutral Kentucky, and the sites and defenses constructed were less than ideal.[8] A reconnaissance report on Fort Henry by Brigadier General Charles F. Smith had helped inspire Grant to propose this expedition. In his January 22nd report, Smith indicated that "two ironclad gunboats could make short work" of Fort Henry.[9] But just one week later, Smith was perhaps getting cold feet as it looked like the expedition would actually be mounted. On January 30th, at the last moment, Smith reported evidence that Fort Henry had been reinforced, bringing the garrison to no less than 6,000 with 15,000 more Rebel reinforcements to come if the fort was threatened. This news from Smith, however, in no way deterred Grant, though he did pass Smith's information along to Halleck.[10] While Foote and Grant's plan for attacking Fort Henry was a coordinated attack by Grant's land force of 15,000 and Foote's water force of three unarmed gunboats and four ironclad river gunboats,[11] the reality of the situation was that flooding at the ill-chosen site of Fort Henry had left the Rebel fort undefendable. Continuing rains also slowed Grant's advance on the fort to a standstill, reducing the road, as John Logan, one of McClernand's subordinates, described it, "to the consistency of soft porridge of almost immeasurable depth."[12]

Grant lacked hard evidence regarding the number of Rebels manning Fort Henry or unfinished Fort Heiman, opposite Fort Henry on the Tennessee River, though he mistakenly believed they might be manned by as many as 10,000. Thus, his deployment of troops to begin the investment of this Rebel guardian on the Tennessee is nothing less than startling. Grant did not have enough river transportation to bring his entire force of some 15,000 men all at once to the environs of the forts, so he first sent McClernand, a political general with no experience other than the "Battle of Belmont," with his command to a position several miles from Fort Henry. McClernand was ordered to take up a position on the road between Forts Henry and Donelson that would prevent Rebel retreat or reinforcement. In his instructions to McClernand, Grant recommended that he bring along all his axes and five or six ambulances. It would turn out that the axes were

General John McClernand (Library of Congress).

not destined to be used for building log defenses, for that was not Grant's intention, but were intended to be used in the destruction of Rebel bridges. Therefore the ambulances would be fully employed.[13]

McClernand was landed several miles from Fort Henry on February 4, 1863, to wait until the rest of Grant's force came up. It would be the early hours of February 6th before the remainder of the Federal force would finish arriving near Fort Henry.[14] Grant, for once, did consider it possible that the Rebels might take the initiative and attack McClernand's isolated force, but he did not seem overly concerned about it. In fact, instead of remaining with McClernand, Grant boarded the gunboat USS *Essex* for a reconnaissance of Fort Henry,[15] while Foote returned to Cairo with the boats that would transport C.F. Smith and his men to join the expedition. Grant did leave Lt. Col. James B. McPherson (USMA, 1853), the engineer that Halleck had sent to keep an eye on Grant, to provide guidance for McClernand. McPherson was a personable young engineering officer who would later become one of "Grant's Men."[16] While most of Grant's cronies were infantry or cavalrymen, with a heavy sprinkling of officers whose experience in the military had been as quartermasters, McPherson broke the mold in that he was an engineer who had graduated first in his West Point class. However, truer to form, like many of Grant's friends McPherson was a westerner hailing from Ohio. In the months to come, McPherson would became one of Grant's inner circle. But McClernand seemingly didn't appreciate Grant's assignment of McPherson to his military staff, and on receiving Grant's orders he immediately questioned whether the direction of his being "under the guidance of Lt. Col. McPherson" would in any way interfere with his authority as *the* commander of the first Federal force embarked near Fort Henry.[17]

The *Essex* with Grant aboard came under fire, and when the vessel was still two and one half miles below the fort, a Rebel shell smashed into the *Essex*'s stern nearly killing Grant and the *Essex's* commander. A visibly shaken Grant returned to move McClernand's force to a safer position.[18] Luckily for Grant, McPherson, and McClernand, the awkwardness and inadequacies of the Confederate command structure in the area, as well as the Tennessee River's inundation of Fort Henry left the Rebels in no position to take advantage of McClernand's inexperience and isolation. And high water negated the threat of the Confederates' floating mines, as Foote returned from Cairo with the command of Gen. C.F. Smith. Thus it turned out that Foote, whose gunboats were to have played a supporting role, ended up taking the flooded Fort Henry without help from Grant. Foote, who realized that the muddy condition of the roads would delay the advance of Grant's infantry, suggested that he postpone the navy's attack until the soldiers were in position, but Grant stubbornly refused. Thus, as historian Cooling observes, on the 6th of February, 1862, when "Foote hoisted his signal pennant to prepare for the battle about 10:20 A.M., Grant's soldiers were still in camp." Grant's men marched at 11 A.M., and promptly became mired in the mud.[19] Under the command of Confederate general Lloyd Tilghman, 100 men out of Fort Henry's original complement of 2,600 had managed to stall the Federal investment of Fort Henry long enough to allow most of fort's defenders to make the trek to Fort Donelson before Ft. Henry capitulated. Most all would straggle in to Donelson in the next two days. And lest we think Confederate commander Tilghman's defense of Henry was perfunctory, as Foote pointed out in his report, the engagement between his four gunboats and the 11 heavy-caliber guns of Fort Henry was spirited. Tilghman and

USS *Essex* (U.S. Naval Historical Center).

his 100 forlorn hope defenders,[20] who had remained behind to buy time for the rest of those abandoning the fort, fought for an hour and a half, the fight ending only after seven of Tilghman's 11 guns were dismounted by the navy's bombardment. So it was that Foote turned Fort Henry over to Grant on his arrival in midafternoon, an hour after the fort had capitulated. General Tilghman must have been experiencing a strong sense of "I told you so." Having argued with the officials who controlled Confederate ordnance that his fort did not have the arms necessary to sustain an attack from the water, the Federals now possessed Fort Henry,[21] along with what Foote's biographer, James Mason Hoppin, estimates as a million dollars' worth of Rebel property. Cooling cites a Memphis Unionist who estimated the value of lost Confederate materiel after the fall of Fort Donelson and Memphis at an even more startling five million dollars. The accouterments and supplies for the 15,000 men who were to have been stationed there did make a tidy haul, and it was of sufficient value that it would prove a major headache for Grant in the days to come. Meanwhile, Rebel supporters warily anticipated another advance by the "Northmen," as the *Memphis Avalanche* called the invading Yankees.[22]

In his report to Halleck on February 6, 1862, Grant gave full credit to Foote for the capture of Fort Henry, renaming the captured works "Fort Foote," but in his reports, with edited copies prepared for the press, Grant made much of the number of guns and amount of materiel he had captured and also praised his troops' pursuit of the escaping Rebels. Sending out only cavalry, Grant, in fact, delivered only 150 prisoners of war out of the 2,600 Rebels that had occupied Fort Henry a few days earlier. And while Grant's report mentioned a number of the commanders of McClernand's division, he did not mention McClernand. Did this prompt McClernand's letter, which he sent directly to Lincoln, regarding the role he and his troops had played in the capture of Fort Henry? McClernand, tit for tat, makes no mention of Grant. But to return to Grant's report, the Fort Henry fortifications he had previously described to Halleck as vulnerable, became "extensive," and giving "evidence of engineering skill, and great labor." Then Grant blithely added that he, Grant, would take Fort Donelson on February 8th.[23]

The capture of Fort Donelson had not been part of the original plan submitted to Halleck by his subordinate, and Grant's rather casual mention that he intended to take another fort somewhat unnerved Halleck, who was still anxious about Grant's ability to handle the expedition, let alone an expanded one. Halleck had already been anxious enough to send Lt. Col. James B. McPherson to keep an eye on Grant, as previously stated,[24] but there were other indications of Halleck's uneasiness over Grant's expedition, and perhaps, rightly so, as Halleck biographer Stephen Ambrose points out. Grant disobeyed a number of Halleck's orders. When leaving Fort Henry to approach Fort Donelson, Grant failed to entrench the small force he had left behind at Fort Henry, and did not leave sufficient equipment to give himself a base to return to should it be necessary. Grant was in the middle of enemy territory with hostile forces to his northeast and northwest. Would General Johnston see this opportunity and take advantage of Grant's vulnerability? Halleck would become so convinced that Grant was in jeopardy and must have reinforcements that when Halleck's requests for help were rebuffed by Buell, Halleck made a radical suggestion. Halleck told Buell several days before Fort Donelson's fate had been resolved that if Buell brought reinforcements Halleck would give Buell command of Grant's expedition, suggesting he would transfer Grant and Sherman elsewhere. Buell didn't budge.[25]

Apparently not sharing any of Halleck's worries, Grant, after Fort Henry's fall, was so confident of taking Fort Donelson that he urged a reporter with his forces to stick around if he wanted a better story than the fall of Fort Henry. When the reporter asked if Grant knew the enemy's strength at Fort Donelson, Grant admitted that he did not, but that he thought he could take the fort, and meant to try.[26] But Grant did encounter several insurmountable barriers to his optimistic projection of delivering Donelson on February 8th. While Foote took his gunboats back to Cairo for repairs, February 8th came and went with rain continuing to make the roads impassable. Cooling points out that "only the gunboat *Carondelet* remained to protect Grant's army huddled in crowded camps awaiting the dry roads. The unruly volunteers continued to loot and destroy property, their officers hugging warmer quarters aboard transports offshore." Cooling suggests, "Grant was in a tight spot — only he would not admit it. With the gunboats gone on one mission or another and his land force with its back against the swiftly flowing flood waters, there was surely reason for concern. A determined counteroffensive by Johnston could have proved disastrous."[27]

Grant's advance finally got underway on February 12th, arriving near Fort Donelson at dusk, where Grant discovered that the fort would be a much greater challenge than Fort Henry. Unlike Fort Henry, Donelson was strongly positioned with an effective field of fire over the Cumberland River, and the fort was well manned with Confederate reinforcements arriving daily. Grant believed the Rebel garrison numbered 30,000, while Rebel prisoners claimed that there were 20,000 to 25,000 Confederates at Fort Donelson.

But the most reliable Confederate statistics indicate there were 17,000 men at the fort at the time of Grant's investiture.[28] While Grant was also receiving reinforcements from the still-recovering William T. Sherman, whom Halleck had assigned to command at Paducah, Grant, with about 15,000 men, was still outnumbered by the fort's Rebel defenders.[29] Sherman offered to do all he could to help hurry reinforcements to Grant, including offering to come himself if he could be of any service, "assuring Grant that he would do so without mention of making any question of Rank with you or General Smith whose commissions are the same date." Sherman wrote the same day that he was anxious about Grant, but "I have faith in you — Command me in any way." Sherman would be quick to send his congratulations and praise to Grant in the upcoming days, forming the first links of the strong bond that would exist between the two men.[30]

Though Grant considered trying to take Fort Donelson before Foote's return, he decided against it and chose to wait for the arrival of Foote's gunboats before making an attack.[31] But Grant, again with apparently no thought for what the Rebels might do, felt it unnecessary for his troops to construct earthworks. Grant mistakenly believed that his former Belmont adversary, Confederate general Gideon Pillow was in command, but while Pillow had been Fort Donelson's commander, he was now second in command to Gen. John Floyd, the former secretary of war under President James Buchanan, and now a Rebel general.[32]

On the cold morning of February 13, 1862, Grant, while sending word for Lew Wallace to bring up his troops from Fort Henry, gave orders for Smith and McClernand to close in on the Fort Donelson perimeter but avoid bringing on a battle. But when C.F. Smith "probed" the Rebel line by opening on it with a battery, then tried to move closer to the enemy earthworks, sending a line of Federals with fixed bayonets to within cannon range of the Confederate right, a fight was under way. Historian Cooling comments, "Why anyone thought this would not violate Grant's orders about a general battle was unclear." To the soldiers who made the advance, it certainly felt more like an assault than a reconnaissance. Later in the day, when the Unionists drew back from their advanced position, things on the Federal left quieted down.[33]

While Smith had moved toward Fort Donelson, the ironclad gunboat USS *Carondelet* was ordered to get up steam and hurl long-range projectiles into Donelson. Though the Confederate gun crews had only two guns capable of answering the distant Federal fire, they nonetheless put one 128-pound shell through the *Carondelet*, while a Federal shot shattered a Rebel gun carriage.[34] On the Union right, as McClernand continued to edge his force toward the river, Confederate artillery in the Rebel outer trenches contested his movement. Perhaps it was Grant's message that Smith's morning action against the Rebels had been repulsed, that led McClernand to believe that he, too, could risk bringing on an engagement, for he sent three of his regiments to rush Confederate batteries and stop the annoying enemy shelling. The attempt, which incurred 147 casualties, failed. In the night that followed, the soldiers within and without Donelson suffered through high wind, sleet and snow.[35]

On the cold, wet morning of February 14th, by 11 A.M., Lew Wallace's division arrived from Fort Henry, and Grant positioned them in the center of the Federal line, between Smith and McClernand. Historian Cooling suggests that Grant was aware of his precarious situation, facing an enemy in a strong, well-manned fortification, and he suspects that it

Fort Donelson and its outer works. From Plate XI, #5, *Official Atlas* (Ned Smith).

was with no little relief that Grant greeted the reappearance of Foote's boats. When Foote returned to Donelson, his gunboats accompanied troop transports loaded with men, who debarked unmolested by the Rebels. These reinforcements brought Grant's numbers up to an estimated 40,000. While posting the new arrivals with Smith and Wallace on the Federal left and center, Grant lost no time adding his own demands to those already made by Halleck and Washington, pressuring the flotilla commander to attack Fort Donelson. Foote advised against what he felt was an ill-prepared assault, stating that his boats were undermanned, at least 600 men short by Foote's estimate, and the mortars he felt necessary for success had not arrived. But Foote was persuaded to prepare to attack on the afternoon of February 14th. Not only did Foote's attack fail to adequately destroy Donelson's defenses, but the flotilla came away with more than 50 killed and wounded, including Foote with two wounds, and all four of his ironclads seriously damaged. By 4:30 P.M., the fight was over, the Fort's water batteries were undamaged, and the Rebel losses were one killed and several wounded. Grant watched the attack from onshore. No land attack had accompanied the river assault, and while the Confederates celebrated their river victory, it was muted by the real threat of the Unionist infantry's investment of Donelson. It seems that the Rebels' commander in the West, Albert Sidney Johnston, had already despaired regarding the fate of the fort and its garrison, and he advised the Rebel commanders, "If you lose the fort, bring your troops to Nashville if possible." The night of February 14th, Donelson commanders, Generals Floyd, Pillow and Buckner, continued to look for a route that would allow them to push past the Union right and escape southward toward Nashville. If Grant had expected Fort Donelson to surrender as Fort Henry had, he was mistaken. But if Grant thought that the Rebels would wait for him while he decided what he should do next, he was *very* much mistaken. Though the Rebel plans were faulty, with different commanders having different understandings of what the break-

USS *Carondelet* (Naval History and Heritage Command Photographic Department).

out on the Rebel left would accomplish, by the first hour of February 15th, the plan was set that the Confederates, leaving only a skeleton force in Fort Donelson, would attack well before the late winter dawn and destroy the Federal right. While Pillow intended that the Rebel force, after crushing the Federals, would return to Donelson's defenses and retrieve their equipment before starting for Nashville, Buckner, on the other hand, assumed that no one would return to the trenches and that the men who had been left in Donelson would be sacrificed. How else could it be viewed, for it was decided that one regiment, the 30th Tennessee, would replace Buckner's entire division in the outer earthworks that they had been holding. While the Unionists, on this dark and stormy night, did not detect the extensive movements taking place in the Confederate lines, when day dawned, the 30th Tennessee alone would be holding three-quarters of a mile of outer earthworks that Buckner had evacuated, and the Tennesseans would be confronting Charles F. Smith's entire division massed on a ridge to the west.[36]

On the morning of February 15th, Grant rode to the river to confer with the wounded Foote, leaving his troops facing Donelson. McClernand held the far right and was charged with cutting off the possible escape route of the Confederates should Donelson be taken. Lew Wallace's division held the center of Grant's line, and when Grant had positioned Wallace's division in his line between McClernand and Smith, he specifically told Wallace not to take any offensive action. Gen. Charles F. Smith held Grant's left, facing Fort Donelson itself.[37] Previously, as the Federals had begun their partial encirclement of Fort Donelson, McClernand, after reconnaissance, had reported to Grant that he had insufficient troops to close a possible escape route for the Rebels between his right flank and the Cumberland River. A brigade from Smith's division was sent to assist McClernand, though his numbers were still insufficient to close the gap between his right and the river or provide a reserve. But Grant assured McClernand that the Rebels would not bring on a battle.[38] As it turned out, McClernand's anxiety was entirely justified, for the Confederates, with the intention to break out of the intensifying Federal encirclement, had already identified the Union line's weakest point and had already decided on forcing open the path to escape between McClernand's right and the river. McClernand's men were short of food and ammunition, since the army's supply trains had not kept up with the army's movement, but they would have far more to worry about than their cold and hunger in the coming day.[39]

At daybreak on the cold, snowy morning of February 15th, five Rebel brigades, some 6,000 men, hit McClernand's right flank. Though Grant heard firing that morning as he conferred with Foote on his flagship, he refused to consider that the enemy had taken the initiative while he had been away from his front. It was another indication of the risk one takes when avoiding worry over what your enemy might do. Leaving no one in charge, and having told his commanders to simply stay in place until he returned, when a strong column of Rebels made a breakout attack on a weak point on the far Federal right, McClernand had varying success getting the other commanders to assist him. With his right flank refused, McClernand put up what the Rebel commander later described as an obstinate resistance, but by 8 A.M., McClernand was in trouble. Sending word that he was under attack by a large force of Rebels, McClernand called upon Wallace for assistance, but Wallace, still under orders not to bring on an engagement, tried to send a message to Grant first, thereby discovering that Grant was not at his headquarters located at the far left of the Union line. Reluctantly, Wallace sent one brigade to McClernand, which McClernand put in his reserve to support his rapidly crumbling front. As the attack on McClernand intensified, the Rebel onslaught was assisted by Nathan Bedford Forrest's cavalry. Their success opened the Rebel's escape route to Nashville. John Logan's 31st Illinois was among those who had resisted stubbornly, but was driven back. As Cooling observes, the Federals on the right had provided a stubborn resistance throughout the morning of February 15th, and some still fought on in isolated pockets. But by 1 P.M., "McClernand's division virtually ceased to exist as an organized fighting force."[40]

Wallace finally realized that McClernand had not exaggerated when he described the Rebel assault as one that threatened Grant's whole army, and, without orders, Wallace sent the rest of his division — seven regiments — at the critical time of about 1 P.M. to help McClernand form a line against the flood of Rebels. Rawlins, who apparently had not accompanied Grant on his visit to Foote, evidently had thought it unnecessary to forward to Grant the division commanders' reports and inquiries regarding the Rebel's dawn attack. Rawlins did finally go to Wallace's headquarters at midday, and soon Wallace and Rawlins witnessed the flood of wounded and stampeded troops, many with empty cartridge boxes, fleeing from McClernand's front. Wallace recalled having to restrain Rawlins, who, on witnessing the flight of one panicked Federal officer, began drawing his pistol to shoot him down. Together the men of Lew Wallace's division and McClernand's survivors formed a line that would turn the tide. About the time that the Rebel onslaught began to again encounter stiff resistance, and their drive began to lose steam, Pillow, in accordance with his version of what would happen next, began to order the Confederates back into Fort Donelson. With visions of victory still dominating his perception, Pillow believed his men would pack up the equipment and supplies that earlier would have encumbered them while they fought, but which they could now take and march past the defeated Yankees to Nashville. It was a fool's dream. Buckner argued vehemently with Pillow regarding a return to the fort, but the coercive Pillow was able to convince the ever-wavering Floyd, who was after all the man in charge, that it was the right thing to do.[41]

Though Grant had finally returned to his headquarters on the Union left around 1 P.M., (about the same time Rawlins was being inspired to shoot his own men), it was near 1:30 before Grant came to see what was going on on his right. Red faced with agitation, Grant at first ordered Wallace and McClernand to await reinforcement, but on second thought, Grant calmly ordered Wallace and McClernand to retake what they had lost. The only other visible display of Grant's dismay at the surprise the Rebels had given him was in his message to Foote, in which he confided that "all may be defeated" if the gunboats did not open fire.[42] Grant then rode to instruct General Smith, who had sat idle on the Federal left, to attack what was believed to be a weakened Rebel defense on his front. Smith's division easily took the Rebel's outer works, driving out the 30th Tennessee, but since Buckner's troops were just coming back into the inner fortifications of Fort Donelson, the Federal assault bogged down.[43]

McClernand and Wallace would later dispute who had led the attack to regain control of the road to Nashville that they had lost to the Confederates, but Cooling describes Gen. Lew Wallace as leading his men, much as C.F. Smith was doing, into the attack. In the five-hour fight to resist the Rebels that morning, McClernand had lost 1,500 of his

8,000 men and all of his division was low on ammunition, so it seems evident that it was with Wallace's fresh seven regiments and a brigade from General Smith that the Federals were finally able to start closing the door to Nashville. Lew Wallace's assault proved so effective against weakening Rebel resistance that Wallace resented the order he received from Grant, instructing him to pull back from Donelson, move out of cannon range and construct earthworks. Considering the realities regarding the practicalities of Wallace's assertion that he could have attacked the fortification, he may have been, to borrow a phrase from the good general, merely "blowing smoke."[44]

It seems inexplicable why the Rebels, instead of taking advantage of their breakout, began to return to the dubious safety of Fort Donelson. But the commanders' differing understandings of what the goals of the breakout were, and the ambiguities of who was in charge, with the passive Floyd in the role of overall commander seeming secondary to the outspoken Pillow, all lend insight into what happened next. As the men of the Rebel infantry endured another freezing night in Fort Donelson, many believed that they had won a victory. But Floyd's report that the Federals had received reinforcements that night that increased their numbers to 80 regiments (the Unionists had in fact half that) began to shake the confidence of those in command and turn their focus to another breakout. Orders for the next morning were actually given to make another attack on the Federal right, but Simon Bolivar Buckner (USMA, 1844), who had argued against returning to the fort, now argued against attempting to break out again. Buckner, apparently, was the first to propose surrender, and as Floyd and Pillow began to get cold feet about breaking out, it appeared that Donelson's fate was sealed. Generals Floyd and Pillow, in turn, passed command of Fort Donelson to General Buckner, while Nathan Bedford Forrest refused to be party to the capitulation and fled with his cavalry from the fort. The Confederate garrison, shocked at their generals' plan to surrender, cursed their commanders and began to slip away from Donelson, with about 1,200 Rebels making an escape from the Federal besiegers.[45]

Cooling mentions that a number of Rebels escaped under Federal noses when Grant's terms allowed them access to the battlefield to bury their dead. Grant later regretted it, for many Confederates who came out onto the field kept right on walking. Then, too, the exultant Federals were distracted, looting the abundant Rebel supplies and searching for souvenirs. Even the teetotaler Rawlins, the guardian of Grant's sobriety, was said to have made several celebratory toasts. But the celebration at Grant's headquarters was coupled with bewilderment, for it puzzled the Federals why the amount of enemy supplies found at Donelson, particularly the warm clothing, had not been distributed to the suffering Rebels. Preventing pilfering of these abundant supplies became an impossible job. So chaotic were things in the days after the battle that when Buckner offered to help with the overwhelming job of dealing with the many prisoners, he was able to convince Grant to allow Federal guards to acknowledge passes with Buckner's signature on them, no doubt adding to post-surrender escapes. Criticism over how Grant handled the flood of prisoners, wounded, dead, and confiscated Rebel property at Donelson would come back to haunt him in coming days.[46]

Grant would later say that he owed his success at Donelson to Gen. Charles F. Smith. One could also make the opposite case that Smith almost lost Donelson for Grant by his stubborn refusal to send aid to McClernand when he was attacked during the Rebel's attempted breakout.[47] And when Confederate commander Buckner, an old friend of Grant's, asked for terms of surrender, it was on General Smith's advice that Grant demanded "unconditional surrender," though Grant softened some of the harsh words suggested by Smith, who would later refuse to shake Buckner's hand at the surrender. Grant's words would capture the nation's imagination and make U.S. Grant famous throughout the country.[48]

Depending which account you read, Smith, when he finally led an attack on the left at Donelson, either drove the Rebels back into their fortifications, or captured an outer work, taking the enemy's redan.[49] After being resupplied with ammunition, McClernand and Wallace did recapture the ground that had been lost to the Rebels that morning, but it was Smith whose reputation, largely because of Grant's attention, seemed to be most enhanced regarding his performance at Donelson. Grant later forwarded General McClernand's report on Fort Donelson to Halleck,[50] but with the comment that McClernand's account of his First Division's conduct was "highly colored." Grant also denied McClernand's assertion that, when Grant finally came on the field at 1:30 P.M., it was McClernand's idea for an advance along the whole line. On the face of it, on considering other reports and accounts, including very positive comments by Halleck's observer, Lieutenant Colonel McPherson,[51] it seems that McClernand's report is a fair representation of what his division went through on February 15th. McClernand offers that his division had, by far, the greatest loss of the three divisions, stating that more than 1,500 of his 8,000 men engaged were killed, wounded or captured, and he proudly lists the brave behavior of his many officers and men. But McClernand also tallies up all the men and materiel taken from the enemy upon the fall of Donelson, a rather presumptuous and excessive inclusion in a division commander's report, for it was Grant's army, not McClernand's division, that must be credited with the large overall capture of prisoners and stores. Among the promotions being handed out, Lincoln approved and signed Grant's nomination as a major general, dated February 17, 1862. Several days later, his friend Elihu Washburne sent a telegram to Grant informing him that the Senate had confirmed his promotion.[52]

The results of Grant's victory at Fort Donelson were impressive. Nearly 15,000 Rebels were taken prisoner at Donelson and sent north, including Confederate generals Buckner and Bushrod Johnson, while some 3,000 Confederates escaped.[53] Because of the nature of prisoner exchange, most of the Confederate regiments captured at Fort Donelson would be back in service in seven month, but as Larry Daniel, author of *Shiloh*, points out, those captured men awaiting exchange were not available to Gen. Albert. Sidney Johnston when he needed them most, at Shiloh. Grant took 20,000 stands of arms, 48 pieces of artillery, 17 heavy guns, 2,000–4,000 horses and large quantities of commissary stores. Of the 27,000 Federals that Grant had brought to Donelson, 500 were killed, 2,108 were wounded, including Col. John Logan, one of McClernand's regimental commanders, while 224 men were captured or missing, for a total of 2,832.[54]

On February 22nd, Grant reminded Representative Washburne that not a single brigadier general had been appointed from the southern part of Illinois. While reminding Washburne that he would never recommend promotion for a man for any reason other than the best interest of the army, he credited John Logan with bringing many men from that part of the state into the Union army, and citing his bravery, Grant urged promotion for Logan. On March 3rd, Lincoln directed Stanton to appoint Brigadier Generals Don

Carlos Buell, John A. McClernand, Charles F. Smith and Lewis Wallace as major generals. Lincoln also instructed that Col. John Logan be appointed a brigadier general.[55] But on a broader scale, the fall of Forts Henry and Donelson set bells ringing in celebration across the North. It would be some time, however, before the full potential of Grant's victories was realized. The Tennessee and Cumberland Rivers were now open pathways into the Confederate heartland. In the coming weeks, Albert S. Johnston's troops would be driven back 100 miles.[56] As Forts Henry and Donelson historian Cooling observes, beyond the Confederate leaders' doomed determination to hold on to so much territory, "muddled indecision" at Johnston's headquarters, as well as animosities that existed among the Rebel officers, were all responsible for this great blow that was delivered to the Confederate cause.[57] And as Larry Daniel points out in the preliminary chapters to his book *Shiloh*, it was the inept leadership of Floyd and Pillow that gave Grant his victory at Fort Donelson,[58] but nonetheless, for his victory at Donelson, Grant received a promotion to major general of volunteers and the new stature he attained with the *nom de guerre* "Unconditional Surrender Grant."

While Lieutenant Colonel McPherson assured Grant of Halleck's delight at Grant's finally taking Donelson,[59] mutual admiration had so far developed between Grant and McPherson, whom Halleck had sent to keep an eye on Grant, that Grant asked to be allowed to keep McPherson with him for all future movements. But Halleck's plans for reorganization of his force did not include Grant. While Grant was maneuvering for Donelson, Halleck had been maneuvering for command in the West, having written to McClellan suggesting that either Buell or Halleck himself should take command of Grant's Cumberland Expedition. Halleck went on to propose a thorough reshuffling of districts and commands that would result in Buell remaining where he was and Gen. David Hunter (USMA, 1822), whom Halleck was feeling indebted to since Hunter sent Halleck reinforcements when Buell would not, would be given another department in the West. Then, Halleck recommended, that either Gen. Ethan Allen Hitchcock (USMA, 1817), an intimate friend of Lieutenant General Scott, Stanton and Lincoln,[60] or Gen. William T. Sherman, whom Halleck stated was now in good health, should have the third district.[61] In order to avoid all the conflict and confusion over who had what districts, Halleck suggested an overall commander in the West, himself. Grant's name was notably missing from the list of potential candidates for future Western command, except for being named as the officer whom Gen. Hitchcock would replace, should McClellan like Halleck's plan. McClellan didn't.[62]

The country north of the Mason-Dixon line, hungry for good news, embraced the announcements of Grant's victories at Forts Henry and Donelson with great enthusiasm, and no one celebrated more joyously than those at Halleck's headquarters at St. Louis.[63] After Fort Donelson's fall, Halleck, completely willing to take advantage of Grant's victory to further his own career, with even greater confidence continued his campaign to take command of the West. Apparently awarding himself much of the credit for Grant's victories, Halleck wrote to McClellan on February 17th, "Make Buell, Grant, and Pope major-general of volunteers, and give me command in the West. I ask this in return for Forts Henry and Donelson."[64]

It is at first surprising that Halleck recommended Buell for promotion, but it was a carrot on a stick, though not really one that was Halleck's to give. Halleck was attempting to win over his rival and gain his cooperation, and at first, Buell seemed to be interested, even suggesting on February 18th that he meet with Grant, Halleck's subordinate, to "study the ground."[65] Halleck had also considered how to keep the political generals out of his way, while he placed the regulars he wanted in command over volunteers. Halleck declared that it was decided in the Mexican War that "regulars ranked volunteers without regard to dates. This decision, if sustained, makes everything right for the Western Division." Another item Halleck put on a want list that he communicated to Stanton was 50,000 soldiers to be transferred from the Army of the Potomac to Halleck in order for him to subjugate both Tennessee and Missouri.[66] On the 17th, Halleck had also been juggling his human resources, assigning Grant to a newly constituted District of West Tennessee, while he sent General Sherman, the subordinate so deeply in his debt, to take command of Cairo, Paducah and Smithland.[67] So while Grant perceived that Nashville was ripe for the taking and longed to act on it, squabbles being mediated in Washington over who had authority to take the Tennessee capital, prevented Halleck, Grant, and Foote from moving on Nashville. It seems everyone had a plan or idea on what should happen next, while Lincoln, who usually took an active interest and role in military planning, was incapacitated that February by the death of his little son Willie. This personal loss, along with the serious illness of his son Tad, left Lincoln struggling to cope.[68]

While Sherman continued to assist Grant in getting the wounded out of Donelson and trying to prevent worried families of the wounded and missing from filling up the boats that would transport them, Grant shared his frustration with Sherman over his own inability to move on to Nashville.[69] In the midst of it all, Grant wrote to Elihu Washburne on February 21, 1862, answering Washburne's inquiry about a place on Grant's staff for his younger brother, Cadwallader Washburn. (Elihu Washburne for unknown reasons added a final "e" to his name that the rest of the family did not use.) Grant assured Washburne that he had a place on his staff for Cadwallader, and he personally thanked Washburne for the opportunities that the representative's continued support had given him. Cadwallader is a good example of the power of political influence. A wealthy politician from a family of wealthy and influential Republican politicians, he is reputed to have given adequate service, but his rise from colonel in February of 1862 to brigadier general of volunteers in July of 1862, and to major general by March of 1863, to date from November 1862, could be termed meteoric.[70]

On February 24th, three boats arrived at Federally occupied Clarksville, Tennessee, with a division that constituted Buell's advance under the command of Brig. Gen. William "Bull" Nelson. Grant immediately sent them to occupy Nashville. Johnston had abandoned the city, and conflicting reports placed Johnston at Murfreesboro, some 35 miles southeast of Tennessee's capital, while later reports had Johnston's troops at Chattanooga.[71] Thus, Halleck, while not able to claim the occupation of Nashville, could take some credit for its acquisition, inevitable after the fall of Fort Donelson, and add to his list of accomplishments the fall of Columbus, Kentucky, which was evacuated on March 2nd. On March 8th, another of Halleck's commanders, Brigadier General Sam Curtis (USMA, 1831), fought and won the pivotal battle of Pea Ridge, Arkansas, a victory that would consolidate the Union hold over Missouri for the next two years. But the credit for the occupation of Nashville still eluded Halleck, for after Gen. William Nelson occupied the city, it was Buell who arrived (some would say came waltzing in), unopposed, to accept Nashville's surrender.[72]

Whoever should have accepted the laurels, McClellan didn't fall in with Halleck's plans, for he was not about to let Halleck supersede his man Buell.[73] Failing to convince McClellan that his plan for the West was best, as February was drawing to a close, Halleck took his appeal for there to be one commander in the West directly to Secretary of War Stanton, saying they were missing a golden opportunity that could only be taken advantage of if Halleck was given control over Buell's army.[74] But instead of the news he wished to hear, Halleck would learn that Lincoln had signed the order to promote only one of Halleck's nominees for major general, sending the name of U.S. Grant to the Senate for confirmation. When the Senate confirmed Grant's promotion to major general to date from February 16, 1862, Grant outranked everyone in Halleck's command except for Halleck himself.[75] The very next day Halleck wrote what his biographer Stephen Ambrose described as a "masterfully composed letter which appealed to McClellan's vanity, his fear and hatred of abolitionists, and his desire for new honors." Halleck declared that Radical Republicans were actively supporting the promotion of officers with antislavery sentiments, and were working to see one of their men become lieutenant general. Halleck suggested a plan that would make it possible for McClellan to see that there would be only two generals. McClellan would become a brevet lieutenant general when he took Richmond (history tells us that that should have been a hypothetical — though Halleck did not write it so to McClellan), while Halleck "would come in for it" at the close of the war. Assuring McClellan that Halleck's name would never be used in opposition to McClellan's, Halleck praised Little Mac's character and military skill.[76]

Halleck was also able to draw on his antebellum experience as an expert in international law at this time to bring together the precedents to justify the U.S. government declaring martial law over the captured forts and towns of Tennessee. On March 3, 1862, Lincoln appointed Tennessee Senator Andrew Johnson a brigadier general, and after Senate confirmation, Edwin Stanton appointed Johnson the military governor of Tennessee.[77]

After Fort Donelson, Grant, feeling that the Rebels were ready to relinquish Tennessee, was anxious to move forward, but he lacked the authority as well as the supplies to advance at that time. He had had little opportunity to enjoy his victory, for he was arranging for transportation of the sick and wounded, and coping with the prisoners he held, a duty so onerous he began contemplating a way of paroling the prisoners to be rid of them as soon as possible. Despite captured supplies, some of Grant's own men were suffering without blankets or greatcoats in freezing temperatures, and needs had to be addressed. In the midst of all this, Grant had to arrange for the policing of his own garrison, for plundering at Donelson was rampant.[78] Despite the thievery, Grant's troops were still desperate for some supplies. For instance McClernand reported that his men were suffering from camp diarrhea because of their limited diet of salt beef and no vegetables. While supplies were reported to be available to be sent to Grant's force, there were no ships to transport them, and supplies that were sent, often went astray. Grant begged for supplies and requested that a quartermaster be assigned. What Grant got to help with the overwhelming paperwork after Donelson was a new aide-de-camp. A mutual friend of Rawlins and Representative Washburne, Lt. William R. Rowley was a fellow Galena citizen who, unbeknownst to Grant, was reporting directly to Washburne regarding Grant's behavior. Rowley assured the congressman that February that Washburne would "have no cause to be ashamed of the then Brigadier you have manufactured." Meanwhile, a fawning letter from Grant's staffer Rawlins to Washburne late that March resulted in a promotion to major for Rawlins.[79]

But in spite of all the burdens upon him, Grant was unwilling to remain inactive. A February 24th letter to Julia says it all. " 'Secesh' is now about on its last legs in Tennessee. I want to push on as rapidly as possible to save hard fighting. These terrible battles are very good things to read about for persons who loose [sic] no friends but I am decidedly in favor of having as little of it as possible. The way to avoid it is to push forward as vigorously as possible." Grant then added optimistically, "Gen. Halleck is clearly the same way of thinking and with his clear head I think the Congressional Committee for investigating the Conduct of the War will have nothing to enquire about in the West." But Grant's mind was uneasy. He urged Julia to save some of the money he was sending her "against accident," although he was now earning a very comfortable $6,000 a year.[80] Nor was he happy with the number and condition of his troops. Besides the causalities he had endured, men had to be assigned to guard prisoners, garrison the captured forts, and at the same time, his numbers were being depleted by illness. And as Washington pressured Halleck to become more jailer than host to his Rebel prisoners, Halleck, who had to abandon all hope of charming the Southern sympathizers in the Border states, took out his frustration on Grant.[81] At the time, while Grant still expressed confidence in Halleck, professing him to be "one of the greatest men of the age," Grant confessed to Julia that he wished he had an independent command. And as Grant told the ever-supportive General Sherman, he had no idea what Halleck intended to do next, and he was growing anxious to know what that next move would be, Sherman was keeping Grant in on the gossip and news of what was happening beyond Grant's reckoning.[82]

When the opportunity presented itself for Grant to meet with Buell in occupied Nashville to discuss future offensives and learn what information Buell had of the enemy, it no doubt was irresistible. Grant started for Nashville on February 26th, but waited all the next day without hearing from Buell. As Grant went to the river to return to Fort Donelson, Buell finally turned up to meet with him.[83] While Buell, Halleck's chief competitor for command in the West, was interested for the most part only in occupying Nashville, he had somehow commandeered C. F. Smith's division from Grant's force for his own use. Buell also ordered Smith's division to remain and support him, for Buell feared an attack by Johnston could catch him at a disadvantage before his whole force was consolidated. Grant responded that he would likely need all of his own force, including Smith, since he expected any day to be ordered to make an advance. But Buell was not convinced, as Grant was, that the Rebels were more than willing to leave the area. When Halleck discovered that Smith's division was with Buell, he was dumbfounded, and he was furious that Grant had met with Buell. As it was, Grant's meeting with Buell had been less than satisfactory.[84]

Halleck's continued pleas to McClellan for sole command in the West were rejected,[85] with Halleck commenting, "Believe me General, you make a serious mistake in having three independent commands in the West." Halleck began to take his frustration out on Grant, who was also a handy scapegoat on whom to blame anything that McClellan or anyone else might find to criticize. And while Grant's message to Halleck had clearly stated his intention to go to Nashville unless ordered not to, in a document that exists in the official records,[86] Halleck angrily reported to McClellan that Grant had traveled to

Nashville without Halleck's permission or knowledge. And though other messages from Grant to Halleck, written the last days of February, can also be found in the records, Halleck reported to McClellan that since he had had no communications from Grant, he must charge his subordinate with neglect and inefficiency. Halleck commented, "It is hard to censure a successful general immediately after a victory, but I think he richly deserves it." McClellan thereby authorized Halleck to place Grant under arrest. While Halleck did not deem it necessary to arrest Grant "at present," Halleck did order Grant to turn his command over to Gen. Charles F. Smith[87]

On March 4th, Grant received Halleck's order to remain at Fort Henry and turn over his command to General Smith for the Tennessee River advance. Grant was "in utter amazement, wondering at the cause, as well he might," Smith observed.[88] While Grant had been coping with the aftermath of wounded, prisoners, and stores at Donelson, he had allowed himself to indulge in a sense of accomplishment, but the semblance of security that Grant had begun to feel was misplaced. Still caring what his father thought, Grant had also written to Julia in late February saying that he was anxious to receive a letter from his father to see his criticisms. Grant also quipped, now that he was a major general, "Is father afraid yet that I will not be able to sustain myself?" Ironically, that awful moment when Grant received Halleck's telegram informing him of his removal from command was made more painful by the presence of his father at his headquarters.[89] But Halleck wasn't done with Grant yet. Halleck was particularly piqued by a suggestion from McClellan that Halleck was unready for larger command since he didn't even know his own troop strength.[90] So on the same day, he also reported to McClellan rumors that Grant had begun drinking since his victory at Donelson. There were similar accusations made by discontented subordinates that a number of Grant's enemies were ready to use.[91] Next, telegrams from Halleck to Grant angrily accused him of neglecting to send reports Halleck had requested; it is unclear whether Grant did not receive the requests for reports or whether Grant's reports were not transmitted to Halleck. When Grant tried to discover the cause of his woes, Halleck lied outright about the source of Grant's troubles, with Halleck claiming that it was McClellan who had made the accusations against Grant. Eventually it was discovered that some of the trouble regarding communications had been caused by a telegraphic operator who failed to transmit all of Halleck's and Grant's wires.[92] But the treacherous accusations Halleck had sent to McClellan regarding Grant had many causes other than the unreliable telegraphy of a Rebel partisan. Nor did Grant suspect the truth when Halleck asserted that he was the one who defended Grant against McClellan's suspicions.[93]

In the spring of 1862, Gen. George McClellan (USMA, 1846), was the 36-year-old who, as a regular army captain, had resigned in 1857 to go into the railroad business. He went from captain to major general of volunteers in one leap, then to a regular army major general, only to become general in chief of the armies in November of 1861. But his reign as General-in-Chief was short, for on March 11, 1862, after McClellan's poorly executed Peninsula Campaign, Lincoln removed him from overall command and ordered him to confine his attention to commanding the Army of the Potomac and capturing Richmond. When McClellan fell into disfavor, the roadblock he presented to Halleck's ambitions was removed. Washington perceived success in Halleck's department and it meant opportunity for Halleck. Lincoln instructed Stanton to ask what he would like a new Department of the West to look like, and Halleck became the commander of the new Department of the Mississippi, encompassing most of the area west of the Alleghenies. Halleck, confident that his own star was in the ascendance, addressed a letter to McClellan that was full of spleen, referring to McClellan's failure to direct reinforcements to Halleck during his recent campaigns. Halleck then suggested that McClellan had allowed his friendship with Buell to interfere with military needs. He told McClellan, "You will regret your decision against me on this point," adding, "So be it." Several days after McClellan's removal as general in chief, Halleck was appointed sole commander in the West.[94]

In March and April Halleck could claim more successes, with Gen. John Pope's force taking New Madrid, and then the Confederate stronghold Island No. 10.[95] Halleck's command style with Pope was a demonstration of that which he used throughout the rest of the war, and the one that would keep him firmly in the halls of power. While directing Pope to invest New Madrid and Island No. 10, he then stood back and let all planning and responsibility fall upon the shoulders of the commander in the field. While the commanders could usually count on Halleck for supplies and reinforcements, they would not be receiving specific orders from Halleck, should they want them or not. Nor would Flag-Officer Foote unhesitatingly follow the army's orders from now on. Dismayed by Halleck's lack of planning and his quickness to accept credit for himself and the army, Foote withheld what had previously been full and unquestioning cooperation.[96]

In the first weeks of March 1862, Grant, distraught and feeling disgraced, was ill with a severe chest cold and headaches.[97] Different newspapers gave different commanders credit for the Federal success, among them Halleck, Stanton, McClellan and Buell, none of whom were shy about accepting the accolades. Meanwhile, as historian Cooling observes, Grant and his army seemed lost in the shuffle, and total exploitation of Grant's victories on the twin rivers was neglected. Luckily, the Confederates seemed equally unable to take advantage of opportunities.[98] Caught on the sidelines in this power struggle, Grant applied three times to Halleck to be relieved from duty.[99] But now that Halleck was going to get what he wanted, that is, command of the Department of the Mississippi, created by merging the Department of the Missouri and the Department of the Ohio, Halleck informed Grant on March 13th that he could rejoin, though not yet take command of, the Tennessee River expedition. After all, Halleck did not want Washington to take a closer look at his accusations against Grant, and Washburne, Grant's political ally in Washington, was asking questions. Grant wrote to Washburne, asserting that it had been his idea to attack Forts Henry and Donelson, and asking whether Halleck and McClellan would have given him command of the expedition if they had not had confidence in him.[100] Meanwhile, Halleck continued to allow Grant to believe that it was he, Halleck, who had rescued Grant from the accusations made against him. Yet, Grant still did not have a real command. Later in his memoirs, Grant would confess he suspected that Halleck thought Smith a better commander than he was, and sometimes Grant thought so too.[101] To add to the strain, when Grant had turned command over to Smith, McClernand had challenged the admired Smith's seniority and right to command, a presumption that likely deeply rankled Grant. Meanwhile, on the home front, Grant continued to worry about money and agonized over how hostile newspapers abused him, hurting his family and friends. Then, too, he heard from Julia that, after an argument with the women in Grant's family, she must move herself and the children.[102] When the demoralized Grant again applied to be relieved and was making arrangements to go home, Halleck finally restored Grant to command, and Grant, on March 14, 1862, accepted.[103] It would take some time for Grant to get over his temporary removal from command. And though returned to command, Grant would not be spared from Halleck's scolding, for on the same day he was restored, he received a dressing down from Halleck regarding his medical department. Grant replied with a letter to Halleck addressing many of the accusations that had resulted in his past troubles, including the thievery at Fort Donelson, which Grant amazingly blamed on the Sanitary Commission. He also suggested that Nashville wasn't really outside his district, permission to travel there wasn't really needed, and last but not least, Grant assured Halleck that he had sent his reports and had done his duty.[104]

Lincoln had nominated Charles F. Smith as a major general of volunteers for his service at Donelson in early March, and after Smith had replaced Grant, he had started the advance up the Tennessee River with Halleck's instructions to avoid major confrontations and simply destroy Rebel communications. Smith occupied Savannah, Tennessee, on March 11, and William T. Sherman and his division were given permission by Halleck to join the expedition. Sherman occupied Pittsburg Landing, Tennessee, on the 15th, when it was found that the small river settlement had a direct road to Corinth, just 19 miles from that perceived future Federal objective. It was believed that 50,000 to 60,000 Rebels occupied Corinth, and Halleck, ordering Buell to move toward Grant's army, wanted no significant fighting until Buell and Grant united.[105] On April 2, 1862, Smith relinquished command to Grant per Halleck's orders. Smith later died on April 25, 1862, at Grant's headquarters at Savannah, Tennessee, on his sickbed, able to hear the thunder and crash of the battle a few miles to the north. He died from infection of an abraded shin that he had injured jumping from one boat to another; his condition was aggravated by dysentery.[106]

While Halleck was hardly enthusiastic about U.S. Grant, did Sherman feel he had Halleck's confidence? On February 24th, Halleck was annoyed that Cairo did not have the blank forms they needed. Halleck commented, "There is a screw loose in that command; it had better be fixed pretty soon or the commander will hear from me." The commander was Gen. William T. Sherman, and since Sherman was recovering from what most historians describe as a nervous breakdown, it's unlikely Halleck could have chosen words that would have discouraged Sherman more should he have heard of them.[107] Meanwhile, Grant, with one of the biggest battles of the war ahead of him, was still obsessed with getting reports from his subordinates and getting information and returns to Halleck. Still struggling to regain his health on March 10, Grant got Halleck's permission to rejoin the Tennessee River expedition, and his staff presented him with the sword that now rests in the Smithsonian. It was presented with the sentiment, "At this moment when the jealousy caused by your brilliant success has raised up hidden enemies who are endeavoring to strike you in the dark, it affords us an opportunity to express our renewed confidence in your ability as a commander." Grant, overcome with emotion, was unable to reply.[108]

Asserting that he began to feel better as soon as he was back with his troops, Grant arrived at Savannah, Tennessee, on March 17th, reporting to Halleck the next day that he was ordering all troops to concentrate at Pittsburg Landing, the landing place chosen by Smith for its access road to Corinth and its adjoining plain, so ideal as a campground for large numbers of troops. Buell, who had left Columbia, Tennessee, in mid–March was detained rebuilding a bridge the Rebels had destroyed. Though still approximately 75 miles from Savannah,[109] Buell was leading his 35,000 man army in Grant's direction, as Grant evaluated Pittsburg Landing's suitability. Grant also offered Halleck his preliminary opinion that the Rebels numbered fewer than 40,000. Grant had Halleck's orders to bring on no general engagement until his numbers were sufficient to ensure success. When Buell's and Grant's armies were united, Halleck would arrive and take command of the Federal advance on Corinth. Grant's orders to both Smith and Sherman were to "fortify himself partially and to make no stand against a superior force should he be attacked...," but there apparently was no attempt to entrench. Perhaps Grant's concern for enemy aggression was somewhat allayed when Sherman, whose reputation was for exaggerating threats, made little of the constant Rebel activities on the fringes of the Federal army. And as if there wasn't enough to take Grant's mind off the coming confrontation with the enemy, on one of his many trips to Pittsburg Landing, a fall with his horse left his ankle bruised and the commander hobbling around. Meanwhile Grant wished for and asked for more specific instructions from Halleck, but he did not get them.[110]

Questions were asked at the time, and are still being asked, as to why Grant impatiently crossed his army to the side of the river where the enemy was — the side opposite to where his reinforcements, Buell's vanguard, would be arriving? Why did Grant not fortify himself as Halleck ordered?[111] Is it possible that Grant had no wish, despite Halleck's orders, to delay an encounter with the enemy until Buell could arrive? Is it possible that Grant wished to fight the Rebels before Halleck could come and supersede Grant? And why would Grant later insist that he hadn't needed Buell's assistance to fight the enemy successfully the second day at Shiloh? As Ambrose Bierce points out, it took the combination of what was left of

Cairo to Shiloh. Adapted from Plate CXXV, *Official Atlas* (Ned Smith).

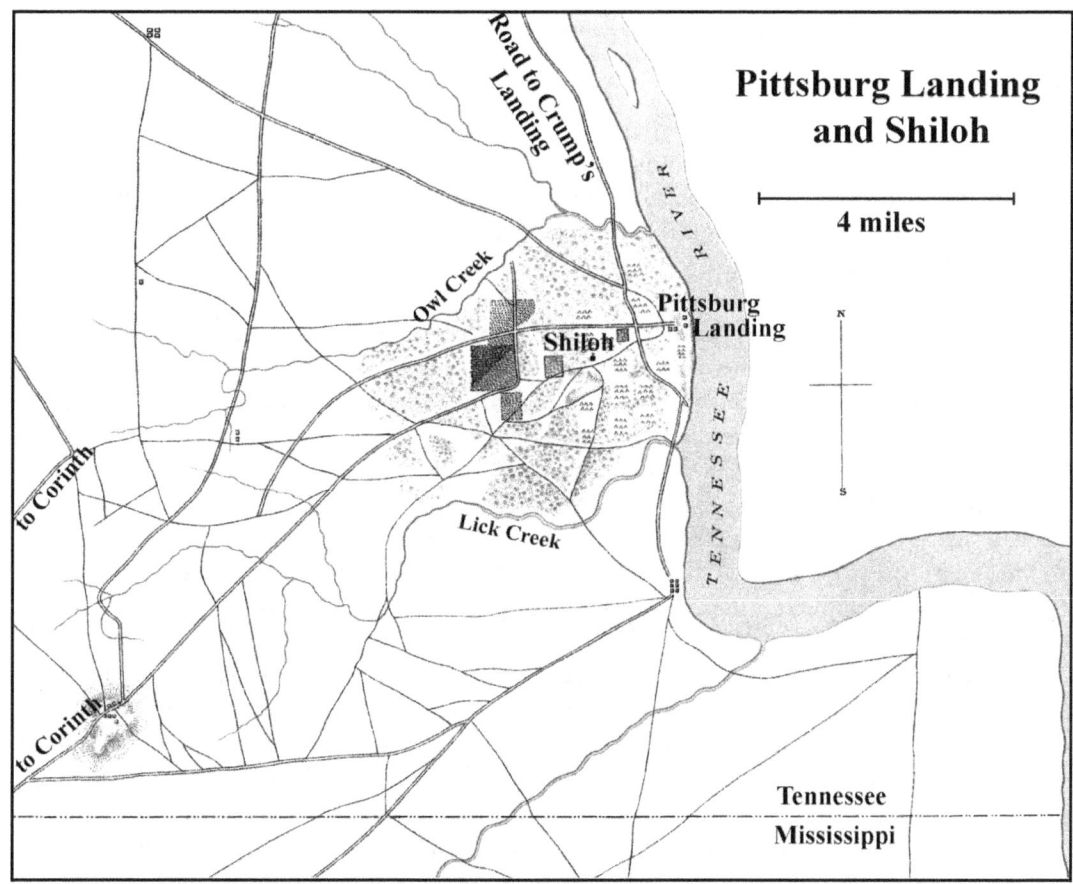

Pittsburg Landing and Shiloh. Adapted from *Official Records*, Ser. 1, Vol. X, Pt. 1, 392 (Ned Smith).

Grant's tired army and Buell's 30,000 fresh troops a whole day of terrible fighting to recover the death-filled ground that Grant had lost the day before and to send the Rebels on their way to Corinth.[112] And so, did Grant intentionally attempt to engage the enemy before either Buell or Halleck could arrive? One often hears that the waiting before battle is the most difficult part of warfare. Was Grant's often-stated desire to attack or engage in battle immediately, without disposition or knowledge, the result of his inability to wait until it made sense to attack?

But with the inevitability of a large and momentous battle looming ahead of him, it should be remembered that Grant also had plenty to distract him from what he should have been focused upon at Savannah and Pittsburg Landing. While at Savannah, Grant was still fretting over details of captured stores that had been stolen at Donelson, and was promising to get reports to Halleck. And Grant continued to ponder over and fret about the two weeks after Donelson when his and Halleck's communications went missing. As Grant wrote to his friend, Representative Washburne, on March 22, 1862,

> After geting [*sic*] into Donelson Gen. Halleck did not hear from me for near two weeks. It was about the same time before I heard from him. I was writing every day and sometimes as often

as three times a day. Reported every move and change, the conditions of my troops &c Not getting these Gen. Halleck very justly become [*sic*] dissatisfied and was, as I have since learned, sending me d[a]ily repremands.

While Grant observed that many were making claims about whose idea it was to attack by way of the Tennessee and Cumberland Rivers, Grant demanded that Washburne consider that "as to how the battles should be fought both McClellan and Halleck are too much of soldiers to suppose that they can plan how that should be done at a distance.... The job being an important one neither of the above Generals would have entrusted it to an officer who they had not confidence in."[113]

But his troubles with Halleck did not all concern things of the past. On March 24th, Halleck was raking Grant over the coals regarding "irregularities" in his medical department, including another accusation that Grant had ignored Halleck's orders, giving Grant more to worry about besides his troops and their disposition. Several days later, members of an expedition sent from Sherman's command to confiscate cotton were accused of stealing livestock and burning a house. Sherman defended his troops, denying any improper actions, but he also suggested that, since the Rebel cavalry were burning cotton and stealing horses and wagons, perhaps the Federals *should* anticipate the enemy and take them first. It is an interesting question that will get very different answers later in Sherman's career and in later days of the war.[114]

On March 25th, Grant sent Halleck a map delineating the placement of Smith, Hurlbut, Sherman and McClernand's divisions around Pittsburg Landing, with Wallace six miles away. It would become significant later when questions were raised about just who had placed the divisions and who was aware of their locations. Meanwhile, Grant, still trying to placate Halleck, frantically demanded an answer from McClernand on how a man had a pass to board one of the steamers with what was suspected to be a stolen horse. Sorting through the tangled chain of command, it turned out that the pass, which had been given to a scout, somehow had been amended to include a scout and a horse. McClernand declared himself sympathetic to Grant's concerns and awkward position, for all blame was falling on Grant when things were not done according to Halleck's orders. Days later, Grant was still trying to sort out the problems of passes initiating from commands other than his own headquarters. Grant made the peevish excuse that this army was mostly new to him, and he was receiving "such feeble support from many officers." Grant also mentioned that, in many cases, passes had been issued to allow the sick to leave the army, for they had been without necessary medicine for a week, despite properly made requisitions. In fact, Grant and his staff were suffering from the same diarrhea, chills and fevers that were afflicting the troops. Grant was also ordered to investigate a report that the 21st Missouri, while on the river between Paducah, Kentucky, and Pillsbury, Tennessee, took potshots at innocent civilians along the shore. And then there were the accusations that McClernand's men were carrying off Negroes and Grant's scouts were stealing horses. One is forced to wonder, under such conditions, who would want to be commander of an army, and how did Grant stand it?[115] On March 27th, McClernand provided further diversion by again questioning Smith's seniority, demanding to know what the dates were on his and Smith's promotions to major generals. Grant referred the question to Halleck, and Halleck referred the question to the secretary of war. Grant, meanwhile, who had been waiting for Buell at Savannah, prepared to move his headquarters to Pittsburg Landing to take command, and defuse the difficulties between Smith and McClernand.[116]

In the spring of 1862, though Gen. Albert Sidney Johnston continued to face a buildup of Federal forces with numbers superior to his own, Davis failed to send him significant reinforcements. Even the shock waves that the fall of Forts Henry and Donelson had caused in the Confederate capital resulted in fewer than 10,000 men being sent to bolster Johnston's western force. Another gesture made was Davis's assignment of Gen. P.G.T. Beauregard to Johnston as second in command. Davis distrusted Beauregard, who had tried to establish that after the Rebel victory at First Bull Run, he had wanted to capture Washington, D.C., but Davis had prevented him. But Beauregard's name also had good propaganda value, and the thought of exiling the fractious Creole away from the Confederate capital may also have appealed to Davis. Since serving as second in command for Gen. Albert Sidney Johnston was not a demotion, as he went west on February 24, 1862, Beauregard might have fancied the idea that he would rescue Rebel interests in the West.[117]

Bolstered by reinforcements that Beauregard had solicited from all over the Confederacy, the fate of the Mississippi Valley was seemingly going to be the stakes for this one aggressive Rebel throw.[118] Albert Sidney Johnston's army of just over 40,000 began its advance from Corinth to Pittsburg Landing on April 3rd, as Grant was confidently reporting that his army could go anywhere it wanted without bringing on an general engagement *except* for approaching the enemy's railroads. Contact had been made by telegraph with Buell's vanguard, and it, under Gen. Bull Nelson's command, was expected to arrive on Saturday, April 5th. While Grant realized that a terrible battle was in the offing, he did not expect it to begin until he, Grant, began it. Though they were constantly in the presence of enemy pickets, he was convinced that the enemy would await them at Corinth or, at the worst, would fight them along the 19 miles of roads that led to Corinth once the Union army began its advance. On April 4th, the day before the Rebels' general attack, Johnston's army probed the Federals, and Sherman believed that the rough handling they had given the Rebel reconnaissance would prevent any further enemy incursions. Though Grant now estimated the enemy force at 80,000, twice their actual number, he was still confident that the Rebels remained at Corinth. With more of Buell's force expected the next day, Grant sent his engineer, James McPherson, to Hamburg, four miles from Pittsburg Landing, to find a suitable campsite for Buell's men. When the time came for Grant's and Buell's combined armies to advance on the Rebels, a good road connected Hamburg to Corinth. Meanwhile, Sherman reiterated his conviction that the enemy would not attack.[119] So while Sherman undoubtedly influenced Smith's decision to occupy Pittsburg Landing, later Sherman was in charge of placing more and more of the troops as they arrived. And though Sherman had given instruction for the forces to encamp in proximity to one another, and facing in the direction that allowed defense, Sherman's instructions were widely ignored and nothing was done about it.[120] And even though Grant himself became fully aware of the arrangements of the forces at Pittsburg Landing, he failed to change them or take any precautions by way of defensive works or a better placement of troops to receive an attack. What Sherman's critics see when they look at the deep creeks that formed the sides of Sherman's position is the trap the Union army placed itself in at Pittsburg Landing. Sherman's supporters defend the site with its deep, swift-running creeks as having ready-made barriers to keep the Rebels off the Union army's flanks. And Sherman, it must be remembered, had made suggestions to Grant that some the troops be placed at sites other than Pittsburg Landing. But as the Rebels approached Pittsburg on the morning of April 6th, they were astonished that they found no outposts and no pickets until they were veritably right upon their Unionist foes.[121]

Grant often proposed that he who attacked first had the advantage. It was one of the most important principles hammered home by Professor Dennis Hart Mahan at West Point, who said,

> Speed is one of the chief characteristics of strategical marches, as it is of the ordinary movements on the battle-field. In this one quality reside all the advantages that a fortunate initiative may have procured; and by it we gain in the pursuit all the results that a victory on the battlefield has placed in our hands.... No great success can be hoped for in war in which rapid movements do not enter as an element. Even the very elements of Nature seem to array themselves against the slow and over-prudent general. The chevalier Folard has very well remarked, "that the slow and heavy in war will partake of as little of the glory of this world, as the lukewarm will of that of the world to come."[122]

It is interesting how the administration, as the war went on, changed its attitude toward confiscating or withdrawing protection from Rebel property owners, which facilitated the army's ability to travel faster and lighter. But while Mahan urged speed, he also warned in his treatise the importance of being prepared for what the enemy would do,[123] a lesson Grant did not seemingly take to heart. Mahan stated that neglecting to protect one's columns from surprise had brought about some of the greatest disasters in history. So while Grant seemingly often heeded Mahan's advice on the importance of attacking first, he surely should have kept in mind that he must be prepared should the enemy be the one who managed to attack first with all the advantages that could provide his foe.[124] It is interesting to ponder on Grant's penchant for headlong, often unprepared attack. Many participants in war have described the great stress of waiting for the moment, perhaps just the right moment, to attack. Perhaps the waiting was more than Grant could stand.

There are many "what-ifs" about Shiloh, as there are about all battles. What would have happened if Johnston had been able to get his army up to attack the Federals on April 4th as originally planned, well before Buell was at hand to bring fresh reinforcements to Grant? Difficult terrain and torrential rain slowed the Rebel advance, to the point that Beauregard, despairing of any element of surprise, ultimately advised Johnston against attacking at all. But Johnston was determined to carry through, and on the morning of April 6th, Johnston's orders for his army's attack should have smashed in the Federal army with the heaviest Rebel force to assault the Yankee left, pushing the Unionists back against Owl Creek and cutting them off from their only line of escape, the Tennessee River. But as author James Lee McDonough in *Shiloh* points out, the Rebel army did not follow Johnston's plan, an occurrence that can be explained by Johnston's orders having been changed by his second in command, Pierre Gustave Beauregard, who instead pushed the Confederate reserves toward the Federal center rather than its left. When Albert Sidney Johnston went to the front, Beauregard was left holding the reins of the Confederate attack.[125] Or was it Braxton Bragg's stubborn series of futile attacks on the Union center, vainly spending the lives of his men at the Hornet's Nest when his assignment had been to assault that all-important weak Federal left, that ultimately gave the gift of the battle to the Federals?[126] And what if Sherman had placed the troops with experience (those who had fought at Donelson) in the most exposed or isolated positions instead of placing his greenest troops, those with no battlefield experience and little training, where the threat was the greatest? The estimated 7,000 Federals who fled the field at Shiloh during the terrible surprise of the Rebel attack were, it is suspected, from these raw regiments, while Sherman's veterans had thoughtlessly been positioned back by the river. And when the green regiments that first bore the brunt of the Confederate attack had sent back warnings to Sherman's headquarters, they were ignored, for Sherman believed these newly mustered soldiers were easily stampeded. The "what-ifs" may add up to the possibility that the Rebel army could conceivably have destroyed Grant's army that first day at Shiloh, a battle "what-if" that can be forcefully argued and imagined. Errors made by the Confederate leadership, however, let Grant survive the Rebel onslaught with enough of his army to fight again, with reinforcements, the next day. While it seems that both Sherman and Grant protested way too much regarding whether or not they were "surprised" at Shiloh, the fact remains that the battle did turn out, despite many blunders, to be another nail in the Confederacy's coffin. The controversies of Shiloh are still argued today, and it will be highly surprising if they are not argued in the future.[127]

Heavy firing from the direction of Pittsburg Landing was Grant's first indication that his army had been attacked. Sending a message from Savannah to Buell, who had approached close enough to Grant's army to hear the fight for himself, Grant commented that he had been expecting an attack but had thought it would not come until April 7th or 8th, and that he was leaving Savannah for Pittsburg Landing. A message from Grant, after he arrived on the field at Shiloh, to another of Buell's commanders stressed the difference the arrival of fresh troops on the field could make, and Grant estimated that the number of Rebels attacking was 100,000 men. It was, in fact, around 40,000.[128] Grant had already ordered Nelson's newly arrived division to march for the place on the river opposite Pittsburg Landing. Grant also ordered Lew Wallace's force, stationed at Crump's Landing, to enter the fight, but uninstructed, Wallace set out on a road that, prior to the Rebel attack, would have led his division to the lines of his own army. But because the Federals had been driven back, Wallace's initial advance would have led him, unknowingly, to behind the Rebel lines where his force was too small to attack the Rebel rear independently. If he had, Wallace's force would likely have been captured or destroyed. Messengers from Grant eventually warned Wallace of this danger, necessitating a long and time-consuming countermarch, resulting in Wallace not reaching the field until after dark, missing that day's battle all together. The Grant-Wallace disagreement over who was right and who was wrong regarding this day, and who was responsible for the delay, would continue for years.[129]

That night, Buell and another division of his army arrived, with another division arriving the next day.[130] Early on the morning of the April 7th, Grant counterattacked, and the day long fight drove the Rebels from the field. After the battle, Grant told Buell that his troops were too tired after two days of fighting to pursue the enemy. Grant commented that he would not move more than one day's march from his current position at Pittsburg Landing. (One wonders how they would have fared after *three* days of battle, like the Army of the Potomac at Gettysburg?) On the 8th, Grant reported to Halleck that

Federal cavalry supported by infantry was pursuing the enemy fleeing toward Corinth as far as Pea Ridge. On April 9th, Halleck responded that he was coming with reinforcements to the field, and to avoid another confrontation with the enemy.[131] In a letter to Julia after Shiloh, Grant described what he perceived as a battle unlike any other that had ever been fought on their continent, a terrible two-day battle with, what Grant thought at the time, was an attack by an enemy of 162 regiments of Rebels, double the actual number that had attacked at Shiloh on the first day. He estimated that the heavy losses were 20,000 all together — very near the real figure.[132]

In Grant's April 9th report, he described that when the Rebels attacked his pickets, all five of his divisions responded by drawing into a line of battle, and he admitted that the enemy then drove that line nearly halfway from their camps to the river. When the Rebels tried to take the Federal right and Pittsburg Landing, Grant credits the gunboats and Nelson with driving them off. While criticizing Lew Wallace, Grant was vociferous in his praise of Sherman, and Grant also extols McPherson's reconnaissance and direction of troops to their proper positions, a puzzling observation since McPherson was one of those who apparently misdirected Wallace. Having accurately stated in the letter to his wife that he thought he had lost 10,000, Grant in his report understated his losses as 1,500 killed and 3,500 wounded, while claiming Rebel losses were greater than they actually were. Grant does not mention division commander Benjamin Mayberry Prentiss's stubborn defensive fight at the Hornet's Nest, holding off the Confederates for six hours, which gave commanders, including Sherman, enough time to form the last of the army's defensive lines. Prentiss is mentioned in Grant's report, but the only distinction accorded him in comparison with other commanders was the comment that Prentiss had been taken prisoner. By May 1st, Sherman would have his second star for his services at Shiloh. Two weeks later, McPherson became a brigadier general, and by October, he would have his second star. The captured Prentiss was exchanged in October, and while he was made a major general the next year, he resigned in 1863 when he felt he had been "shelved" with his assignment to the District of East Arkansas.[133]

By the end of the first day, Grant, although his troops had been pushed back two and a half miles, had been able to finally patch together a reasonably solid defensive line. The line was made up of McClernand and Sherman's troops, who had fallen back earlier in the afternoon, as well as those of Prentiss's troops who had been able to avoid capture. While Nelson, who arrived with the vanguard of Buell's troops at Pittsburg Landing, credits himself with saving the day, it does not seem accurate. At the end of the first day, the Union army was in a good position with fresh reinforcements. And most of all, when both Sherman and McPherson assumed their army would withdraw, Grant seemed incapable of knowing when he was beaten — that gift or curse that would drive him on upon many another battlefield. And why not? Reinforced, Grant now had 40,000 to 45,000 men to meet the 20,000 to 25,000 Rebels at Shiloh. Beauregard, who assumed command after Johnston's death, slept that night in Sherman's captured headquarters tent, and seemingly did not suspect what the dawn of April 7th would bring.[134]

Despite the disorganization and exhaustion of the Confederate force, the Federals' dawn attack was no walk in the park. Despite overwhelming Unionist numbers, stubborn Rebel resistance brought the Federal advance to a standstill by 8 A.M. Fierce fighting took place over some of the same fields as the first day's slaughter, the battle eventually turning in the Federals' favor in the afternoon. Sherman did not begin his pursuit of the exhausted Rebels until the following day, and its purpose seemed more to establish that the enemy had left the field rather than inflicting any further damage on the Rebel army. Repelled by Nathan Bedford Forrest's cavalry, acting as the Confederates' rear guard, Sherman turned back to his camp at Shiloh.[135]

Some Northern newspapers made much of the surprise Grant had received at Shiloh, and spoke of how fearfully the Federal army had been battered. Such reports temporarily bolstered Beauregard's insistence that Shiloh had been a great Confederate victory, but that did not last. Grant's actions after the battle at Shiloh, an apparent reaction to the hot water he had experienced after Fort Donelson, were designed to avoid or forestall controversy and criticism. In General Order No. 34 Grant congratulated his troops. In General Order No. 22, division commanders were ordered to make out and send field returns without delay. They were to report the part taken by each division, and take notice of those officers and men who disgraced themselves by their cowardice, stating what charges would be brought against them. While Sherman had acquitted himself well that first day, the ground he initially defended and then surrendered was more favorable than that occupied by Prentiss, who received the full impact of the Rebel attack. But it was Prentiss's stubborn resistance that can be described as ultimately saving the day for the Federals at Shiloh.[136]

Grant issued strict orders on who could leave or enter his encampment after the battle, and Grant refused to give Beauregard access to the battlefield, stating that the Rebel dead had already been buried. Grant was still overestimating the number of Confederates nearby, believing that they still possessed 162 regiments, though Grant also believed the Rebels would not be able to mount another general attack for several weeks. Grant did, however, uncharacteristically suggest that it might be necessary for his force to retire across the river if Federal reinforcements weren't received soon.[137]

In mid–April, Halleck had taken command of all the forces at Pittsburg Landing, leaving Grant at least nominally in command of the Army of the Tennessee. After issuing a general order praising the troops for their victory at Shiloh, Halleck bragged to his wife that on his arrival the army's officers were very glad to see him, that Grant's army was undisciplined and very much disorganized, its officers incapable of maintaining order, and he, Halleck, had been hard at work straightening things out. Informing Grant that his army was "not now in a condition to resist an attack," Halleck demanded that Grant reorganize his artillery, complete and forward his returns and send them through proper channels so intermediaries could add comments, perhaps a more reasonable and pertinent request than the demand that letters to Halleck's headquarters should address only one subject. There was also the complaint made by his headquarters regarding whether or not official correspondence was being folded properly. But in case the commanders had not yet given in to despair, Halleck also ordered them to begin drilling and holding inspections, to establish strict control in the area around the Landing, and when the commanders were not reporting, folding, and patrolling, they were to establish a defensive line with the Army of the Ohio with its left on Lick Creek, and the Army of the Tennessee with its right on Owl Creek, and then send work parties to repair bridges and roads in the area.[138]

It was one of these work parties that gave Grant his first contact with Phil Sheridan. Though Sheridan recalled that his first meeting with Grant was in the fall of the year,

Grant noticed that spring a work party standing in the rain outside his headquarters, waiting for one Philip H. Sheridan to come and take command of the road repair crew to which they'd been assigned. When Sheridan didn't show up, Grant dismissed them and reported the delinquent Sheridan to Halleck's headquarters. Halleck already knew Sheridan well. Sheridan, as a sort of personal quartermaster to Halleck, had supplied headquarters with the comforts that Halleck and his chief of staff, George Washington Cullum (USMA, 1843), demanded.[139]

Sheridan, while pursuing a regular source for ice from the medical department, met Grant's former surgeon, Dr. John Brinton, and he invited Brinton to share his quarters. They came to know each other well as they frequently rode out to forage together for their and Halleck's headquarters' table. Another of Halleck's orders, that any officer who neglected to do his duty when in command of a work detail should be arrested and court-martialed, was apparently not enforced when it came to his own headquarters staff.[140]

The incident regarding the work detail standing out in the rain was not the only time Grant had an unpleasant incident with Philip Sheridan in his early acquaintance with the man. Well after the war, Grant related an incident when he had requested that Sheridan and his regiment, which had been assigned elsewhere, stay with Grant's command. Grant observed that Sheridan's reply, that "he would rather go than stay ... was brusque and rough, and annoyed me. I don't think Sheridan could have said anything to have made a worse impression on me." While Grant described watching Sheridan's subsequent military career and seeing that there was "something in him," it hardly explains Grant's postwar comments that he would rank "Sheridan with Napoleon and Frederick and the great commanders in history." Grant followed this startling accolade with a description of the spy network Sheridan developed in the Shenandoah Valley and Sheridan's "magnetic quality of swaying men." While Sheridan certainly swayed Grant, it still doesn't explain Grant's attitude toward the now infamous incident when Sheridan was a cadet and was suspended from West Point for attacking an upperclassman. Of that, Grant commented when he was President that he tried to get the unfair rules at West Point changed, such as the one that had been inflicted on "poor Sheridan." Grant's seeming blindness to any of Sheridan's faults will be a recurring theme in our considerations of the Overland Campaign.[141]

Captain Philip Sheridan (*Personal Memoirs of P.H. Sheridan*, New York: Charles L. Webster, 1888).

On April 17th, Halleck also ordered

Grant and Buell to appoint boards to investigate the character and capacity of volunteer officers, most particularly their conduct in the recent battles. In all cases of improper conduct, the boards decided whether an officer should simply be dismissed or tried for cowardice. John Logan headed the board of investigators, and General Sherman submitted charges against five officers in his division, all of whom were dismissed or resigned.[142] In the meantime, an inquiry on April 23rd from Stanton and the President, asked why Halleck had made no official report on Shiloh, and they wanted to know whether any neglect or misconduct by General Grant or any other officer contributed to the "sad casualties that befell our forces that Sunday."[143] Halleck replied that there had been bad conduct on the part of some Federal officers who were unfit to command, but Halleck also attributed the high casualties to the "numbers and bravery" of the enemy. Stating that he would not elaborate before receiving the reports of his division commanders, Halleck asserted, again incorrectly, that the enemy had suffered greater losses than he had. Many of the participants at Shiloh would remember the horrors of that battlefield above all others. While many soldiers pondered over whether or not they would live to see home again, after this battle Sherman pessimistically wrote to his wife that he did not expect to survive the war.[144]

Grant, though his real authority had been much diminished by Halleck's presence,[145] still received Washburne's support. Grant heard from Washburne that he had given a speech in the House of Representatives on the subject of Grant's "glorious victory" at Pittsburg Landing. Washburne commented that Grant's critics, still vociferous after Shiloh, were undoubtedly the cowardly scoundrels who had fled the field during the battle. Washburne also sent his regards to Rawlins and Rowley.[146] Meanwhile, Lew Wallace provoked Grant with his report on Shiloh, which Grant disputed. Wallace seemingly places all the blame for his failure to arrive at Shiloh in time for the battle squarely on Grant and his aides. Wallace claimed that at 11:30 in the morning of April 6th, he was given a verbal order to march to the Federal right, and he was well on his way before Grant's aide Rowley arrived in midafternoon to tell Wallace, apparently for the first time, that the Federal right was not where it used to be. At that point, Wallace learned that he was marching toward the rear of the Rebel line where his division would be in danger of being completely cut off. While Wallace insisted that neither Rowley nor subsequent messengers from Grant carried any orders for him, Wallace knew of no option but to countermarch and take another road, which kept his division from reaching the field until long after the battle was over. Grant would claim that Wallace had been told to take the proper road along the river in the first place, and the argument as to who was at fault would continue for the rest of Grant's life. Wallace would comment that many lies were told about his force and his actions, including some newspaper reports that stated that he had a force of 19,000 men, whereas he put the number at 4,500. Wallace was also criticized for failing to attack the Rebel rear, but as he caustically pointed out, the newspaper account describing his death in the battle was an indication of journalistic unreliability.[147]

Halleck's command style was one of constant threat. By way of example, on April 15th, Grant was informed that his army was in no condition to receive an enemy attack and that it must be reorganized and all deficiencies corrected. Halleck again reminded Grant that reports must be forwarded through proper channels in order to give intermediaries the opportunity to add comments, and Halleck again insisted that all reports must be properly "folded and endorsed." Further, since Halleck deemed most of Grant's army deficient in drill and discipline, he reiterated the need for all division commanders to establish rigorous schedules for drill and inspections.[148] And Halleck's orders were not only meant to be obeyed, but to be obeyed promptly. On April 24th, Grant received an order from Halleck to move his command to a position near to and forward of Shiloh Church. On the next day, when Halleck felt his order had not been completely complied with, he not only ordered Grant to report immediately, but also directed him to arrest all officers who had not carried out the order. After explaining why everyone in his command had not moved exactly as Halleck had ordered, Grant then received a letter from Halleck chastising him for not obeying his orders with the "same promptness of the commanders of the other Army Corps." Grant wrote to his wife Julia, "I am no longer boss." While expressing some relief and the hope that maybe the newspapers would now leave him alone, it is a gloomy picture that Grant paints, one of incessant rain, General Smith dying at Grant's headquarters from his infected wound and dysentery, and Julia, at home, apparently having money problems. To round off this tale of woe, in a letter to a friend Grant denied, as he would many times, that he had been surprised by the Confederate attack at Shiloh, claiming again that his 35,000 men had been attacked by a Rebel force of 80,000, with Grant still erroneously doubling the number of his attackers.[149]

When Halleck had arrived at Pittsburg Landing on April 11th, he had brought reinforcements to the Federal army, and with them he could put an army of 100,000 men in the field. Yet it would be nearly three weeks after the Battle of Shiloh before Halleck began his slow and cautious advance on Corinth. When Halleck finally reached Corinth, the Federal investment left Beauregard with no choice but to evacuate the city, and on May 30th, in the face of a hesitating Union army, he managed to do just that. Beauregard managed to convince the Federal advance that the boisterous welcomes the Rebels were giving all the trains that came into Corinth were noisy greetings for butternut reinforcements. The real purpose of the trains was to remove the Confederate army from Corinth.[150] Meanwhile, Halleck continued to send orders to the division commanders through Grant. For example, there was a demand from headquarters that a missing brigade report on transportation in McClernand's division should result in the arrest of the offending brigade commander. Then Grant must see that the missing report be delivered in the next 24 hours. Yet while Grant acted as a conduit for Halleck's micromanaging, he still believed that Halleck had defended him and continued to do so.[151] He wrote to Julia the last of April saying that he suspected a good deal of the bad press he was still receiving over Shiloh originated from soldiers who wanted an excuse for their bad behavior during the battle or by officers who were jealous of his success. Grant was quick to point out that he did not think Halleck was one of these, and he looked upon Halleck as "one of the greatest men of the age."[152] But by mid–May, when Halleck made Grant his second in command, he removed Grant from command of the Army of the Tennessee, replacing him with Gen. George Thomas, now calling that army the "Right Wing."[153] At that point, Grant had had enough. While still smarting from Halleck's rebuff when Grant had offered recommendations as the army approached Corinth,[154] Grant expressed his great dissatisfaction at being thus sidelined. Halleck responded that he was much surprised by Grant's displeasure, declaring, "In the last three months I have done every thing in my power to ward off the attacks which were made upon you. If you believe me your friend, you will not require explanation." But before and after the taking of Corinth, Grant again contemplated resigning, or asking to be reassigned to some distant post where there would be no superior officer or newspapermen second-guessing him.[155] Once again, when Halleck realized he had pushed Grant to the point where he would resign or go on a furlough from which Grant would arrange not to return, Halleck relented and restored Grant to his former command. Halleck sweetened the assignment by returning Gen. George Thomas to the command of his former division and adding that division to Grant's army. With his new headquarters at recently captured Nashville, Grant gleefully sent for Julia and the family to join him.[156]

Those who had remained loyal to U.S. Grant benefited from his good fortune. Grant praised Rawlins, who made himself indispensable by taking most of the burden of paperwork off Grant's shoulders.[157] And Grant continued to sing McPherson's praises, resulting in McPherson's promotion to colonel on May 1, 1862. Fourteen days later, McPherson became a brigadier general. But it was Sherman who benefited most from the good turn in Grant's fortunes. Sherman declared his allegiance to Grant with his warning to Grant regarding his newly won fame: "The moment you obtained a just celebrity at Donelson, by a stroke of war more rich in consequences than the battle of Saratoga, envious rivals and malicious men set their pack of hounds at you, to pull you from the pinnacle so richly attained."[158] And among the many ways that Sherman had demonstrated his loyalty to Grant was his determination to convince Grant to stay with the army when he longed to leave it all behind.[159] In his message of congratulations to Grant on his decision to remain, Sherman condemned the press as the "public enemy" that wished to pull Grant down.[160] Sherman and Grant also came up with their own version of what happened at Shiloh and supported each other unstintingly. Grant observes that with green troops, Sherman had been steadfast that Sunday, gushing, "There has been nothing like it on this continent, nor in history.... He [Sherman] kept his Division in place all day, and aided materielly in keeping those to his right and left in place — He saw me frequently and received, and obeyed, my directions during that day." Grant and Sherman stuck by each other regarding what happened on those fateful days at Pittsburg Landing, and for his services at Shiloh, Sherman was made a major general. So tenaciously did Sherman cling to his position that when he came down with malaria in July, he refused to go home, and he did not allow anyone else who was sick in his command to leave.[161]

One who had not felt any inclination to become one of "Grant's Men" was Philip Sheridan, though he may have come to regret it. When Grant expressed an interest in Sheridan at the seizure of Corinth after Shiloh, Sheridan chose to cast his lot with General Buell's army. Buell's future apparently looked brighter than Grant's at the time. Sheridan therefore ended up with Buell at Perryville, and missed being with Grant at Vicksburg, where Grant's fortunes rose considerably.[162] Meanwhile, Grant's ever-faithful champion in Washington, Elihu Washburne, made his May 2nd speech in Congress, defending and praising Grant. Washburne also alerted Grant to which way the wind was blowing, as Congress began to insist that stronger measures be taken to dismantle slavery. Grant wrote to Washburne assuring him that he felt it was every soldier's duty to obey orders without regard for their own political opinions.[163]

In July, war news from the East was all bad. McClellan had severe losses but was holding his own, according to Halleck, who was worried that some of his own troops might be ordered east to reinforce McClellan. On July 2nd when Lincoln asked Halleck to come to Washington, Halleck used the specter of an impending Rebel attack to refuse,[164] while privately stating that he did not want to get involved in what he saw as a dispute between Stanton and McClellan. But Halleck claimed that a messenger told him that, he, Halleck, was the only one who could reconcile the current difficulties in Washington, and Lincoln ordered Halleck to the capital to assume command over McClellan and all the other generals of the army. While Halleck, no doubt, felt it a high compliment, he still hesitated to accept a promotion that would bring him into conflict with McClellan's powerful friends. And while Halleck apparently assumed that Grant would be taking over command in the West and had summoned Grant to Corinth, Halleck nonetheless queried Stanton as to whether the secretary of war had someone else in mind to appoint.[165]

It must have been a nervous time for Grant when he was summoned to Halleck's headquarters without explanation. They had just had another unpleasant exchange, with Halleck accusing Grant, after the Rebels destroyed a Federal locomotive, of listening to rumors and being stampeded rather than sending out reconnaissance and getting facts. Halleck had also implied that Grant was in some measure responsible for the Confederate incursion. Grant, after describing what precautions he had taken against such attacks, pointed out that both Halleck and McPherson, the latter in command of Federal trains, had given orders to Grant's Army of the Tennessee without his knowledge, in some cases countermanding Grant's orders, so he hardly thought he could be held responsible for this Rebel attack. Halleck's answer was that he hadn't implied that Grant was responsible for the train, but had merely wanted Grant to investigate, and Grant had taken offense. Putting Grant in his place, Halleck added, "I shall, whenever occasion requires it, exercise the right of issuing orders direct to any detached command, or to any undetached command, if I deem it necessary." Halleck's smarmy parting shot was, "I must confess that I was very much surprised at the tone of your dispatch and the ill-feeling manifested in it, so contrary to your usual style, and especially toward one who has so often befriended you when you were attacked by others."[166] It would be 15 years after the war ended before Grant found out about Halleck's duplicity. Halleck, apparently, had the correspondence in which he made accusations against Grant to McClellan removed from the War Department files, and it was well after Halleck's death that Grant found out that Halleck, the man who had claimed to be his friend and defender, had been his enemy. There is also the story that Lincoln, when told that Halleck had backed down when proof of Grant's failings was demanded, smiled and told Stanton to let him know "when Grant's army demoralizes again, and he resumes his bad habits and captures another army, you just send the news over to me, please." It would appear that Lincoln was well aware of Halleck's ability to dissemble, and Lincoln, by bringing Halleck to Washington, had plans to use this wily conniver. There was a place in Washington for a man with brains, military experience, organizational aptitude and a talent for deceit and lying. Lincoln, against Stanton's advice, made Halleck general in chief, commander of all the United States' armies.[167]

On July 17, Grant took command of the District of West Tennessee with his headquarters at Corinth, Mississippi, with Sherman in support at Memphis.[168] Grant had command of 78,870 soldiers, but they were scattered all over his department, which extended from Cairo to Mississippi. Though Halleck had previously been a great believer in consolidating his troops in one place, after taking Corinth he scattered his soldiers all over the district in an attempt to meet the many Rebel incursions and raids.[169] So while troops in the West repaired railroads and attempted to control enemy geurrilla activity, supposedly in preparation for the next big push, there was no indication of when or where that big push would occur. There was only Halleck's warning to Grant when he was leaving for Washington that Grant must be ready to assist Buell, the other commander in the West, should the Rebels threaten from Chattanooga. Meanwhile, Representative Washburne kept Grant up to date on another change in the political climate in Washington regarding policies toward the enemy and their possessions. Washburne reported that the administration was adopting the long-demanded stance of prosecuting the war by seizing Rebel property, including slaves. Washburne advised Grant that the general who best embraced and adopted the administration's new policy would receive the people's esteem. Grant, pragmatically, adopted such a stance, putting escaped or confiscated slaves to work as laborers for the Union. In the meantime, the new general in chief encouraged Grant to clean out his district of Southern sympathizers, sending them south. Halleck suggested that Grant "handle that class without gloves and take their property for public use."[170]

One of Halleck's first unofficial assignments as the government's hit man was to present George McClellan with an ultimatum. McClellan was now the man who had greatly outstayed his welcome, according to the view of many politicians. While Halleck biographer John Marszalek believes that Halleck was reluctant to fire or even offend his former commander, remembering Halleck's previous threat to McClellan, that he would rue the day he had crossed Halleck, suggests that Halleck may have enjoyed every minute of his interview with McClellan. While Halleck observed to his wife that McClellan did not "understand strategy and should never plan a campaign," now holding all the cards, Halleck went to McClellan and gave him a choice: attack on the Peninsula on his own, or withdraw and send reinforcements to Pope. McClellan had reluctantly assured Halleck he would attack the enemy even though Halleck had refused to give him the large infusion of reinforcements that McClellan had insisted he needed. But by the time Halleck got back to Washington from the Army of the Potomac's headquarters, McClellan was already dragging his feet. One of Halleck's attempts to coax McClellan into cooperation took the form of a fawning attempt to sympathize with McClellan's view that the imbecility of Washington was all that was thwarting McClellan's efforts. Halleck also tried agreeing with McClellan that making the eradication of slavery one of the war's goals was a great mistake on the administration's part. Ultimately, Halleck's cozening efforts to win McClellan's favor did not move McClellan, literally or figuratively.[171]

This time, with Halleck at the controls, McClellan's excuses were not accepted. Halleck, taking his cue from Lincoln, again ordered McClellan to advance on Richmond immediately, or withdraw his army from the Peninsula and unite with Pope. McClellan still, apparently, did not get the message. When McClellan entreated Halleck to rescind the order, Halleck reminded McClellan that it was his own reports, the inflated number of 200,000 Rebels standing between Pope and McClellan, that made it necessary to concentrate the Federal forces, lest the Confederates destroy them before they could unite. If McClellan would reinforce Pope — Halleck dangled the bait before McClellan — then McClellan could take command of the big reconstituted army. Wouldn't McClellan be getting what he had been asking for all along? By adding Pope's army to his own, wasn't he getting the reinforcements he had wanted? But McClellan did not agree to hurry to Pope's assistance.[172]

While Halleck had avidly sought full command of the West, and he stated that he would have gladly stayed in the West if he had been allowed, he found stepping up to command all of the armies daunting and frankly frightening. There was no place to hide if things went badly, as they seemingly were. Pope and his army were vulnerable and McClellan refused to cooperate. In the West, the navy had abandoned its investment of Vicksburg because of a lack of army cooperation, Buell refused to move, and Grant was struggling with Rebel guerrillas. And everyone was looking to Halleck to do something about all of these things. Halleck complained to his wife, "this war has developed so little talent in our generals. There is not a single one in the West fit for a great command." Meanwhile impatient politicians saw that the stress on Halleck was beginning to tell, and when Pope asked Halleck whether he should withdraw or attack, Halleck insisted that that was a decision that only the commander in the field could make. All Halleck could do was make suggestions.[173]

Though some of McClellan's troops had been sent to bolster Pope's army, Pope was roundly defeated on August 29th and 30th. Even though Halleck personally blamed McClellan's lack of support as a major factor in the defeat at Second Bull Run, the administration, with no one else to turn to, again put McClellan in command of the Union army in the East. As McClellan took steps to defend the capital, Halleck suffered what had all the appearances of a breakdown. Without sleep for days and suffering from what is described as a severe case of hemorrhoids, Halleck became the subject of all sorts of rumors, including ones that ironically accused Halleck of drunkenness or the use of opium to treat his diarrhea. Whatever the case, when McClellan arrived in Washington, Halleck completely surrendered authority to him.[174]

After Second Bull Run, the Rebels were on the offensive, and Lincoln called upon the army to prepare to meet the enemy incursion into Maryland without weakening the defense of Washington. With Pope dismissed from command, McClellan was in charge of both his former command, the Army of the Potomac, and Pope's Army of Virginia, so McClellan finally had the numbers he had demanded, though he would ask for more. While McClellan acquired what seemingly should have been the upper hand when a copy of Lee's orders were found, he nevertheless moved so cautiously to meet Lee at Antietam, committing his large Federal force piecemeal, that the battle resulted in a draw. Lee withdrew his army from that blood-soaked field to retire unmolested to Virginia. More than 22,000 men, Federal and Confederate, were killed, wounded, captured or missing after the battle, with only an estimate available in the chaotic aftermath of a fight of such catastrophic proportions. Meanwhile, McClellan saw himself, once again, as the savior of the country, and couldn't understand the waves of disapproval he sensed from his bosses at Washington. Hadn't he once again prevented the enemy from marching on Washington? As the administration again contemplated firing him, McClellan thought about quitting in a huff. And once again, McClellan refused to move against the enemy.[175]

A consideration of McClellan and his interaction with the administration is useful in understanding Lincoln's affections, frustrations and predilections as far as his commanders were concerned. A look at a few other of Lincoln's generals, this time in the West, should provide additional insights. The next chapter will consider the days leading up to and during the Battle of Perryville, and presents an incapsulated view of the turmoil taking place within the command structure in the West, both within the Federal and the Confederate armies. It is important not only to consider the strengths and weaknesses of the Union commanders, but the talents and faults of their Rebel counterparts as well. The next chapter also revisits and introduces many officers who will play major roles in the war in the East in the coming years under the command of Lt. Gen. U.S. Grant.[176]

Three

It Takes Buell and Bragg to Make Grant Look Good

With such turmoil in the East, discussion was nonetheless taking place within the administration regarding what the next move should be in the West. Much as his mentor McClellan had done, Buell refused to move, and perhaps Grant's rise in the military structure is as much attributable to Buell's recalcitrance as to any outstanding talent of Grant's. To understand why the seemingly mediocre Grant became such a presidential favorite, it is necessary to look back and consider Buell in the summer and fall of 1862. While many are familiar with the glacial pace of McClellan's campaigns, fewer are familiar with Buell, who many would see as a more likely candidate for command dominance in the West than Grant. To take a step back, Halleck had won out in 1862 over his rival Buell to take command in the West in the Department of the Mississippi. But Halleck scattered his western forces after the capture of Corinth in a vain attempt to securely hold what he had taken, while coping with determined Rebel guerrillas and raiders. Yet Halleck, nonetheless, decided to go on the offensive. It likely gave Halleck no little satisfaction to choose his former uncooperative rival, General Buell, as the unenthusiastic commander of the Unionist force that would at last move into East Tennessee and confront the Confederates. When Buell began this unwelcome trek, much as he had predicted, the foe in the form of Bedford Forrest and John Hunt Morgan destroyed Buell's supply lines and made his life miserable, while the route Halleck insisted Buell use resulted in Chattanooga being made a gift to the Confederates.[1]

Buell's movement, however, did goad into action the ever-vacillating Confederate general, Braxton Bragg, who had replaced Beauregard as commander of the Army of the Mississippi in late June of 1862.[2] This was no small feat, for as historian James McDonough said of Bragg, he "seemed a Confederate Hamlet, unable to make up his mind." Meanwhile, Bragg's ambitious and underhanded second in command, Kirby Smith, who Noe observes compared himself "alternately to Cortes, Hannibal, and Moses," abandoned any pretense of cooperation and pursued his own plans. Instead of attacking the Federals at the Cumberland Gap as he had agreed to do, Kirby Smith bypassed them and marched on to capture Lexington, Kentucky, from which he was soon issuing pleas to Bragg for help. Thus began Bragg's late summer of 1862 invasion of Kentucky. As Bragg abandoned Chattanooga to march north, Buell, finally justified in ignoring Halleck's demand that he concentrate on Chattanooga, turned his eyes once again to Nashville. Instead of sending the two divisions he had borrowed from Grant's army forward to an intended defensive stand against Bragg, Buell sent them to Nashville. Drought and a region already picked clean of food and forage were the reasons Buell gave for keeping his lifeline to Nashville open, though it seems that Buell's disgruntled soldiers were finding and seizing plenty to eat. Meanwhile, when Buell's Army of the Ohio fell back, anger at their commander was becoming the dominant emotion in the Federal ranks, while rumors were running rampant regarding Buell's alleged incompetence or treachery.[3]

The indomitable Gen. George Thomas was one of those subject to General Buell's orders that summer and fall, and Thomas entreated Buell to consider that the Confederates might not be headed for Nashville as Buell was sure they would. Thomas continued to make a case that the Rebels would pour into Kentucky, and urged Buell to concentrate at the railhead and supply depot, McMinnville. But Buell ignored Thomas and ordered concentration at Altamont, a place with little water, no forage, and roads that were impassable for artillery. In late August, heartened by Buell's withdrawal, Bragg set out with his Confederates for Kentucky, just as George Thomas had predicted he would, while Buell withdrew his poorly fed, footsore soldiers back to Nashville. Ignoring Thomas's suggestions for an attack on Bragg, Buell instead tried to explain to Halleck and Washington why he had not met the Rebel incursion. Halleck's exasperated response was "march where you please, provided you will find the enemy and fight him."[4]

Considering that Washington was still smarting from the defeat inflicted on Pope at Second Bull Run, it's not hard to understand the uneasiness regarding what Bragg and his sizable force were up to, for it wasn't known with any certainty where Bragg was. Yet Buell, citing lack of supplies, gave no assurance that he would take these worrisome matters in hand. Before he did anything, Buell announced he would essentially abandon Tennessee by withdrawing the Army of the Ohio altogether from the state, some 45,000 men, to challenge Bragg in Kentucky. When Andrew Johnson, Tennessee's governor, protested loudly, Buell agreed to leave behind in Nashville the one man who seemed to know what was going on, George Thomas, and his division of 5,000 men. Bragg's Army of the Mississippi, having skirted Nashville, then continued north, but with news of Kirby Smith at Lexington and Richmond, Kentucky, at the end of August, the ever-vaccilating Bragg turned his eyes toward Louisville. That goal was snatched away from Bragg when Buell, at great cost to the hungry and footsore men of his army, managed to outrace Bragg and take possession of the city with its web of roads and railroads. After the fight between the opposing forces at nearby Munfordville, Bragg accepted that he simply could not maintain his army in this destitute area, and he began to move again toward Kirby Smith. And for the Federals, at last some good news came from the East. It was reported that McClellan had bested the Rebels along a creek called the Antietam in Maryland, while Buell's exhausted army not only had not won a victory, but had yet to have the fight they sought and had marched so hard to find.[5]

On July 11, 1862, the reluctant Henry Halleck had been ordered to Washington to take the role of commander in chief of the armies. And as mentioned earlier, he commented to his wife, Elizabeth, "One of the messengers said that I was the only man in the United States who could reconcile the present difficulties," an affirmation of his abilities that Halleck apparently thought quite apt. But Halleck was still apparently loath to get embroiled in the power struggles in Washington.[6] But as these scenes between Buell and Bragg played out, Halleck took hold of the many problems facing the far-flung Federal armies, and one of his first actions was the reorganization of the Department of the Ohio. Though Buell kept command of his army, most of the Department was given to Maj. Gen. Horatio Wright, an officer who would later play a major role in the war in the East as one of Grant's corps commanders. An engineer and career officer (USMA, 1841), Wright was made in the mold of Halleck, a great organizer who didn't particularly inspire his men. But Wright went West with the knowledge that Halleck and the administration were dissatisfied with Buell and that Buell would probably soon be removed.[7] Wright also knew how to get rid of competitors for command. He had not been in the West a week before he commented to Halleck that they should replace Gen. Bull Nelson, who didn't like serving in Wright's department, and Wright thought Nelson too prone to be influenced or stampeded by shaky reports.[8] Wright didn't like to change his mind, for he proved to be yet another of the western officers who, once he decided he knew what the enemy would do, refused to accept any other scenario. When Kirby Smith took Richmond, Kentucky, Wright refused to believe it, but once Wright had finally accepted the news, he was quick to deny any responsibility for the defeat. Trying to deal with the disorganized remnants of the Federal force after the Richmond fight, Wright, when faced with a lack of general officers willing to deal with the mess, took it upon himself to appoint a captain as acting major general. Major General Charles Champion Gilbert, who was quick to put two stars on his uniform, was a graduate of West Point (1846) but had no more than company command experience. Desperate for officers, Wright also asked at this time for the services of Brig. Gen. Philip Sheridan, who was advancing quickly up the military ladder.[9]

General Henry Halleck (Library of Congress).

The march of the defeated Federal garrison from Richmond to Louisville under General Gilbert became known as "the Hell March," the exhausted soldiers greeted with derision for their capitulation when they joined their army comrades in Louisville. Wright put Gilbert in command of the troops in and around Louisville, while calling on Halleck for reinforcements from Generals Sam Curtis or Grant, though Wright stipulated that whatever force came from Grant, he did not want Grant himself. Wright feared Kirby Smith would advance on Cincinnati, but eventually accepted that the Confederate threat would be against

Louisville, and Wright's slim Federal force braced itself for a Confederate attack. Buell's force finally staggered into Louisville, and the men of the Army of the Ohio were, according to one diarist, "the hungriest, raggedest, tiredest, dirtiest, lousiest and sleepiest set of men the hardships of this or any other war ever produced." The sight of these filthy veterans undoubtedly cowed the "fresh fish," as the new recruits who were waiting for Buell in Louisville were known, and when the veterans made off with the well-supplied recruits' blankets and camp equipment, it added injury to the veterans' frequently hurled insults. Nor was Wright happy to be yielding command to Buell, and Wright was slow to obey orders. Finally, the administration had had enough. Washington looked at the unstable muddle of dissension taking place in Louisville before a congressional election and sent instructions for Gen. George Thomas to replace Buell. On the very day the

General Horatio Wright (Library of Congress).

order for Thomas to replace Buell arrived in Louisville, squabbling underlings brought matters to a head. A volatile argument had developed between two Federal commanders, the bombastic Bull Nelson and Jefferson C. Davis. While Nelson was Buell's man, Davis was under Wright's command, and while seen as a lackey of Halleck's, was also a strong favorite with the Army of the Ohio's rank and file. That acrimony culminated in Davis confronting and then shooting and killing Nelson, and it was during this turmoil that orders came for Thomas to replace Buell. George Thomas, stating that it was unfair, apparently to both himself *and* Buell, to replace a commanding general just as his army was ready to take the field, turned down command of the Army of the Ohio. Halleck's reaction was, once again, to lie. When Thomas turned down the command, Halleck countermanded the order, assuring Buell that replacing him had not been his idea and that it had been done against his advice. At any rate, the order taking command from Buell was rescinded.[10]

Before Buell left Louisville to advance on the Rebels, he appointed the newly minted major general Charles Gilbert to replace the murdered corps commander Bull Nelson. Phil Sheridan, protesting at being assigned to serve as one of Gilbert's brigade commanders, managed to get himself assigned to the command of a division instead, with the previous appointee, Jeremiah Boyle, delegated to remain behind in Louisville. In the upcoming fight, Phil Sheridan was about to give an example of his leadership and command style. Journalist William Shanks said of Sheridan, meaning it as a compliment, that he was "born a belligerent." While Sheridan was capable of being more than a little aggressive on the battlefield, his belligerence when fighting for command, power and recognition within the army should be considered legendary.[11]

As Buell prepared to advance on Bragg in three columns, the Rebels learned that the Federals had left Louisville on October 1st with 75,000 men and were moving in their direction. In the severe drought that year, Perryville was one of the few places in the area that still had a limited amount of water, and since the town lay at a crossroads as well, it would prove attractive to both Federals and Confederates. On October 7, 1862, the roads leading to Perryville were filled with Buell's soldiers. The Unionists were tired, disgruntled, thirsty, and trying to cope with Rebel cavalry strikes, which increased in frequency and intensity as they approached nearer the enemy. But the chief trouble was a lack of water — the Rebel army having consumed it — while lack of food and sheer exhaustion also added to their distress. But many of the men of Gilbert's corps so detested their corps commander and his harsh treatment, that threats were made that they would shoot him during the coming battle if given the chance.[12]

Many of the Confederates who had marched through Perryville in the days before the battle were full of optimism. Weren't they close to uniting with Kirby Smith, at which point there would be a great battle in which they would whip the Yankees? But Smith was not nearby, and an irresolute Bragg decided once again that he should march toward Smith. Oblivious to the nature of Buell's forces approaching Perryville, Bragg ordered his army to start north, while one of his corps commanders, William J. Hardee, was left to hold Perryville and to delay what Bragg suspected was a minor Unionist thrust. Hardee, meanwhile, placed his three brigades and a battery to defend Perryville and, more particularly, to control the nearby roads and the water of Doctor's Creek and Bull Run.[13]

General Don Carlos Buell (National Archives).

As Hardee's cavalry skirmished with Federal horsemen, the Confederate general was soon convinced that he had a large enemy force in his front, and he began to send pleas for assistance to Bragg, who responded by sending Polk and one division to Perryville. Buell, meanwhile, having experienced a bad fall with his horse during an angry confrontation with one of this own soldiers, who was foraging against orders, would remain supine for the rest of the battle, traveling in an ambulance or quietly resting and reading at his headquarters. As for Bragg, while sending a force back to assist Hardee, he still believed they would meet the bulk of Buell's army elsewhere, and his army continued to march toward

Kirby Smith and away from Hardee and Perryville. During a night remembered for its full moon and the beauty of the countryside, the combatants of the opposing armies poured into Perryville and the surrounding area, while two dozen Federal officers from Crittenden's and Gilbert's corps met secretly to sign a letter drafted to Lincoln asking for Buell's removal in favor of Thomas. Buell, unaware of the restiveness among his officers, but fully aware that he was facing removal if he did not score a victory against the enemy, sent out orders for preparations for an attack on the enemy the morning of October 8th. Where the Federals could acquire water for their army was the problem, and Buell ordered Gilbert to send a brigade to secure the area where there was a limited amount of that precious commodity. Gilbert gave the assignment to Sheridan, and what followed was a less than admirable step by Sheridan on his climb to high command.[14]

Sheridan, newly appointed division commander, instead of giving the assignment of securing the water source at Doctor's Creek to his seasoned soldiers, gave it to Col. Daniel McCook's men.[15] While McCook was a veteran of Wilson's Creek and Shiloh, he was commanding four regiments of green, untried recruits. McCook was also instructed to consult with the less than reliable captain and acting brigadier general Ebenezer Gay, another of Wright's questionable new appointees. While McCook searched for Gay and his cavalry at Buell's headquarters, Buell himself made the offhand suggestion that young McCook might want to ask Sheridan for artillery to accompany his advance on the water hole. It wasn't until McCook was well on his way that he found out that the hill he was to acquire, Peters Hill, which dominated the water sources, was already occupied by Rebels. Within 15 minutes, performing well against a spirited defense by the enemy, McCook's men, with assistance from nearby units, took Peters Hill. But the enemy was going to fight for the water. Under Confederate bombardment while the Rebels formed to retake the hill, McCook believed himself outnumbered, yet his inexperienced men behaved well and sent the Rebels back where they came from. But when McCook saw enemy cavalry on his left flank and dust clouds indicating enemy movement on his right, McCook sent back to Sheridan for help. Sheridan's response was to come have a look. When joined by corps commander Gilbert, young McCook was directed to do nothing until Gilbert went and talked with Buell, though Gilbert did order the less than effective Gay's cavalry to clear the Rebels out of nearby woods. Sheridan was not completely idle, for he did send a brigade of veterans and a battery to act as McCook's reserve, with instruction to its commander, Bernard Laiboldt, to shoot McCook's green troops if any of them ran. Gay was exceedingly reluctant to take his cavalry into the woods; instead he insisted that McCook's infantry should do it. When Gilbert insisted that Gay advance, Gay's attack failed, and it became clear the cavalry could not or would not do it alone. Sheridan finally sent in his veterans, who drove the enemy before them.[16]

Whether or not Rebel commander Polk was beginning to suspect what his troops at Perryville were facing, he ordered the Confederates to fall back and regroup nearer the town in response to this Federal advance, and, as several Perryville historians attest, Hardee and Polk thereby relinquished the opportunity to destroy Gilbert's isolated Federal corps. And while Sheridan sought to pursue the Rebels as they withdrew, Gilbert insisted that Sheridan retire and defend Peters Hill, for hadn't Buell indicated that he wanted no general engagement until all of his slow-moving forces came up? Buell's orders for the next day's attack inexplicably did not reach his corps commanders until just before dawn of that day, causing confusion and delay to dominate the proposed movement, and making it likely that the Federal attack would have to wait until the following day, November 9th.[17]

Meanwhile, Bragg, who had instructed Polk to make short work of the unknown Federal force at Perryville and then follow him toward Smith, became uneasy, and he decided to find out for himself what was going on, and rode with his staff to Perryville. There Bragg discovered that his orders to attack had been ignored, and the Rebel force at Perryville had taken up a defensive stance rather than attacking as they had been ordered. Thus Bragg, ignorant of the rest of the nearby Federal force and aware only of what he could see at Perryville, made preparations to attack the Unionists. The artillery duel that preceded the fight led several Federal commanders to fear it was a preliminary to a Rebel attack, though others insisted the Rebel fire was simply covering the enemy's retreat. Bragg watched unaware that he was facing the entire Army of the Ohio, but as Noe points out, at least Bragg knew about the battle. For Buell, the combination of his bruising fall and an acoustic shadow left the Union commander unaware that his army was engaged at Perryville. Though he heard artillery, he did not hear musket fire, so as Gilbert and Buell dined together that evening, they simply discussed the attack they would make the next day.[18]

When the Confederate attack came, William Lytle's brigade of Alexander McCook's 1st Corps was one of the units that bore the brunt of it, and they were in serious trouble, outnumbered and running out of ammunition. They had appealed to nearby forces for reinforcements and were refused by Gilbert's 3rd Corps, which included Sheridan's division, which stood by on the 1st Corps's right as a spectator to the fight. In fact, Sheridan placed Dan McCook's brigade of rookies on the left of his division, giving the younger McCook a ringside seat on what was happening to his older brother, Maj. Gen. Alexander McCook's corps. Noticing a gap between Gilbert and McCook's corps, at least the young McCook got permission from Gilbert to send a regiment into the hole between the Federal corps. When Confederate artillery turned their attention on Sheridan's position, he had his batteries exchange shots with the Confederates, but when the Rebel guns turned back to assail Lytle, Sheridan's guns again fell silent. When McCook asked Sheridan to look to the safety of his beleaguered corps' right flank, Sheridan did nothing.[19]

Sheridan may have hesitated because he expected an attack on his own front. When an attack did come much later that afternoon, it was only a Rebel brigade attacking his dug-in and well-supported division. "Sheridan's panicked pleas for reinforcements" were answered with fresh troops, allowing Sheridan to later brag about what he had done to the enemy on his own front, exclaiming that he had "whipped them like hell." The Confederates had sent this feeble force to attack Sheridan because they understandably believed that Alexander McCook's corps *was* the enemy's right flank, for surely there could be no infantry to the right of McCook, or they would have come to their beleaguered comrade's assistance. Then, too, it has been suggested that perhaps Sheridan, fully resenting serving under Gilbert, simply sat there in a fit of pique. There are those who criticize corps commander McCook for not sending a distress call to Buell earlier, but likely McCook also found it beyond belief that the unengaged corps on his right flank would refuse to assist, and sit passively by and watch him be destroyed. Nor did Thomas, in position with Crittenden's Corps on Gilbert's right, send assistance to McCook. Thomas sent an aide to Buell's headquarters with questions about the sounds of battle he heard but was told not to worry about it. Perhaps this misinformation, and the already strained relations and communications between Buell and Thomas, lead Thomas to accept headquarters' orders to prepare for the fight planned for the next day, and take no more initiative to find out what the fighting beyond Gilbert on his left was really about.[20]

Lytle's fight with the Rebels entered its second hour, and when the ammunition was gone, the battle turned into a hand-to-hand fight that lasted for another hour. But the Confederates were reinforced when Patrick Cleburne brought his brigade of butternuts up to replace Bushrod Johnson's men, exhausted from their assault on the Yankees. Cleburne sent his colors in with his skirmishers letting the depleted Unionists expend their last few rounds on his skirmishers while his main line was still to come. The Federals withdrew or broke according to the condition of their cartridge boxes and their spirits. The gallant Lytle was shot and captured. Later exchanged, he was able to testify at the Buell Court of Inquiry, stating that up until the last he had believed that reinforcements would come from another corps.[21] As the sun started to go down on the fight in more ways than one, reinforcements finally came to succor what was left of McCook's 1st Corps, the fresh troops forcing the stubborn Confederates back. As the moon rose over Perryville, one last Rebel assault failed. Though firing would be heard until midnight, McCook could finally report that his line was stable.[22]

Colonel William Lytle (National Archives).

Braxton Bragg, knowing that during that day he had pushed the enemy back nearly a mile, still did not realize that, far from winning a great victory, he had been fighting only part of Buell's army. Why, he asked himself, was the beaten foe not leaving the field, for if more of his enemy's army was present, wouldn't the Yankees have utilized more of their men? As reports came in and the reality of his situation finally became apparent, Bragg prepared his army to abandon Perryville during the night and move again toward Kirby Smith. Though the Rebels were still leaving the town after daylight, the Federals did nothing to impede their departure. On the morning of the 10th, Kirby Smith and Bragg met to discuss what should be done. They considered how to meet the Federal offensive they felt was surely coming, but Buell remained in Perryville, slowly sending forth cavalry and infantry with orders to avoid a battle. After the fighting on October 8th, Buell refused to accept that McCook's corps had endured a severe attack, and Buell continued to make plans to attack the Rebels the next day. It also was not until noon on October 9th that Buell finally accepted that the enemy was gone. The Federal loss was 4,211 (845 killed, 2,851 wounded and 515 missing) or 7 percent of the Army of the Ohio, while the Confederate loss was 3,396 (510 killed, 2,635 wounded and 251 missing) or 21 percent of the Army of the Mississippi.[23]

Journalist William Shanks would add his own twists to what happened at Perryville in his 1866 book, declaring that Gen. Alexander McCook began the "unnecessary" Battle of Perryville against Buell's orders. In fact, it was Gilbert's orders to Sheridan, who dispatched young Col. Daniel McCook's men to take the water source, that kicked off initial fighting. Shanks accused Alexander McCook of refusing to call for help, wishing to keep all the fame and glory for himself. It is likely that after the enemy launched itself at General McCook's corps with such a vengeance, that the General may have been willing to share some of that sort of "fame and glory" with Gilbert and Sheridan. McCook did call on Gilbert for assistance, but was refused or ignored. Shanks further offers that Sheridan begged to go to McCook's assistance, but Gilbert refused to let him do so — a complete fiction.[24]

When Buell eventually pursued the Rebels, and Thomas was finally allowed to advance upon and confront Smith's and Bragg's united forces near Danville, Kentucky, Buell refused to let him engage the enemy. Bragg and Smith took advantage of Buell's lack of enthusiasm for a fight and escaped from Kentucky with their armies intact to fight again.[25] Buell, when he had been asked to make good on his advantage in numbers that October, claimed to Halleck that the nature of the area made it impossible to go on the offensive, and he refused to go into East Tennessee as Lincoln desired. Buell announced his intention of spending the winter in Nashville, and he told General Halleck that if this was not satisfactory, it would be a good time for someone to replace him as commander.[26] Stanton ordered a military commission to look into Buell's handling of operations in Tennessee and Kentucky, letting his feelings be known about how Buell let Kentucky be invaded, had failed to relieve Munfordville, and had let the Rebels escape from Kentucky. Sheridan said of Buell that he was not dynamic enough and wasted "precious time in slow and unnecessary tactical maneuvers."[27] Halleck called a halt to the commission at the end of May 1863, stating the commission had found nothing with which to charge Buell, and when Buell was given no further assignment, he resigned from the army on June 1, 1864.

On October 24th, Stanton created the Department of the Cumberland, replacing Buell with Gen. William S. Rosecrans (USMA, 1842), in response to Rosecrans's successes in the West at Iuka and the defense of Corinth. Thomas was astonished at being passed over, and he protested to Halleck that he had not previously refused the command, but merely asked that Buell's replacement be deferred until after the Battle of Perryville. Thomas also objected to having an officer junior to him in rank placed over him. Halleck responded by insisting that he had been responsible for Thomas's promotion and the offer of command, and on that occasion, Thomas has turned it down flat. He also insisted that Rosecrans, in fact, ranked Thomas. Thomas would discover, when Rosecrans arrived to take command and appealed for Thomas to remain, that Rosecrans was indeed his junior in rank, but Lincoln had backdated his commission from August of 1862 to March 21, 1862, in order to give Rosecrans seniority. It was clear, after that, that Thomas had the true measure of Halleck, something it took Grant many years to discover.[28]

While Rosecrans' fight at Iuka earned him admiration in Washington, when Grant, who had sent Rosecrans there to confront the enemy, discovered that Rosecrans failed to block the Rebels' withdrawal southward or pursue the Confederates after the battle, he was less enthusiastic. In October, Rosecrans 18,000 were supplemented by now Brig Gen. McPherson's brigade of 1,500 to defend Corinth from assault by Gen. Earl Van Dorn. Rosecrans again earned Grant's displeasure when he allowed Van Dorn to escape. Rosecrans' taking Buell's place as the commander of the Army and District of the Ohio spared Rosecrans and Grant further conflict at that time.[29]

While Ulysses Grant retained his command on the Mississippi, back east McClellan was fired and replaced with Gen. Ambrose Burnside, and Gen. Nathaniel P. Banks was sent to replace the controversial Gen. Benjamin Butler in the Deep South. One of McClellan's corps commanders, Gen. Fitz-John Porter, commander of the Army of the Potomac's 5th Corps, was also charged with failing to obey orders at Second Bull Run, and was cashiered and replaced by Gen. Joseph Hooker. Porter's disgrace was a politically loaded condemnation. Porter was seen as one of McClellan's supporters, and the members of the 5th Corps would not soon put the controversy behind them. Halleck had not performed up to the people's expectations, and it was Halleck who seemed to be the one receiving, intentionally or not, much of the public's and politicians' disapprobation, a service that Lincoln may well have appreciated. Halleck biographer Curt Anders gave an apt description of the service that the general in chief provided for Lincoln, calling Halleck, "a lightning rod for absorbing the inevitable criticism and condemnation the Radicals would fling at him."[30] Things had seemed to be looking up as General Burnside submitted his plans to the administration for his advance on Richmond by way of Fredericksburg. But Burnside's stunning defeat at Fredericksburg in December brought about calls for the administration to dismiss both Halleck and Burnside. Yet Lincoln did not know who could replace them. It was a command-structure disaster, for Halleck made it clear to Lincoln at this point that he would not issue orders to commanders in the field, in practice distancing himself from blame and responsibility, but the press and the public nonetheless heaped blame upon Halleck and Stanton, and the Committee on the Conduct of the War demanded to know who was responsible for the Fredericksburg debacle. While Burnside accepted blame, he also pointed out that Halleck had failed to get pontoons for bridges to him when he needed them.[31]

Meanwhile, General Rosecrans in the West resisted all encouragements to move from his army's position at Nashville to challenge General Bragg's army until he had reorganized and reequipped his discouraged army and cavalry. Halleck, in turn, claimed that Rosecrans had asked for more supplies than the government could furnish him, and while making it clear that the administration was dissatisfied and Rosecrans was risking being replaced, Halleck refused to order Rosecrans to move. As Halleck biographer Marszalek observes, "The commanding general continued refusing to command." Some relief from the seemingly unending news of defeat came when Rosecrans finally moved the Army of the Cumberland (a.k.a. 14th Corps until after Stone's River) against Bragg, whose subordinates continued to be as unenthusiastic with their commander as Buell's disgruntled officers had been at Perryville. Rosecrans achieved a costly tactical draw at Stone's River at Murfreesboro, Tennessee, during the last day of 1862 and the first few days of 1863. The two armies had nearly identical plans to attack each other's right, but Bragg chose to attack before breakfast while the Federal commanders were still enjoying their bacon and eggs.[32] The opposing forces were nearly equal in number, and Rosecrans came near losing this fight against Bragg's consolidated and newly designated Army of the Tennessee. Rosecrans, by eventually forcing the Confederates to retreat to Chattanooga, was considered by some the victor, and Sheridan's fighting withdrawal, which allowed Rosecrans to redeploy his army, is credited with saving the day. But Sheridan paid a heavy price, losing two of his brigade commanders, 64 other officers, 1,566 men or 32 percent of his division. Less well known and far less trumpeted is William Hazen's fight, where his brigade fought stubbornly against the Rebels flanking the Union army and threatening Rosecrans's trains. When his men ran out of ammunition, Hazen ordered them to fix bayonets, and those who did not have bayonets were ordered to club their muskets is the phrase the soliders used. Hazen held off the Rebels while Sheridan's men fell back, resupplied themselves with ammunition, and rejoined the fight. Rebel general Polk declared that the Confederates had carried every position on the Federal right except Hazen's key position, which would become known as Round Forest. Though Bragg telegraphed Richmond that "God has granted us a happy New Year," by January 3rd, Bragg was retreating south. Bragg reported losses of 9,000 dead and wounded and 1,000 missing. Rosecrans lost 9,000 killed and wounded and a loss of almost 3,500 prisoners. While Halleck enthusiastically greeted the news about Stone's River from Rosecrans, he was less pleased with that commander's failure to follow up and pursue his enemy. However, Sheridan, in his memoirs, concedes that Rosecrans's army was in no condition to follow Bragg.[33] Hazen ordered an unprecedented memorial to be built at Stone's River to commemorate the 56 dead of his brigade who were buried on the field where they fought.

Beyond Bragg's choice of the less than defensible Murfreesboro for the consolidation of his army, Stone's River historian Peter Cozzens makes much of how restive Bragg's subordinates remained regarding their commander. Cozzens particularly questions Bragg's choice of Joseph Wheeler as chief of his cavalry over the more experienced Nathan Bedford Forrest. Bragg handed over Forrest's cavalry corps to Wheeler, leaving Forrest with one regiment and one artillery battery.[34]

Colonel William B. Hazen (Library of Congress).

Though his losses were dire, Rosecrans gave the administration a victory when all the other news had been bad, and they most needed a positive stroke at the same time as the Emancipation Proclamation was to take effect at the beginning of 1863. A week after Stone's River, Rosecrans's army was renamed the Army of the Cumberland, the name they would carry for the rest of the war. The right, center and left wings became the 14th, 20th and 21st Corps under Thomas, McCook and Crittenden, respectively.[35]

Later in the war in 1865, Grant,

who was no friend of Rosecrans, would declare that "Murfreesboro [Stone's River] was no victory, and had no important results."[36] One would think that by 1865, Grant would have understood that there were battles that the administration could consider victories in a political sense beyond their military significance. Yet Grant goes on to make one's head spin when he still later declares that his friend Sheridan's role at Stone's River was "a wonderful bit of fighting" and that "Sheridan in that battle saved Rosecrans' army."[37] It's not possible to follow Grant's reasoning here.

Another major worry for Halleck was the activities of political general John McClernand, whose previous success as a division commander under Grant, coupled with his amateurish enthusiasm and untrammeled ambition, had all greatly irritated Grant. And now McClernand was lobbying Washington for an independent command for himself in the West. While McClernand offered to bring much needed recruits to the army, which he wished to personally lead in battle, Halleck recommended that the new soldiers McClernand recruited should be sent to the existing armies in the West, allowing veterans to take on an important challenge like Vicksburg. Encouraging McClernand to send his recruits on to the army, Grant, who was planning his own advance against Vicksburg, was informed by Halleck that the recruits he was receiving were his to do with as he wished. Grant had Halleck's permission to use McClernand's recruits before McClernand arrived in the field to take command of them. Grant gave Sherman command of the expedition that would go from Memphis down the Mississippi to land north of Vicksburg, while Grant marched overland to attack Vicksburg from the east. Sherman's three divisions left Memphis in December of 1862 with a force of 32,000 to move by boat to invest Vicksburg, while Grant occupied Confederate general John C. Pemberton's attention in the middle of the state. Grant's plan failed miserably. The Federal supply base at Holly Spring was destroyed by Gen. Earl Van Dorn, now commanding Rebel cavalry, and, unknown to Sherman, Grant was unable to join him for his attack on the Confederates north of Vicksburg. Sherman's defeat at Chickasaw Bayou was an embarrassing loss.[38] In Steven E. Woodworth's book, ironically named *Nothing But Victory*, the author observes that "Sherman stands out for exceptional ineptitude on the tactical offensive.... Sherman simply did not have the knack for planning and executing successful assaults."[39]

As National Park Service historian emeritus Ed Bearss points out in his work on Vicksburg, *Receding Tide*, Grant can not have been in a very good mood at this point. Having to withdraw from Mississippi after his retrograde from Oxford and Holly Springs, along with Sherman's defeat at Chickasaw Bayou, Grant's force was fetching up at Milliken's Bend, Louisiana. As Bearss points out, "All that those poor soldiers can look forward to is a cold winter in the wetlands along the Mississippi River," but Grant feared that his career, and perhaps Lincoln's, couldn't afford another movement that would be considered a retreat.[40] It could not have improved Grant's mood when McClernand arrived to take command of his troops in Mississippi, the troops who were with Sherman and who had already been defeated. McClernand immediately pursued them, found his force and took command, though Admiral David Porter, who disliked McClernand, refused to cooperate with him. Porter agreed to cooperate with Sherman, and the force that had been defeated at Chickasaw Bayou experienced success on January 11th at Arkansas Post.[41] McClernand, oblivious to Halleck's duplicity, wrote to him on January 16th, 1863, "I believe my success here [Arkansas Post] is gall and wormwood to the clique of West Pointers who have been persecuting me for months. How can you expect success when men controlling the military destinies of the country are more chagrined at the success of your volunteer officers than the very enemy beaten by the latter in battle?" But, in spite of McClernand's success, Grant and Halleck won out in the end. Because Grant was the only officer in the West who outranked McClernand, Porter and Sherman both urged Grant to take command of the expedition against Vicksburg himself. Faced with a chorus of disapproving voices, many of them Grant's supporters, McClernand was replaced as commander of the Vicksburg expedition when Grant arrived to take charge.[42]

While Grant and Sherman were impressed with Halleck's influence and what he was able to finagle, Halleck continued to be a target for the public's deprecation and the press's displeasure. While Rosecrans dithered in Tennessee, and Grant tried in vain to dig a canal that would help him bypass Vicksburg's formidable defenses, Burnside planned another winter advance on the Rebels that none of his division commanders supported. While Burnside offered to resign, he recommended to Lincoln that he get rid of Stanton and Halleck, too, as they had no one's confidence. When Lincoln insisted that Halleck approve or disapprove Burnside's plan, Halleck asked to be relieved. Lincoln disgustedly acknowledged "General Halleck's habitual attitude of demur." Burnside's advance, which is best known as the "Mud March," accomplished nothing and led to further recriminations from Burnside's subordinates. When Burnside offered his resignation again, Lincoln accepted it and replaced him with Gen. Joseph Hooker. Though Gen. George G. Meade had also been mentioned, Hooker was the ranking officer. There was a long-standing mutual dislike between Halleck and Hooker, with Hooker accusing Halleck of shady business deals in California, a contention that Stanton supported. Meanwhile, Halleck accused Hooker of an immoral lifestyle. Hooker managed to convince Lincoln to allow him to report directly to the president, bypassing the general in chief.[43]

Rebel guerrillas became more and more of a problem in the West, and Halleck received complaints about Gen. Horatio Wright, who at the time was a commander in Kentucky. Halleck prefaced his message to Wright with his usual mantra, "I have always, whenever it was possible, avoided giving positive instructions to the commanding generals of departments, leaving them the exercise of their own judgment, while giving them my opinion and advice." Halleck then dished out this dubious wisdom. "Domestic traitors, who seek the overthrow of our Government, are not entitled to its protection and should be made to feel its power.... Make them suffer in their persons and property for their crimes and the sufferings they have caused to others.... Let the guilty feel that you have an iron hand; that you know how to apply it when necessary. Don't be influenced by those old political grannies, who are only half way Union men.... Their policy will soon ruin you and ruin Kentucky.[44] We can only assume that Halleck offered similar advice to some of his other generals.

In the spring of 1863, Halleck would make these policies official. Based on the results of a committee Halleck had appointed to make recommendations, he released a chilling document, General Order No. 100, Instructions for the Government of Armies of the United States in the Field. While torture, poisoning or wanton destruction were still barred, expelling noncombatants who consume supplies needed by the army in disputed areas was allowable. The seizure and destruction of property, as well as withholding food from the enemy was permitted if a military necessity, but starving or mistreating prisoners of war was not allowed. Martial law in all disputed areas allowed the trying and execution of captive prisoners if urgency demanded it on the approval of the commander in the field. Halleck informed Grant that the rules of warfare had changed, and while most citizens of the Union States probably never heard of General Order No. 100, citizens of the Confederacy did, and the Rebels denounced this documentation of the new Federal barbarity that carried the war to the Southern and Border State civilians.[45]

At this time, there are other insights to be gained regarding Grant, his popularity with Lincoln, and his growing popularity with Halleck. While Grant seemingly cooperated, others didn't. Rosecrans demanded cavalry and arms of all sorts, Gens. David Hunter and J.G. Foster squabbled over jurisdiction in the Carolinas, and Gen. John Schofield was threatening to resign because General Curtis wouldn't let him advance on the enemy in Missouri. Grant, seemingly, just went ahead and got the job done with what he had. Somehow, Halleck continued to blame interfering politicians for the difficult prosecution of the war, in spite of the fact that West Point–trained Hooker was the biggest thorn in Halleck's side. Hooker refused to tell Halleck what he was doing and continued to ignore Halleck's unsolicited advice. The advice was the same as always, that the Army of the Potomac was responsible for seeing that Washington and Harpers Ferry were protected, and beyond that, Hooker could do whatever he deemed advisable. When a disgruntled Halleck thought about resigning in the spring of 1863, his friend, military theorist Francis Lieber, reminded Halleck that if he quit, someone terrible like McClellan or Butler might take over. It was enough to keep Halleck glued to his desk. Instead he fired off a message to Hooker, Grant and Rosecrans in March of 1863 suggesting that of the three commanders the first to win a major victory would have as his prize the vacant major generalship. Rosecrans was outraged that anyone would think the he would be influenced by the seeming auctioneering of this honor.[46]

Hooker's inglorious defeat at Chancellorsville in the spring of 1863 rather strengthened Halleck's hand, giving him an opportunity to tell the president and anyone else who would listen, "I told you so." But it was Halleck whom the public and press generally blamed for another Union defeat. While Lincoln might have to endure complaints about the incompetent Halleck, he had, nonetheless, found a scapegoat extraordinaire, the military leader most everybody loved to hate. Many stories of Halleck's rudeness and abrasive personality only added fuel to the fire.[47]

When Grant arrived to take command from McClernand in the campaign against Vicksburg, it is no surprise that friction rose up between the two generals. But McClernand was only one of Grant's problems as he strove to get at the enemy stronghold at Vicksburg. The possibilities were to either find a way to the high ground east of the city, or perhaps to get Federal boats into the river south of the city. But Vicksburg wasn't called the "Gibraltar of the Mississippi" for nothing, and Grant would spend the first six months of 1863 trying to reach this illusive goal. His men did 12-hour shifts digging canals, shoring up levees, hauling boats over dry land, removing trees and clearing deadfalls in wet, swampy conditions, which put many on the sick list, or worse yet, into the camp cemeteries.[48] After arriving in January of 1863, Sherman led the canal project, and although he made use of black labor, he employed many soldiers. Vicksburg historian Ed Bearss points out that while the Federals were digging their canal, the Confederates were relocating several big guns, positioned to cover nearly half of the canal's length. So if the Yankees had ever finished their canal, the boats would have been "like ducks sitting in a puddle." By March 27th, Grant ordered work on the canal to stop.[49]

McPherson led the Lake Providence expedition that March, using a small steam tugboat that McPherson named the *J.A. Rawlins*, after Grant's chief of staff, to try to open up a route by breaching levees and flooding existing waterways. A stand of virgin cypress trees and a shallow swamp put an end to McPherson's project.[50] Meanwhile, in late January, a newcomer to Grant's circle, Lt. Col. James Wilson, investigated the possibility of reopening the old Yazoo Pass. Wilson would play a leading role in the conception and dissemination of every nasty rumor or accusation that swirled through Grant's headquarters, and was ready to take the credit for success and blame others for his frequent disasters. For instance, on the Yazoo Pass mission, Wilson blamed the navy for their failure to move forward quickly enough to prevent the enemy from building the defensive fortifications that were forever blocking Wilson's progress. Wilson urged the sailors to use their vulnerable gunboats against the Rebels' heavy guns, whatever the cost, though they had already lost four killed and nine wounded trying to accommodate him.[51]

Yet another attempt to approach Vicksburg, the Steele's Bayou expedition, designed to take the pressure off Wilson's Yazoo Pass expedition, was put forth by Admiral Porter after his personal reconnaissance of the Yazoo River. Sherman, who was to support him with infantry was far less confident of the plan's feasibility. When Porter's fleet became trapped in a narrow channel, the enemy having dropped trees in front of it and sunk a coal barge behind him to prevent withdrawal, Porter called on Sherman to save him from the Rebel force threatening him. Sherman's force rescued Porter just before he acted on his intention to blow up his boats to avoid Rebel capture. Thus, the Steele's Bayou expedition ended in anything but glory.[52] Grant's high hopes for the Yazoo Pass expedition, indicated by Grant's message to Halleck in March that he would take Vicksburg that month, were also doomed to be dashed. Though Grant would claim in his memoirs that he had never had much confidence in the "experiments" that he conducted at Vicksburg, historian Ed Bearss suggests that Grant's writings in the 1880s were benefiting from hindsight.[53]

The plan that eventually worked—and allowed Grant to capture Vicksburg to run the fleet past Vicksburg, cross the river below Vicksburg, establish a base at Grand Gulf, and move into the interior of Mississippi—was appar-

General James Wilson (Library of Congress).

ently opposed by all of Grant's subordinates, including Wilson.[54] Bearss makes note of Wilson's claim later in his life that the plan that succeeded was actually his idea, rather than Grant's. As Bearss points out, "Of course, Grant, Sherman, McClernand, McPherson, Rawlins, and just about everyone who was at Vicksburg is dead when Wilson publishes this tall tale in 1912, so who can argue?"[55]

With the character of James Wilson already called into question, let us pursue that subject, taking into account some of the things Wilson, in later years, had to say about Grant, Rawlins, and his relationship with them during the war. A window is thrown open in William Styple's book *Generals in Bronze,* a consideration of the notebooks of artist and sculptor James Edward Kelly, who was Wilson's friend and confidante in the early 1900s. Kelly, perhaps best known for his sculpture of Gen. John Buford at Gettysburg and his etching of Meade's Council of War at Gettysburg, also interviewed a great many of the Civil War's generals before and while he sketched them. Wilson is the one he became closest to, and Kelly's notebooks on his conversations with Wilson, bring us such gems as: Wilson recounting to Kelly, sometime in the first decade of the 1900s, a story about what happened when he first reported to Grant's headquarters. "I remember the time I called to report to Gen. Grant. It was down at [LaGrange, Tenn.- Styple's note] I went in a tent and asked for General Grant of a man who was sitting with his back toward me. He [Maj. John A. Rawlins- Styple's note] turned round and said, 'Gen. Grant has gone to ——.' And when I gave my name, he jumped up and grasped my hand saying; 'I am G——D—— glad to see you. I have been expecting you and I want to see you. The man you have come to report to is a drunkard. The Sword of Damocles is hanging over his head and may fall at any moment. He is a good man, he may pull through. I want to form an alliance with you to save him.'" Wilson then observed to Kelly, "Now that could never be published—people would not want it. One can't put down history as it really happened—people don't want it—it would shock them. People have formed their own ideas in regard to history and they do not want them dismembered." In his 1912 memoir, Wilson told much the same story, adding that the immediacy of the Rawlins-Wilson friendship was based on Rawlins's relationship with Wilson's grandfather and on a hearty recommendation from McPherson, whom Wilson had traveled with from California to the east and the seat of war in 1861. Wilson appar-

Charles A. Dana (Library of Congress).

ently clung to his assertion that people didn't want the *real* history, for he makes less mention of Grant's alcoholism in *Under the Old Flag*, commenting vaguely in a quotation that Wilson attributes to Rawlins, that, "'Grant was a good man' and that we could 'win with him if we could stay him from falling.'"[56]

McClernand, bitter about the troops he had raised being used by Grant and Sherman on their abortive Chickasaw Bluffs campaign, and still demanding independent command, continued to send protests to Washington. The assigning of Charles Dana to Grant's headquarters, specifically to report back to the administration about Grant's actions and character may have occurred because of McClernand's complaints. Dana, who was appointed because he had favored Stanton with positive press when Stanton was first appointed secretary of war, was officially assigned to be a special commissioner of the War Department sent to investigate the army's pay department in the West, but it was commonly known that he was there to observe Grant and report back to Washington. If it was part of McClernand's plan that Dana would endorse his condemnation of Grant, the plan backfired badly. Dana became, in short order, one of Grant's staunchest supporters and a member of his inner circle, literally dining in Grant's mess, while Grant kept Dana up to date on his latest plans for campaigns. As for Dana's reliability, as the late great historian Glenn Tucker commented about Dana, "Had Stanton combed the country it is doubtful if he could have chosen one less suited than Dana by training and temperament to give a balanced estimate of the abilities of the commander of a great army in action."[57]

Among those whom Dana became closest to was Lieutenant Colonel Wilson, who arrived, true to form, telling tales to Grant that McClernand, who was from Wilson's hometown, had told Wilson in Washington about his devious plan to get Grant's command, or at least, a command independent from Grant. It was the first of many reports Wilson would bring to Grant revealing just who, according to Wilson, were Grant's enemies. Dana cooperated by sending a stream of negative reports to Washington regarding McClernand.[58] Dana, a former managing editor at Horace Greeley's *New York Tribune*, parted ways with the newspaper when Greeley objected to Dana's warmongering. Dana was an advocate, if not one of the originators, of the "On to Richmond" movement that led to that premature and disastrous encounter for the Federals at Bull Run. What was in it for Dana? As early as August of 1863, Dana was commenting on Grant's great potential as a presidential candidate.[59] But Dana also commented in his memoirs and correspondence that he'd rather see the United States under a military government after the war than have two or three countries subject to war and despotism. One can only wonder what role Dana fancied for himself in a military dictatorship in a postwar United States.[60] Between Dana and Wilson, no one was safe from their criticism and disapproval, and though historian Eliot Cohen writes that Dana, the administration's eyes and ears at the front, was trustworthy, one only has to note the difference between what Dana wrote during the war and what Dana wrote after the war. It is glaringly apparent that Dana, when he realized that *President* Grant was not going to present him with the lucrative political appointment he felt he deserved, fast became an enemy of the man he had previously praised and supported. As editor of the *New York Sun*, Charles Dana would quickly accuse Grant and his cabinet in the first days of that administration of corruption, not that there wasn't justification for such criticism in the days to come. But it is unnerving to see Dana turn overnight from being the supporter of Grant, the one he called "the most disinterested, and the most honest man I ever knew,"⁶¹ to calling Grant in the press, again and again, the immoral leader and author of the corruption that plagued Washington.⁶² Back at Vicksburg, Plan B, or was it Plan F or G, was on Grant's drawing board, and it called for Porter to run the river past the Vicksburg batteries. The Federal ship *Queen of the West* had run the river in February, as had the ironclad *Indianola*. But the *Queen of the West* ran aground and was captured, and the Rebels had used it to capture the *Indianola*. But then Porter successfully ran the batteries on April 16th with 12 boats, losing one. Several days later, transports and barges full of supplies ran the river, losing one transport and six barges. Movements made by Sherman and Benjamin Grierson were designed to distract the enemy attention from McClernand's advance on Milliken's Bend and from Porter's move south on the river. Now it was Grant's job to begin moving his infantry.⁶³

On March 29th, Grant had sent McClernand, who was still agitating for independent command, to Milliken's Bend to open a road to the river south of Vicksburg. Bearss suggests that McClernand was chosen because he was the only one of Grant's subordinates who had any enthusiasm for Grant's plan. Grant crossed unopposed at Bruinsburg, as McClernand made a good job of adapting to the need to move further south to Grand Gulf, building roads as he went. To confuse the Confederates, Grant had set so many hares in motion, including Grierson's cavalry heading south and a request to Sherman to return to the Yazoo for a diversion near Vicksburg, and it all worked. The Rebels were utterly confused as to just what was Grant's true target.⁶⁴

It should be remembered that once south of Vicksburg, Grant's orders from Halleck were to continue south, joining Gen. Nathaniel Banks in Louisiana to assist him in his investment of Port Hudson. Then Banks, who ranked Grant and would be in command, would return the favor by assisting Grant to take Vicksburg. But against orders and the advice of his subordinates, Grant decided to attack Vicksburg instead, figuring that, as he moved beyond telegraph communications, he had a good two weeks before Halleck would get news of Grant's plan and express disapproval.⁶⁵ Grant was on his way to Vicksburg, but he had to fight his way there. McPherson fought the Rebels at Port Gibson, and Pemberton, confused by Sherman's feint, Grierson's raid and then Grant's crossing of the river at Bruinsburg, withdrew to near Vicksburg. Bearss notes that Sherman's force, which included soldiers who had been taken prisoner at Shiloh and had just been exchanged after six months in Rebel prisons, were looting and burning houses. Sherman acknowledged his inability to control these men.⁶⁶ As Bearss comments, Grant's willingness to overlook his friend's faults, what Bearss refers to as cronyism, will get Grant into trouble when he is president. (It could be argued that it got Grant into trouble well before that, but he also became skilled at covering up his friends faults, and allowing others to take the fall.) So while Sherman and McPherson and their men were burning and pillaging and looting their way near Port Gibson, McClernand was doing good service the whole time conducting reconnaissance and keeping Grant apprised with reports. But McClernand's performance would not change Grant's animosity toward McClernand. It didn't work that way.⁶⁷

Grant once more received assistance from the Confederate government and those in command of the Rebels in the field. Pemberton, commander at Vicksburg, was told by the Confederate commander in the West, Joseph E. Johnston, to evacuate Vicksburg, then unite with Johnston to defeat the Federals in the field. At the same time Pemberton was told by President Jefferson Davis to hold Vicksburg at all cost. Pemberton would try to do both and ultimately be able to do neither.[68] While the approach of Johnston's army could have provided a confounding variable for Grant, it didn't, for on the May 13, 1863, after fighting at Jackson, Johnston realized that Grant was between his force and Pemberton's. Johnston decided that he must withdraw his supplies from Jackson and escape north with his army. The fight at Champion's Hill followed, where Grant turned on Pemberton east of Vicksburg, and Pemberton failed to stop the Federal onslaught. Pemberton's next stand on the Big Black River also ended in failure, and on May 19th, all of Grant's forces were free to invest Vicksburg.[69]

Army of the Tennessee historian Steven Woodworth, writing of McClernand's performance at Champion's Hill, states that he was unworthy of command because of his unwillingness to disobey Grant's order not to bring on an engagement when McPherson was attacked a half mile away. It brings strongly to mind McClernand's day-long struggle at Fort Donelson, when Grant favorite, Gen. Charles Smith, refused to come to McClernand's aid because of similar orders from Grant not to engage.[70] Meanwhile, Dana began to send a steady stream of condemnation regarding McClernand to Washington, and although Stanton warned Dana "to avoid giving any advice in respect to commands that may be assigned, as it may lead to misunderstanding," Dana continued to report McClernand's failings, both real and manufactured, and on May 6th, Stanton sent word to Grant through Dana that Grant had the authority to remove McClernand from command if he thought it necessary.[71]

Grant invested Vicksburg on May 18th and prepared to attack, and on May 20th, Dana confidently reported to Stanton that Vicksburg would fall the next day. It did not, and who else but McClernand would be blamed. When the Federals failed to take the Rebel fortifications, Grant accused McClernand of having sent a false report claiming to have made a breakthrough on his front, one that caused Grant to order an attack all along his line, and the attack failed.[72] The Federals settled down to a siege that would last well into the summer. While Dana sings the praises of Generals Grant, Sherman, McPherson, and Captain Cyrus Comstock, Grant's new chief engineer, he declares that McClernand was not fit to command a regiment, let alone a corps or an army. Though he had no military experience, Dana was not at all shy about pronouncements on who was or wasn't fit for command. Dana was lavish with his praise when he took to someone, proclaiming Wilson "brilliant" though unpopular because he believed in doing one's duty as opposed to those who liked to do little work. And Dana said of Col. Giles Smith, to whom he took a shine, that "there are plenty of men with generals' commissions who in all military respects are not fit to tie his [Col. Smith's] shoes." But Dana was equally outspoken if he didn't like someone, or, since Dana was spending a great deal of time with the caustic Lieutenant Colonel Wilson, perhaps he was really sharing the ambitious views and prejudices of Wilson and others. For instance, Dana reported to Stanton and Lincoln that Gen. A.J. Smith was not to be trusted with independent command, and he reported that Grant's siege of Vicksburg was suffering because of the incompetence of his chief of artillery, Lt. Col. William L. Duff. Regarding Duff, Dana commented of Grant that "it is one of his [Grant's] weaknesses that he is unwilling to hurt the feelings of a friend, and so he keeps him on." Dana went on to describe other various officers as "pretentious," "not destined to greatness," and "totally unfit to command — a very good man but a very poor general." Of Gen. Cadwallader Washburn (Congressman Washburne's brother, who spelt his name with no final "e") Dana decreed that the general was a better politician than a military man.[73]

In June of 1863, Lee began his incursion into the North, and Hooker submitted a plan to Lincoln that more or less would have abandoned Washington to its fate while Hooker attacked Richmond. Hooker did not particularly want but, nonetheless, could not get any orders from Halleck. When Lincoln ordered Halleck to give Hooker orders, Halleck would not. The problem of what Hooker was going to do remained unresolved as Lee moved into Pennsylvania, and when an exasperated Hooker offered his resignation, it was accepted. At this critical time, as Lee's invasion spread shock waves through the North, Hooker was replaced by Gen. George Gordon Meade. The most recent commander of the 5th Corps was now commander of the Army of the Potomac.[74] After three days of fighting at Gettysburg, Meade's victory would find Halleck complaining that Meade had not followed and destroyed Lee's army when he had the opportunity. Though one could cite numerous battles in the West after which the Union armies were too exhausted or depleted or exhilarated to follow the enemy, including Halleck's bloodless victory at Corinth, few opportunities were missed to criticize George Gordon Meade and the Army of the Potomac. But was Halleck simply acting as a conduit between Lincoln and Meade, allegedly expressing the president's, as opposed to his own, great dissatisfaction? Halleck biographer Marszalek offers evidence that Halleck, urged by a distraught Lincoln, still hesitated to offer any directions or orders to Meade, while nonetheless demanding that Meade pursue Lee. Immediately after Gettysburg, the New York draft riots led to troops being sent from the Army of the Potomac to quell the violence. The uprising so startled and worried Halleck, that he eventually told Meade not to go on the offensive against Lee in case more troops would be needed if trouble flared up in other cities.[75]

Though William S. McFeely wrote an extensive biography on Grant, he is no particular fan of the general, and McFeely observes regarding Vicksburg and Gettysburg that

> General Grant, of Vicksburg, and not General Meade, of Gettysburg, emerged as the hero of the day despite the fact that Gettysburg was the scene of a greater battle than Vicksburg. Indeed, the taking of Vicksburg, the culmination of the campaign to open to the Union a river route through the Confederacy, was not achieved through a battle at all. It was completed not with colors handed gloriously over parapets, but with the ignominious starving out of a small town. The action at Gettysburg, by contrast, had the gory majesty of the storied battles of eighteenth-century and Napoleonic Europe, yet its victor, George Gordon Meade, never caught the eye of the public the way Grant did.[76]

As the rewards for the Battles of Gettysburg and Vicksburg were being considered and handed out, Grant became a major general in the regular army at the same time that Meade was promoted to a brigadier general. The more prominent candidates for additional regular brigadier-generals were Sherman, McPherson, Thomas, Sedgwick and Hancock; Halleck was of the opinion that the promotions should go to Sherman and McPherson. Grant later commented that he had been offered command of the Army of the Potomac after Gettysburg and had refused it.[77]

Grant, Halleck and Dana had another reason to celebrate after the fall of Vicksburg. Supported by Dana's stream of caustic criticism of McClernand,[78] Grant found a way to get rid of his least favorite corps commander and perceived competitor. Accusations had continued that McClernand had misled Grant, Sherman and McPherson during the May 22nd attacks on Vicksburg by issuing false reports of success. Grant's engineering officer, the always-ready-to-bear-tales James Wilson, reported later to Grant that when he delivered an order to McClernand, he heard McClernand say that he'd be damned if he would comply with any more of Grant's directives. Wilson claimed to have challenged McClernand to apologize at once, or face a fist fight on the spot. Perhaps of more consequence, Grant had also learned that a congratulatory message McClernand wrote to his corps had been leaked to the press, and McClernand had neglected to submit the obligatory copy to headquarters first. On June 18th, Grant had Rawlins write the order for McClernand's dismissal. It goes to show just what kind of person James Wilson was that he volunteered, despite the fact that he had once been a favorite of McClernand's, to personally hand him the order relieving him from command. Wilson, snake like to the end, in his 1912 memoirs, written when all involved were dead and could not comment, stated that Sherman and McPherson were as much to blame as McClernand for the failure of Grant's May 22nd assault at Vicksburg.[79]

If Halleck thought little of Meade's accomplishments at Gettysburg, perhaps it was because Halleck so firmly believed that the important battles of the war were being fought in the West.[80] It is necessary only to refer to James McPherson's masterly *This Mighty Scourge* to set the record straight. Leaving behind any animosities or jealousies that existed between the soldiers of the East and the soldiers of the West, McPherson looked at the cold hard facts. To quote McPherson, "The war was won by hard fighting, and the Army of the Potomac did most of that fighting. Of the ten largest battles in the war (each with combined Union and Confederate causalities of 23,000 or more), seven were fought between the Army of the Potomac and the Army of Northern Virginia. Of the fifty Union regiments with the largest percentage of battle causalities, forty-one fought in the Eastern theater." As far as inflicting casualties on the enemy, McPherson observes, "Of the fifty Confederate regiments with the highest percentage of combat casualties, forty were in the Army of Northern Virginia. In terms of fighting prowess, therefore, the 'band box' soldier in the Army of the Potomac more than held their own."[81] It seems foolish to have to say it, but the war was not won in the East or won in the West, it was won by the blood and sacrifices of soldiers in battles, large and small, in both theaters.

Regardless of what Halleck thought about whose fight was more significant, the preponderance of the U.S. population and the press in the East, watching the drama being played out in their backyard, doomed Halleck's western slant to be treated with some degree of disparagement. But hadn't Halleck insisted that one Vicksburg was worth 40 Richmonds?[82] So while near 50,000 casualties were incurred on both sides at Gettysburg, Halleck was focused on Grant's investment of Vicksburg, which, after more than six months of fumbling, finally fell on July 4, 1863. One could say that Meade's and Grant's July 1863 victories received fairly equal attention with mixed reviews from the public and the administration. But Halleck, made clear how he felt about Grant's eventual victory at Vicksburg. As previously stated, Grant was made a major general in the regular army, dated July 4, 1863, while Meade would not achieve that status until August of 1864. Halleck also gushed that at Vicksburg it was "in boldness of plan, rapidity of execution, and brilliancy of results, these operations will compare most favorably with those of Napoleon about Ulm."[83]

Halleck's feelings toward another of his commanders, Rosecrans, were very different, as Halleck chided Rosecrans for his slowness and refused to satisfy Rosecrans's repeated requests for men and supplies.[84] When Grant finally took Vicksburg on July 4th, Stanton announced the event to Rosecrans, adding, "You and your noble army now have a chance to give the finishing blow to the rebellion. Will you neglect the chance?" Rosecrans' response to this painful jibe was, "Just received your cheering telegram.... You do not appear to observe the fact that this noble army has driven the rebels from Middle Tennessee. I beg in behalf of this army that the War Department may not overlook so great an event because it is not written in letters of blood."[85]

At the end of August, Rosecrans had occupied Chattanooga without a fight, and after Burnside captured Knoxville, despite direct orders to reinforce Rosecrans, Burnside refused to move. After taking Vicksburg, it was Grant's responsibility to detain Johnston and prevent him from reinforcing Bragg, but Grant seemed unable to do so. Grant also had other things on his mind. Halleck and Dana had apparently stalled an effort to bring Grant east to take command of the Army of the Potomac, a delay Grant distinctly approved of, not wanting the assignment at that time. It's not hard to hazard a guess that Halleck and Dana had much bigger plans for Grant than a mere change of command.[86]

Even before Confederate reinforcements from the East began to arrive outside Chattanooga, Bragg's army outnumbered Rosecrans's force. And though Washington knew that James Longstreet's corps was being sent west, neither Halleck nor anyone else informed Rosecrans.[87] Halleck did make feeble attempts to call upon other Western commanders to send reinforcements to Rosecrans, but without results. Rosecrans, though he had asked many times for more troops and supplies, would have to make do with whatever he had when he drove Bragg out of Chattanooga.[88] Rosecrans was kept so much in the dark by Halleck, that during the Battle of Chickamauga, Rosecrans angrily refused to believe Rebel captives who stated they were from Longstreet's Corps.[89]

Rosecrans outmaneuvered and forced Bragg out of Chattanooga, a feat that historian Glenn Tucker describes as one of the great strategic achievements of the war. Then Rosecrans took up his pursuit of Bragg. Tucker, in his description of the remarkable river passage that was part of Rosecrans's campaign, takes note of Sheridan's part, which was less exemplary. Sheridan, who was then one of McCook's division commanders, rebuilt a trestle bridge at Bridgeport, Alabama, which promptly fell down and had to be built again. The ever-enthusiastic Sheridan supporter, journalist William Shanks, tells an anecdote of this time when Sheridan invited General Thomas to come and see his bridge-building preparations at Bridgeport. The six-foot conductor of the train Sheridan and Thomas were traveling on refused to obey Sheridan's command to start the train, commenting that he took his orders only from the military superintendent of the road. Shanks writes admiringly, "Without giving him time to finish the insulting reply, Sheridan struck him two or three rapid blows, kicked him from the cars and into the hands of a guard, and then ordered the train forward." Considering the outcome of Sheridan's bridge-building efforts, perhaps more attention to bridge-building and less attention to a short major general's outraged dignity might have been appropriate.[90]

Meanwhile, another veteran was musing on the seriousness of an upcoming confrontation with Bragg. The cynical author and war raconteur Ambrose Bierce observed that, at the time, "We knew well enough that there would be a fight; the fact that we did not want one would have told that, for Bragg always retired when we wanted to fight and fought when we most desired peace." Rosecrans, under persistent goading from Halleck and Lincoln, determined to go on the offensive, and dispersed his troops for a complicated approach against the enemy along a very long front. But the scattered nature of Rosecrans's troops and the vulnerability of his communications proved irresistible. Though Rosecrans finally realized the danger, and had nearly completed the consolidation of his forces for his offensive, Bragg beat Rosecrans to the punch, attacking with his army of 71,500 to Rosecrans's 64,500 Federals.[91] Interestingly, while Rosecrans was relying on pitifully inadequate maps and reluctant locals regarding the area around Chickamauga, Bragg was quite familiar with the area, having been stationed at Camp Missionary Hill in 1838 during the enforced migration of the Cherokee.[92]

Dana, who had arrived unannounced at Rosecrans's headquarters on September 11th, was not taken into Rosecrans's inner circle as he had been at Grant's headquarters. Rosecrans's staff saw him as a "Bird of Evil Omen," sent to spy on their chief, and that was just what he was.[93] Dana was there to report, though he did not report accurately, what happened to Rosecrans's outnumbered Federals. Rosecrans experienced a painful, if not complete, defeat at Chickamauga Creek on September 19th and 20th, when Longstreet, Rosecrans's former roommate at West Point, found and exploited a gap mistakenly left in Rosecrans's line, allowing Braxton Bragg to break and scatter the entire right of Rosecrans's army. The rout included Sheridan and his men who had fought tenaciously at Stone's River, but the dauntless General Lytle, who Sheridan reportedly ordered to go to General Thomas, never made it away from Sheridan's overrun position. Lytle was mortally wounded trying to stem the enemy inundation. If Lytle believed at Chickamauga, as he had at Perryville, that if he held, help would come, he was, once again, mistaken. As historian Glenn Tucker points out, "'Little Phil' was rarely at his best when the odds were even," and Tucker suggests that while Lytle did the heavy fighting, Sheridan might have rallied his four other brigades in the rear, and brought them back to do some real damage to Longstreet who would later turn on

Charles A. Dana (Library of Congress).

Thomas. Though Thomas sent an aide to request that Sheridan return to assist him, Sheridan insisted on continuing onward toward Rossville on the way to Chattanooga and away from Thomas.[94]

Back on the abandoned Federal right, General Lytle's body was viewed on the captured field by a Rebel commander seemingly out of place and time, for it was William C. Oates of Round Top–Gettysburg fame who had come west with Longstreet. Oates and his Alabamians were among the stormy ocean of gray that had enveloped and destroyed the Federal right at Chickamauga. But on the left, Gen. George Thomas's troops stood firm, earning their commander the sobriquet the "Rock of Chickamauga." Thomas, along with Hazen and Granger and their men, maintained whatever honor or composure was left for the discomfited and flustered Federals, until Thomas was ordered to withdraw into Chattanooga with the rest of Rosecrans's army. A panicky dispatch from Dana to Stanton was "leaked" to the press, and it was never satisfactorily explained how it was that the cipher Dana used failed. Dana, though unaware of the real situation on the battlefield, wrote to Stanton, "My report today is of deplorable importance. Chickamauga is as fatal a name in our history as Bull Run.... Our soldiers turned and fled. It was wholesale panic. Vain were all attempts to rally them. Our wounded are all left behind."[95]

Dana had become separated from Rosecrans during the battle and then became lost. As Tucker observes in *Chickamauga*, since Dana's descriptions of times and events during his flight to Chattanooga don't make sense, it is likely that "though he [Dana] was to become a boldly assertive New York newspaperman, he was at that moment a very badly frightened Assistant Secretary of War."[96] On the field, Dana encountered Col. John T. Wilder's mounted Federal infantry, who, dismounted, had formed that rare formation for this war, the hollow square, during their attempt to reach Thomas. Dana incorrectly informed Wilder that Rosecrans was either killed or captured and that Wilder's was the only brigade left on the field. Dana demanded to be taken to Chattanooga, and Wilder sent Dana off accompanied by several scouts, where Dana would send his panicked message to Stanton.[97] Wilder, meanwhile, was another of the more tenacious officers on the field at Chickamauga who later reported asking Sheridan to come up and support him. Sheridan, whose men were retreating in disorder though not pursued, replied that he could not rally his men, and Sheridan advised Wilder "to get out of there." Casualties at Chickamauga were roughly 35,000.[98]

For the political side of Rosecrans's eventual downfall, oh, what a tangled web had been woven. Rosecrans, before Chickamauga, was being looked at by the Salmon Chase–Ben Wade radical Republicans as a potential candidate for president, and Dana's nemesis, his former employer, publisher Horace Greeley, was actively working to develop Rosecrans as a replacement for Lincoln. Meanwhile James Garfield, who the administration had finagled into place as Rosecrans's chief of staff, was reporting in most uncomplimentary terms directly to Secretary of the Treasury Salmon P. Chase regarding Rosecrans. Meanwhile, Dana, Washington's malicious and inept eyes and ears, recognized that Rosecrans was standing in the way of *his* choice for future presidential candidate, U.S. Grant. Ironically, Rosecrans had no political ambitions. But then neither, supposedly, did Grant.[99]

The repercussions of Chickamauga were immense. The military careers of Rosecrans and his commanders on the Federal right — Negley, McCook, Crittenden and Van Cleve — never recovered from the disgrace of leaving the field. Rosecrans's first reports from Chattanooga showed demonstrably that he had lost his self-confidence, and although Dana admitted that Rosecrans had displayed nothing but gallantry on the field in his attempts to rally his troops, Dana sent a constant stream of reports to Washington describing Rosecrans as unfit for command. Finally, Dana's fabricated report that Rosecrans was preparing to retreat from Chattanooga resulted in Grant, who was given command of the Military Division of the Mississippi on October 18th, replacing Rosecrans with Thomas one month after Chickamauga. Roy Morris in "Bird of Evil Omen"[100] suggests that Halleck and Stanton, unnerved that they might be blamed for the debacle at Chickamauga by their failure to reinforce Rosecrans and keep him informed, were more than willing to support Dana's efforts to supply scapegoats for the disaster. Dana upped the ante by suggesting that Rosecrans, in his upcoming report on Chickamauga, was going to place the blame for the disaster on Halleck and Stanton. Rosecrans' report does not, in fact, mention either of his worried superiors. In Dana's report to Stanton dated September 27, 1863, while declaring that Generals Palmer, Sheridan, Wood, Johnson and Hazen felt deeply the "desertion" of the commanders who left the field at Chickamauga, Dana avers that his commanders and men had lost all confidence in Rosecrans. Dana urges that Rosecrans, McCook and Crittenden be removed from command, and as a replacement for Rosecrans, Dana suggests "some Western general of high rank and great prestige, like Grant, for instance, would be preferable as his successor to any one who has hitherto commanded in East alone."[101]

Oddly, Sheridan, though he left the field with the rest from the Union right, did not suffer at all, but as Chickamauga historian Bob Redman points out in his well-defended "Sheridan's Ride at Chickamauga," the others didn't have Little Phil's "robust pr [public relations] instincts and effrontery to fake a return to the field."[102] While Glenn Tucker suggests that Sheridan may have taken a long, roundabout route toward Thomas's fight, he agrees that Sheridan arrived so late that he provided no assistance.[103] Hazen suggested that it was absurd to think Sheridan joined Thomas in the fight on Snodgrass Hill, for Davis, who started directly toward Thomas about 5 P.M. didn't reach Thomas until he was already withdrawing. Sheridan went six miles further before turning toward Thomas, and Sheridan admits that it was 6 P.M. before he encountered Thomas, whose order to his wing to withdraw was issued at 5 P.M. The reality is that Sheridan met Thomas, not on the battlefield as he claimed, but several miles outside of Rossville during Thomas's retreat. Hazen, who stood by Thomas, was made a major in the regular army for his role at Chickamauga.[104]

After Chickamauga, Bragg had initially believed Rosecrans would give up Chattanooga and withdraw beyond the city, but Bragg hesitated before laying siege to the stronghold, while the Federals busily improved and increased their defenses. Halleck and the administration, while they had done little to add to the outnumbered force Rosecrans had had in the field at Chickamauga, now pulled out all the stops to send men to Rosecrans, while Bragg, though he occupied the heights around Chattanooga, allowed them the time to do so, much to the frustration of some of his commanders and soldiers. Gens. O. O. Howard and Joseph Hooker with 20,000 men set out for the West on September 25, 1863, and began to arrive seven days later. Sherman moved from Memphis to Vicksburg in order to bring four divisions to Chattanooga. But most importantly, in mid–October, Halleck, under orders from Lincoln, appointed Grant commander of all the military departments between the Appalachians and the Mississippi. As the new leader in the West, Grant in turn named Sherman to replace him as commander of the Army of the Tennessee, and Grant had permission from Halleck to replace Rosecrans with George Thomas, though the ever-loyal Thomas protested.[105] Rosecrans, contrary to Dana's deceptive missives to Washington stating that Rosecrans intended to give up Chattanooga, had been making plans to go on the offensive and improve supply lines to Chattanooga. After Grant relieved Rosecrans, Rosecrans shared his plan with the new commander in the West for breaking the seige, the plan that he himself would now never get to execute. Meanwhile the foe that the Federals was facing, Braxton Bragg, was seemingly at war with his own subordinates, and the region's depleted supplies made for much misery in the ranks. Longstreet, among others, pleaded with Richmond to replace Bragg, suggesting that Robert E. Lee come west, leaving the Army of Northern Virginia to act on the defensive while he was gone.[106]

While Halleck was still subject to disparagement in the East, he now had two commanders in the West who still admired him. As Sherman became a brigadier general in the regular army, he gushed to Halleck that "you alone can grasp the mighty questions of government that are now at issue in America." Interestingly enough, Sherman also wrote to his congressman brother, John, that Grant had qualities that Halleck didn't, but they weren't enough to equip Grant to command the whole army.[107] Grant and Sherman with the Army of the Tennessee, fresh from their much-praised taking of Vicksburg, managed to bring reinforcements to Chattanooga through Bragg's porous seige line. Halleck saw to it that Grant got the reinforcements that he had neglected to send to Rosecrans, including Hooker, Howard and two corps from the Army of the Potomac. Dana, his work done, left for Washington, commenting, "The Tycoon of the war Department is on the warpath; his hands are red and smoking with the scalping of Rosey."[108] Turning from political dirty work, what was really at stake at this point in the war was the Unionist retention of the rail hub at Chattanooga, which was nothing less than a pathway into the southeastern Confederacy and a necessary widening of the opening for the Federals to bring in additional reinforcements.[109]

Grant, on crutches from a fall suffered at New Orleans, arrived at General Thomas's headquarters in Chattanooga on October 23, 1863, wet and tired. Horace Porter, one of General Thomas's staff, said that Grant, who had taken command of the western armies on October 19th, had unexpectedly arrived at Thomas's headquarters during a storm, where, according to Porter, he was made welcome. Porter went on to serve on Grant's staff, and Porter's book *Campaigning with Grant* is an ample testimony to his dedication to Grant.[110] The troublemaker James Wilson, however, was solely responsible for the report of the "coldness" of the reception given Grant by General Thomas on Grant's arrival.[111] This is one of many opportunities to view Wilson's adept manipulation of events, describing offensive behavior where none was meant or offered, as well as insults or disobedience manufactured by Wilson's malicious imagination. But whether Thomas was enthusiastic at his new commander's arrival that night or not, Grant began to address the dire supply situation that the Chattanooga garrison was experiencing. Grant was soon impressed with Gen. William F. "Baldy" Smith's (USMA, 1845) grasp of the surrounding topography and Smith's detailed proposal to open up a line of communication. With the army's animals dying of starvation and the soldiers on half or even quarter rations, Grant would not forget Smith's role in alleviating the army's hardship in the days to come. Grant would also remember, up to a point, Smith's efficacy in breaking the back of the Rebel siege. Not only did the Rebels lose any possibility of starving out the Federals, but seemingly oblivious to the buildup of Federal troops he would be facing, Bragg consummated his feud with Longstreet by sending him away to confront Burnside at Knoxville. While Bragg had hoped that Longstreet's investment of Knoxville would force Grant to send part of his force to Burnside's aid, Bragg was sending away a sizable part of his force when he most needed it.[112]

Grant countermanded orders from Halleck to Sherman to repair railroads that would have delayed Sherman's passage to Chattanooga, and Grant also had to fend off demands from Washington that he send Sherman to assist Burnside in Knoxville. On Sherman's reunion with Grant, once the stage was finally set for the Unionists to take the offensive, Sherman was supposed to have played the leading role in the attack on Bragg's Confederates in late November of 1863, while Thomas played a supporting minor role of distracting the enemy. The Confederates, who had taken up positions on Missionary Ridge, Lookout Mountain and in the Lookout Valley, proved impervious to Sherman's assaults. Unable to make his superior numbers tell against Rebel Patrick Cleburne's well-placed troops on the Rebel right, Sherman failed to complete his part in Grant's plan. Though there were others who substantiated Sherman's apparently incorrect claims that Cleburne was heavily reinforced,[113] the fact remains that Sherman, with a corps and two divisions (Howard and Davis), could not dislodge Cleburne's division, consisting of two brigades and two regiments. Meanwhile, Hooker unexpectedly took Lookout Mountain and Thomas took the strategically important Missionary Ridge, and Bragg's army fled. There are many stories about Grant's displeasure with Thomas's behavior on Orchard Knob that day, with accusations of tardiness and recalcitrance. We can thank Wilson, once again, for this tale of ill will. Wilson claimed in his memoirs that he, Wilson, had egged on Rawlins, who, thanks to Grant's patronage, was now a brigadier general,[114] to insist to Grant that he make the reluctant Thomas attack. Baldy Smith saw the same situation quite differently, for it was Smith's understanding that the Rebel center was still considered too formidably manned for an attack there to be advisable. As historian James Lee McDonough points out, Grant's reputation is better served when the gilding of his having planned things this way all along is discarded, for if Grant had ordered an assault on the center of the Confederate line, it would have been a reckless gamble indeed.[115] It is interesting to consider that Wilson outlived just about all of his Civil War contemporaries. There was no one left to counter or deny the claims he made for himself and his own military prowess. For instance, in his 1912 memoirs, Wilson, while taking the opportunity to criticize Sherman's slowness and poor

General William F. "Baldy" Smith (Library of Congress).

General Joseph Hooker sitting on Lookout Mountain (National Archives).

performance at Missionary Ridge, did not hesitate to give himself, Wilson, full credit for the actions taken that day that led to the Union victory. Wilson undoubtedly had Grant's attention and confidence. (Hadn't Grant, himself, administered the customary oath to Wilson several days earlier when Wilson received his commission as brigadier general?) But Wilson recounts that he got the outspoken Rawlins to urge Grant to insist that his orders were carried out at once.[116]

Grant would also forevermore deny that Hooker's taking of Lookout Mountain the day before deserved to be called a battle. As Chattanooga historian Glenn Tucker observes, those who died or were wounded in the fight might disagree.[117] Grant would, however, praise Sheridan's role at Missionary Ridge to high heaven, although fellow commander General Hazen argued, again forevermore, that it was his men, not Sheridan's, that took the enemy's guns.[118] Sheridan wrote that "General Hazen and his brigade employed themselves in collecting the artillery from which we had driven the enemy, and have claimed it in their capture." But McDonough in *Chattanooga* observes that the account of 3rd Division commander, Brigadier General Thomas J. Wood, is supported by "an impressive array of eyewitness testimony."[119]

Wood's account of Missionary Ridge reports that his division, including Hazen's 2nd Brigade, not only got to the top of the ridge first, but well before Sheridan made it to the top. But Sheridan's assertion, that he got there first and took the guns, because it was supported by Grant, carried much weight. As an example of Grant's continuing support for Sheridan's version of things, Grant wrote in the 1880s for the *Battles and Leaders* series about Chattanooga and Missionary Ridge, "To Sheridan's prompt movement the Army of the Cumberland and the nation are indebted for the bulk of the capture of prisoners, artillery, and small arms that day." Grant also wrote that while Sheridan pursued the enemy after reaching the crest, neither Wood nor Granger joined in. He implies in his account that it was his own plans that were being carried out this day and that Thomas's assault in the center up Missionary Ridge was part of that plan. Grant also seemingly blamed Hooker's delay in coming up on the Federal right for whatever deviation there was from his original plan.[120] Hazen, who advanced up Missionary Ridge with his men while Sheridan hesitated, remained in the army after the war, and found he had made a firm enemy in Sheridan, who, according to Hazen, hampered his career at every turn.[121] There are also those who point out that it was the disgruntled soldiers of Thomas's Army of the Cumberland who made the decision and took it upon themselves to ascend Missionary Ridge, by no order or any particular inspiration from Sheridan. In fact, historian Lloyd Lewis suggests that when Sheridan's 2nd Division took the enemy's rifle pits at the bottom of the ridge and kept right on going, Sheridan, far from leading them, actually tried to stop his men and get them to come back. Sheridan then took the time to send back a messenger to see if they were supposed to take the rifle pits and stop, or continue.[122] But his men saw, if their commander did not, that to stay in the area of the Rebel rifle pits would be to stay in a slaughter pen, and when Sheridan realized that the rest of Thomas's force was on their way up the ridge, he and his men joined their climbing comrades. While a number of witnesses confirm Hazen's claims, perhaps the most interesting is a report of a Confederate commander, William Bates, that confirms that Hazen's men broke the Confederate line on Missionary Ridge and reached the summit, while the Rebels had been able to hold back Sheridan's advance. The last of the enemy's artillery was captured by Hazen's men when Sheridan was still halfway up Missionary Ridge. Hazen lost 92 men killed, 430 wounded, and 7 missing. Hazen's brigade captured 382 men, 2 stands of colors, 18 pieces of artillery, and 650 stands of small arms.[123]

It came to Hazen's attention that Sheridan was claiming credit for the capture of several of the artillery pieces that Hazen had. Hazen then wrote to Sheridan saying that he would be glad to consider whatever facts Sheridan had, so that if Sheridan was correct, the situation could be rectified. But when Sheridan came to Hazen's headquarters on Missionary Ridge that night and "insisted imperiously upon an unquestioning giving up of the guns, I stood upon my written proposition." Hazen's commanders argued against giving up the guns they had taken before Sheridan reached the top of the ridge. In his report, Sheridan claimed that others took the guns. In later years, when Hazen preferred charges against a Sheridan favorite, Gen. David Stanley, Sheridan took the opportunity to testify against Hazen, accusing Hazen of lying in his report that he and his men were first on top of Missionary Ridge and had captured the enemy's guns.[124] After the battle at Chattanooga, Sheridan also stated in his report that after the ridge was taken, it was he, Sheridan, who pursued the Rebels relentlessly. Sheridan described his troops as harassing the enemy on into the moonlit night. The Rebels tell it a bit differently, stating that after an hour's fight fending off a following Federal force, the Confederates retreated at their leisure.[125]

Though nothing went according to Grant's plan at Chattanooga, Sherman, who declared that Thomas's attack was the original plan all along, would also gush, "It was a great victory — the neatest and cleanest battle I was ever in — and Grant deserves the credit of it all." Grant, too, in his memoirs indicated that everything went according to his orders. Later, Grant would continue to add real insult to injury by perpetuating the fiction that General Thomas was somehow slow and inept. Grant uses the sobriquet "Slow Trot," that Thomas's enemies intentionally misinterpreted; impetuous cadets had given the name to Thomas when he curbed them from riding their mounts recklessly during cavalry training at West Point. Grant would add, "Thomas is too slow to move, and too brave to run away."[126]

Perhaps writer and veteran Ambrose Bierce's description of Grant on that day at Missionary Ridge goes some way to explain the muddle. Bierce, no stranger to imbibing himself, said of Grant,

> It was my privilege to be close to him for six or seven hours, on Orchard Knob — him and his staff and a variable group of other general and staff officers, including Thomas, Granger, Sheridan, Wood and Hazen. They looked upon the wine when it was red, these tall fellows — they bit the glass. The poisoned chalice went about and about. Some of them did not kiss the dragon, my recollection is that Grant commonly did. I don't think he took enough to comfort the enemy — not more than I did myself from another bottle — but I was all the time afraid he would, which was ungenerous, for he did not appear at all afraid I would. This confidence touched me deeply.

The author doesn't wish to add myself to the list of many who blamed Grant's faults on his fondness for the bottle, though Bierce also commented that those who were insistent about Grant's adoption of total abstinence were themselves "abstainers from the truth."[127]

McDonough comments in his masterly work *Chattanooga* that Grant was understandably impatient to attack, but almost made a terrible blunder before the Missionary Ridge victory. On November 7th, when Grant found out that Longstreet was marching to invest Knoxville, Grant impulsively ordered George Thomas to attack Bragg at Missionary Ridge the next day in the vain hope of forcing Longstreet to return to Chattanooga. Thomas and Baldy Smith were able to convince Grant that such an attack would fail and should not be made until Sherman's arrival. Though Grant implied in his reports to Washington, then and later, that it was Thomas's fault, in some way, that the attack was not made, McDonough also observes that Thomas and Smith saved Grant from making one of the worst mistakes of his career. This is one of many examples of Grant's impatience to attack, which produced results ranging from triumph to disaster. But beyond impatience, perhaps Grant's most seriousness weakness was refusing to blame his friends when they didn't live up to his expectations, while he extravagantly criticized anyone who made his chosen few look bad by succeeding where they failed.[128]

Halleck was effusive in his praise of Grant, though the way in which the fighting at Missionary Ridge had played out in no way reflected Grant's plan. With the perception that victories were happening in the West, while nothing was happening in the East, Halleck began to relish the success of "his" western generals, Sherman and Grant.[129] Meanwhile, Granger, the hero that had marched to the sound of the guns and stood by Thomas at Chickamauga, was sent, along with Hazen, to go to Burnside's assistance. Wilson in his memoirs tells a very strange story regarding Granger and Thomas, his commander, a story he likely told to Grant. According to Wilson, Thomas was very slow to order Granger to move toward Knoxville, and Granger all but refused to go, declaring that he, Granger, thought it a very bad move to make. Grant, unaware that Burnside had already repulsed Longstreet without assistance, was outraged. What sort of a commander would he be to let a division commander argue with him about orders? Wilson, once again, seems to be the only source available for this bit of insubordination perpetrated by Thomas and Granger. Wilson acknowledges in his memoirs that Granger, among his other faults, took liberties with orders because of his "swelled head."[130] Grant informed Sherman about the leader of the column he sent to Knoxville, stating, "Granger is on the way to Burnside's relief, but I have lost all faith in his [Granger's] energy or capacity to manage an expedition of this importance." Grant therefore sent Sherman to take command from Granger, and upon arriving in Knoxville, it was discovered that Burnside was in no particular distress, and Sherman prepared to return to Chattanooga.[131] When Burnside asked Sherman to leave Granger and Hazen behind, Sherman ignored Granger's protests, and ordered him to remain. Sherman commented that Granger "most unreasonably, I thought, remonstrated against being left; complaining bitterly of what he thought was hard treatment to his men and himself." Sherman, claiming that it made a very bad impression on him, declared that he was determined that Granger should eventually be replaced.[132] Meanwhile, at Knoxville, both Hazen and Sheridan protested the lack of warm clothing and reduced rations for their men, but a serious vacuum in command left them in limbo. While Grant waited for confirmation of his promotion to lieutenant general, Burnside went east to serve with the Army of the Potomac. The buck of command was then passed to Generals Foster, Parke, Granger and finally to Sheridan, who was in command when Hazen was put under arrest for making a report that Sheridan thought of as being intentionally "ironical and irritating." Meanwhile the garrison at Knoxville endured a winter of receiving sometimes as little as quarter rations.[133] But that would not be the new military triumvirate's problem. In the spring of 1864, Lieutenant General Grant went east, Sheridan went with him to command the Army of the Potomac's cavalry, Gen. John Schofield replaced Foster, Granger was replaced by Oliver O. Howard, and William T. Sherman was given command of the western armies.

After Grant's success at Chattanooga, communications between Grant and Halleck had grown so cordial that Grant dared to make suggestions to Halleck regarding the possible movements of the eastern armies, and Halleck encouraged Grant to write him freely and fully regarding his opinions on these matters.[134] And Halleck discussed the subject of reconstruction with Sherman, who declared that the war must continue until all the armies of the rebellion had been defeated. In late summer of 1863, the glowing reports Secretary of War Stanton was receiving from the assistant he had sent west to report on Grant, Charles Dana, led the secretary to seriously consider having Grant come east to take over the Army of the Potomac. It was an idea that had been talked about since July of 1863, but, intriguingly, Grant, Halleck, Lincoln, Wilson and Dana were opposed to it *at that time*. But it was an idea that did not go away. For those with bigger plans for Grant, his coming east might be part of the plan, but how large and powerful his role would be when he got there was a matter of ultimate importance. In the Badeau-Wilson letters at Princeton University, Wilson's friend Adam Badeau was speaking of Grant as a presidential candidate as early as October 28, 1863. Badeau also spoke of the likelihood of the conflict ending in a military dictatorship, while commenting that all who want power, fortune or fame must be soldiers.[135]

In July of 1863, Halleck had written to Grant that "Meade has thus far proved an excellent general ... the only one who has ever fought the Army of the Potomac well. He seems the right man in the right place." It is likely that the positive assessment Halleck reported to Grant that July would have surprised Meade, for he had been hearing no such praise.[136] But by December of that year, attitudes toward Meade had hardened significantly in Washington. With Meade's failure to successfully assault Lee's Army of Northern Virginia, Meade's star was fading. At the end of 1863, Charles Dana, having just met with Lincoln, Stanton and Halleck, wrote to Grant from Washington that Grant's idea that either Sherman or W.F. "Baldy" Smith replace Meade as commander of the Army of the Potomac had been listened to with interest. Smith was the administration's choice, especially after Dana gave them reassurance regarding Smith's disposition and character. Dana reported that all agreed with Grant that Smith was a better choice than Sherman.[137]

By February of 1864, the House of Representatives was calling for Grant to come east, and the congressmen were also offering the new rank of lieutenant general, a rank that had been previously held only by George Washington and Winfield Scott, and one which would place Grant above Halleck.[138] Yet others, including Dana, continued to speak of Grant as a possible candidate for president, but Grant's assurance that he had no interest in holding office gave Lincoln enough encouragement to agree. Stanton told Halleck to order Lt. Gen. U.S. Grant to come to Washington. Sherman feared what would become of his friend Grant in or near the capital, declaring that "no man can do anything so near Washington as the Army of the Potomac. That army can do nothing till the Closing Scenes. It would be cruel & inhuman to take Grant or any western officer there." And while Grant apparently took Sherman's warnings about Washington to heart, he chose to travel with the Army of the Potomac, the army that would confront Lee's Army of Northern Virginia. Some have said that those who supported Grant's promotion did it as much for their detestation of Halleck as any fondness or appreciation for Grant. But Halleck, far from resenting Grant's ascendence, seemed to relish the idea that with his promotion, Grant would take all the responsibility from his shoulders. Halleck functioned in a role not unlike that of Grant's military secretary in Washington.[139]

Halleck was finally comfortable at being able to offer his opinions and advice while taking no responsibility for the outcome. In a long letter to Grant in February of 1864, Halleck reminded his soon-to-be commander that whatever his plans were for the armies, they could be modified by Lincoln. One wonders if this led Grant to keep his plans from Lincoln, who cooperated by allowing Grant to chart his own course. Offering his own opinions on which of Grant's plans for operations might or might not work, Halleck stated that "Lee's army is by far the best in the rebel service and I regard him as their ablest general." Halleck challenged Grant to consider, since little else could be accomplished beforehand, how he would destroy the Army of Northern Virginia. Though Grant would later dispute that Lee or his army deserved their vaunted reputation, it is interesting that Grant chose to accompany the Army of the Potomac and be present to oversee their assignment.[140]

Sherman took Grant's place as commander of the western armies, and James McPherson took Sherman's former command. On March 12, 1864, Halleck was relieved at his own request as general in chief, and was assigned to the post of chief of staff of the armies under the direction of Lieutenant General Grant and Secretary of War Stanton. One of Halleck's aide's cynically observed that Halleck would, while remaining the intermediary between the administration and the generals, "remain the scapegoat for others people's blunders and interference." Halleck would continue as an administrator, that being his cup of tea, while Grant pursued his own supposed forte, command in the field. In Grant, Lincoln felt that he finally had a general who was willing to command.[141]

There is one last member of Grant's inner circle to meet, perhaps the most eccentric of them all, which is saying something, considering "Grant's Men." Lt. Col. Adam Badeau joined Grant's staff on March 29, 1864, as Grant's military secretary in the field. Badeau is described by James Wilson as a "short, stoop-shouldered, redheaded man who wore glasses," and Grant himself described him as "a pale, blue-eyed man, who wore spectacles and looking like a bent fo'-pence."[142] Badeau was a New York journalist and theater critic before the war, and he was an intimate of and a mentor to the famous actor Edwin Booth. A recent Booth biography describes Badeau as a man of independent means with an openness about his homosexuality that was rare in nineteenth century New York. But Badeau was a man about town who could open many doors for Edwin Booth, doors that ordinarily would have been closed because of his lack of education and his profession. Badeau's worshipful reviews also added considerable impetus to Edwin Booth's rise to fame.[143] And when Badeau was shot in the leg at

Adam Badeau (National Archives).

General U.S. Grant with staff officers. Standing left to right: Colonel Adam Badeau and General Cyrus Comstock. Seated left to right: General Grant and General John Rawlins (National Archives).

Port Hudson in May of 1863 while serving as an aide to Gen. Thomas W. Sherman, Edwin Booth nursed Badeau back to health at his house on 107 East 17th Street in New York with the help of his brother, John Wilkes Booth. Though Badeau perceived John Wilkes as being sympathetic toward him, and J.W. had kept the family provisioned during the New York draft riots, John Wilkes Booth would laughingly comment afterwards to his and Edwin's sister, Asia Booth Clarke, "Imagine me helping that wounded Yankee with my rebel sinews. If it weren't for mother, I wouldn't enter Edwin's house."[144]

Badeau, who had previously served as an aide to Halleck, was also a friend of James Wilson, and it was Wilson who recommended Badeau to Grant as a secretary. Although Badeau was only with Grant during the last year of the war, he quickly became part of the cadre of officers who sought prominence for Grant and themselves.[145] The Badeau-Wilson relationship is an interesting one, and perhaps historian Charles Shattuck's assessment of Badeau is most apt. With admirably responsible awareness of the differences between male relationships in the nineteenth century and those of today, Shattuck observes that Badeau's "youthful attachment to male companions, as expressed in his letters to Booth and to his soldier-friend Harry Wilson, ranged from generous affection to maudlin and even hysterical possessiveness." When Badeau went into the army, he wrote to Booth that "he had found 'real and exquisite happiness' in conferring his 'profound and tender and anxious love' upon a young soldier." While Badeau referred to Edwin Booth as his "Right Arm," he referred to James Wilson as his "Left Arm."[146] James Harrison Wilson's placement of such a close friend as Badeau into Grant's inner circle, indeed, someone who would be at Grant's very elbow around the clock, gave Harry, as Badeau called him, unique access to and knowledge of all that was going on at Grant's headquarters. In letters found in the Wilson-Badeau Collection at Princeton, Badeau, urging Wilson to influence Grant, comments that Grant "has not been hammered yet to the right heat. There is only one sledge at work, and that is Rawlins."[147]

Meanwhile, Grant's man in Washington, Halleck, greeted Grant's new appointment and his own new duties as chief of staff with enthusiasm. After patting himself on the back in his final report for the wonderful job he had done as a commanding general, Halleck settled into the part of the job he liked best, administration and giving advice, while Grant was left to carry all the responsibility of issuing orders and commanding in the field. Sherman was in charge in the West with Thomas's Army of the Cumberland, Schofield's Army of the Ohio, and McPherson's Army of the Tennessee under his command. Sherman was facing Joe Johnston, who had replaced Bragg, while Longstreet had rejoined Lee in the East. With everyone under orders to move against the enemy simultaneously, the two largest movements would be commanded by Grant and Sherman. Grant would fight bloody battles pitting the Army of the Potomac against Lee's Army of Northern Virginia throughout the spring of 1864. Grant's attitude was that the Army of the Potomac had "never been thoroughly fought."[148]

While Grant moved with the Army of the Potomac, Sherman and his army would attempt, unsuccessfully, to flank Johnston, as he made a slow passage between Chattanooga and Atlanta.[149] Hazen biographer Edward S. Cooper describes "Sherman's brilliant strategy" as,

> at almost every place that Confederate General Joseph E. Johnston fortified positions, Sherman would bring up the bulk of his army, begin skirmishing, and then send McPherson's troops on

a wide flanking movement. Johnston had no choice but to retreat. Sometimes McPherson had to pull out of line and march across the entire rear of the Federal army to flank Johnston. The men might grumble, but they knew that marching was far better than major assaults against fortified positions. Sherman tried to avoid frontal assaults, knowing that the Rebel defensives were identical to those they themselves prepared. It was only when rains made maneuvering impossible and delay intolerable, that Sherman felt compelled to assault opposing lines.

One of those places was at Resaca, Georgia, where Hazen was serving under O.O. Howard in George Thomas's army. Hazen, ordered to attack a Confederate works, lost 120 men in 30 seconds.[150]

It was Halleck's job to keep everyone — Grant, Sherman, Butler, Banks, Sigel, and others — well supplied, and to keep all interested parties informed. Halleck also watched Grant's back for him in the jungle that was Washington politics.

Four

The Army of the Potomac Carries Old Baggage into the Wilderness

WHEN LT. GEN. ULYSSES S. GRANT came east in 1864 to take command of all of the U.S. armies, Gen. George Gordon Meade suspected that Grant would be choosing one of his own western generals to replace him as commander of the Army of the Potomac. One would think that Meade, the victor of Gettysburg, would have no cause for worry. He was the general who had had command of that army thrust upon him just days before the three-day battle in 1863, who by his decisive defeat of Lee in Pennsylvania had sent the audacious Rebel leader fleeing back to Virginia with his battered army. Surely all this would assure Meade of receiving his country's accolades and support. But it did not. Though one can cite numerous examples of western commanders failing to mount postbattle pursuit, Meade's failure to set his own tattered army in motion to prevent Lee's retreat set the pattern of constant criticism that condemned Meade for not moving on the wounded but still dangerous Army of Northern Virginia in the weeks and months after Gettysburg. While Grant allowed Meade to maintain his Army of the Potomac command, Grant was not immune from criticizing Meade's performance at Gettysburg. While Grant commented after the war that, after all, Meade had just taken command of the Army of the Potomac at the time of the battle, Grant also added the caustic comment that if "Sherman or Sheridan had commanded at Gettysburg, I think Lee would have been destroyed."[1]

One cannot follow the fate of the Army of the Potomac in the spring of 1864 without becoming aware of the tensions that existed between Gen. Gouverneur K. Warren, then commander of the Army of the Potomac's 5th Corps, and Gen. George G. Meade, the Army of the Potomac's commander. A strained relationship would also quickly develop between Warren and Grant, when the new general in chief of the armies chose to travel with the Army of the Potomac during the Overland Campaign. The conflicts that arose among these officers were often exacerbated by the animosities of such men as the ambitious, one could easily say ruthless, Generals Sheridan and Wilson, who had served with Grant in the West and were among the trusted associates who had become known as "Grant's Men." But it was not just these commanders' own destinies that were at stake, for their actions guided the fate of the thousands of men who served under them as well.

A consideration of the Meade-Warren relationship prior to the Grant's 1864 Overland Campaign provides many insights on what was to become of the Army of the Potomac and its commanders in 1864 and 1865. In late June of 1863, when General Meade had suddenly had the command of the Army of the Potomac thrust upon him, General Gouverneur K. Warren, serving as Meade's chief engineer, distinguished himself on the second day of Gettysburg by directing the timely occupation of Little Round Top on the vulnerable left of the Union line. It was an action that brought Warren considerable recognition, and one that could only have strengthened the apparent confidence his commander, General Meade, had in him. Meade proposed that the 33-year-old Warren be commissioned a major general, and when Gen. Winfield S. Hancock's Gettysburg wound absented him from the field, though Warren had experienced no more than brigade command, Meade gave Warren temporary command of the 2nd Corps.[2]

Lieutenant General U.S. Grant (Library of Congress).

As mentioned, Meade had had little time to enjoy his victory over Lee at Gettysburg in the summer of 1863 before criticism arose of his handling of the army, both during the battle and in its aftermath when the Army of Northern Virginia slipped from his grasp.[3] Within two days of the battle, one of Meade's chief critics, the wounded general Dan Sickles, fresh from the battlefield after losing a leg, was in Washington telling family friend, President Lincoln, how Meade had botched the Battle of Gettysburg.[4]

Coupled with Lincoln's and Halleck's expressed disappointment upon Lee's escape, other rivals for Gettysburg accolades or who coveted Meade's very command of the army, were hard at work disputing his fitness for command.[5] Nor had Meade's maneuvering for an advantage in the months after Gettysburg resulted in a decisive battle that could restore his beleaguered reputation.[6] Meanwhile Halleck's interests were directed ever westward, for even before Chickamauga, Halleck had ordered Sherman to leave Vicksburg and bring four divisions to Chattanooga. Ever mindful of Lee's loss of Longstreet and his corps, sent west to reinforce Bragg that September, Secretary of War Stanton, critical of Meade's efforts in the East, urged Lincoln to transfer the Army of the Potomac's 11th and 12th Corps to Rosecrans. Lincoln, reluctant to handicap Meade by this loss of more than 20,000 men, finally yielded, sending that same month two corps under Gen. Joseph

Hooker's command to Chattanooga. Halleck would support this fresh infusion of men to bolster the Army of the Cumberland's efforts in the West.[7]

One of the few bright spots for the Army of the Potomac that fall, although it apparently was not bright enough to defer criticism, was Meade's encounter with Lee in October near Bristoe Station, where Meade discovered that Lee was well on his way to turning the right flank of the Army of the Potomac in preparation for an attack. Meade withdrew to the Rappahannock, not only taking up a better position to receive an attack but also placing his army between Lee and Washington. General Warren, with the 2nd Corps, was assigned to protect the Army of the Potomac's withdrawal while fending off Lee's advance. As Rebel general A. P. Hill's corps hurried to catch the rear echelon of the Federals headed for Centreville, Warren laid what Hill biographer James I. Robertson described as "one of the neatest traps of the war." Unaware of Warren's presence, or perhaps, simply the extent of his 2nd Corps numbers, Hill unheedingly pitched only two brigades of his men headlong after the retreating Federals, at which point he was very roughly handled by three divisions of the 2nd Corps on Hill's unprotected flank.[8]

Warren had been told to expect some assistance from Sykes and the 5th Corps in handling not only Hill's Corps but Ewell's Corps as well, who was coming up behind and in support of Hill. But by the time Sykes and the 5th Corps arrived, Warren had dealt with Hill's corps on his own. Warren had pushed Hill back with heavy Confederate loss, and although Rebel general Richard Ewell was coming up to form his own line of battle, luckily for the 2nd Corps, darkness brought an end to the day's fighting. Warren and his corps, now facing two corps of Lee's army, made their way silently to safety with the rest of the Army of the Potomac at Centreville. It is not the last time Warren as corps commander would face Lee's army on his own. One can speculate just how much Warren's unexpected blow on Hill's corps affected Lee's mind-set as he contemplated his next move, for his scouts told Lee that Meade had taken up a stronger position at Centreville, and with Confederate supplies running low, Lee was reluctant to lengthen his supply lines. Much to Meade's disappointment, Lee would turn away.[9]

Lee, after destroying the railroad upon which Meade was dependent for provisions, fell back to a new line at the Rappahannock,[10] and Meade realized that, though Warren had done well, he and his army had failed to bring on a battle with Lee that Wash-

General Gouverneur K. Warren (Bangor Public Library).

ington was demanding. Meade confessed to his wife, "This was a deep game and I am free to admit that in the playing of it he has got the advantage of me."[11] While Halleck implied to Meade that he was allowing Lee to bully him, Warren, the day after his Bristoe Station triumph, was also encouraging Meade to go on the offensive. Warren offered to push the 2nd Corps forward to test what Lee was doing, but although Warren skirmished with the enemy the next day, Meade remained puzzled and cautious regarding Lee's movements.[12] A caustic message from Halleck advised Meade that he had better fight instead of running away, and Meade responded with the observation that Halleck had made no suggestions as to how this could be done to advantage. Meade, experiencing his own disappointment that Lee had refused to attack him in his stronger position, suggested that if his judgment was not approved he should be relieved. Halleck did not reply.[13] So while Warren's star was in the ascendant, Meade's was falling. Demonstrating this, is a comment by 2nd Corps aide Frank A. Haskell, who after Bristoe Station wrote of Warren, his new commander, "Such men as he are required to end this War — men who will not hesitate to strike when a chance occurs, and who will *hanker* after a chance, and run forward to meet it." Haskell, who remained with the 2nd Corps, became colonel of the 36th Wisconsin, and died leading his men at Cold Harbor in the 1864 Overland Campaign.[14]

After Bristoe Station, the Army of the Potomac attempted to follow Lee as he retired, and strove to anticipate what Lee would do next. As one 5th Corps wag described it, for several weeks the Army of the Potomac "oscillated" between Fairfax and Centreville, and back again.[15] But when Meade, citing Lee's destruction of his supply line, the Orange and Alexandria Railroad, suggested to the administration that the year's campaigning was over, he was summoned to Washington to discuss the situation. Accepting no excuses, while the Unionists' railroad was being swiftly rebuilt, on October 24, Meade was ordered to prepare to attack Lee's army.[16]

After anxiously searching for a weak point in the enemy's line, Meade, on November 2nd wired a proposal to Halleck. Convinced that an attempted crossing of the Rappahannock and frontal assault on Lee would be a very costly venture, Meade suggested a move around Lee's right flank, moving the entire Army of the Potomac across the Rappahannock near Fredericksburg. Meade assured Halleck that he could easily make a smooth change of base, obtaining his supplies by either rail or water. Halleck rejected Meade's proposal out of hand. "Any tactical movement to turn a flank or threaten a communication is left to your own judgment, but an entire change of base under existing circumstances, I can neither advise or approve." This "change of base" is precisely what Grant would do at the beginning of the Overland Campaign, when he relinquished hold on the Rapidan crossing, and adopted the same waterborne supply line that Meade had advocated. One difference was that Grant didn't bother to ask Halleck. He just did it, and stood back to receive the applause.[17]

On November 7, 1863, Meade put the only plan seemingly still open to him into action, approaching Lee's defenses along the Rappahannock. Unexpectedly, Major General John Sedgwick (USMA, 1837), commanding the 5th Corps and part of the 6th, administered a strong blow to Lee's defenses at Rappahannock Station. It was an attack that surprised and shocked Lee and led him to hurriedly withdraw his army away from the Federal incursion.[18] An eyewitness to the meeting of General Sedgwick with several of his subordinates, including one of his temporary corps commanders, Gen. Horatio Wright, tells that Sedgwick asked for their opinions of the chances for making a successful attack on the enemy. Telling quite a different story, our old acquaintance from the West, General Wright, credited himself with coming up with the idea and suggesting the attack at Rappahannock Station, as Wright would state in his after-action report.[19] On that November day, Lee lost more than 2,000 irreplaceable veterans in the fighting at Rappahannock Station and at nearby Kelly's Ford, where the losses were inflicted by Federal general William French's force, consisting of the Army of the Potomac's 1st, 2nd and 3rd Corps. Federal losses to Sedgwick and French's forces were 419 and 42, respectively.[20]

One who was less than impressed with Meade's accomplishments at Rappahannock Station was Secretary of War Stanton. Though the victory of November 7th had caused great excitement in Washington, enthusiasm became tempered by the news that Lee had withdrawn beyond the Rapidan. Stanton's anger was unfortunately expressed by his refusing to receive the honor guard sent to deliver the enemy colors captured at Rappahannock Station when they were brought to the capital. The honor guard was led by one of the successful, wounded commanders, General David A. Russell (USMA, 1845), who would later be killed while serving in the 6th Corps with Sheridan in the 1864 Valley Campaign.[21]

It is unfortunate that following Sedgwick's victory, Meade either did not realize or did not dare to take advantage of the Army of Northern Virginia's vulnerability as Lee hurriedly sought a feasible new line of defense. Realizing the jeopardy he and his army were in, Lee, on the night of November 8th, retired with his army across the Rapidan, taking up a strong position south of the river that included a line along the banks of a little-known creek called Mine Run. Both the Orange Plank Road and the Orange Turnpike (two roads that will be heard of again in the next year's campaigning) ran roughly parallel to Lee's lines, giving him great ease of movement for men and materiel behind his position.[22]

Given the administration's mandate that Meade not change base of supply, and not uncover his line of communication with Washington, there were really few options left to Meade, ones of which Robert E. Lee would certainly have been aware. Given the strong new position of the Army of Northern Virginia, Meade's only course was to try to get around one of Lee's flanks, and when reports were received that the lower fords of the Rapidan were unguarded, it seemed to invite the Federals to make the attempt on the Confederate right flank. And there was also the knowledge that the Orange Plank Road and Orange Turnpike behind the Rebel lines had not been obstructed, further encouragement for Meade's plan to attempt to gain the enemy's right flank and rear. These undefended avenues leave Mine Run historians Martin Graham and George Skoch puzzling over how Lee had overlooked these threats to his army, while others believe that Lee, feeling he could not prevent the enemy's crossing of the Rapidan, simply chose to wait and engage the enemy on his own side of the river. Considering that little obstructed the Federals' crossing of the Rapidan other than rain-swollen waters, this seems to be the case. Meade was also mindful of what turned out to be accurate reports of Confederate strength, telling that there was about 50,000 Rebels confronting the Army of the Potomac's 80,000.[23]

As Meade would describe in his official report,

The plan I decided on was to cross the Rapidan at the lower fords, in three columns, and by a prompt movement seize the plank road and turnpike, advancing rapidly toward Orange Court House, thus turning the enemy's works, and compelling him to give battle on ground not previously selected or prepared, and I indulged the hope that in the execution of this plan I should be enabled to fall on part of the enemy's forces before he could effect a concentration.[24]

The Army of the Potomac's movement was executed on the morning of November 26th, starting at 6 A.M. Gen. William H. French, commanding the 3rd Corps and leading the column on the Army of the Potomac's right, crossed the Rapidan at Jacobs' Mill and was to march to meet with Warren's 2nd Corps, who, having crossed at Germanna Ford, marched to Robertson's Tavern. Sykes's 5th Corps was

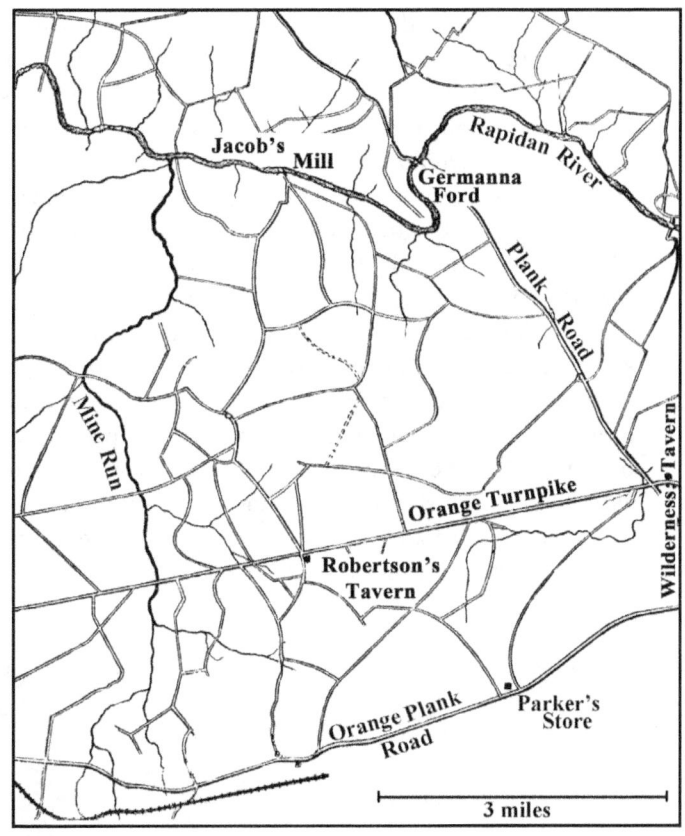

Mine Run. Adapted from Plate XLVII, *Official Atlas*, and Walker's *History of the Second Army Corps*, page 371 (Ned Smith).

to make for the plank road from Culpeper Ford, and continue as far as Parker's Store, or if possible, reach the road toward Robertson's Tavern. The army's cavalry supported the movement and guarded its trains. Since Meade expected the most resistance from the enemy against his own right, Meade had Sedgwick's 6th Corps following and supporting French's corps, while part of the 1st Corps supported Sykes's column on the Federal left. The columns movements would be simultaneous, and all depended upon surprising the enemy, but before the first Federal moved out of the winter camps, Robert E. Lee heard from one of his scouts in Culpeper on November 25th that the Army of the Potomac's 1st Corps had received eight days' rations and their marching orders, leaving little doubt that a Unionist movement was planned.[25]

While the 5th and 2nd Corps reached the Rapidan between 9 and 10 A.M. on November 26th, French's 3rd Corps," from causes not yet explained," as Meade later commented, did not arrive on the river until noon, delaying the advance of the entire army, which was under orders to make a simultaneous crossing. Since Lee apparently already knew the Federals were coming, it's difficult to know how critical French's creeping advance was, but it is tempting to suggest, as author and veteran Ambrose Bierce commented on such things, French's tardiness was bad enough to "acquaint the enemy with our intention to surprise him."²⁶ No one reached Robertson's Tavern before nightfall, and the advance was left to continue early on the next day. By 10 A.M. on November 27th, Warren and the 2nd Corps found themselves confronting two divisions of Ewell's corps, at which point Warren was ordered to hold his ground until the anticipated imminent arrival of French and the 3rd Corps. But French, out on the wrong road and either lost or having forgotten his orders, reported that he was waiting for Warren, and at 1 P.M., French sent word to Meade that his right flank was being assaulted by the enemy. At 2:30 P.M., French received Meade's peremptory order to advance at once, with his whole force if necessary, in order to throw forth his left and unite with Warren. Though French was informed that Warren was engaged with the enemy and being in need of support, French declared that Meade's order was hazardous to his command and attempted to get the officer carrying Meade's order to rescind it. Further delay and confusion in the 3rd Corps left French still skirmishing with the enemy. Rebel general Edward Johnson's command, some 5,000 soldiers, aided by the confusing and confounding conditions of the Wilderness, blocked the advance of the Federal 3rd and 6th Corps, some 32,000 soldiers, until darkness fell.²⁷

Far from executing the advance as Meade had planned it, Warren had been forced

Generals of the Army of the Potomac. From left, General Gouverneur K. Warren, General Samuel G. French, General George G. Meade, General Henry J. Hunt, General Andrew A. Humphreys, and General George Sykes (Library of Congress).

to spend the day on the defensive, awaiting the arrival of French and the 3rd and 6th Corps. And though Lee was still unsure of exactly what Meade intended to do as he entered the densely wooded region known as the Wilderness, Lee prepared for what he saw as the two most likely targets. Lee prepared to make an attack on the Union left flank if Meade should strike out for Richmond, or, should Meade try to gain the rear of the Rebel line, Lee prepared a strong defensive line. Thus, by the time the 2nd Corps advanced early the next day, November 28th, they found that the enemy had withdrawn into formidable earthworks on the stream called Mine Run.[28]

The forces that Lee deployed to delay the advancing Federals, in combination with the glacial pace of Meade's 3rd Corps commander, General French, gave the Army of Northern Virginia enough time to consolidate at a strong position on the bank of Mine Run, where the Rebels displayed the speedy efficiency at fortification that would thwart the Federals for many months to come.[29] Faced with a strongly entrenched enemy, Meade, with Warren's encouragement, began a turning movement late in the afternoon of May 28th. Under Warren's command, the 2nd Corps and Terry's division of the 6th Corps strained through the day of the 29th to gain the unprotected Confederate right flank. Coming up on Lee's right at the last light of day, Warren decided against an attack, but his report of the weakness of the Rebel flank convinced Meade to issue orders for the next day. Reinforced with two divisions from the 3rd Corps, Warren was to attack the Confederate right with 26,000 men, supported by strong demonstrations along Meade's entire front.[30] A biographer describes that Warren, by personal, daring reconnaissance, knew well before a frigid dawn confirmed it, that overnight, Rebels had transformed their thinly held line into stout breastworks, bristling with muskets and containing a battery of 14 guns. Warren's grim soldiers wrote their names on slips of paper to pin to their breasts so that their bodies could be identified. The order that would send his men to useless destruction was one Warren decided he could not give. Too far from Meade's headquarters to seek his commander's counsel, Warren made his decision alone.[31]

Captain Thomas Livermore of the 2nd Corps, stating that he felt Warren's decision against attack took more boldness than it would have taken to attack, was witness to Warren's dilemma, and would later write,

> In command of nearly one half the army, the youngest major-general in it, with the hopes of General Meade resting upon his action, when to do nothing was almost as bad as a defeat; with such orders that the responsibility of defeat would have rested wholly or in great measure on General Meade; with a command full of courage, and believing that he would be the greatest man in the army, if he succeeded, he, as he afterwards said in my hearing, when he rode along the lines on that frigid morning and saw the enemy's position, thought of the wounded who were frozen at Fredericksburg and determined that he would not risk a defeat.[32]

The officer who fielded the unenviable task of carrying Warren's terse message to Meade on the morning of November 30th, was Captain Washington Roebling of Warren's staff. Roebling, a civil engineer who had served with Warren on Round Top at Gettysburg, brought Meade news of Warren's startling decision. Roebling carried Warren's words regarding the enemy scribbled on a paper, reporting, "Position and strength seem so formidable in my present front that I advise against making the attack here. The full light of the sun shows me that I cannot succeed." But it was Roebling's verbal message, that Warren had suspended the attack on his front, that visibly disconcerted Meade, who exclaimed, "My God! General Warren has half my army at this disposition." At Captain Roebling's urging, Meade sent aides to suspend the supporting attacks scheduled to begin shortly all along his line.[33]

On riding to Warren's position, Meade, who was described as "looking as savage as anyone could," looked over his young commander's situation, and though Warren offered to make the attack if Meade ordered him to, Meade decided against overruling Warren's initial decision. On the ride back to his headquarters, Meade was confronted by General French. Still angry that two of his divisions had been given to Warren for the morning's canceled movement, French taunted Meade with the question, "Where are your young Napoleon's [Warren's] guns; why doesn't he open?"[34] It is hard to imagine being able to accomplish much in the way of teamwork with a teammate like Gen. William French.

In Meade's report on Mine Run, he fixes much of the blame for the failure of the movement on Gen. William H. French, the new commander of what had been Sickles' 3rd Corps. Meade cited French's still unexplained delays as having destroyed the plan that had demanded speed and surprise in order to succeed.[35] However, Meade did not let Warren off the hook. Though in other venues, mostly private ones, he agreed with the 2nd Corps commander that an attack would have been futile, Meade blamed Warren for talking him into putting most of his troops into the abortive flanking attack on the Confederate right. And what Meade states in his report seems to fix the blame on both French and Warren, for he declares that "after the enemy, through these culpable delays, had been permitted to concentrate on Mine Run, I have reason to believe, but for the unfortunate error of judgment of Major-General Warren, my original plan of attack in three columns would have been successful, or, at least, under the view I took of it, would certainly have been tried." In his report, Meade also did not let the administration forget that they had refused to allow him to make the movement according to his own plans and judgment.[36]

Warren's independent decision to abandon what he considered a costly and useless attack on the morning of November 30th would have long-lasting repercussions.[37] Warren not only drew criticism on himself, but unquestionably brought criticism down upon Meade, damaging and undermining their relationship. Though Meade ultimately endorsed Warren's stand against senseless slaughter, it was Meade who had to endure the ignominy of withdrawing his army without a fight. For this, he expected no less than removal from command, and though his critics grew more vociferous, Meade would be spared that ultimate embarrassment.[38] But relations between Meade and Warren would never be the same. While Meade could sympathize with Warren's reluctance to wantonly expend the lives of his men, issues of subordination and the necessities of obedience to orders had been introduced. When the Army of the Potomac renewed its advance upon Lee the next spring, fighting of unimaginable intensity and duration would bring such issues to the front again and again, further straining the relationship between Meade and Warren.

While Meade was already known for his sensitivity to slights, real or imagined, when he felt his orders or opinions were not being given sufficient weight, Warren's calling off the attack at Mine Run unquestionably upset Meade. Meanwhile, the stresses of command and his enemies' continued sniping at his abilities and character were undoubtedly having an effect as well. That November of 1863, 6th Corps commander John Sedgwick commented that "Meade is twenty years older than when he took command." But Confederate commander Robert E. Lee was also feeling his age. It gives a new perspective to Meade's and Warren's decision not to press their attack to know that after Mine Run Lee expressed his frustration at being unable to tempt Meade into a foolish assault. Lee commented to his staff, "I am too old to command this army; we should never have permitted those people [the Army of the Potomac] to get away."[39]

Lest one imagines that Meade's suspicion that he would be replaced in the weeks and months after Mine Run was a baseless anxiety, in the spring of 1864, Congress's Joint Committee on the Conduct of the War began hearing testimony from Meade's harshest critics, Gens. Daniel Sickles, Daniel Butterfield and Abner Doubleday among others, who denigrated Meade's performance at Gettysburg. Not satisfied to merely disagree with Meade's handling of the Army of the Potomac, a disgruntled Doubleday, who had been removed from command of the 1st Corps by Meade, suggested that Meade belonged to one of the "proslavery cliques controlling that army ... men who, in my opinion, would have been willing to have a compromise in favor of slavery." There were those, however, who testified in defense of Meade's performance at Gettysburg. In his testimony before the Joint Committee, Gouverneur K. Warren, while critical of some of his fellow corps commanders, for the most part defended Meade's actions.[40]

While partisan testimony questioned Meade's very patriotism, further provocation was provided by anonymous letters that were being published in the *New York Tribune* under the name "Historicus." They accused Meade of planning to abandon his position at Gettysburg before the battle, and credited Dan Sickles with making all the good decisions on that field.[41] It's little wonder that Meade suspected he would be removed from his command. Nor was the *Tribune* the only paper attacking Meade. As he commented to his wife in late December of 1863,[42] "The *Herald* is constantly harping on the assertion that Gettysburg was fought by the corps commanders and the common soldiers, and that no generalship was displayed. I suppose after awhile it will be discovered I was not at Gettysburg at all." Another contribution to Meade's uneasiness was made by General Hancock, who, partially recovered from his Gettysburg wound, had returned to the Army of the Potomac in late December. Hancock carried word that the administration had indeed been planning to replace Meade, in all likelihood with Hancock, himself. Supported by Meade's report on Mine Run and those of his corps commanders, however, Halleck claimed that *he* was the one who had been able to save Meade's command of the Army of the Potomac. Seemingly, the one bright spot in Meade's life early that spring of 1864 was his confirmation as brigadier general in the regular army.[43]

Ultimately, Meade would not only retain command of his army, but Lincoln and Grant would leave the reorganization of the Army of the Potomac in Meade's hands, and several commanders of that army disappeared along with their corps. The reorganization of the Army of the Potomac sent the depleted regiments of the 1st and 3rd Corps to swell the ranks of the 2nd, 5th and 6th Corps. Gen. Hancock had returned to command of the 2nd Corps, and Warren replaced Gen. George Sykes as commander of the 5th, an indication that Warren retained at least some part of Meade's confidence.[44]

Grant's only "personal" choices for the Army of the Potomac were fateful ones indeed. They were made with seemingly no consideration of the appointees' experience or expertise, nor any consideration for the valuable skills and knowledge of the men they were displacing. Gen. Philip Sheridan, whose cavalry experience consisted of two months as a

From left, General Henry E. Davies, General David M. Gregg, General Philip H. Sheridan, General Wesley Merritt, General A.T.A. Torbert, and General James H. Wilson (Library of Congress).

cavalry, regiment and brigade commander, was appointed to replace Gen. Alfred Pleasonton (USMA, 1844) as head of the Army of the Potomac's cavalry. It was in some ways unfortunate timing, for as cavalry historian Eric Wittenberg observes, "The Army of the Potomac's Cavalry Corps had enjoyed success under Pleasonton's leadership in the summer and fall of 1863. With such able subordinates as Buford and Gregg, Pleasonton's horse soldiers scored their first victories over the vaunted Confederate cavalry and gained respect in the eyes of both the infantry and the enemy." But the ill-fated Kilpatrick-Dahlgren raid in early 1864 caused irreparable harm to both Pleasonton's and Kilpatrick's reputations, as well as inflicting severe loss on Kilpatrick's 3rd Cavalry Division. So with the trauma of Gen. John Buford's death, came Kilpatrick's exile to Sherman's army and Pleasonton's removal from command. The Army of the Potomac's Cavalry Corps would, as Wittenberg comments, "be starting over again."[45]

When Philip H. Sheridan was chosen by Grant to command the Army of the Potomac's Cavalry Corps, Pleasonton was not the only veteran cavalrymen who was replaced or displaced. Another choice for senior cavalry command was Grant's former aide in the West, Gen. James H. Wilson. A close friend of Grant's military secretary, Adam Badeau, and Grant's chief of staff, John Rawlins, Wilson also had the patronage of Undersecretary of State Charles Dana. It was Dana who had apparently recommended Wilson to Secretary of War Stanton as the best possible man to go to Washington and straighten out irregularities that had been discovered in the operations of the Cavalry Bureau. In his brief tenure as Cavalry Bureau director, less than four months, Wilson, as he later reminisced, lived with and apparently spent all his available time with Charles Dana, enjoying the amenities of the wartime capital. While Wilson attempted to improve the way cavalry horses and supplies were purchased, as Cavalry Bureau director, Wilson made what was perhaps his greatest contribution to that branch of the service by seeing to it that the Army of the Potomac's cavalry was armed with the very effective Spencer carbine.[46]

But James Wilson had never commanded troops in combat other than those pioneers and sailors he had futilely tried to force through the swamps of Vicksburg under stubborn Rebel artillery fire. Thus Wilson's appointment to the command of the Army of the Potomac's 3rd Calvary Division is said to have enraged Gen. George Armstrong Custer, who had commanded that division throughout the summer and fall of the previous year, and who outranked Wilson. The inconvenience of Custer outranking Wilson was dealt with by moving Custer's brigade to the 1st Division, and bringing Gen. George Chapman's brigade from the 1st to Wilson's division. Another 3rd Division commander, Henry E. Davies, who also outranked Wilson, was reassigned to the 2nd Division, and then, and only then, was it possible for James Wilson to have command of the 3rd Division of the Army of the Potomac's Cavalry Corps. Cols. J. B McIntosh and G.H. Chapman were the unfortunates who served as Wilson's brigade commanders.[47]

Gen. Alfred T. Torbert, though his experience had been limited to infantry command, was given Sheridan's 1st Division. Torbert was an "Easterner," but was a friend of Sheridan's who affected a rather dandified, elaborate costume, though it would be difficult to outdo the get-up George Armstrong Custer was partial to, one that a Meade aide described as "a circus rider gone mad."[48] Torbert's appointment as division commander meant that well-respected brigadier general Wesley Merritt, who had commanded Gen. John Buford's men since the latter's death, was relegated to brigade command under Torbert. Merritt was assigned to command the reserve brigade, which included four small regiments of veteran regulars. The reshuffling also meant that the experienced cavalrymen Col. Thomas Devin and Brigadier General George Armstrong Custer, now shifted to the cavalry's 1st Division, were put in brigade command under Torbert. Only veteran Army of the Potomac commander Gen. David Gregg had managed to retain division command under Grant's and Sheridan's reorganization, and as such, Gregg was Sheridan's only experienced division commander. Gen. H. E. Davies and Col. J. Irvin Gregg were David Gregg's brigade commanders.[49]

When the Army of the Potomac again crossed the Rapidan on May 4, 1864, they were but a part of Grant's grand strategy that sent Gen. William T. Sherman against Gen. Joseph E. Johnston's army in the West, Gen. George Crook in West Virginia was to destroy Rebel communications, while Gen. Franz Sigel with Gens. Edward Ord and William Averell to confiscate vital supplies in the Shenandoah Valley. Gen. Benjamin Butler would move to the James River, with Richmond and Petersburg as his goals. The Army of the Potomac, which Grant would accompany, had Lee's army as its objective.[50]

As Grant historian William McFeely points out, at the beginning of his Overland Campaign, Grant had placed General Meade, the victor of Gettysburg, in the same awkward position he himself had found intolerable at Corinth with Halleck, that of being second in command and without real authority.[51] Though Grant was usually careful to issue no orders to the Army of the Potomac except through Meade, it is not a circumstance that any military commander would recommend: having the commander of all the armies looking over his shoulder. And it is evident that Grant did a good deal more than look over Meade's shoulder.[52] Given Grant's penchant for impulsive frontal attacks, ones in which no time would be "wasted" on reconnaissance or preparation, it is not difficult to guess why it suddenly became Meade's style as well. In the first days of the campaign, Grant was of the opinion that, should anything happen to Meade, General Warren would be his choice to succeed him. Grant's high opinion of Warren would not last.[53] And while the members of Meade's staff, predisposed to be critical of this western usurper, warmed toward Grant and the tactful confidence and deference he seemingly expressed toward Meade, as time went on the same could not be said about their feelings for some of Grant's former western associates.

Five

The Wilderness

Early on May 4, 1864, Lt. Gen. U.S. Grant, accompanied by his patron, Congressman Elihu B. Washburne, began the first fateful steps of his "Overland Campaign." With the Federal incursion clearly visible to the Rebel signal station on Clark's Mountain,[1] Grant's message to General Halleck, Lincoln's chief of staff, now seems eerily naive. Grant reported, "The crossing of Rapidan effected. Forty Eight hours now will demonstrate whether the enemy intends giving battle this side of Richmond." While Grant's account of the Army of the Potomac's first clash with Lee's army admits that in the dense forest of the Wilderness "all the conditions were favorable for defensive operations,"[2] he does not address the question of whether his battle in this nightmarish setting of tangled second growth, which destroyed all possibility of unit cohesion, had been foreseen or intended. Gen. Adam Badeau, Grant biographer and former aide-de-camp to the general, insists that meeting the enemy in the Wilderness was intentional, while Gen. Andrew Humphreys, chief of staff of the Army of the Potomac at the time, expresses disbelief that anyone would purposefully choose such ground for a battlefield.[3]

While it's true that the 5th Corps infantrymen were fresh from their winter camps, it's also true that they had been on the move since midnight of May 3rd–4th, moving to reach their Germanna Ford crossing place by 6 A.M. Having been notified by Wilson at 5:50 A.M. that he had a pontoon bridge established and his men were nearly all across at Germanna Ford, Griffin, Warren's advance, on reaching the ford found Wilson had, in fact, not crossed the river. Only after putting their own pontoon bridge in place, and allowing Wilson to use both bridges, his own and Warren's, was the 5th Corps able to cross an hour later at 7 A.M. The 6th Corps, which followed the 5th, hadn't begun their movement until daylight on May 4th. The four divisions of Hancock's 2nd Corps, preceded by Gregg's Cavalry, crossed the Rapidan at Ely's Ford that same morning.[4] But was it wise to halt at a point in the day when a continuation of the march would have taken them beyond the terrible environs of the Wilderness? By mid-afternoon of May 4th, all of the Army of the Potomac had crossed the Rapidan but their trains, with Warren's 5th Corps, ordered to halt at Wilderness Tavern. Warren's aide and engineer, Washington Roebling, many years later was still bemoaning the fact that the 5th Corps halted, as ordered, when there was still four hours of daylight left. He went on to fume about the spot in which they were ordered to encamp, a swampy hollow surrounded by high ground,

A view of the Wilderness (National Archives).

when half an hour's march away lay the key to the battlefield, a hill known as the Chewning Farm that overlooked the whole area.[5]

The 2nd Corps, crossing at Ely Ford, reached Chancellorsville by 9:30 in the morning, with their corps completely across the river by two o'clock in the afternoon. Burnside's 9th Corps, at this point not officially part of the Army of the Potomac, was also under Grant's supervision, not Meade's, in order to avoid the awkwardness of the present Army of the Potomac's commander giving orders to that army's former commander. Of course, Grant giving separate orders to the less than reliable Burnside ended up creating an awkwardness of a whole different sort. So as the 5th Corps began crossing at Germanna Ford on the morning of May 4th, Grant telegraphed Burnside, some of whose divisions were 40 miles from the Rapidan, to start his distant corps toward Germanna Ford.[6]

Credited with coming up with the plan for the Army of the Potomac's passage through the Wilderness, Gen. Andrew A. Humphreys, Meade's chief of staff for the Army of the Potomac, had pondered over the logistics of getting the army past that tangle of the woods in one day. Humphreys saw no obstacle to the Federal columns marching the 30 miles that would carry them all beyond the heavy, confounding growth of the Wilderness. The Unionist corps had made marches that long before, and could do it again, and the benefit of being able to fight on ground of their own choosing where they could take advantage of their superior artillery was well worth the effort. The midnight start of

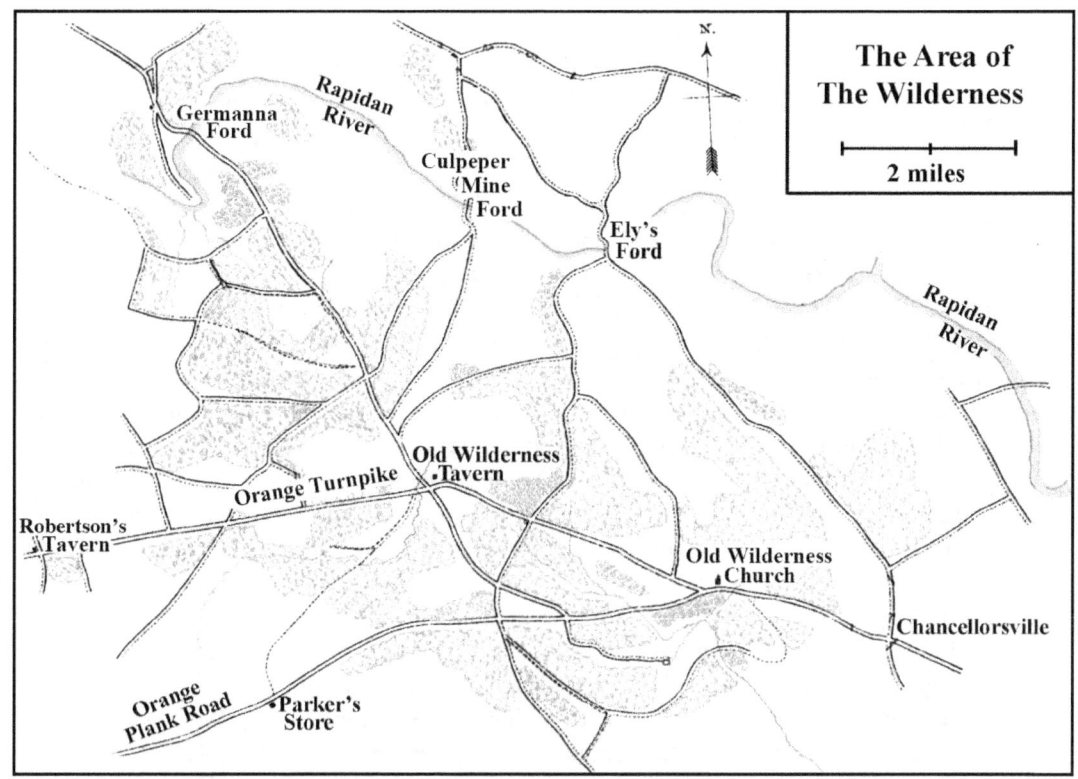

The area of the Wilderness. Adapted from Plate XCIV, #6, *Official Atlas* (Ned Smith).

the 5th Corps was one element designed to hide the army's motion as long as possible from Lee's attention. Grant's eventual choice of moving on Lee's right flank, as opposed to his own right where Grant's army would be crossing open country, was, again, a concession made to ease the transport of supplies and hurry the change of base that would take place on the Army of the Potomac's projected route. Burnside's approach to join the Army of the Potomac was timed to provide additional protection for both Washington and the army's trains. But all this went wrong in the first days of the campaign when the cavalry, instead of acting as a screen and warning system for the army and protection of the army's trains, failed in its mission and was then pulled away for unconsummated battle with the Rebel cavalry. And when the cavalry's role in these first steps of the campaign began to change from protecting the army's supply wagons, the trains became a dragging anchor on the army that could not be ignored.[7]

Everything changed with intercepted Rebel signals and reports from Sheridan's cavalry late in the day of May 4th. While the information in Sheridan's reports would prove to be false, they apparently reinforced both Meade's and Grant's belief that Lee's army had not advanced to confront the Federal incursion. Though Lee was well aware of the Army of the Potomac's crossing of the Rapidan, Lee was puzzled over what Grant's intentions might be. Although he was ever ready to pitch into his foes, Lee hesitated, unable to read what Grant might do. As Wilderness historian Edward Steere observes, "However eager Lee may have been to hit at the flank of the long Federal columns as they threaded their way southward through the depths of the woodland beyond Mine Run, there was nothing as yet to justify a belief at Confederate headquarters that Grant would expose his forces to the perils of such a situation."[8] Put another way, Lee couldn't believe that Grant would do something that put his army at such a disadvantage. For as Lee's aide, Charles S. Venable, later wrote, Lee was delighted that Grant "had not profited by General Hooker's Wilderness experiences, and that he seemed inclined to throw away to some extent the immense advantages which his great superiority in numbers in every arm gave him."[9]

Historian Steere gave careful consideration to what few copies of Lee's Wilderness orders survived, for much of the Confederates' records and reports were lost during the Army of Northern Virginia's retreat to Appomattox the next year. But taking into account the Rebels' movement and the recollections of other Confederate commanders, Steere concludes that Lee, while anxious to delay and harass the Federal incursion, wanted to avoid a battle until Longstreet could bring up the remainder of his force. But since there was some question as to where Grant was headed, Lee initially hesitated to send orders to Longstreet, thus waiting to commit himself to just where Longstreet should go. While Lee assumed that Grant would push through the Wilderness to Fredericksburg or toward Mine Run, the possibility that he would pause in the Wilderness did not seem like a viable option, but that was exactly what Grant did. The answer to the question of where Grant intended the two advancing columns to go the next day, May 5th, can be answered by saying, not very far. Warren's 5th Corps had orders to move at 5 A.M. some four miles to Parker's Store on the Plank Road, with Sedgwick's 6th Corps taking Warren's place at Wilderness Tavern. Hancock's 2nd Corps was to move at 5 A.M. to Shady Grove Church, where he would extend his right toward Parker's Store and the 5th Corps. On the morning of May 5th, while Meade was at 5th Corps headquarters, Grant waited impatiently at Germanna Ford for the first elements of the 9th Corps to arrive. One can only guess what Grant would have done next, once his army was united, for they would never get to complete this creeping advance.[10]

With the Army of the Potomac's first steps into the Wilderness so closely resembling Meade's own ill-fated advance on Mine Run in late 1863, one can't help but wonder what regretful memories or doubts may have plagued General Meade. But in the days to come, he would come to trust Grant. Meade would live to regret it, much as Grant would one day rue the trust he had put in Henry Halleck.[11] Grant biographer William McFeely, commenting on the relationship between Grant and Meade, said that it took Meade a year to realize what Grant had been doing to him. In the spring of 1865, "after Sherman and Sheridan had been promoted ahead of him, Meade realized that he had been killed with kindness. Grant needed a general he could ignore. He wanted an army that would obediently press the enemy, and Meade was never insubordinate.... By the war's end Meade knew that Grant, who so often said he agreed with his ideas, had merely listened and ignored them...."[12] But all that was a year away, and on a spring morning, Meade and Grant and the Army of the Potomac were taking the first steps on what would become known as the Overland Campaign of 1864.

Federal cavalry would play a rather astonishing and highly significant role in the Wilderness, and indeed, by their presence or absence, have a very strong impact on the entire Overland Campaign. To begin at the beginning, Edward Steere's *The Wilderness Campaign*, is strongly recommended for while other works exist, none are so reliable or thorough as Steere's. It is of interest that Steere spends much time considering the cavalry's role, and particularly revealing that Steere additionally dedicated an entire chapter, "The Misadventures of Sheridan's Cavalry,"[13] to provide the details that make it clear that Sheridan and his cavalry did not perform well at the Wilderness. A case in point is James Wilson. Off schedule and making inaccurate reports from the start, General Wilson and his cavalry preceded the 5th Corps across the Rapidan on May 4th with orders to keep his troopers out on both the Orange Turnpike and Plank Road to alert the Federals to any Rebel activity. On the night of May 4th, Wilson reported to Warren's 5th Corps headquarters at the Lacey House near Wilderness Tavern that he had patrols on both roads. And as a Rebel report Lee received that night indicates, a Federal cavalry contingent led by Gen. James Wilson had been encountered on the Turnpike. While Wilson reported to Warren that he had driven the Rebels that he had met some six miles toward

General George Meade (Library of Congress).

Mine Run, the Rebels reported that when they encountered Wilson, he withdrew, and while doing so was overheard loudly "instructing his party to return to within closer supporting distance of the main body near Wilderness Church."[14] Many years later, in his 1912 memoirs, Wilson would cast some doubt upon the efficiency of his troopers by making the snide comment that "my division was as nearly ready as volunteer cavalry ever is." He would also try to explain away his extraordinary failure to provide vital information for the army by suggesting that he had expected the infantry to relieve his cavalry detachments and throw out their own cover to protect their flanks. Considering Wilson's orders and his report to Warren that he had men out on both the Plank Road and the Orange Turnpike, Wilson's story makes no sense. Nor does it explain why, if Wilson imagined that his men were to be relieved, he had left no one there for the infantry to replace.[15]

As far as the cavalry was concerned, very little would go as planned on May 5th. Torbert's cavalry, retained across the Rapidan to guard the crossing of the army's trains, was supposed to have joined forces with Wilson to screen the army's front and flank on May 5th.[16] But acting on what turned out to be erroneous reports of a division of Confederate cavalry outside Fredericksburg, Sheridan received Meade's permission to send both Torbert's and Gregg's divisions away. Though Sheridan would later assert that it was

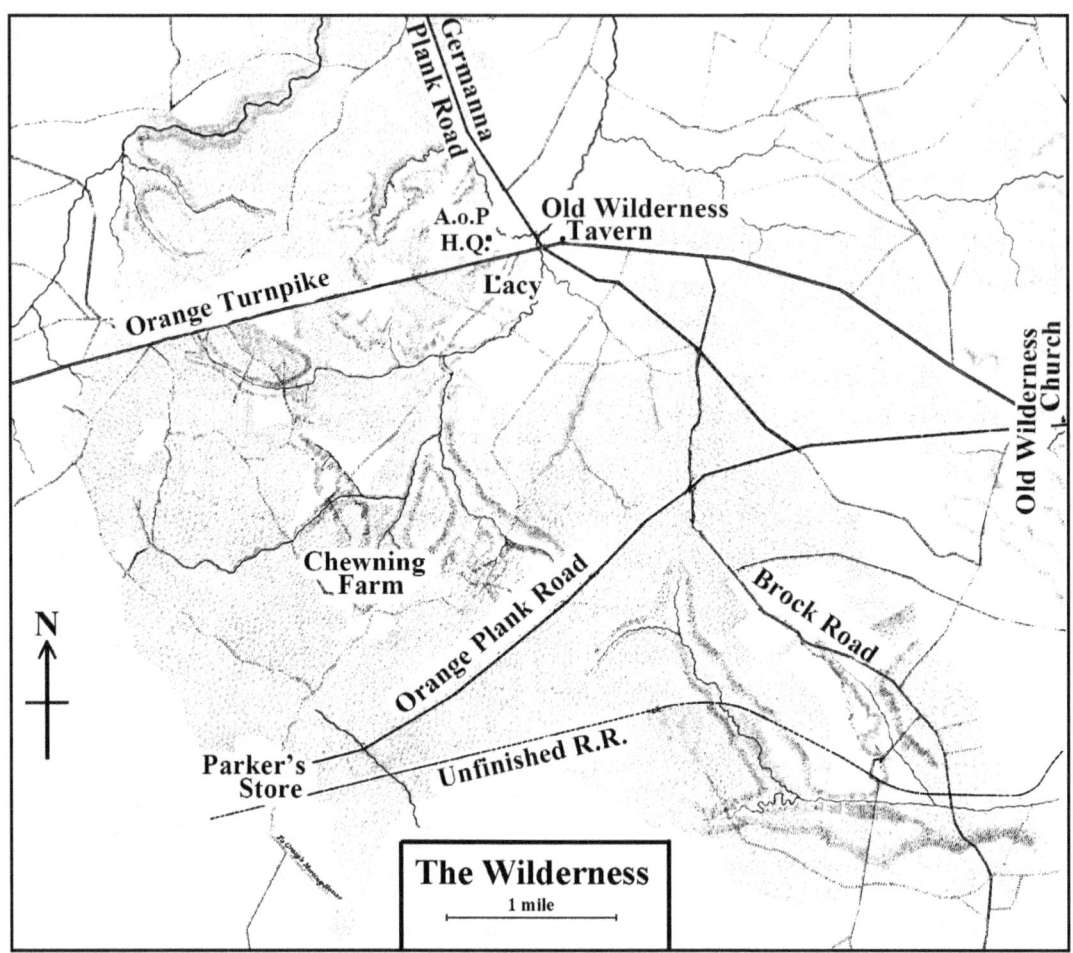

The Wilderness. Adapted from Plate LV, #1, *Official Atlas* (Ned Smith).

Meade's fault that he went off on this wild goose chase, it was clearly his own reports that sent the cavalry away from the army at this critical time. It was a movement that, had it been completed, would have taken nearly three-fourths of the cavalry corps to Hamilton's Crossing and away from the approaching enemy.[17] The Hamilton's Crossing expedition, while tying up the greater part of the Federal cavalry, came to naught, for whatever Rebel force had been detected was long gone by the time the Federal cavalry began its approach. Thus Wilson was left as sole provider of advanced warning for the Army of the Potomac, which, in essence, meant no warning at all, for Wilson, who claimed that he never received the additional orders Meade sent to him on the morning of the 5th, orders reminding him, once again, to keep his parties out on both the Turnpike and Plank Road, began following the orders he had received on May 4th. Thus Wilson left one regiment of cavalry on the Plank Road, the soon-to-be-proven intrepid 5th New York, whereupon Wilson led his division south toward Craig's Tavern where Confederate cavalry and infantry soon cut off Wilson's division from the rest of the Army of the Potomac.[18]

When the 5th Corps advanced on the Orange Turnpike and Plank Road on the morning of May 5, 1864, they unexpectedly began to encounter the enemy in force. Still believing the Rebels were merely trying to delay them with no intention of giving battle, Meade ordered the entire 5th Corps to attack. At 8:30 A.M., Grant endorsed Meade's 7:30 A.M. order directing Warren to attack with his whole corps, while Grant added that Warren should do so without giving time for disposition of his troops.[19] When Grant reached Meade at around 10 A.M. on the morning of May 5th, the attack had not been made, and reports were coming in of Rebel cavalry on the 5th Corps right, and a sizable Rebel force coming down the Plank Road on the 5th Corps' left. No cavalry was available to meet any of these incursions. Wilson was lost, while Gregg and Torbert were still responding to the nonexistent threat at Hamilton's Crossing.[20]

Washington Roebling (Roebling Collection, Institute Archives and Special Collections, Rensselaer Polytechnic Institute, Troy, New York).

On the 5th Corps' left, Crawford's division, followed by Wadsworth's and Robinson's, had advanced on a narrow woods road toward Parker's Store, and had arrived at the Chewning Farm, located in a field on a commanding plateau, when they heard firing ahead at Parker's Store. Washington Roebling, Warren's aide and scout, who always seemed to be in the right place at the right time, recognized that the field they had reached was of key importance, for if the 5th Corps could hold that field, they could split Lee's army in two if he attempted to come down the Plank Road and the Turnpike at the same time. Nor could Lee pass by the 5th Corps to attack the 2nd Corps. Roebling saw to it that Crawford's division was put in position with two batteries, as Roebling rode ahead to find the 5th New York Cavalry, the small remnant of Wilson's force he had left behind, skirmishing with Rebel infantry, accompanied by Robert E. Lee, himself, coming down the Orange Plank Road.[21]

On May 5th, having left the 5th New York behind to do the job his whole division was supposed to have done, the rest of Wilson's contingent rode off and was literally chased away from the Army of the Potomac by the Rebel horsemen of Rosser's cavalry, who were operating on the Confederate right that day. By noon on the 5th, Sheridan had no idea where Wilson was and sent Gregg's Division to find and/or rescue Wilson. By 2:15 that afternoon, Gregg found Wilson falling back away from the enemy to Todd's Tavern. Gregg's mission was not an easy one, for while he would attempt to assist Wilson by shoring up his rearguard, as it passed by with Rosser in hot pursuit, but as Steere describes it, "Wilson's rear was trying to catch the advance." But however inglorious Wilson's actions were on May 5th, he had done one thing right before he rode off to meet his own embarrassing fate. Wilson's choice of John Hammond's 5th New York Cavalry as the regiment he would leave at Parker's Store that morning was inspired, for this intrepid regiment had held off, or at least slowed down, the advance of Hill's corps that was coming down the Orange Plank Road. But by the time Roebling was able to bring up Federal infantry support, the 5th New York was gone, fleeing toward Chancellorsville, while Rebel infantry flooded down the Plank Road. As Steere observes, it was remarkable what one cavalry regiment, in this case the 5th New York, had been able to do, and Steere ponders over what Sheridan might have accomplished if he had not dismantled Meade's original plan with his futile diversion to attack a nonexistent enemy. If Torbert had been allowed to place his whole corps on the Federal left, what could Torbert's 3,000 dismounted cavalrymen have accomplished against Hill's column? "Instead," Steere comments, "Wilson's screen was torn to tatters, while the preponderance of Sheridan's powerful force stood immobile in the rear."[22] But despite the great importance of possession of the Chewning Plateau, with great reluctance, the 5th Corps' left was pulled back from the Chewning Farm to meet the demands by Meade and Grant for a massed frontal attack by the 5th Corps. The next day it was belatedly realized that holding the Chewning Farm was critical. Both Hancock and Burnside were sent to try to recover it and failed.

As Steere comments, "There is no difficulty in accounting for Grant's reaction to such a situation. When his flanks were in jeopardy, it was not his habit to solve the difficulty by retreating; if he could not threaten the enemy's communications, he threw everything at hand into a frontal assault." But that's a puzzling statement in a way, for Warren was not advocating retreat, just an assault where the enemy was threatening his flank. But Grant directed Meade to send orders simultaneously to the 5th Corps' Griffin and Wadsworth, and the 6th Corps' Wright and Getty for an immediate attack regardless of condition of their flanks. With orders for the 5th Corps to make a frontal assault immediately, to Roebling's great disgust, shortly after 2 P.M. Crawford was withdrawn from the Chewning Farm, sent to rejoin the 5th Corps and bolster Wadsworth's exposed left flank. When the Rebels took and held the vital ground at the Chewning Farm, Hancock would be ordered to march to Parker's Store to support Getty's attempt to try to regain the commanding position at Chewning's.[23] Though at 10:30, Wright was again ordered to come up and attack on the 5th Corps' right, it would be 3 P.M. before Wright managed to bring his men up to meet the enemy on the 5th Corps' flank.[24]

General Charles Griffin (Library of Congress).

While the 5th Corps' left was extricating itself from the Chewning Farm, on the 5th Corps' front, 1st Division commander Gen. Charles Griffin could see what his corps and army commanders could not, that he was facing a considerable body of the enemy with more Rebels pouring down the Orange Turnpike, deploying to the right and left to face his own division's hastily dug defensive line. While Griffin demanded that an assault be delayed until reinforcements came up on his flanks, Warren, faced with Meade and Grant's imperative orders, insisted that the frontal attack be made as ordered, at once. Word made the rounds that Grant, when he found out that the attack proposed for earlier that morning had yet to be made, had apparently questioned the courage of Warren, the 5th Corps and Meade's Army of the Potomac. While Sedgwick's 6th Corps was ordered to come up to the 5th Corps' aid, Gen. Horatio Wright's Division was reportedly unable to come up on the 5th Corps' right because of the density of the woods. Meanwhile Wadsworth's division was struggling to come up toward Griffin's left flank, though a gap still existed between Wadsworth's division and Crawford's division working its way back from the Chewning Farm out on the Plank Road.[25]

While the 5th Corps' 1st and 4th Divisions struggled to get in position to make their early afternoon attack alone, Grant was sending messages urging speed to Burnside's 9th Corps, the vanguard of which had first started crossing the Rapidan at 8:30 that morning. Though the 9th Corps' role would be no more dramatic than relieving 6th Corps units who were guarding the army's communications, it would free up the 6th Corps to join the fray and help prevent Lee from driving his army between the two columns of the Army of the Potomac. But Grant's hopes that the 9th Corps would make a speedy arrival was overly optimistic, for Burnside, as Grant would come to know, was not known for his speed. Or as one of Meade's aides put it, Burnside "had a genius for slowness."[26] Meanwhile, Hancock was still ten miles away with his 2nd Corps stopped, but stretched out in a line six miles long on a road leading to Spotsylvania. The communication between Army of the Potomac headquarters and the 2nd Corps was difficult and slow, and by midday, Hancock had just received orders to halt. Later, Hancock would receive word to turn and move the 2nd Corps to reunite the army in the rather belated hope that they could prevent Lee from driving his forces between the Army of the Potomac's two columns. At least Hancock's arrival would promise more assistance to the battered Federal corps than Burnside would offer.[27] While Burnside dithered and Hancock waited for orders, Warren faced the prospect of making an attack on an unknown enemy in a hellish tangle of woods with both flanks of his battle line in the air. As Steere observes, "The tragic nature of this situation was soon to be revealed — one which would bring about a savage and indecisive battle."[28]

The 5th Corps attacked "impetuously" at midday on May 5th, as Warren described it,[29] with whatever elements of the Corps he had been able to cobble together, with Griffin's division bearing most of the responsibility. With thick undergrowth making movement and communications nearly impossible, all unit cohesion vanished as the advance lurched forward. One soon lost contact with the units on the left and right, and many eventually lost all sense of direction. Griffin's division at first seemingly experienced some success, driving the enemy's skirmishers back, but when Griffin reached the enemy's main line, he realized that the Confederate line outflanked his own by what looked like a full division. It was, in fact, Gen. Edward Johnson's division, including the vaunted

Stonewall Brigade, whose line stretched off into the woods well beyond Griffin's own. When the two Confederate divisions Griffin had been fighting were reinforced, Sanders Field, one of the only open spaces in the tangle of scrub pine and foot-grabbing vines, fast became a killing ground. By 2:00 in the afternoon, Griffin on the right, was being forced back with the loss of two of his guns. Eventually Wadsworth and Crawford on the 5th Corps' left, receiving the Rebel fire on their flank, were also forced back with heavy losses. The broken 1st, 3rd and 4th Divisions ended up where their advance had begun early that morning, and they straggled back bloodied and angry.[30]

As Warren aide Washington Roebling described it, "Griffin's Div.[ision] made a splendid attack, losing most of his regulars, gaining a few hundred feet of worthless ground & inflicting small loss on the enemy." When Roebling wrote this account more than 40 years had passed since the battle, but the anguish he still experienced is evident. He described the carnage, the experience of fighting an invisible enemy in dense woods, and the fires that burned the wounded alive and choked the survivors with smoke. But Roebling's most shocking revelation is his blunt statement regarding the response Warren received to his request that he be allowed to attack further south, where the enemy in force was turning the 5th Corps' position, instead of making another futile frontal attack. Roebling unequivocally states that, though no staff officer from Meade or Grant had been up to their position, let alone Meade or Grant themselves, the answer from the army's headquarters came back quickly. "Unless Genl. Warren attacks instantly at the point indicated he shall be cashiered on the spot in face of the whole army." Thus, in the first hours of the first day of the campaign, Grant and Meade's expectations for swift and unquestioning obedience to orders had been stated very clearly. Warren sent Crawford's division forward into the undergrowth, where, Roebling records, their line bent in upon itself as it moved through the dense thickets, and the division suffered more casualties from friendly fire than from the enemy. The outraged and outspoken Roebling comments, "I mention this incident because it marked the beginning of Grant's reckless murderous methods of hurling troops at fortified positions and other impossible places, without regard to human life, when better results could be achieved by proper maneuvering on the field of battle."[31]

As Steere observes regarding the Federal attacks of May 5th, they were hurried and, lacking preparation, were piecemeal. The Rebel lines they were attacking were sufficiently dug in to resist the attacks, for, as Steere points out, Lee unlike Grant, had told his corps commanders to avoid a confrontation until more of their force had come up.[32] Once the Rebel line had reformed and been reinforced, they counterattacked with devastating effect. As Steere points out, the Federals threw around 18,300 infantrymen against the Rebels roughly 14,300. If Grant had allowed more time for deployment and for bringing up the 2nd and 6th Corps as they were converging on the 5th Corps' left and right, respectively, their participation in the assault would have allowed Meade to have thrown 26,000 men against Ewell's 14,500.[33] It might have avoided such an exercise in costly futility.

When Hancock approached the battlefield midafternoon, he received the same treatment from Grant and Meade that Warren had been subjected to, receiving orders from army headquarters around 2 P.M. to attack immediately, although only two of his five divisions were formed for an attack, while the other three were still moving in column of march. In his memoirs, Grant would criticize Hancock, remarking that, while the woods and narrow roads prevented Hancock from getting into position for attack, he was not as prompt as he usually was. He also made note that when Hancock had not attacked by 4 P.M., Getty's division, which Hancock had been called upon to rescue, was ordered to attack by themselves.[34] Nonetheless, Hancock, with assistance from Getty and Wadsworth who was sent from the 5th Corps, managed by the end of May 5th to push back and partly envelop Hill's corps, a situation that seemed to promise success for the next day. But one feat which Hancock had been unable to accomplish was the recovery of the Chewning Farm from the enemy. When Meade and Grant realized that Rebel reinforcements were pouring through there to join the assault on Hancock, Wadsworth, anxious to redeem his division's honor after the morning's disaster, volunteered to launch an attack on the enemy column's flank and rear. Wadsworth and his division would fight their way toward the 2nd Corps until darkness brought an end to the day's battle. Wadsworth took up a position in heavy woods in advance of the 2nd Corps line to await daylight.[35]

Meanwhile, on the 5th Corps' right, the advance through the woods made by Wright's division was so slow paced that it took over three hours to advance one and a half miles to confront the main line of Ewell's Confederates. So while Warren had been attacking the Rebels in the early afternoon of May 5th, it was two hours later, around 3 P.M., before Wright's division approached the enemy and drew any attention away from the beleaguered 5th Corps. When Wright finally attacked he met stiff resistance, and ultimately both Hancock's 2nd Corps' and Sedgwick's 6th Corps' attacks were indecisive, for similar reasons. For once again, the hurried attacks were hindered by lack of preparation, and the lines they were attacking had been strengthened.[36]

Though the vanguard of Burnside's 9th Corps had begun arriving at Germanna Ford at 8 A.M. on May 5th, it was after dark that night before elements of the 9th Corps were expected to take their place in the Federal battle line. Unionist adjustments and movements were hampered by darkness, so attempts to find and gain position on the Rebel flanks, as well as the probing for the alleged gap in the line at the Confederates' center, would have to wait for the next day's first light.[37] With the day having ended with no decisive results, Grant and Meade issued orders for early the next day, May 6th. The hour Grant first stipulated, 4:30 A.M., was deemed too early in that there would not yet be enough light to find and get into position before dawn. Burnside was having difficulty in understanding what was expected from him as he took up a position between Hancock's 2nd Corps and Warren's 5th Corps, with the 9th Corps facing the gap in the Rebel line. Wadsworth, still assigned to Hancock, would attack with the 2nd Corps. The 5th Corps' order for the next day was another frontal attack by Warren's whole corps on the same line he had attacked that day. The Federal cavalry was ordered to protect the army's trains while seeking out any opportunities for harassing the enemy. Sheridan's reply was, "Why cannot infantry be sent to guard the trains and let me take the offensive."[38]

Delayed orders and changes to orders continued to come into the 5th Corps headquarters until well after midnight on May 5th. In his journal, Warren recorded the results of this, his first day of campaigning with Grant. With marked restraint, Warren described the assaults that Meade and Grant had ordered elements of the 5th Corps to make that first day, when they "impetuously" attacked what turned out to be Ewell's corps. Warren describes heavy losses in the thick, disorienting woods, and the failure of Wright's 6th Corps division to come up and assist them.[39]

That night, Warren's 1st Division commander, Gen. Charles Griffin, an old regular who had served on the frontier and throughout the war, came to Meade's headquarters and joined in an informal council of war taking place. Griffin denounced that day's attack, describing his heavy losses as useless slaughter and declaring that it was an inexcusable blunder to fight from such a disadvantageous position. Griffin implied that Wright's failure to come up on his right deserved censure, and Griffin was also angry with Warren, for in passing along Grant and Meade's insistent orders to attack without waiting for support on his flanks, Warren had also earned a portion of Griffin's wrath. Grant, ignoring the import of what Griffin was saying, began to question Meade as to why he was tolerating such public criticism from a subordinate, at which point Griffin withdrew. Grant's chief of staff, the always outspoken Rawlins, suggested that Griffin should be put under arrest for such treasonous language, and Grant seemed to agree. Meade went out of his way to soothe Grant and passed Griffin's words off as it just being Griffin's way.[40] One would think from this occurrence that Grant was a stickler for soldiers treating their commanding officers with respect, but as will be shown, it depended on who was being insubordinate. Grant would have a great deal of patience with, if not amusement from, Sheridan's confrontation with Meade several days later.

Fighting the next day, May 6th, was chiefly borne by General Hancock, his 2nd Corps reinforced by units from other corps until he had command of six divisions. With success seemingly assured and the destruction of Hill's corps likely, as Hancock was making a breakthrough on the enemy line, the vanguard of Longstreet's corps began to arrive, pushing back the 2nd Corps and turning the tide against Hancock. Participating in Hancock's assault, 5th Corps division commander James Wadsworth was killed leading an attack, his body taken by the enemy. A lightening flank attack by Longstreet drove Hancock back into his starting place at his earthworks, while dire reports on Hancock's situation caused Meade to draw the cavalry away from their fight at Todd's Tavern to again protect the trains.[41] While Hancock lost this engagement on May 6th, James Longstreet came near losing his life when he was shot and wounded by his own men while reforming them after a successful attack on the Federal line. Lee, nonetheless, succeeded in getting Longstreet's 1st Corps back into action for a renewed attack. Burnside, who eventually managed to come between the 2nd and 5th Corps, contributed little to the day's fighting, and Steere attributes Hancock's defeat to the sluggish inactivity of Burnside that day. To add insult to injury, late on the night of the 6th, Sedgwick's 6th Corps, on the Union right, sustained a night attack by the enemy that threatened to become a rout before it was contained.[42]

When Grant assigned Gen. Edward Ferrero's black division of the 9th Corps to guard the army's trains, the cavalry was still expected to maintain a position between the enemy and the army's vital supplies. Freedom from exclusive responsibility for protection of the trains undoubtedly gave the cavalry some of the additional latitude Sheridan had been demanding. But with it, Sheridan also received orders on the morning of the 6th from Army of the Potomac headquarters to make an attack on Longstreet's flank and rear on the Brock Road. But the enemy's cavalry kept the Union cavalry quite busy, and Sheridan's troopers remained on the defensive all during May 6th. When Custer's

1st Brigade, 1st Division, moved out on the Brock Road to make dispositions to engage Longstreet, they received a formidable attack from Rosser's Rebel cavalry, one that demanded the intervention of the 2nd Brigade under Devin, which rode in to assist Custer just before he was overwhelmed by Confederate horsemen. Custer, with Devin's help, drove back Rosser, but had orders *not* to pursue the enemy, for at midday, as Steere observes, even the most efficient of Sheridan's divisions were "contained" at Todd's Tavern by Fitzhugh Lee, who also kept an eye on Wilson's division in the hinterland. The Confederate cavalry served its army well this day. While Sheridan was quick to blame Meade and his anxiety for the trains as the reason why his movements were curtailed, Sheridan himself was reporting to headquarters at midday on the 6th regarding his own qualms about the safety of the trains. It was a missive that did nothing to ease Meade's apprehensions and worries, and the Federal cavalry's inability to apprise Meade and Grant of the situation on the Union flank on May 6th had dire consequences for the 2nd Corps.[43]

While fighting raged on the Federal left, danger still lurked for both armies at the center of the opposing lines. The Confederates had initially been unable to close the gap between Ewell and Hill, until remnants of Hill's division as well as a brigade from Longstreet's corps filed through the Chewning Farm and filled the hole as Burnside's skirmishers were approaching. Roebling describes the long discussion that took place between Burnside and Grant's engineer, Colonel Comstock, as displaying no enthusiasm for trying to retake Chewning's by assault. An hour of discussion was punctuated by increasingly heavy fire from Wadsworth's direction, and at last it was decided that Burnside would move to the left, somewhere between Chewning Farm and Wadsworth's front. Engaged indecisively about noon, the 9th Corps toward evening fell back and entrenched.[44]

May 6th had proved to be another difficult day for the 5th Corps commanders. Wadsworth was shot while rallying his men to repel a Rebel counterattack, and he was captured and died behind enemy lines. The 5th Corps' 2nd Division, led by Robinson, was then sent up to take Wadsworth's place on the 2nd Corps' right flank.[45] Back on the 5th Corps front line, Griffin's 1st Division of the 5th Corps had no more than heavy skirmishing on the 6th, but an eyewitness described "Fighting Jack," as Charles Griffin's soldiers called him, coming into camp that night with tears running down a powder-begrimed face. Receiving reports from his brigades, Griffin began to fully realize his division's losses in the last 24 hours, and Griffin's anger had turned to sorrow. He remarked that night to Warren, "General, I have lost four thousand of my boys in that cursed hole."[46]

Cavalry commander James Wilson in his 1912 memoirs would claim that he "perfectly screened Grant's advance" engaging the enemy "wherever we encountered him and making good our hold on the important points of the field." Wilson boasted he had fought three Rebel brigades, but Wilson had, in fact, been demolished by Rosser's Confederate cavalry, which Wilson outnumbered three to one.[47] In the height of cheek, Wilson also complained in his 1912 reminiscing that "not withstanding the successful operations of the cavalry, ... nearly all historical accounts ignore or minimize the part played by the cavalry."[48] So let's give James Wilson all the credit he deserves. Left vulnerable by General Wilson's far from perfect screen, the 5th Corps was confronted with, then attacked by Ewell's Corps without warning on the morning of May 5, 1864. Far from being the Rebel attempt to delay the Federal advance that Grant and Meade were expecting, Ewell was the vanguard of the Army of Northern Virginia that Lee was bringing to confront Grant's incursion. Of the four infantry corps that fought at the Wilderness (the 2nd, 5th, 6th and 9th Corps) the 5th Corps sustained one-third of the casualties. Out of a total of 17,666 Army of the Potomac officers and men who were killed, wounded or captured the 5th Corps lost 5,132. But it is likely that we will never know the real numbers of killed, wounded or captured at the Wilderness or anywhere else during Grant's Overland Campaign. For as Morris Schaff, one of Warren's aides, testifies, Warren was obliged to underreport his losses. The Army of Northern Virginia's losses were estimated at 11,500. Though it is not difficult to attribute the Army of the Potomac's unexpected encounter with the Army of Northern Virginia in the Wilderness to the incompetence of 3rd Division cavalry commander James Wilson, in the coming weeks, Grant would recommend Wilson for the rank of brevet major general of volunteers in recognition for his service at the Wilderness.[49]

Grant's reports from the battlefield to Washington were terse, and while downplaying his casualties, Grant implied a number of times that the enemy was on their last legs. Grant forbade the journalists who had accompanied the army from using the telegraph, so when the news of what was really happening in Virginia and the long lists of casualties were released, it only made the shock of the battles and the extent of the losses that much more appalling. It was not news conducive to keeping Lincoln in office in the election he faced later in the year. Nor was it a fulfillment of the promise and excitement the public had felt when Grant first took command.[50]

Six

On to Spotsylvania

THE FEDERALS' POSITION AT THE END of the fighting on May 6th at the Wilderness was not one of strength. Lee's aggression was unchecked, and as 5th Corps commander Warren pointed out, the Rebel position on the Chewning Plateau overlooked his entire line. The line that was held by Burnside's 9th Corps was too long and too thin, and Hancock realized that the Rebel line opposing his 2nd Corps extended beyond his own. Edward Steere concludes his book on the Wilderness with the conviction that Lee was the one who held the advantage on that field, or at most, the battle was a draw.[1] Spotsylvania historian Bill Matter agrees with the latter, commenting that it was not at all obvious after the Battle of the Wilderness which army had been victorious. The Wilderness is not a battle that one thinks of as benefiting the fortunes of anyone or either side. Of the many wounded left behind, the "fortunate" ones were the ones who were in the unburned area, for some of their comrades, when the woods caught fire from small arms and artillery fire, burned to death, a circumstance that added an additional element of horror to this already terrible battlefield.[2]

After this ominous beginning, Grant next determined to move again to the left, and while many credit Grant's decision to his indomitable spirit, Steere takes a somewhat more cynical view. After Gordon's successful May 6th night attack on Sedgwick on the Army of the Potomac's far right, Meade felt compelled to refuse, or bend back his army's right flank. This left the army's line of communication back to the Rapidan in jeopardy, and Steere suggests that Grant therefore had a change of base forced upon him. This, along with Lee's threatening position at the Chewning Plateau, did not bode well for the Federals. Yet Steere also acknowledges that Grant, after all, had Lee's Army of Northern Virginia as his target, and whatever situation Lee had forced upon Grant, that goal remained.[3] So Grant's decision was made, but May 7th was a day of unease. The Rebels and Federals probed each other's positions throughout the day, with both sides apprehensive of attack, and all reports, except an erroneous one by Burnside, indicated that the two armies still lay confronting one another. Matter comments that Warren on this day demonstrated his "maddening propensity to forward to headquarters unsolicited opinions and advice concerning both tactical and strategic matters that lay outside of his own immediate area of operations and knowledge." In that, Matter is correct, but it is also possible to understand why Warren, Meade's former chief engineer, who had served him

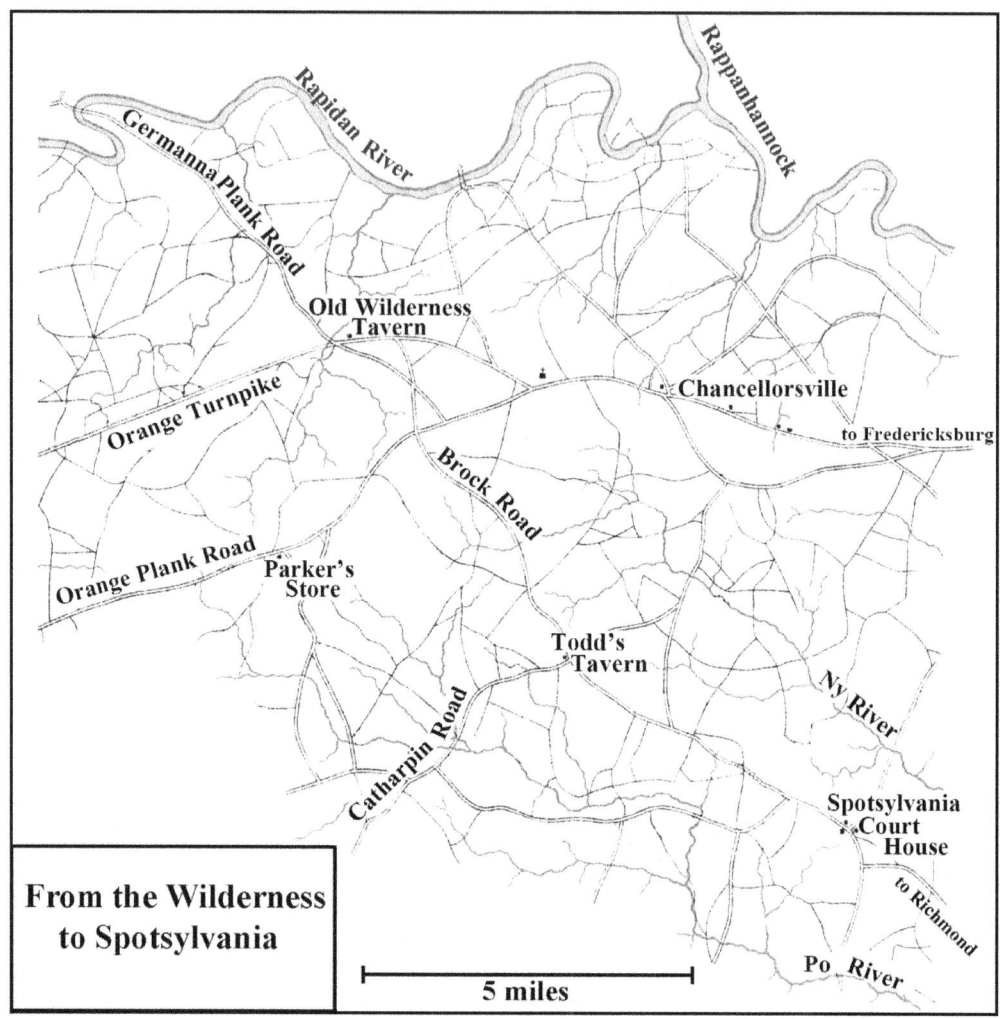

From the Wilderness to Spotsylvania. Adapted from Plate LXXXI, #1, *Official Atlas* (Ned Smith).

well a year earlier at Gettysburg, continued to offer advice, however unwanted, to his chief.[4]

Did Lee ever anticipate that Grant, defeated, would withdraw across the Rapidan? Matter suggests that by the morning of May 7th, when Lee realized that the Federals weren't defending their communications back to the Rapidan as they had been, Lee knew that Grant was planning a change of base. The removal of the pontoon bridge at Germanna Ford was a bit of a give away. The actions of the Federal cavalry somewhat mystified Jeb Stuart and Lee initially, for while skirmishing with them during the 6th, Sheridan had withdrawn from Todd's Tavern for no apparent reason, then inexplicably returned. But Sheridan's persistence in skirmishing with the Rebel cavalry at the tavern was another confirmation that a Federal movement would come that way.[5] While some exclaimed over Lee's intuitive ability to guess Grant's next move, Matter suggests that his intuition was bolstered by simple logic, for there were really only two choices if Grant wasn't going to go back the way he had come. The Army of the Potomac could either go to Fredericksburg, where it would have a number of options, or move through Todd's Tavern to Spotsylvania and then toward Richmond, and the Federal cavalry's continued interest in Todd's Tavern could very well have been a red flag to Lee. But whichever of these two possibilities the Army of the Potomac chose, Fredericksburg or Richmond via Spotsylvania, Spotsylvania was the right place for the Army of Northern Virginia to confront them.[6]

At 6:30 A.M. on May 7th, Grant sent Meade orders for the Army of the Potomac to prepare for a night march that would bring the army and Burnside's 9th Corps to a position extending from Todd's Tavern to Spotsylvania Court House by May 8th. Grant then hoped to deploy by May 9th at the North Anna to await Lee's arrival on the 10th or later.[7] Needless to say, Grant was, in fact, falling hopelessly behind schedule as far as his own presupposed agenda was concerned. As historian William Glenn Robertson observes, it is popular to blame Butler for the failure of his Army of the James to accomplish much with their advance on the Rebel capital, but Butler was only supposed to be operating by himself for less than a few weeks. For Grant and the Army of the Potomac, according to Grant's original plan, were expected to join Butler's force to finish the job at Richmond and Petersburg, but it would be more than a month before the Army of the Potomac was able to fight its way to Petersburg.[8] Things would work out far, far differently than what Grant intended, much as his plan for moving through and past the Wilderness before engaging Lee had gone. But whatever the men of the Army of the Potomac thought of the military judgment that had sent them into nightmare struggles in the Wilderness, when the 5th Corps saw that they were turning to the south for an advance, not to the north for a retreat, the boys in blue cheered.[9] One of the most eloquent explanations of the Army of the Potomac's willingness to fight comes from then Captain Charles Francis Lowell, Jr., commander of Meade's headquarters cavalry escort. It was written on May 29, 1864, several weeks later and several battles later, but I believe it is apropos to the severe treatment that the Federals had just been dealt at the Wilderness. Lowell wrote,

> These two great armies have pounded each other nearly to pieces for many days; neither has achieved any real success over the other on the field of battle. Our loss has probably been greater than theirs, for ours has been the offensive.... The enemy, I think, outfight us, but we outnumber them, and finally, in the last three days one witnesses in this Army as it moves along all the results of a victory, when in fact it has done only barren fighting. For it has done the one thing needful before the enemy — it has advanced. The result is wonderful. Hammered and pounded as this Army has been; worked, marched, fought and reduced as it is, it is in better spirits and better fighting trim today than it was in the first day's fight in the Wilderness. Strange as it seems to me, it is, I believe, yet the fact, that this Army is now just on its second wind, and more formidable than it ever was before. This I see on every march and I attribute it to movement in advance after heavy, though barren fighting.[10]

While Grant issued orders for his next move, Lee, too, was preparing for a move. Lee had ordered a road cut from his infantry's right to facilitate movement, and at midmorning on the 7th, it was noticed that Federal wagons once visible from the Rebel lines were gone. Humphreys, Meade's chief of staff, had been apprehensive that the enemy would notice the movement of the Army of the Potomac's trains, a clear signal that something was up. Along with the army's crushing amount of supplies needing transport, more than 10,000 wounded needed to be moved to Fredericksburg and then on by train to Washington. Despite 325 of the army's wagons being detailed to join the 488 ambulances available for the transfer, more than 900 wounded were left behind in the Wilderness, either because they were too seriously wounded to be moved, or there simply wasn't transportation for them.[11] On May 7th, Lee was also considering who would replace Longstreet as commander of the 1st Corps, and he chose Gen. Richard Anderson, one of Hill's division commanders, but a former subordinate of Longstreet's. On the night of May 7th, Anderson and his 1st Corps, with help from Stuart's Cavalry, would play a crucial role in obstructing the upcoming movement of the Army of the Potomac.[12]

The 5th Corps led the movement as ordered at dark on May 7th, though, as mentioned, the movement of the Army of the Potomac's trains that had began on the afternoon of that day had already signaled the enemy of Federal intentions.[13] The 5th Corps would leave its position on the army's right and move to the left, passing behind and beyond the lines of the 2nd Corps, and moving on the Brock Road to Todd's Tavern and on to Spotsylvania. The 2nd Corps would follow hard upon the 5th Corps' heels, with the hardworking John Hammond and the 5th New York Cavalry remaining at the Wilderness Tavern until all of the 2nd Corps had withdrawn. The 6th Corps, followed by the 9th Corps, would be moving on the Plank Road and Turnpike toward Chancellorsville.[14]

The cavalry's role, now that Ferrero's infantry had assumed a good part of their duties regarding the trains, was to see that the route along which the army would be moving was secure. By midday on the 6th, Sheridan was still trying to dislodge the Rebels from the Brock Road, the 5th Corps' proposed route into Spotsylvania, and they would still be disputing the Brock Road with the Confederates that night, when Confederate horsemen, dismounted, settled into earthworks several miles from the tavern. Sheridan no doubt intended to try and dislodge the Rebels the next day. But Stuart added to the Union horsemen's woes by sending another contingent of his troopers against the Federal cavalry west of Todd's Tavern on the 7th. At dusk, Sheridan withdrew his force back to Todd's Tavern, leaving the Brock Road in Rebel hands. As Matter noted, every yard that the Federal cavalry relinquished that afternoon of May 7th, would have to be fought for and regained, and the time it would take to do that would make all the difference in the next day's fight.[15]

While Sheridan's orders, to maintain a presence on both the army's flanks as it withdrew from the Wilderness battlefield, are crystal clear, Sheridan's actions on the day and night of May 7th are a confused mess. Though there is no record of such an order, Sheridan claims in a subsequent report, that early on the morning of the 7th, he received and tried to follow an erroneous order from headquarters that forced him to halt the army's trains in order to prevent them from moving into enemy territory. And while, as just seen, Sheridan had failed to clear the enemy from the Brock Road, Sheridan inexplicably reported that he had done just that. Contrary to the real situation on the Brock Road and the approach to Spotsylvania, Sheridan's last messages to Meade at 6:15 and 8:00 P.M. on the night of the 7th, not only implied that he had won a complete victory against the enemy, but he reported to Meade that they had driven the enemy, "in confusion toward Spotsylvania Court House." It makes one wonder if Sheridan was, as has been postulated, unaware of his orders to support the infantry's passage to Spotsylvania. Otherwise, surely, Sheridan would have realized that the Federal vanguard would notice that the Brock Road was full of Rebels. Sheridan's last message had been sent from Todd's Tavern, where he had congratulated his division commanders, but did not inform either of the Federal cavalry commanders, Wesley Merritt or J. Irwin Gregg, of the infantry movement that was taking place that night, another indication that Sheridan's headquarters did not bother to forward Meade's orders to their errant commander. Then Sheridan left to return to his headquarters at Alrich's more than three miles away. In his book, Matter acknowledges the conjecture of a number of historians that perhaps Sheridan did not know of the infantry advance until his return to his headquarters at Alrich's. It is, perhaps, possible that his staff failed to get Meade's 3 P.M. orders and instructions to their commander. But if Sheridan left Todd's Tavern some time after sending his last 8:00 P.M. communication, surely, by 9:00 or 10:00 P.M., when he returned to his headquarters, Sheridan had gotten Meade's orders. Yet, at midnight, when Meade arrived at Todd's Tavern, none of Sheridan's calvary, though their commander was within several miles of his men, none of Sheridan's cavalry were safeguarding the intended route of their army, nor did they have orders to do so.[16]

As dark settled over the Wilderness, Sheridan had two brigades at Todd's Tavern, while the rest of his force was in bivouac scattered over an area within a mile of the tavern. Where Sheridan had spent the day of the 7th and what he had been doing is unknown except for his night messages to Meade, but his counterpart in the Army of Northern Virginia, J.E.B. Stuart, it is known, had had a busy day. Beyond the hard time he gave Sheridan's cavalry on both of the Federal flanks, Stuart kept Lee apprised of Unionist movements, and his horsemen scouted the area for roads on which Lee's infantry could move. Stuart also made arrangements for a number of his men to act as guides along the roads.[17]

Robert E. Lee, having received a constant stream of reports from his cavalry and infantry commanders throughout the day, late in the afternoon of May 6th went to the Chewning Farm, where they had set up a naval telescope to look at what they assumed was Grant's headquarters. They considered the large number of couriers coming and going, and they watched a group of Federal heavy guns leave and head toward the Confederate right. Richard H. Anderson, who now commanded Longstreet's 1st Corps, was given orders to withdraw from his front after dark, and at 3:00 A.M. he began his march to Spotsylvania Court House. Thus, the adversaries were set upon converging paths, and both would be striving to reach Spotsylvania and beyond before the other. Anderson had the advantage of moving his corps on roads that had been scouted by the Confederate cavalry, and after he received orders for his move, Lee also ordered Stuart to provide a guide to facilitate the 1st Corps' passage. While Stuart offered to escort Anderson himself, one of Stuart's staff ended up leading the Confederates down the road Lee had chosen in the event that his army needed to move quickly to Spotsylvania. Starting out at 11:00 P.M., Anderson had planned on finding a clearing after a few hours where his men could stop and rest, but burning woods and dense undergrowth kept his 1st Corps in motion. At approximately 1 A.M., Anderson's advance, accompanied by Rebel cavalry, was crossing Corbin's Bridge, roughly a mile from Todd's Tavern. They marched for two more hours before a space, approximately three miles from Spotsylvania, was found that was adequate to accommodate this corps of tired Confederates.[18]

Warren supervised the risky work of withdrawing his corps from the enemy's front, with the skirmishers the last to leave, while the head of Warren's column began moving up a rough road in the darkness. Meade and Grant rode ahead of the 5th Corps column,[19] as it moved to the left from its position on the right of the army, passing behind and past the 2nd Corps position. Grant and Meade took a fork in the road that unexpectedly led them close to the Rebel lines. Doubling back, they left a guide at the fork to direct the 5th Corps.[20] It was the first, but hardly the last time in this campaign that the Army of the Potomac would be moving blindly into unknown territory. As one of the army's topographical engineers commented regarding the maps that the Federals depended on during the Overland Campaign, they were wholly inadequate for attempting to maneuver against "a brave and ever watchful enemy." There were roads shown on the maps that didn't exist, and many roads that existed were not shown.[21]

As the army began its withdrawal and night march, Sheridan, as has been noted, had orders to keep sufficient forces out on the army's flank to protect it and alert the Federals to enemy movement.[22] But when Generals Meade and Grant arrived around midnight at Todd's Tavern, they found both Gregg's and Merritt's cavalry divisions encamped with no orders. Though it seems clear that both Meade and Grant arrived at the Tavern, what would happen in the next hours inexplicably became a confrontation between Sheridan and Meade with no known input from Grant until the aftermath. Did Grant retire after their night ride leaving Meade to deal with the cavalry? If the diary entry that night of Grant's chief engineer, Comstock, is any indication of the concerns at headquarters, Grant was not worried about the Army of Northern Virginia. Comstock, seemingly confident that Lee was falling back, merely poses the question of how far Lee would fall back — a little, or to Mine Run?[23] When no orders had arrived an hour later, at 1 A.M. on May 7, Meade issued orders for Merritt to move down the Brock Road to beyond Spotsylvania Court House, clearing it and keeping it clear with pickets for the passage of the 5th Corps. Meade directed Gregg to attend to Corbin's Bridge, watching the roads to the north that lay between Spotsylvania and the enemy, as well as seeing to any Rebels that might follow the 2nd Corps on their withdrawal from the Wilderness battlefield. At the same time he issued these orders, Meade notified Sheridan of the two orders he had given to Merritt and Gregg, advising Sheridan that he could alter them after the passage of the infantry. Coincidentally, at the same time in the first hours of May 8th, Sheridan was finally getting around to issuing his own orders to Merritt and Gregg, though it is difficult to know when they were received. But as Matter points out, it would make little difference, for it was already too late for the 5th Corps to make an undisputed passage to Spotsylvania. Though Meade gave his orders to Merritt and Gregg at 1 A.M., it would be close to 3 A.M. before Merritt was under way, and, inexplicably, Gregg did not attempt to remove Rebel cavalry from Corbin's Bridge until near 8 A.M. on May 8th.[24]

Ironically, Wilson's was the only cavalry division that ended up well out between the enemy and the Army of the Potomac on the morning of the 8th. Early on May 7th, when Meade requested a cavalry reconnaissance force to watch the Germanna Plank Road, Wilson was ordered out on the Federal right by Sheridan.[25] Wilson, on finding no Rebels, had stayed out on the right until he and his division received orders on the night of the 7th to proceed in the morning to Spotsylvania Court House, driving a small force of the enemy out of the village. Wilson became aware of large forces of Rebel infantry approaching his position at the Court House, and one of his brigade commanders had actually attacked the rear of a Rebel force before being ordered to stop. Wilson, on reporting to

Sheridan where he was and what he was seeing, told Sheridan that "everything was all right" with his command, but shortly a courier came from Sheridan, who was alarmed by Wilson's isolated position, at least in regard to other cavalry, and he ordered Wilson to withdraw immediately from Spotsylvania and return by a circuitous route to the cavalry's base. Thus the town that would become the epicenter of the next weeks' battles, the village at Spotsylvania Court House, was relinquished. Could a division of cavalry behind the enemy's lines have assisted the 5th Corps' fight as they tried to deploy from the Todd's Tavern Rd.? We'll never know, but when Wilson left Spotsylvania, as we shall see, the enemy force he had been facing turned it's attention to the 5th Corps coming down the Brock Road from Todd's Tavern. Carswell McClellan, in his 1889 response to Sheridan's memoirs, questions why the pugnacious Sheridan, if he was so anxious to fight the Rebel cavalry, did not do so on May 8th at Spotsylvania, where he withdrew Wilson from an advantageous position and allowed Stuart's horsemen to extend the Confederate infantry's lines confronting the 5th and 6th Corps, unopposed.[26]

The night of May 7th–8th was a long one for the 5th Corps. Artillery and supply trains, and finally, part of Meade's entourage in the road caused delay after delay. Conceding that Warren would have made short work of this last blockage if he had been at the head of his column, in his account of that night, Humphreys defends Warren's decision to remain at the 5th Corps position on the front line until his exhausted pickets were withdrawn and out of jeopardy. Warren, when he reached the head of his corps, found the road blocked a second time by Meade's headquarters escort. Warren rode ahead of his column arriving at Todd's Tavern at that all significant time of 1 A.M. on May 8th. It is known that Warren conferred with Meade, but where Grant was at this point is unknown. Warren proceeded down the Brock Road to see how Merritt's taking possession of the road was progressing, but Warren arrived at Merritt's headquarters at 3 A.M. to find Merritt's troopers just mounting up to make their first efforts to clear enemy cavalry from the Brock Road.[27]

At daylight, with the arrival of Robinson's Division, the vanguard of the 5th Corps halted behind Gen. Wesley Merritt's troopers. Delayed by barriers of fallen trees the enemy had dropped across the road, Merritt's troopers were just beginning to try to clear the road of Gen. Fitzhugh Lee's Confederate cavalry which stood in the way.[28] Apparently still having some faith that Sheridan's cavalry was alert to the movements of the enemy, General Griffin assured his men that, after the Rebel cavalry ahead was brushed aside, they would stop and rest after their all night march and have breakfast.[29] But Merritt's cavalry failed to dislodge the Confederates who blocked the way, and at 6 A.M., Merritt suggested that the infantry could make better progress removing this obstruction for themselves, and that's just what the weary 5th Corps did.[30]

Robinson's division, still in the lead, was roused to take to the road again, and when they approached the skirmish line the cavalry was holding, they were met by, of all people, Sheridan, who ordered the infantrymen to deploy on either side of the road. Sheridan, who took such exception to Meade giving orders to his men, did not, apparently, find it at all improper to give orders without authority to someone else's corps. While the 5th Corps had endured a good deal on the first day of the Battle of the Wilderness, another bad day, provided courtesy of the Federal cavalry, lay before them. Beyond the Rebel cavalry that blocked the way on the morning of the 8th, as previously mentioned, Anderson's, formerly Longstreet's, 1st Corps, had halted several miles from Spotsylvania, the strategic junction of railroad lines and a number of roads.[31] When word came from Fitzhugh Lee to Confederate cavalry commander J.E.B. Stuart that his Rebel horsemen were preventing Federal infantry from coming down the Brock Road toward Spotsylvania, Anderson and the 1st Corps, though his orders had been to proceed to Spotsylvania village, had hurried men forward to assist the Confederate cavalry and take up a defensive position against this Yankee incursion. Urged on by messengers from the cavalry, the Rebel infantry were literally running to reach the makeshift barricades their cavalry had erected. It was a near thing, but they managed to possess them just before the Yankees could get there, as J.E.B. Stuart himself placed the arriving infantry in the Confederate defenses.[32]. Meanwhile, another message had come to Stuart that Federal cavalry was nearby, entering Spotsylvania from the east. This was the wandering Wilson, and if the results for the 5th Corps were not so tragic, it would be funny. Stuart sent a brigade to entertain Wilson, while Wilson received word that a large body of the enemy were moving in his direction. Wilson, to his credit, began to dig in at Spotsylvania village, where he was providing at least some distraction to Rebel concentration on the Federal movement

Philip H. Sheridan and his staff. From left: Sheridan, Jos. Forsythe, Wesley Merritt, Thomas C. Devins, and George A. Custer (Library of Congress). This was taken in 1865 and doesn't reflect their 1864 ranks.

on Brock Road, but the order from Sheridan recalled Wilson to the safety of the fold at cavalry headquarters.[33]

Having successfully delayed the Federal advance on Brock Road, the Rebel cavalry withdrew, and the 5th Corps vanguard believed they had finally dispersed the enemy obstruction. When Robinson's division advanced, they expected to encounter only a remnant of the enemy's dismounted cavalrymen. But Stuart's men had been replaced by Anderson's infantrymen, and when the first elements of the 5th Corps deployed from a narrow woods road on the morning of May 8th, a good part of the Confederate 1st Corps was there to meet them. Grant's chief engineer, Comstock, while disparaging Warren's "slowness" in getting up to Spotsylvania, registers real surprise in his diary for May 8th. Comstock commented, "It turned out however that Ewell's [sic] corps was there & prisoners said they began moving from Wilderness at 11 P.M."[34]

We've followed in some detail the movements of the 5th Corps of the Army of the Potomac and that army's cavalry on the night of May 7th–8th because the results of this night would have tremendous impact on the fate of all the participants involved, from the general officers to the men in the ranks. Grant, as stated in his memoirs, accepted Sheridan's insupportable excuses for his failures, stating that it was Meade's changing of Sheridan's orders to his cavalry commanders that caused all the trouble. A confrontation between Meade and Sheridan took place at Meade's Headquarters, with Meade accusing Sheridan of being responsible for delaying the 5th Corps advance.[35] But Sheridan was adamant that he had not received Meade's orders regarding the army's movement, and whether the order was lost, not forwarded to Sheridan by his staff, or was simply ignored is unknown. Meade apologized, but Sheridan, seemingly determined to inflame the situation, commented regarding Meade's former command that he "saw nothing to oppose the advance of the 5th Corps; that the behavior of the infantry was disgraceful." After bragging that he and his cavalry could whip Stuart if Meade would only let him, Sheridan declared that since Meade insisted on issuing orders to the cavalry without consulting Sheridan, henceforth Meade could command it himself.[36]

When Meade reported Sheridan's behavior to Grant, the Lieutenant general, far from disapproving of Sheridan's clear insubordination, was apparently intrigued by Sheridan's assertion that he could whip Stuart. As Matter comments, perhaps Grant, realizing that Meade and Sheridan would have great difficulty serving together, chose to focus on the idea of sending Sheridan away on an expedition as an easy fix for this dilemma. There apparently was no thought to reining in his mouthy subordinate, and there were no repercussions for Sheridan's failures or tirade to Meade. On the contrary, within hours Sheridan had exactly what he wanted, an independent command with orders to take his cavalry division, all 10,000 of them, and pursue the Rebel cavalry. While ultimately Sheridan's expedition did draw off roughly half of the Confederate cavalry, Lee retained the other half to provide himself and his army with reconnaissance and screening.[37]

One cannot consider the actions of the Confederate and Union cavalries during these initial days of the Overland Campaign without realizing that the Rebel troopers were consistently outperforming their Federal counterparts. While Sheridan fumed about having to protect army trains, he was occupied trying to fight off attacks by his ever-active opponents, while Stuart's horsemen were scouting, launching probes and attacks, apprising Lee of Federal incursions and screening Confederate movements. It seems that the Rebel cavalry, not adhering to Sheridan's definition of what was the proper role for cavalry, was doing it all, and doing it well. When Sheridan, finally free from what he saw as the impediment of interfering army commanders, rode off at the beginning of the fighting at Spotsylvania, he took with him, with Grant's approval, nearly all of the army's cavalry, and the Army of the Potomac would begin a long period of moving blindly without protection through a territory of hostile inhabitants and unknown terrain. The enemy would be at no such disadvantage.

Sheridan's report, written two years later, after he'd had a chance to think it over, blamed the failure of his cavalry to provide protection and information to the infantry during the night of May 7th and 8th on, of all people, Meade. According to Sheridan, if Meade hadn't changed Sheridan's nonexistent orders on that night, the army would likely have reached Spotsylvania before the enemy, and all would have been well. Sheridan also still insisted that Meade did not notify him of the change. Despite the fact that duplicates exist and the text is presented in the *Official Records*, is Sheridan claiming that this is yet another lost communiqué?[38]

Matter draws our attention to Grant's memoirs, and though he is somewhat reluctant to contradict Grant's version of the events, Matter observes that Grant obviously relied on Sheridan's report and also on the ever-unreliable account of Adam Badeau. Matter also suggests that Grant apparently didn't consult, or chose to ignore, any information or views contrary to his own. Matter also questions Humphreys's assertion in his *The Virginia Campaign of 1864 and 1865* that the cavalry's failure during the night move had little impact on the outcome. But Humphreys is simply emphasizing that it was neither Sheridan's nor Meade's orders that kept the Army of the Potomac away from Spotsylvania, but the all too effective presence of Fitzhugh Lee's Cavalry at the mouth of the Brock Road on the night of May 7th and the morning of May 8th. Buttressed by nearby elements of Hampton's cavalry and additional oncoming enemy infantry, there was no question how this was going to end. Thus Humphreys makes it very clear in his 1883 history that Badeau's assertion, that Meade could have and would have occupied Spotsylvania if he hadn't changed Sheridan's orders, is ludicrous. As Humphreys testifies, at the hour Sheridan was issuing orders, orders that Badeau insists would have denied Rebel access to Spotsylvania, the Confederates were already on and in control of all of the roads leading to their next confrontation with the Army of the Potomac.[39]

Meade's report, written in the fall of 1864, regardless of the many things he could have said regarding the cavalry in the night-move debacle, mentioned only James Wilson's brief sojourn at Spotsylvania Court House on the morning of May 8th. As Matter comments, Meade did not enter in the affray, staying above the war of competing postwar accounts, and as Meade died in 1872, he did not have to endure having to see Badeau's and Grant's and Sheridan's later accounts written in the 1880s. Matter comments that he feels that if Meade had seen Grant's version of the night move to Spotsylvania, it would have been "especially painful."[40] But another who did challenge the many contradictions was Carswell McClellan, formerly an aide to General Humphreys, who authored *The Personal Memoirs and Military History of U.S. Grant Versus the Record of the Army of the Potomac* as well as a refutation of Sheridan's memoirs. McClellan commented rather floridly that, while he was reluctant to contradict his illustrious former commander, Grant, "...there are voices calling from other graves; there are memories shrining other names precious to comrades and countrymen; and it were craven to stand in acquiescent silence while bias strives anew to mar the record of manly effort with detraction." Carswell McClellan then went on to say that the details of Grant's brief writings about the night of May 7–8, 1864, were obviously drawn from Sheridan's report and Badeau's account. McClellan goes on to elucidate the faults, fictions and fallacies, which have been pointed out in the above account.[41] Carswell McClellan also wrote a scathing rebuttal to Sheridan's memoirs, pointing out that Meade didn't change Sheridan's orders on the night of May 7–8, 1864, since Sheridan sent his orders to his cavalry commanders after Meade had issued his. McClellan also observes that the positions Sheridan ordered his cavalrymen to take up were already occupied by heavy columns of advancing Rebels.[42]

Seven

Spotsylvania: Laurel Hill, Again and Again

THE 5TH CORPS WAS ONLY "apprised" of the enemy's presence in force at Laurel Hill, when the vanguard of the 5th Corps, John C. Robinson's division,[1] expecting a confrontation with enemy cavalry, ran headlong into the fire of entrenched infantry. The narrowness of the road that the division had to travel was delaying the arrival of Robinson's brigades and their deployment, so Robinson advanced with what he had in hand, just one of his three brigades. Lyle's brigade, significantly reduced in numbers, as was all of Robinson's division from their fighting at the Wilderness, walked into two unexpected Confederate volleys. It was Peter Lyle's misfortune to face the 3rd South Carolina of Kershaw's brigade,[2] which was one of two brigades that had replaced J.E.B. Stuart's horsemen at the barricades at Laurel Hill.

When the 2nd South Carolina added their flanking fire to the 3rd South Carolina's volley, Lyle's men broke and fled. One of the Carolinians would remember the carnage of that 30 minutes, commenting that they never fought braver men than Lyle's. Lyle lost 131 men, while the 3rd Carolina reportedly lost one member. When Robinson realized he was facing enemy infantry, he asked Warren for time to allow his other brigades to come up before advancing again, but Warren was impatient. Warren was reported to have said, "Never mind cannon! Never mind bullets! Press on and clear this road."[3]

At the time of Lyle's attack, Warren had gone back to hurry Robinson's other two brigades forward, sending two more brigades and a battery of Napoleons to aid in Robinson's assault. About the time some of Lyle's men came tumbling back, the next assault went forward. The Yankees, without orders to the contrary, stopped to answer the fire they were receiving from the enemy line, and in the delay to reload, Federal casualties mounted. Fifty yards from the enemy works, Robinson and his second in command, who had been leading the assault on the right, were shot from their mounts, their wounds serious enough to cost these officers a leg and an arm, respectively. Roebling attributes the coming disintegration of this division to the early wounding of their commanders and the rush with which the division was put on the field.[4] For when the third and fourth officers who tried to assume command were shot down, as well as every member of the Maryland Brigade's color companies, the division turned and fled, though Warren attempted to rally the fleeing troops. There were so few members of Robinson's division left after the Wilderness and Spotsylvania that Robinson's division would be disbanded the next day, with what was left of its brigades being doled out to other divisions. Gen. John Robinson was severely wounded; a Rebel bullet in the knee would cost him his left leg and his field command.[5]

The next division to file out from the confines of the Brock Road was Griffin's 1st Division, their gruff commander having, far too optimistically, promised his boys breakfast once they had brushed aside what he, too, believed was enemy cavalry. Many of the 5th Corps men went into battle that day with their knapsacks still strapped to their backs, so unaware were their commanders of what they were walking into. Having driven in the enemy's skirmishers, Griffin's men received the same sort of treatment as Robinson's, with heavy fire cutting down many of the division's officers and color companies. Though many Federals made it to within yards of the Rebel barricade, the remnants of the 1st Division soon fell back, where, despite evidence of enemy activity on their flanks, Warren and Griffin began the work of rallying and reorganizing their men. Crawford's 3rd Division and Wadsworth's 4th Division, now commanded by Lysander Cutler, in turn advanced and were eventually driven back. Though Cutler's division included the dauntless Iron Brigade, the heavy Rebel fire and evidence that the enemy was clearly flanking them sent Cutler reeling back. The 5th Corps fought alone until 10:00 A.M., when Wright's division of the 6th Corps began to come up on the 5th Corps' left.[6]

While the 5th Corps divisions came up and deployed in the fateful trickle allowed by the narrow road on which they had arrived on, the Rebels were gaining in numbers as Field's division completed their night march and came up to reinforce Anderson. And when word came that the James Wilson's cavalry had abandoned the village at Spotsylvania, the Confederates turned their full attention on Warren's 5th Corps. At midday on May 8th, when Grant and Meade still assumed that they were facing only two enemy divisions, orders went out for two divisions of the 6th Corps to join the 5th Corps in an assault on the Rebel line at Laurel Hill. Meanwhile, Grant was composing a report to Halleck stating that the results of the Wilderness had been decidedly in their favor. Grant also reiterated his plan for the Army of the Potomac to continue on to join with Butler's force near Richmond, and, apparently oblivious to the resistance Warren was facing at Spotsylvania, Grant went on to prepare orders for the Army of the Potomac to march to the North Anna on the following day. Grant also declared his intention to Halleck to be prepared to meet the enemy wherever they might intervene,[7] displaying a rather startling unawareness of how often and with what determination Lee would, in fact, intervene. On this morning of May 8th, Confederate cavalry and skirmishers, finding the Yankees had departed from the Wilderness, were marveling at the amount of equipment and supplies they had left behind. They also found a number of Federal stragglers and wounded, and made them prisoners, but on encountering black soldiers for the first time, the 9th Virginia Cavalry gathered them up and shot them before marching off their white prisoners. It was this sort of response to black troops that would have lasting repercussions for both white and black prisoners in the upcoming days of the war.[8]

Another significant encounter, one that would also cost many of the Army of the Potomac's infantrymen dearly, was the confrontation that took place when Sheridan, the cavalry's commander, turned up at Meade's headquarters at noon on May 8th. When Meade confronted Sheridan regarding his troopers' delay of the 5th Corps' night march,

Sheridan angrily denied ever receiving Meade's orders regarding the army's movement. Meade supposedly apologized, but when Sheridan went on to say that the 5th Corps had let very little enemy resistance stop them at Laurel Hill, Meade engaged Sheridan in a very public shouting match. Sheridan went on to accuse Meade of endangering Wilson when Meade gave Merritt and Gregg orders the previous night, and Sheridan told Meade that if he insisted on giving his cavalry orders without consulting him, Meade could command it himself. But when Meade reported this pithy bit of insubordination to Grant, also mentioning Sheridan's boast that he could defeat Stuart if only Meade would let him, it was only the latter that got Grant's attention. Grant instructed Meade to give Sheridan the orders he had demanded, and before 2 P.M. Sheridan was withdrawing his cavalrymen from their positions, and ordering them to prepare for departure the next morning. A lesser-known animosity that came to a head in that passage from the Wilderness to Spotsylvania, was the ill will that Sheridan bore Gouverneur K. Warren. Many years later, Washington Roebling, Warren's aide and scout, would declare, "Sheridan's hatred of Warren dates back to the night march from the Wilderness to Spotsylvania when Sheridan's cavalry got in the way and prevented the 5th Corps from reaching Spotsylvania in time. Warren complained of him at HdQrtrs and Sheridan never forgot it."[9]

In Grant's memoirs, Warren and the 5th Corps would be assigned all of the blame for the Army of the Potomac's failure to reach Spotsylvania before the Confederates. He would also be blamed for his inability to successfully assault the Rebels dug in at Laurel Hill, as well as the failure to coordinate an attack with the 6th Corps on the enemy earlier on May 8th.[10] Considering the chaos that was taking place that day, was the criticism of Warren and his corps justly assigned? The 6th Corps had had no better luck than the 5th Corps on their night march from their front line at the Wilderness. Leaving at 9:30 P.M. on the 7th, it had taken them seven hours to make the five and a half miles that brought Wright's division to Chancellorsville by dawn, but the 6th Corps soldiers, although numb with fatigue, were nonetheless ordered and urged on in the growing heat of the morning of May 8th. Faulty maps again played a part, but there was also a puzzling dispersal of the 6th Corps that seemingly was an attempt to have Sedgwick's corps attempt the impossible tasks of providing support to both the 5th Corps and the approaching 2nd Corps, while also giving some protection to the trains. But after all, there'd be no more screening or scouting from the Federal cavalry, for Sheridan was already consolidating his force to leave on their expedition the next day. So on May 8th, as Hancock's 2nd Corps, then near Todd's Tavern, began to cope with the vanguard of Jubal Early's approaching Confederate 3rd Corps, Hancock was informed by Federal cavalry brigade commander J. Irwin Gregg that the cavalry was being withdrawn. On Sheridan's departure, the five regiments of cavalry assigned to Burnside were all that was left of the Army of the Potomac's cavalry, but even these were unavailable to the army for scouting or other duties during the next ten days. The 22nd New York Cavalry, with two months' service, was assigned to escort the trains of wounded being transported to Fredericksburg, while the remaining four cavalry regiments guarded the army's rear and escorted the army trains.[11]

Meanwhile, a morning of costly fighting bought the 5th Corps no more than a position immediately in the enemy's front. Reporting that he was out of infantry ammunition, Warren informed Meade that he would not be able to attack the two enemy divisions he faced without support. Hancock, with problems of his own, had been ordered by Meade to support the 5th Corps, and he did send one division down the Brock Road, but regarding Warren's report to Meade that his troops were out of ammunition, Hancock reported that he had no ammunition to spare. Meade informed Warren that the entire 6th Corps had been ordered up to Warren's support, and as soon as Sedgwick arrived, the two corps were to attack together without delay. Though Meade withdrew the support of the 2nd Corps, a new infusion of Federal troops by way of the 6th Corps, plus the promise of ammunition and the realization that the Rebels were likely as exhausted as the Federals were, raised Warren's hopes.[12]

While three brigades of Wright's 6th Corps division had been placed in support of Warren at 10:30 that morning, Upton's brigade did not come in until early afternoon, with another division arriving at 3 P.M. As Grant and Meade once again grew impatient for an assault, it apparently took an interminable amount of time for the 6th Corps units to be positioned, with Meade giving additional orders to help speed Sedgwick's men on their way. Grant and Meade had unrealistically hoped that the assault by the two corps would take place at 1 P.M. But with the last of Sedgwick's divisions not arriving until 5:00 P.M., the attack by elements of both corps did not take place until 6:30 P.M. Then, too, the ever-practical Sedgwick had demanded, and since he was in fact the senior commander on the field, he got a lengthy description from Warren of what was going to take place before he would place his brigades. According to Roebling's report, only the Jersey Brigade of Neill's Division, 6th Corps, advanced against the enemy, and were speedily repulsed by the enemy. As it began to grow dark, Crawford's division of the 5th Corps advanced and, surprising a moving column of Ewell's men, drove them three-fourths of a mile, taking 100 prisoners before Crawford fell back, leaving a skirmish line well out. But this brief success by no means provides any explanation for the failure of the 6th and 5th Corps to make a combined assault on the Rebel works. Reports of additional fighting that took place on 5th and 6th Corps' fronts in the gathering gloom at the end of the day on May 8th, are confused and piecemeal, while simultaneous attacks thrown forward by both Federals and Confederates resulted in chaos. While the plan for the Federal attacks was for them to be made *en echelon* from left to right, troops on the right never got the orders to advance. Regarding Crawford's advance, Roebling commented, "Had the attack been made in stronger force as was initially intended, it would under the circumstances have doubtless been successful."[13] When the fighting was over, both sides took advantage of the dark to move closer to the enemy, searching for advantages in the terrain, digging in, and placing their batteries.[14]

Grant, who commented in his memoirs that he had "not yet learned the special qualifications of the different corps commanders," would express regret that Warren had led the advance on Spotsylvania, for he felt that Hancock would not have been so slow and would have crushed Anderson. And while offering that Sedgwick was probably "unavoidably detained" from getting his whole force on the field, Grant blamed Warren for the failure of the May 8th afternoon attack, though Sedgwick, the commander of the 6th Corps, as senior, was in command of the field. Grant admitted in a memo to Halleck that their "movements were terribly embarrassed by our immense wagon trains," trains that now had to be guarded by the Federal infantry instead of the cavalry. Grant also believed that Lee was moving away from Spotsylvania to interpose himself between the Army of the Potomac and Richmond. Once again, no cavalry meant no accurate information on where the enemy was and what he was doing. It would be another 12 days before Lee began moving away from Spotsylvania.[15]

There is also a story that has been repeated for many years that when Warren was ordered to "cooperate" with Sedgwick on the afternoon of May 8th, as opposed to having one or the other of them in command of the assault on the enemy, Warren, in a huff, refused to cooperate with anyone. The only source this author was able to find for this supposed Warren tirade is James Wilson, who, to this author's knowledge, was not there, but asserts he was told this tale by, of all people, Gouverneur K. Warren. Wilson reports that when Meade, on the afternoon of May 8th, told Warren to cooperate with Sedgwick, Warren replied, "General Meade, I'll be God d——d if I'll cooperate with Sedgwick or anybody else. You are the commander of this army and can give your orders and I will obey them; or you can put Sedgwick in command and he can give the orders and I will obey them; or you can put me in command and I will give the orders and Sedgwick shall obey them; but I'll be God d——d if I'll *cooperate* with General Sedgwick or anybody else." Wilson comments that Meade took no notice of this speech, and Wilson reports telling Warren that he thought Warren should have been sent to the rear under arrest. Wilson adds that Warren commented to that by saying he knew to whom he was talking, General Meade, and Wilson assures us that Warren added, "with pensive sadness," that if he had been arrested it would have saved him from later misfortune. Here Wilson is referring to Sheridan's removal of Warren of command of the 5th Corps at Five Forks a year later. Wilson, adding insult to injury, suggests that Warren, while a capable corps commander, was "cautious and impatient of control, and perhaps became more and more accustomed to the use of violent language as he beheld with what fatuity the Army of the Potomac was commanded." Wilson comments that Warren became incapable of receiving an order "which he did not criticize nor a suggestion which he did not resent." It is the same song and dance regarding General Warren that will be sung and danced to for many years by "Grant's Men."[16]

It is true that Warren was distressed by the outcome of the combined efforts of the 5th and 6th Corps that day. He did, in fact, write a personal letter to Meade, stating that if the 6th Corps had been allowed to maintain its original schedule, instead of changing it for minor considerations, it would have permitted the 5th and 6th Corps to have struck the enemy at noon instead of at twilight. Warren also suggested that Meade accompany the van of a column advancing to a critical point, to be on the spot to give necessary orders. Warren commented that whether he had Meade's confidence or not, he doubted the capabilities of his fellow commanders, offering that Sedgwick won't do anything unless he is ordered to do so and that Hancock gave a poor performance at the Wilderness. This letter, written on May 9th, the day Sedgwick was killed by a Rebel sharpshooter, was never sent but found later in Warren's papers.[17]

After his confrontation with Meade that day, Sheridan hurriedly prepared to "cut loose" with most of the cavalry of the Army of the Potomac, near 10,000 horsemen. With them, he assured Grant that he would "protect" the army's flanks and rear by drawing off the Rebel cavalry. It was what Sheridan had advocated from the very beginning of his service with the Army of the Potomac, and while he did draw away Gen. J.E.B. Stuart and Gen. Fitzhugh Lee's horsemen, Lee retained Gen. Wade Hampton and Gen. Rooney Lee's cavalry to help support and defend his army in ways that only cavalry can. For the next 16 days the Army of the Potomac, on the battlefield or moving through enemy country, would have to look after itself. The cavalry reported 250 wounded on the morning of May 8th, the day of fight at Laurel Hill, while they did not fight on the 9th. The 5th Corps reported wounded for the days of May 8th and 9th, as 1,419 wounded; Humphreys estimates roughly 443 were killed, mostly during the assaults at Laurel Hill.[18]

Assistant Secretary of War Charles Dana, the ever-unreliable eyes and ears of the administration, arrived at Grant's headquarters sometime on May 7th, and he reported on May 8th and 9th regarding the Army of the Potomac's attempted move to Spotsylvania, that "a body of rebel cavalry resisted our movement there, but without any considerable effect. There are no indications that Lee has moved in any direction, and General Grant is decidedly of opinion that he remains in the old place. If this be so we are much nearer Richmond than he is." Dana ended his May 8th telegram with "'On to Richmond!' Spirits of men and officers are of the highest pitch of animation."[19] Apparently feelings at Grant's headquarters on May 8th were entirely different from that at 5th Corps headquarters, or was Grant trying to be as optimistic as possible, knowing that all he said would soon be transmitted by Dana's telegrams to Lincoln's and Stanton's ears? It would be of great interest to think that Dana, there at Grant's headquarters, was privy to the thoughts and attitudes of the lieutenant general, but Dana proves so unreliable in his reports that one must consider them cautiously.

Dana's telegram to Washington on May 9th was a bit more subdued. He began in earnest, however, to attack Warren, for Dana could always be counted on to puff the role and reputation of his friends, while attacking anyone who got in their way. Warren was definitely not one of Dana's friends. Dana reported that James Wilson had occupied Spotsylvania on May 8th, but "as Warren's corps had not yet made its appearance," Wilson had to fall back to cavalry headquarters. Though Dana acknowledges that two divisions of Anderson's Confederate corps were already positioned at Spotsylvania, he contributed,

> General Grant at once gave orders for attacking these troops with the whole of Warren's corps, to whose support Sedgwick was hurrying up, in order to destroy them before the rest of the rebel army could arrive. Warren, however, proceeded with exceeding caution, and when he finally did attack, sent a single division at a time, and was constantly repulsed. The general attack which Generals Grant and Meade directed was never made, for reasons which I have not yet been able to learn, but successive assaults were made upon this and that point in the rebel positions, with no decisive results. The last assaults were made just before dark, when the fighting was very sharp.

Dana added that he did not know the number of casualties but, on visiting the hospital, was surprised that it wasn't more.[20]

The 9th of May was spent by the exhausted combatants of both sides adjusting their lines, entrenching and catching their breath. Only the sharpshooters and skirmishers were active, and on the morning of the 9th, General Sedgwick was killed while laughingly telling his men that they were beyond the enemy's range. Gen. Horatio Wright was then given command of the 6th Corps.[21] At noon at Todd's Tavern, Hancock, when his false alarm regarding a potential enemy attack had been disproved, was directed to move three divisions down the Brock Road to a position on Warren's right. Hancock's earlier concerns of a potential enemy attack on his position at Todd's, as well as misinformation from Burnside, had caused Meade and Grant to make erroneous assumptions regarding the 2nd Corps' position and movements.[22] And while Hancock had been raising alarms, Burnside was reporting an enemy presence on his front at the far left of the Federal line, which would later prove to be a single Rebel division. There, on the Union left, was the golden opportunity that Grant had been looking for, but unfortunately, all Meade's and Grant's attention and efforts were focused on the Federal right this day. As Grant would admit in his Memoirs, unbeknownst to him, Burnside had

> got up to within a few hundred yards of Spottsylvania [sic] Court House, completely turning Lee's right. He [Burnside] was not aware of the importance of the advantage he had gained, and I, [Grant] being with troops where the heavy fighting was, did not know of it at the time. He had gained his position with but little fighting, and almost without loss. Burnside's position now separated him widely from Wright's corps, the corps nearest him. At night he was ordered to join on to this. This brought him back about a mile, and lost to us an important advantage.[23]

Reports of enemy activity made bringing Hancock's corps up to the Federal front with the rest of the Army of the Potomac a desirable necessity. Sheridan's cavalry had only left that morning, and the vacuum created by their absence, as far as Federal reconnaissance and screening the army was concerned, was already being felt. For Grant, even the knowledge of the positions of his own corps was less than clear. Hancock, ordered to come up to the right of the 5th Corps, was directed to press forward to the Po River, where there seemed to be little Confederate resistance. With the intention of crossing the river and turning the enemy's left, Hancock would find out that it was a much easier matter to cross the Po than it would be to bring his corps back over the Po.[24]

During the first hours of daylight on May 10th, Hancock sent out scouts, some of whom climbed trees trying to gain information about their position and enemy opposition.[25] It is hard to know whether it was Hancock or Grant's chief engineer, Comstock, who had initiated the idea of sending Hancock's corps into this isolated position, for with the discovery of Rebel opposition on the enemy left, the 2nd Corps experienced an anxious night. But when Comstock came over the next morning "to see if it was a good place to attack," it was decided that it was "impracticable," and Hancock received orders from Meade that morning seemingly canceling his turning movement.[26] Hancock was then ordered to send two of his divisions to Warren for a frontal attack on the enemy at Laurel Hill at 5 P.M. Gibbon's and Birney's divisions were sent to Warren, while Barlow's division remained across the Po. Hancock, who because of his seniority of rank would command the attack by his divisions and the 5th Corps, was examining the ground on Warren's front and right when he learned that Barlow, alone across the river, was under attack by Early's 2nd Corps. While Comstock apparently did not feel that much could be accomplished on the Po, Lee apparently saw the danger and had sent Early to deal with this threat to Confederate communications and the Federal potential for enfilading the Rebel line. Unaware that the Federals had already given up on the movement, it was a threat that the Confederates acknowledged and acted upon.[27]

Army of the Potomac historian Humphreys as well as 2nd Corps historian Francis Walker, though they were both admittedly enjoying the benefit of hindsight, agreed on this point regarding lost opportunities. If Hancock had been ordered to cross the Po after dark on the 9th or early on the morning of the 10th, instead of doing so during daylight on the 9th, thereby alerting the enemy to his presence, perhaps Hancock could have done some real damage on the Rebel left. By the Confederate commander's response to Hancock's incursion, the enemy certainly seemed to think so. It seems feasible that if Hancock had been allowed to complete his attempt to turn the Rebel left, without having his force and his attention distracted by an auxiliary frontal assault on the Rebels' main line on Warren's front, he just might have succeeded. It is this change of plans that Humphreys bemoans as a lost opportunity. But it was Comstock's judgment, as Dana later reported it to Washington, that the ground Hancock had gained "proves to be worthless, however, as the rebels have all got east of the Po, and stoutly hold every point where crossing might be effected."[28]

Being sent to extricate part of his corps also meant that Hancock was unable to attend to the assault to be made by Birney, Gibbon and Warren, for when it was clear that Barlow, alone over the river, was under attack, Meade sent Hancock back to help extricate his division from their sticky predicament. The withdrawal of Barlow's division in the face of the aggressive Gen. Henry Heth's division, intent on engaging the retiring Federals, was a difficult and costly maneuver. But as Badeau later reported, echoing a view of things that Grant would express again and again, and upon which he would base many an order, Hancock's threat to the Confederate left, as Grant saw it, would undoubtedly draw troops away from the Rebel center, thus creating a promising situation for the 5th Corps and elements of the 2nd Corps to make their frontal attack on the Confederate earthworks that afternoon. Did Grant on some level realize the cost that these attacks were inflicting on the Army of the Potomac, for on that same morning of May 10th, Grant sent a demand to Halleck that he "rake and scrape" up 10,000 men from the defenses of Washington to send to Grant.[29]

Though the 5th Corps had spent the day inching closer to the Rebel lines under heavy enemy fire, and the attack the Federals made at 4 P.M. on May 10th was described by the Rebels as a fierce assault, it failed. It is hard to know whether Warren, because of a small success against the enemy's pickets, suggested to Meade that the attack be made before the original time of 5:00 P.M., or if Meade seized upon Warren's small bit of success to order an immediate attack.[30] With Meade and Grant watching from just behind Warren's lines, the 5th Corps, under severe enemy fire, lost heavily and were driven back. Though a few Yankees made it into the Rebel trenches, Confederate reports tell that those who made it to the Rebel line were killed there. It was reported that the Rebels who were manning the earthworks had gathered up the weapons and ammunition of the fallen Federals, and were waiting behind their lines with several loaded muskets each. A second attack was made on the Rebel line at 7 P.M. by five brigades of the 5th Corps and two from the 2nd. Though he had spent the whole afternoon elsewhere and knew nothing of the 5th Corps' disposition, Hancock commanded the assault that ultimately accomplished no more than the earlier one had.[31] A brief breakthrough at one point on the Confederate line went unsupported, ending in another costly failure, and what the Rebels described as terrible slaughter. They reported that they were pained to hear and see the Federal wounded still suffering in front of their earthworks the following day, but Yankee sharpshooters made it impossible for them to reach the wounded.[32]

Dana's report this day to Washington is of interest, for, first of all, Dana made the startling observation that Grant had no idea whether all of Lee's army was at Spotsylvania, or part of it had gone to Richmond, another mystery provided courtesy of the missing Federal cavalry. But the ever caustic Dana goes on to outdo himself with an attack on Warren. Though it has been said that Meade approved Warren's 5 P.M. attack based on

Warren's advice, Dana asserts that Warren was ordered to make the attack at that time in order to provide relief for the beleaguered and isolated Barlow on the Po. It is the sort of command that would be in character for the lieutenant general, and rather has the ring of truth about it. But Dana goes on in his report on Warren's May 10th attack, "I witnessed it in Warren's front, where it was executed with the caution and absence of comprehensive *ensemble* which seem to characterize that officer." Even Badeau, who was also no friend of Warren's, commented that in this case Dana's criticism of Warren was too severe. Beyond the fact that Dana had no military training or experience, is it possible that men with the intelligence and astute judgment of Lincoln and Stanton were unaware of Dana's prejudices in favor of his friends, and his propensity for opposing any who might stand in the way of their advancement? It must be remembered that Dana had favorites, such as James Wilson, who were anxious to become corps commanders, and command of the 5th Corps would have done nicely.[33] The losses for the Army of the Potomac on May 10th at Spotsylvania were 2nd Corps, 1,680; 5th Corps, 767; and 6th Corps, 900, with Humphreys estimating of the total wounded and killed for the army at 4,100. Confederate 1st Corps commander Anderson, in his diary, described those many attempts by the 5th Corps to inch closer to his lines as repeated attacks throughout the day, while Anderson described that last combined attack by 2nd Corps and 5th Corps at 7 P.M., as being "repulsed with great slaughter to the enemy and little loss to us."[34]

Again, Dana's May 10th report to Washington regarding the field returns for the Army of the Potomac is of interest, though because it was sent at 2 P.M. on the 10th, it does not reflect the losses of that day. Dana reported that the Army of the Potomac had 57,710 men, artillery and infantry, present for duty, while thus far in the campaign the total killed, wounded, stragglers and missing was 27,621. Dana noted that Sheridan had an additional 15,000 men elsewhere, while observing that Sheridan had seen nothing of the Rebel Stuart, nor did Grant know where Stuart was. Dana reports 2nd Corps losses as 6,619; the 5th Corps, 11,982; and the 6th Corps, 9,023. For a man who was excused from fighting because of his bad eyesight, Dana had a lot to say about the fighting proficiency and character of others who did fight. In his closing comments on the army's losses, he suggests, "Of course great numbers of men who are lying around in the woods will soon return to their commands, but many of these are worthless for fighting purposes."[35]

The Army of the Potomac and the 9th Corps, once concentrated at Spotsylvania, confronted an enemy that had been hard at work strengthening its breastworks. But the soldiers of the 2nd, 5th, 6th and 9th Corps were sent, again and again, against the enemy's fortifications, probing for weak points or actually attempting to storm the works to their fronts, actions that were becoming trademarks for Grant's campaign. Without Federal cavalry, which could have told Meade and Grant a great deal about the enemy's strength, position and movements, the infantry instead was repeatedly sent in on "reconnaissance in force." The attacks by the 2nd, 5th and 6th Corps on May 10th amply demonstrate Grant's unfortunate predilection for frontal confrontations with the enemy. In his memoirs regarding these days, Grant states his assumption that Lee had weakened his center to defend his left, as if it were fact. Apparently once Grant had adopted a theory, it became and remained to be, in his mind, what actually happened.[36]

While it seems that anyone who witnessed the results of the Federal attacks on May 10th would come up with a plan other than frontal assaults, that was not the case. For there was one seemingly promising event that stood out for Grant in that day of futile assaults. Before the assaults on May 10th, a young engineer, Ranald Mackenzie, had found during his reconnaissance that there was a way to bring a 6th Corps force undercover in a wooded area to within 200 yards of the Rebel works. With young Col. Emory Upton in command, nearly 5,000 men in four lines made a well-planned assault on a salient in the Rebel line on May 10th. Their temporary breakthrough on the Rebel line would have an alarming effect on the direction that Federal strategy would take in the continuing conflict at Spotsylvania.[37]

While all the 6th Corps attacks, including Upton's, ultimately failed, Wright sent word to Grant that Emory Upton and his handpicked force had achieved partial success

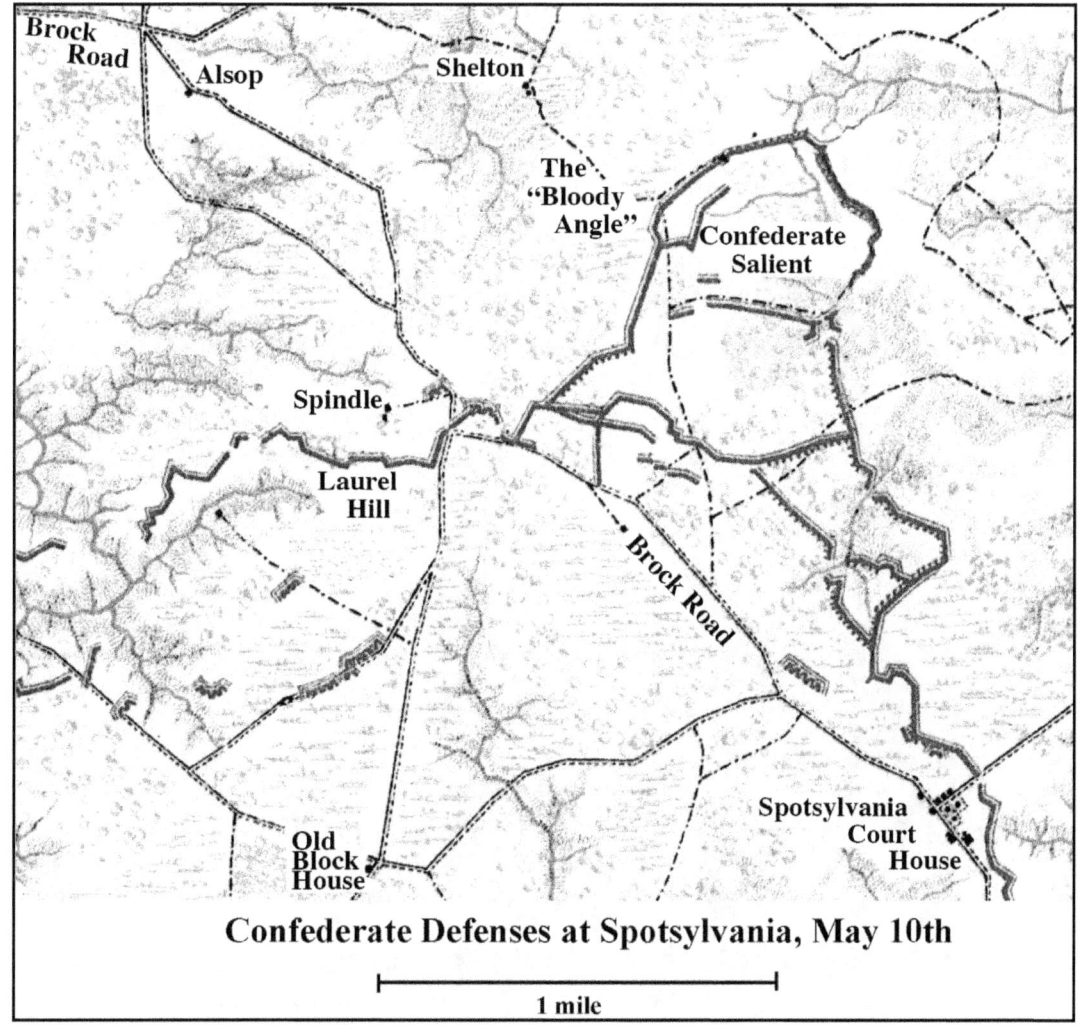

Confederate defenses at Spotsylvania, May 10. Adapted from Plate XCVI, *Official Atlas* and a sketch map by Jed. Hotchkiss, 2nd Corps, Army of Northern Virginia, Library of Congress (Ned Smith).

in their attack on the salient in the Rebel line. Wright reported that Upton's breakthrough had failed only because it hadn't been properly supported. Since Grant seemingly fixated on Upton's temporary success, it apparently provided Grant with the proof he wanted that such frontal attacks had merit. It allowed Grant to ignore the many examples he already had of frontal attacks proving useless, and sometimes disastrous. Historians William Matter, Andrew Humphreys and Francis Walker all puzzle over why support for Upton's attack wasn't expected to have come from the rest of the 6th Corps, rather than just Mott's division from the 2nd Corps. Grant's engineer, Comstock may well have been responsible for Mott being left on his own, for Comstock, after consulting with Wright, reported to Meade and Grant that they need not reinforce Mott with an additional force from the 2nd Corps, for any reserve the army had might be needed elsewhere.[38]

While Wright, on this his first day of commanding the 6th Corps, was reporting the enemy's salient as a tempting target, there are indications that he was extremely reluctant to attack on the rest of his line. While Wright told Dana that there was nowhere on his front that he could attack because it was all a morass,[39] Wright told Meade that there was no place on the 6th Corps' front that wasn't enfiladed by the enemy's flanking fire, and that was, apparently, enough to convince his superiors that only concentrated attacks on the enemy's weak spots should be made on the 6th Corps' front. The conditions on Wright's front and the acceptance by Meade and Grant of Wright's reasons why the 6th Corps could not attack are worth remembering. For when Warren, on the morning of May 12th, sent a very similar message to Meade and Grant, that his front was enfiladed by enemy artillery, he would get a very different response from his commanders.[40]

But to return to the 10th and the Bloody Angle, as the salient became known, 2nd Corps historian Walker, as previously stated, was outspoken in his suggestions that, if Upton's assault held such promise, why was a single divi-

Emory Upton (Salvatore Cillela, *Upton's Regulars: The 121st New York Infantry in the Civil War*, Lawrence: University Press of Kansas, 2009).

sion (Mott's) the only force designated to support a breakthrough. And Walker, who served as adjutant general in the 2nd Corps, questioned why the rest of the 6th Corps was not used in support. Walker, the future first president of MIT, then went on to question why elements of the 5th Corps and Gibbon's 2nd Corps division hadn't been sent for support, instead of engaging them in "bloody and fruitless" frontal attacks on their fronts.[41]

Taking nothing away from the gallant Upton and his initial success at the salient, the fact that his approach was covered by woods gave him the element of surprise, which was a scarce commodity on that field. But that was a factor that seemed to leave little impression on his superiors. Upton was wounded in the spirited attack that took more than a thousand Rebel prisoners and several stand of colors, and though it cost Upton a thousand casualties, the attack was the sort of thing that made Grant's eyes sparkle. Grant enthusiastically bestowed his first field promotion on bold young Upton, making him a brigadier general.[42]

On the morning of May 11th, a calm day between the storms of May 10th, and the upcoming maelstrom of May 12th, Grant wrote enthusiastically to Halleck,

> We have now ended the 6th day of very hard fighting. The result up to this time is much in our favor. But our losses have been heavy as well as those of the enemy. We have lost to this time eleven general officers killed, wounded and missing, and probably twenty thousand men. I think the loss of the enemy must be greater — we have taken over four thousand prisoners in battle, whilst he has taken from us but few except a few stragglers. I am now sending back to Belle Plain all my wagons for a fresh supply of provisions and ammunition, and propose to fight it out on this line if it takes all summer.[43]

In this letter, carried to Washington by Representative Washburne on behalf of Grant, the lieutenant general went on to say that reinforcements were much needed, but he also reported, "I am satisfied the enemy are very shaky, and are only kept to the mark by the greatest exertions on the part of their officers, and by keeping them intrenched in every position they take." Requesting that Halleck send him 10,000 reinforcements, Grant suggested that Halleck get them by sending him troops that were manning the defenses around Washington.[44]

An element of Upton's attack that had *not* gone so well was the failure of the support that had supposedly been arranged for Upton, and all the blame for that failure was heaped upon Gen. Gershom Mott, 4th Division commander in the 2nd Corps. In all fairness, some fault should be assigned to headquarters, and the risky position in which they had placed Mott in the first place. As Matter points out, before the assault Mott had been forced to feel his way through unscouted territory to his left, trying to find and connect with Burnside's right.[45] Then too, responsibility should be placed on headquarters for the confusing orders they issued to Mott that day. Mott, positioned between Burnside on his left and Wright on his right, was told initially to support Burnside and send men if called upon by Burnside for assistance. Later that order was changed to suggest that Mott should attack on his own front, rather than sending troops to Burnside if the 9th Corps was attacked. Mott's next order from headquarters informed him that an engineer was coming to tell him what his role would be in Wright's plan for Upton's assault. Mott responded that so many of his men had been needed out on picket in order to connect with Burnside that he'd have no more than 1,500 men available for an assault. Wright then weighed in, advising Mott to have the men he had out on picket make a frontal attack from where they were. This confusion of orders was bad enough, but the time for Wright's attack had been changed, and as evidence points out below, Wright may have neglected to get that word to Mott.[46]

In Grant's memoirs, there would be no acknowledgment of this stream of confusing orders to Mott, nor any consideration of how unrealistic expectations were on the part of 6th Corps and army headquarters on May 10th. There is no consideration of the very awkward position Mott held on the Federal line, nor his distance from the enemy, or the fact that he was given no time for deployment. Nor is the question asked as to why no one other than Mott was expected to support Upton's attack. Grant blithely lays all the blame on Mott for Upton not having a more complete and lasting success on May 10th. Dana, that expert at blackening names and reputations, reported to Washington, "Mott's division held ground, between Wright and Burnside, we were disgraced by a retreat of that division, without loss, and apparently without any considerable force to oppose them. They advanced into the woods with orders to attack, but came out again at once, like cowards."[47] It is no surprise that Wright would accept no blame for his own failure to provide adequate support for Upton's attack. Wright had already established himself as a man who would not accept blame for his mistakes, but would blame others. But historian Humphreys clearly regrets the criticism that had been heaped upon Mott, with Humphreys describing Mott as a man "well known as a gallant officer."[48]

Hoping to improve upon Upton's assault by enlarging the scale of the tactic, Grant ordered an attack by the 2nd Corps, with the 6th in support, on the salient in the Rebel works near Spotsylvania Court House for early morning on May 12th. On May 11th, Grant sent his staff engineer, Col. Cyrus Comstock, with the officers of Hancock's staff to choose the point of attack for the 12th. Pouring rain made visibility difficult, and Comstock became lost, and after riding many miles, he and the scouting party struck the position of Burnside's corps. By the time they returned to the "Mule Shoe," as the salient would become known, it was near dark, but a line was chosen where the 2nd Corps would make their formation for the attack. The position chosen was on the same front where Mott had made his attack on May 10th. After dark, the 2nd Corps' three divisions moved into position at the Union center along with Mott's 4th Division to assault the enemy salient at first light. Heavy fog, while slightly delaying the dawn advance, enhanced the cover provided by the woods where Hancock initially formed his men. Fortune also smiled on the 2nd Corps in that the artillery from that portion of the Rebel line had been removed when Lee mistakenly believed a Federal withdrawal from Spotsylvania was in the offing.[49] For it was Hancock's reconnaissance on the Federal right, along with Burnside's pointless meandering on the Federal left, that had resulted in Federal activity being reported by Rebel cavalry to Lee. The Confederate commander incorrectly deduced that this Federal flurry of activity indicated that the Yankees were about to move from Spotsylvania, and Lee prematurely prepared to remove his artillery. While this "luck" resulted in Hancock taking a portion of the enemy's trenches at the Bloody Angle, it also resulted in terrible hand-to-hand fighting among the densely packed troops, with appalling casualties for both sides. But Hancock, on securing part of Lee's line, took 4,000 prisoners, 20 pieces of artillery, more than 30 colors and two Rebel generals, which he sent back to a jubilant Grant. Humphreys estimated the casualties for May 12th for the Army of the Potomac and Burnside's 9th Corps to be 6,800 and 800 missing.[50]

The commander of the famed Vermont Brigade of the 6th Corps, Col. Lewis A. Grant,[51] described a visit he made to the Bloody Angle on the day after the battle, May 13th. He was sickened by what he saw, declaring that the salient was worse than the Bloody Lane at Antietam, for at Spotsylvania the dead were piled up several deep and, with the close confines in which the fighting took place, the dead were more torn and mangled. In fact, when Colonel Grant's Vermonters had arrived to reinforce the 2nd Corps men already inside the salient, Lewis sent word, "For God's sake, Hancock, do not send any more troops in here," as soldiers jammed the narrow battlefront.[52] The 2nd Corps and 6th Corps, during the attack at the salient on May 12th, lost 2,043 and 840, respectively. The 5th Corps attacked the earthworks manned by Anderson's corps on their own front, but elements of the 5th Corps also were sent to the salient. Fifth Corps losses were 970 for May 12th, oddly, more than the number lost by Wright at the "Bloody Angle." Burnside, attacking on the Federal far left, sustained 1,250 casualties and the loss of 300 prisoners. It is worth noting, however, that in Hancock's initial report late on May 12th, he estimates his losses in just the 2nd Corps at 7,100. Was Hancock underreporting his casualties, as Warren had at the Wilderness? Such wide discrepancies in the reported number of casualties, especially when the number decreases, seem to indicate that that is so.[53]

While the fight at the "Bloody Angle" on May 12th will forevermore be known as the 2nd Corps' fight, the 5th Corps, 9th Corps and 6th Corps all paid a high price for that 2nd Corps victory. Warren had the 5th Corps line extended to cover his own front as well as that formerly held by the 2nd Corps after their departure to the Union center for the May 12th attack. Roebling, Warren's aide, led some of the newly arrived heavy artillerymen, who had been wrenched from their Washington fortifications by Grant's demands for more men, to a place in Warren's line. Though untrained as infantrymen, the artillerymen were sent to help lengthen Warren's long line, the 5th Corps' original line and that previously held by the 2nd Corps. For Warren was not only responsible for keeping track of all that was happening on the Federal right along his extended line, but he had also been advised to hold his force in readiness to either attack on his front, or be ready to withdraw and send reinforcements to Hancock or Wright. To be prepared to attack or to withdraw are two wildly different scenarios in any commander's mind, but a circular from Meade on May 11th demanded that Warren, Burnside and Wright all make preparations for just such conflicting actions. Headquarters had advised corps commanders Warren, Burnside and Wright to establish how much of their force was necessary to hold their positions, so they could be ready to withdraw and then send some portion of their corps away for use elsewhere.[54]

At 6 A.M. on May 12th, Meade informed Warren that Wright was being ordered in to support Hancock's attack on the Rebel salient and that Warren must be prepared to attack on his front. At 6:30 A.M., Meade sent a circular to all division commanders that their corps could be ordered to attack at any moment. When the order came, it directed that "they were to precede their main lines of battle with a strong line of skirmishers to draw an initial volley from the enemy. After this their main lines were to charge." At 7:30, Meade informed Warren that the right of Wright's corps was under heavy attack and that Wright desired support. While Meade believed that an attack on the 5th Corps front would help relieve Wright, he nonetheless recommended that Warren send part of his force to the 5th Corp's left in case Wright suffered a reverse. At the same time, Warren received a message directly from Wright asking for troops to support the right of the 6th Corps and to be brought up to extend Wright's line.[55] Warren sent that portion of Bartlett's Brigade that was not out on the skirmish line and two large regiments of heavy artillerymen. Matter suggests that Wright, who was not in dire straights at this point that morning, having been engaged only an hour, was likely just apprehensive of what might happen if the Confederates answered his attack with a counterattack, but this is not the message that Wright conveyed to either Meade or Warren. Wright wanted support at his back and on his right, and he wanted it immediately. Meanwhile Warren, who was being asked not only to attack on his front but also to withdraw part of his force and send it to Wright, could very well have been having similar doubts about the security of his own front. What would happen on his long line if the enemy decided to respond to continual advances with their own counterattacks? With Warren's extended line, reduced numbers and no reserve, the 5th Corps would be ill-prepared to handle any Rebel aggression. Matter also observes that it was at this very time that Meade shifted his headquarters from near the fighting at the front to a position some distance from the front, a move that could only have made Meade's knowledge of what was actually going on on the battlefield more tenuous.[56]

At 8 A.M., Grant became involved, sending an order through Meade to Warren to attack immediately with as much of his force as possible and to be prepared to follow up any success gained in the attack with his whole force. In Grant's mind, this attack on Warren's front was intended to occupy Anderson's corps, which Warren was confronting, and prevent him from sending reinforcements to Ewell at the Bloody Angle. Warren complained that the immediacy of this latest order to attack would give him no time to deal with two key points on the enemy line, including one enemy position that would enfilade any advance he made on his front, and which included the enemy opposite the 6th Corps' right.[57] Though Meade received Warren's reply, he ignored it, and Meade notified Hancock that Warren was initiating his attack, and that was just what Warren did. Warren attacked, but as Roebling recalled in his later report, this was the fourth or fifth time that the 5th Corps had been asked to attack at Laurel Hill, and the men showed little enthusiasm. One of Griffin's divisions sent in three regiments, who became pinned on the field, and suffered heavily when withdrawing. One of these regiments, the 32nd Massachusetts, experienced nearly 100 casualties in this 30 minutes' work. Meanwhile, the men of Cutler's division, though they did not make contact with the enemy, inched forward. Perhaps it's not that difficult to explain the division's lack of enthusiasm, for there was ample evidence that the enemy entrenchment on their front, far from being empty, was fully manned. One needs only to consider the condition of one of Cutler's brigades, the famed Iron Brigade. The brigade was one regiment short this day, and would be without the missing regiment permanently. The 2nd Wisconsin, after the losses experienced by Cutler's, formerly Wadsworth's, division at the Wilderness and at Laurel Hill, had dropped to fewer than 100 men. Its field officers were wounded or captured, so the 2nd Wisconsin, or what was left of it, was detailed to provost guard for the rest of their enlistments. Though it is hard to imagine that any of Warren's regiments and brigades suffered nearly as extensively as had the 2nd Wisconsin, there were, apparently, other brigades in Warren's 5th Corps that obeyed the order to advance that day but did not advance far enough to engage the enemy again.[58]

Roebling's report for the 12th of May offers additional insight into the mind and movements of Warren and the men of the 5th Corps on this day. Roebling observes that at 8 A.M., when Meade's peremptory and reiterated orders for an attack along their whole line came, the corps had already been skirmishing and had clear indications that the enemy had been in no way weakened in their front. Nonetheless, the attack was made by the 5th Corps at 8:15 A.M. and "was quickly repulsed as was anticipated." Roebling commented that, considering how many times these men had been asked to attack in the same place, "it is not a matter of surprise that they had lost all spirit for that kind of work; many of them positively refused to go forward as their previous experience had taught them that to do so was certain death on *that* front."[59]

By 9:10 on the morning of the 12th, any chance of constructive communication between Meade and Warren had disappeared, for while Warren was informing Meade that he could advance his lines no further, Meade was being told by Grant, who would have every last word, that the enemy must have weakened their left, in front of Warren, to reinforce their center to sustain the 2nd Corps' attack. Neither Meade nor Grant wanted to hear from Warren that their theory on enemy troop movements was incorrect. Warren, under pressure to attack again, added fuel to Meade's increasingly smoldering temper by also forwarding a message from Griffin that he wanted the brigade that had been sent to Wright to come back. Meade curtly informed Warren that headquarters would decide where Griffin's 1st Brigade was most needed. But the message that seemed to put Meade completely over the edge was one from Warren at about this same time, stating that some of the fire being directed at the 5th Corps was coming from Warren's left from the unengaged enemy on Wright's front. Warren reported, "My left cannot advance without a most destructive enfilade fire until the Sixth Corps has cleared its front. My right is close up to the enemy's works, and ordered to assault. The enemy's line here appears to be strongly held. It is his point-d'appui if he throws back his right."[60] The "point-d'appui" Warren referred to was a particularly strong, well-protected point on the enemy's line that would be used as a pivot point should the enemy find it necessary to throw back one or another wing. But as Matter notes, when Meade received this last message from Warren, he was furious. For while Warren's earlier messages indicated that Warren had complied with Meade's orders to attack, this last one seemed to indicate that he had not made the attack with his whole corps, nor did he want to. Meade then informed Warren through Humphreys, "The order of the major-general commanding is peremptory that you attack at once at all hazards with your whole force, if necessary."[61]

As Warren advanced his right for the attack, the 5th Corps commander no doubt realized that Meade and Grant were making the same mistake they had made on May 10th — the mistaken assumption that the enemy had or would be drawing troops away from Warren's front to send to the point of the Federal 2nd Corps' attack at the enemy's center. Just how many Rebels it would take to adequately man the works Warren was facing was apparently not one of headquarters' considerations, though as Dana's telegram to Washington that very morning reported of the fortification which Warren was demonstrating against, "The rebel works at that point are exceedingly strong." Thus Meade, ignoring Warren's report that the enemy was still in his earthworks in force, pressed on with his own interpretation of Grant's instructions, that Meade have Warren and Wright "hold their Corps as close to the enemy as possible to take advantage of any diversion caused by this attack and to break in if the opportunity presents itself."[62] While no "opportunity" was presenting itself on Warren's front, what Meade would insist upon was a full attack by Warren's whole corps on his front to be made immediately.

Meade sent word to Warren through the Army of the Potomac's chief of staff, General Humphreys, who was a longtime friend of Warren's, that the order for the entire 5th Corps to attack was peremptory. Humphreys, who had made a reconnaissance of the 5th Corps front and was aware of what Warren was facing, sent the message encouraging Warren to get his men across that field of fire as quickly as possible, regardless of the cost. "Dear Warren, Don't hesitate to attack with the bayonet. Meade has assumed the responsibility, and will take the consequences. Your friend, A.A. Humphreys."[63] Did Humphreys's assurance that the responsibility for this 5th Corps attack now fully rested upon Meade now that Warren's protest had been noted, really relieve Warren of his own feelings of responsibility for sending his men against Laurel Hill again? For what Warren was being ordered to do was, as Humphrey's account confirms, to make an attack on a portion of the Rebel entrenchments where the enemy earthworks had already been deemed too strong to take by assault. The assumption of their impregnability had been made on May 10th, and since then, the Rebel works had been strengthened. Humphreys also confirms that the force facing Warren in the Confederate breastworks was Anderson's [Longstreet's] corps, lacking only one brigade. Warren, again ordered to attack, ordered three divisions forward over open ground toward the well-manned breastworks of Field's and Kershaw's divisions, who would report sustaining "two violent assaults" during the morning which were "easily repulsed with great loss to the enemy."[64]

Warren biographer Emerson Taylor attributes the impatience and anger demonstrated in the correspondence between Meade and Warren this day to Grant's presence at Meade's elbow.[65] But it seems glaringly apparent that Meade intentionally inflamed the situation when Meade had sent word to Grant, "Warren seems reluctant to assault. I have ordered him at all hazards to do so, and if his attack should be repulsed to draw in the right and send his troops as fast as possible to Wright and Hancock." Grant sent orders to Meade that, if Warren failed to move promptly, Meade should relieve Warren and put Gen. Andrew Humphreys, Meade's chief of staff, in command of the 5th Corps. Meade left Humphreys with the 5th Corps with his authority to give orders to "attend to the shortening of the line and the sending reinforcements to Wright & Hancock."[66]

Humphreys, believing that further attacks on the 5th Corps front could not succeed, began to send some of Warren's divisions to assist other corps — specifically Griffin's division to the 2nd Corps and Cutler's Division to the 6th Corps. Instead of adding Cutler's division as a reinforcement to his line, as had been intended for the planned assault, Wright used Cutler to relieve one of his own brigades. This, as Matter points out, insured failure for Meade and Grant's attempt to mount a successful assault against the northwest face of the salient while Hancock fought on the other face. At 5:15 P.M. on May 12th, Wright, who apparently had complete discretion as to whether he would attack or not, decided that he did not have enough men. By way of justification, Wright inexplicably suggested that only 1,000 men of his own 6th Corps were available for an assault. In a confirmation of Wright's great uneasiness at what might happen if his attack failed, Wright added the strangest of all qualifiers regarding his views against making an attack, that his concern was "not that it might not succeed, but in view of the disaster which would possibly follow a failure." Meade approved Wright's decision not to attack. In fact, when Stanton asked Meade at this time for recommendations for promotion, Meade recommended the immediate promotion of Wright and Gibbon to be major generals, and he recommended that Wright be given permanent command of the 6th Corps.[67]

It is, perhaps, easy to understand why 2nd Corps commander Winfield Scott Hancock, ready and willing to follow any order without hesitation regardless of the consequences, was a fair-haired boy as far as Meade and Grant were concerned. But it is a matter of real puzzlement why the timid and unreliable Wright seemingly thrived. Other than Halleck's continued preferment for Wright, the 6th Corps commander's performance at Spotsylvania or in the Overland Campaign in general did not recommend him. But Grant, on May 20th, wrote to Halleck, "General Wright is one of the most meritorious officers in the service, and with opportunity will demonstrate his fitness for any position." But while Grant might be willing to boost Wright, he was not willing for Wright to get ahead of his favorite, Sheridan, for Grant added, "But at present I doubt whether Sheridan has not most entitled himself to the vacancy Brigadier Generalcy."[68]

While Cutler's 4th Division was used to relieve Wright's troops on the 6th Corps front, Griffin's 1st Division, which had been sent to the 2nd Corps, had been immediately placed in Hancock's battle line as soon as they arrived from Warren. What Griffin and his men experienced was absolute chaos on the 2nd Corps front, with "a large portion of the 2nd Corps huddled together in one angle of the captured works and firing almost at random. It was intended that as soon as our Corps [the 5th] had joined the 2d that the two were to advance and follow up the enemy, but it soon became apparent that we would do well if we held the captured line and carried off the guns; the enemy still held on firmly opposite the left of the 6th and on the right of the 2d." An attempt by the Rebels to regain their lines was repulsed at 6 P.M., and firing continued most of the night. The night of May 12th–13th was also a nervous one for the 5th Corps back at Laurel Hill, for Warren was holding a long line with just one of his divisions and a contingent of untrained heavy artillery. Warren doubted that Crawford and his division would have been able to withstand an attack from the enemy, and it was with some relief that Warren welcomed back Cutler's and Griffin's divisions at midday on May 13th.[69]

Charles Dana lost no opportunity to denigrate Warren, reporting at the end of May 12th that while Wright and Hancock bore the brunt of the fighting, Burnside contributed several attacks in which his troops bore themselves "like good soldiers." Dana observed,

> Warren alone gained nothing. His attacks were made in the forenoon, with so much delay that both Grant and Meade were greatly dissatisfied, but when they were made they were unsuccessful, though attended with considerable loss. The rebel works in his front were very strong, and finally at about 1 o'clock, the chief portion of his troops were withdrawn from his lines and brought to the support of Wright. It was then intended to attempt a grand assault with a very powerful column under Wright at about 5 P.M., but when the men were brought up they were so tired from the long day's work, and the chances of success were so much short of certainty, that General Wright advised General Meade to postpone the attempt.[70]

Grant suggested in his memoir that the action on May 12th would have been more successful if Warren had been as prompt as Wright. This is an apparent assertion that if Warren had been quicker about making his costly attacks, he could have, upon the failure of those attacks, reinforced the 2nd and 6th Corps with the 5th Corps' survivors more swiftly. Once again, because Grant assumed at the time that Lee would draw troops from somewhere on his line to reinforce his center, Grant insists that those reinforcements came from the Confederate left in Warren's front, sufficiently weakening the line in front of Warren. By way of refuting this point, Dana reported to Washington that although some prisoners taken at the angle were from other corps and divisions, most of them were from Ewell's corps and Johnson's division. Dana also reported that of the 6,000 causalities the Army of the Potomac incurred, 2,000 were from the 5th Corps — high numbers for the corps merely holding a force in place while the 2nd and 6th Corps attacked the Bloody Angle. But regardless of exactly how many of the enemy Warren faced, the Rebels proved that they had more than enough men facing the 5th Corps on May 12th to cause great slaughter. Yet Grant's implied accusation is clear, that it was Warren's fault that Hancock and Wright were unable to accomplish more at the Union center.[71] Interestingly, Walker, the 2nd Corps historian, who had every reason to be sensitive to and cognizant of any help or hindrance his corps had experienced at the salient, had a different view of things. Walker wrote that Meade also reported to Hancock regarding Warren's "reluctance to assault." Walker said about the attacks the 5th Corps made on their front on May 12th, "Warren's attack failed, with heavy loss, as that judicious officer had anticipated."[72]

The fighting at the salient, which amply earned the name the "Bloody Angle," continued on into the night. On the morning of the 13th, it would be discovered that Lee had retired back to a new, stronger line, completely eliminating the salient. The 2nd Corps' attempts to breach this new line would fail. In the end, Grant would sum up the action of May 12th by stating that the enemy's resistance on this day "was so obstinate that the advantage gained did not prove decisive."[73]

As the enemy's withdrawal to their new line in front of the 2nd and 6th Corps was discovered on the morning of the 13th, Meade once again directed Warren to push forward a force to ascertain whether the enemy was still in his front. Warren responded that the enemy had in fact strengthened his lines during the night, with more men than the previous evening and artillery that covered all the 5th Corps' lines of advance. Meade's reaction, eloquent evidence that Meade no longer wanted the opinions of his once trusted lieutenant, was to order Warren to advance. Warren appealed to Humphreys to explain to Meade that the enemy was still in position on Warren's front, his artillery enfilading his advance as it had yesterday and the day before. Warren knew that Grant did not want a battle this day, though he did want his lines pressed forward far enough to determine the enemy's position and strength. Warren asked if he must send out a force, and shortly after, orders arrived directing the 2nd, 5th and 6th Corps to each throw forward a division to determine enemy presence. Warren again appealed to Meade, sending a sketch of his position in line with Wright's Corps, and stating that, unless Wright advanced with him, his advancing line would be enfiladed by the three Rebel batteries that had his line within canister range on his front. Shortly before noon, Meade grudgingly admitted that Warren had complied with establishing the enemy's position and strength on his front and need not advance his line further.[74]

In a letter to his wife this day, May 13th, Meade, while writing of having achieved a decided victory at Spotsylvania, also commented, "Our losses have been frightful; I do not like to estimate them." Yet he did not share such sentiments with Grant when several days later Grant expressed regret at their heavy losses, amounting to more than 33,000 men since the Army of the Potomac had left their winter quarters. Meade, according to Assistant Secretary of War Charles Dana, is said to have replied to Grant, "We can't do these little tricks without losses."[75] Meade's willingness to please Grant would not go unrewarded, or so he thought. On May 13th, Grant wrote to Stanton recommending both Meade and Sherman for promotion to major general in the regular army. Grant commented, "General Meade had more than met my most sanguine expectations. He and Sherman are the fittest officers for large commands I have come in contact with." Grant added that he would not like to see one promoted without the other. But in reality, that is just what happened. Sherman and Sheridan, Meade's subordinate, would both be appointed major generals in the regular army before Meade. In mid–June, when the appointments for Meade and Sherman still had not been made, Stanton commented to Grant that it had been considered that it would be appropriate if the major generalcies were not officially appointed until Sherman took Atlanta and Meade reached Richmond. Grant concurred.[76]

Late on the afternoon of the 13th, orders were issued for the 5th Corps, followed by the 6th Corps, to move after dark, passing in the rear of the army to take up a place on the extreme left flank of the army beyond the Fredericksburg Road. Here they would assault the enemy at dawn.[77] At sundown, the 5th Corps finally left their battleground at Laurel Hill to begin a nightmarish march by farm roads and across country through intense dark, heavy rain, mist and mud. Though Warren posted men and lit fires at short intervals, exhausted men lost their way or fell by the wayside. It was daylight before Warren's advance arrived at the point of attack with little more than a thousand of Griffin's exhausted infantry who had marched as Warren's vanguard. The Rebels, strongly entrenched, awaited them as they approached their new position on the Federal line. Though Meade admitted to Grant that the condition of the men made him doubt the practicality of doing anything that day, when Warren expressed similar thoughts, Warren was ordered to deploy for attack. Not until 9 A.M. did Meade notify Warren that the assault for that morning was suspended. In his report after the fact, Roebling expressed contempt for the original, now discarded, plan to have the 5th Corps "assault the enemy's position which we had never seen, at 4 o'clock in the morning, in conjunction with the 9th Corps who had been whipped the day before, and felt in fine spirits for such work." Historian Matter questioned what criteria Grant was using that made him assess that the army was in the best of spirits. On the contrary, the evidence seems to weigh heavily that in the 5th Corps camp there was a prevalence of exhaustion and a "scornful distaste for what they described as reckless assaults in the open against prepared field fortifications." Only high causalities resulted from these futile assaults.[78]

As the 5th Corps straggled in during the morning of the 14th, Warren's 1st Division commander, Charles Griffin, spotted a hill on the 5th Corps front — variously called Bleak Hill, Gayle's Hill, Jet's House or Myers Farm — that offered a good defensive position and a useful view of the country westward toward the Rebel position. Griffin sent several regiments from Ayres's brigade to drive off enemy cavalry and occupy it, but when the 6th Corps, who had also made the same night march in the wake of the 5th Corps, came up on Warren's left, Meade ordered Upton's brigade, now whittled down to only 800 men, to occupy the hill Griffin had taken. Though Upton was reinforced, when the Rebel cavalry returned with reinforcements they drove Upton's force from the hill. Meade, who was at the front with Wright examining the ground, was cut off from the army. Luckily, a member of Meade's party knew of a ford across the Ni River at their backs, and the two generals escaped to safety. What a coup it would have been for the Rebels to capture Meade and Wright! Meanwhile, Meade ordered Wright to retake the hill immediately, using his entire infantry force if necessary, and Meade authorized Wright to call on Warren if needed. By 7 P.M., knowing of no results other than a heavy cannonading, Meade asked Warren what was happening. Warren replied that the fire Meade heard was from Wright's guns, and it might as well stop as it appeared the Rebels had left the hill. Warren informed Wright that he would again send Ayres's brigade forward as soon as Wright's guns ceased fire. The hill was again occupied, and Ayres handed it over to the 6th Corps men who relieved him. Wright, who was uneasy in the position, asked permission to withdraw, but headquarters refused.[79]

While Meade thanked Warren for his services that day at Myer's Hill, this period of good feelings didn't last long. The next day, Warren received orders that if Burnside's force on Warren's right was attacked, Warren was to attack on his own front. Unaware that elements of Hancock's 2nd Corps were already in reserve in the 9th Corps' rear, Warren annoyed Meade by inquiring whether it would not be better for him to send reinforcements to Burnside, rather than attack on his own front. An exasperated Meade told Warren that, while orders would be given if Burnside was attacked, in the meantime Meade's original order was in force.[80]

As continuing rain curtailed action and movements, the Army of the Potomac was occupied from the 13th through the 17th of May entrenching lines, opening roads, and examining the country and roads around them. But late in the afternoon of the 15th, Burnside became apprehensive of an attack, and Warren was ordered "to attack the enemy's breastworks, full of men as soon as the attack on the 9th Corps commenced. Troops stood under arms from 5 o'clock until 9 P.M. in fact they remained that way all night, making themselves as comfortable as possible" until the order to attack was rescinded. On May 16th Grant informed Halleck that five days of constant rain had made the roads impassable, making it impossible to send out the ambulances with wounded. Grant asked that Halleck inform the president and secretary of war that the army was in "the best of spirits and feel the greatest confidence in ultimate success." Grant added, "Elements alone have suspended hostilities and that it is in no manner due to weakness or exhaustion on our part."[81]

Good news reached Grant on the 15th and 16th. Butler reported having captured the outer works at Drewry's Bluff on the James River near Richmond, while Averell's Federal cavalry had destroyed Rebel supplies and a railroad bridge. News came that Sherman had taken Dalton, Georgia, and was following Gen. Joseph Johnston's army southward. Sheridan's cavalry, meanwhile, had passed through the outer defenses of Richmond, temporarily disrupting Lee's telegraph lines to the capital. But Lee would also be receiving good news, for he learned that John C. Breckinridge had defeated Gen. Franz Sigel's Federal force at New Market, Virginia, and as desperately as Lee wanted reinforcements, he nonetheless encouraged Breckinridge to follow the retreating Yankees northward. Then word came that Beauregard had scored a victory against Butler at Drewry's Bluff and that Butler had withdrawn his force into the safe but limiting confines of Bermuda Hundred.[82]

As far flung actions occupied Grant's thoughts, one wonders if another squabble between Warren and Meade made the lieutenant general shake his head. Midday, on May 16th, Meade received instructions from Grant to order an advance of the corps' pickets to discover if there had been any change in the enemy's positions. Warren answered Meade's order by explaining that his pickets were out as far as they could go, and his aide was on his way to Meade with a sketch of the 5th Corps front. Meade insisted that Warren advance his pickets. While reporting that any further advance would bring on Rebel shelling, Warren requested time to get the wagons that had just come up to issue supplies out of the way. He also mentioned that Gen. Cyrus Comstock of Grant's staff had just been with Warren, and Comstock had thought that the condition of affairs on Warren's front was understood. Warren concluded his message with his intention to make immediate preparation to advance his skirmish line. Meade, more than a little miffed and intent on obeying the lieutenant general's orders to the letter, insisted on referring the matter to Grant, who replied, "All I wanted was to be assured that the enemy retained their old position, or, if they had taken up a new one, to find where it was." Griffin's division, which would have had to cross an open field to approach the enemy line manned by Hill's corps, was spared the great loss he would have incurred.[83] One may also suspect that some of Meade's impatience with Warren was born of the frustrations produced by the awkwardness of the chain of command. Grant frequently dictated tactics and strategy, leaving Meade to implement the movements.[84] But if Meade chafed at having such limited control of his own army, it did not make him hesitate to inflict seemingly much the same restrictions upon Warren and his corps, leaving Warren no opportunity to react or respond to conditions on the field.

During the night of May 17th, the 5th Corps advanced its lines and entrenched, bringing up Warren's batteries under the cover of darkness in preparation for holding most of the army's line in order to free the 2nd and 6th Corps for yet another assault on the Bloody Angle the next morning. A young colonel, Joshua Chamberlain, had just returned to the army after months of hospitalization and sick leave after he had collapsed from malaria at Rappahannock Station the previous fall. Since Gen. Joseph J. Bartlett had been given command of Chamberlain's brigade during his absence, the colonel returned to the command of his regiment, the 20th Maine, but on the night of May 17th–18th, Chamberlain was given a special force that Warren had put together to build platforms and position the 5th Corps' 26 guns to assist in the assault.[85]

On the night of May 17th–18th, the 2nd and 6th Corps took up their positions for their early morning attack. On the morning of the 18th, the Rebels had their pickets up so close to the Federal lines that by the time the enemy's pickets were driven in, the Confederates had more than adequate warning that an assault was under way. Thus, when the 2nd and 6th Corps advanced on the morning of May 18th, they found a well-prepared enemy waiting for them. They also discovered that the enemy's defenses had been strengthened since the May 12th attack, and the Federal assault was easily halted and broken by the Rebel artillery fire alone. Then, too, it was noted, that circumstances on the field were not such that would hearten the men making an attack. The sight and stench of the dead from the fight of the 12th, many of whom were still on the field, were enough to dishearten the most experienced soldiers.[86] After the fact, Meade would comment, "Even Grant thought it useless to knock our heads against a brick wall, and directed a suspension of the attack." Meade also pointed out, when visiting politicians, Senators Sherman and

Sprague, commented that Washington knew these were Meade's battles, that "such was not the case; that at first I had maneuvered the army, but that gradually, and from the very nature of things, Grant had taken the control; and that it would be injurious to the army to have two heads."[87]

The failure of the May 18th attack was not the only discouraging news Grant received this day. News came that Union general Franz Sigel's troops, having been defeated by Breckinridge at New Market, were fleeing the Shenandoah Valley. Breckinridge and an estimated 5,000 men were now free to reinforce Lee. And with General Butler's defeat at Drewry's Bluff, Lee could now send for Gen. George Pickett and his 5,000 men to be sent from the defenses of the Rebel capital, while Gen. Robert Hoke would bring 1,200 from Petersburg. But Grant, too, was receiving reinforcements. Some 6,000 men had been stripped from the heavy artillery regiments in the defenses around Washington, suddenly finding themselves sent to the front as infantry.[88] While there were doubts concerning the usefulness of these raw artillerymen to the infantry, they soon proved their worth.

With orders issued for the Army of the Potomac to begin withdrawing from Spotsylvania the night of the 19th, in preparation for another movement by the left flank toward Richmond, the Federals began moving to the left, leaving Warren on the army's right flank. As Lee became aware that the Army of the Potomac was moving toward his right, he ordered Ewell to advance his corps and find the Union right flank. Lee sent his Rebel cavalry to see just where the right flank of the Federal army now was, and when Warren's midday report told of this Confederate incursion, five large Federal heavy artillery regiments under the command of Gen. Robert O. Tyler were sent toward the Union right. When the Rebel cavalry probe was followed by an enemy infantry advance, it would be these untried Yankee artillerymen who confronted Ewell's force of 6,000. What the artillerymen lacked in training and finesse, they made up for with their numbers and angry determination. Meade ordered both Hancock and Warren to send troops to assist Tyler. Despite a demonstration by Early's Rebels on his own 5th Corps front, Warren sent his aide Roebling with his corps' Maryland Brigade, and they were the only reinforcements sent that were actually engaged before the "Heavies" fight ended at dark. By chance, the men of the 1st Maryland Regiment, who had reenlisted and were returning from their furlough home, were coming down the road from Fredericksburg when they found their comrades from the Maryland Brigade fighting alongside the "Heavies." Without orders, the returning veterans of the 1st Maryland pitched in with their battling comrades. Ewell's attack was stopped in its tracks, and in the night, the Confederates withdrew back to their original lines.[89]

Regardless of what actually happened on Tyler's front, in his memoirs, Grant would credit Hancock's speedy reinforcement, rather than the courage and determination of the "Heavies" and the Maryland Brigade, with saving the day. It was a feat that 2nd Corps historian Francis Walker did not claim for his corps, whose members arrived when the fight was essentially over.[90] But Grant would also state that Warren, when ordered to get on Ewell's flank and rear to prevent him from retiring to his line, made so feeble an effort that the enemy was allowed to withdraw unmolested. General Humphreys, Meade's chief of staff, denies that Warren was ever given such an order, but was with his two divisions on his line, under orders to attack the entrenchment's in his front if there was promise of success. Warren, in fact, received an attack on his right front by one of Gen. Jubal Early's brigade's, ordered up by Lee in hopes of relieving the pressure on Ewell, who was some two miles away from Warren at the end of the battle. So Warren was not only fending off an attack by Early, but Ewell's movement was well beyond Warren's reach. It was pure fancy on the part of Grant's military secretary, Adam Badeau, that the 5th Corps was in a position to attack Ewell on May 19th.[91] It reinforces suggestions that Grant relied on the accounts of Badeau when writing his own accounts. Otherwise such similar mistakes are rather inexplicable. As for the apparent negativity of both Grant and Badeau toward Warren, historian Francis Walker would later say of Badeau and his unstilted criticism of Warren, among others, "That person is so eager to sacrifice reputations, as a burnt offering of sweet savor upon the altar of Grant's fame, that we may well disregard his imputations."[92]

Soldiers determined to kill and wound one another on the 19th were, by the next day, making jokes and exchanging newspapers on the picket line.[93] Friendly pickets often warned each other when the situation was changing. Bloodshed was narrowly avoided on the morning of May 21st, when Meade, upon receiving reports of sounds of movement on the Rebel line during the night, ordered 5th and 6th Corps pickets to advance and drive in those of the enemy to investigate.[94] Meade was understandably anxious to know of any Rebel movements or changes in the Rebel line, for Grant, hoping to tempt Lee out of his entrenchments, had sent Hancock's 2nd Corps on a march toward Richmond that would isolate them about 20 miles away from the rest of the Army of the Potomac.[95] But the 5th Corps had ample evidence that the enemy was still manning the breastworks in front of them in force. General Griffin of the 1st Division, known to speak his mind, offered, "The enemy is in force in my front, his artillery in plain sight, and before I advance my pickets, I desire this fact to be known. A far stronger force than my picket-line is visible." When Warren forwarded this comment to Meade, he snapped back that if they were satisfied that they knew the force and position of the enemy, they need not advance, but he could see no objection to them pushing out anyway. Warren, quite able to see an objection, directed Griffin to have the "pickets fire away occasionally at the enemy's, and ascertain all they can and report."[96]

Later that morning, with Burnside and Wright prepared to hold the lines at Spotsylvania, Warren and the 5th Corps began a ticklish daylight withdrawal from their front. The results were such that one might wish that the Army of the Potomac's attacks and advances during this campaign were as well thought out as their withdrawals. Russell's division, 6th Corps, charged with covering Warren's withdrawal, was well placed to surprise and check the Rebels who had followed the last departing elements of the 5th Corps off the field.[97] Lee was not only alerted to Army of the Potomac's movement by Warren's withdrawal from Spotsylvania, but his cavalry was already keeping tabs on Hancock and the 2nd Corps. Although Lee began his own withdrawal at midday on the 21st, he would not strike at the isolated Federal corps, but would instead interpose his army between the Army of the Potomac and Richmond, taking up a position that would protect the all important Virginia Central Railroad that connected the capital with the most fertile areas of Virginia.[98] As the armies, corps by corps, withdrew from the fields they had fought upon, the fight for Spotsylvania was over.

In movements that would place the corps of the Army of the Potomac three to four miles from one another, the 9th and 6th Corps withdrew to follow their army. The

Federals could only have been glad to leave Spotsylvania behind, a battlefield that had claimed nearly 18,000 of their comrades. Confederate losses are estimated at 9,000 to 10,000, half of which were Rebel prisoners captured on the 10th, 12th and 20th of May. Humphreys lists the total Federal losses, killed, wounded, captured, missing and sick sent to hospital over the period of the Wilderness and Spotsylvania as 37,335.[99]

One of Warren's biographers, Emerson Taylor, commenting on Warren and his service at Spotsylvania, observed that he was "a man of special gifts and temperament, a scientific soldier, he takes part in a rat fight. Again and again he is compelled to order frontal attacks against entrenchments, which could succeed only at a ruinous cost, when, as he is perfectly aware, sounder tactical methods would accomplish better results." Taylor goes on to suggest that the effect of the carnage, as well as the knowledge that he had lost the confidence of his commanders, had a very negative effect on Warren.[100] Did Warren suspect that in order to succeed in Grant's armies, one must do what one was told, do it quickly and without comment, and do it without regard to the consequences for one's men? By the time the Army of the Potomac was leaving Spotsylvania, it was very clear that neither Meade nor Grant were interested in hearing ideas or suggestions from Warren. Nor did they want any questions or comments regarding the orders sent to the 5th Corps. While Grant would listen to all of his friends from the West — Sherman, Sheridan, Rawlins, Horatio Wright, James Wilson and Baldy Smith — he did not want advice from Gouverneur K. Warren. Nor was Grant paying much attention to Meade's advice, though Meade did not yet fully realize it.[101]

Speaking of listening to Sheridan, Grant had allowed the cavalry commander and his troopers, after their poor performance at the Wilderness, to start out on May 9th on a raid with the expressed intent of fighting the Rebel cavalry. J.E.B. Stuart and three Rebel cavalry brigades, roughly 4,500 horsemen, had been dispatched to confront Sheridan's 10,000. By May 11th, Sheridan reported that he had ripped up ten miles of railroad track and destroyed two locomotives and three trains, along with a large amount of Rebel provisions. By happy accident, Sheridan had also recaptured 500 Federal prisoners of war on their way to Confederate prisons.[102] In addition, Stuart was mortally wound on May 11th. While the loss of Stuart was arguably of significance to the Confederates, it is debatable whether the damage Sheridan was able to do to Rebel property was lasting enough to be worth the sacrifices that the Army of the Potomac made as they struggled to fight and maneuver without cavalry at Spotsylvania and beyond. While Grant would continue to report that his Rebel foes were "whipped," Lee, as the armies left Spotsylvania, was convinced that the Army of the Potomac could only be disheartened and shaken by the bloody repulses they had received during their repeated attacks on Confederate entrenchments. Leaving the Rebels in possession of the field, the Union army left their dead unburied at Spotsylvania, as they had at the Wilderness. Rebel ordnance officers gathered up muskets, and reportedly collected 122,000 pounds of lead, which was recast at Richmond into balls that would be fired at the enemy again before the Overland Campaign was over.[103]

Lee did not give Grant the open-field battle he was hoping for as he left Spotsylvania. And Meade, still haunted by the criticism he received for Mine Run, commented, "Instead of coming out of his works and attacking us, he [Lee] has fallen back from Spottsylvania Court House, and taken up a new position behind the North Anna River; in other words, performed the same operation which I did last fall when I fell back from Culpeper, and for which I was ridiculed." And had Meade heard the rumors of political opposition in Washington that was blocking his promotion to major general? While Grant succeeded where others had failed at such things as diminishing the mass of manpower defending the capital in order to reinforce his army, an indication of his considerable influence, even he had his limitations. His choices of Meade and Sherman for promotion were meeting resistance, for there were politicians who urged consideration of the mind-boggling duo of Butler and Sickles for the appointments, defending these candidates with their theories regarding the necessity of diminishing "West Point influence."[104]

Eight

The 5th Corps at the North Anna and the Totopotomoy

After the 2nd and 5th Corps left Spotsylvania, and the 6th and 9th Corps withdrew to follow their army, the movements that Grant directed for his corps eventually positioned the corps three to four miles distant from one another. The country the combatants were moving into was open and well-cultivated, but cut by many streams and swamps that would present new difficulties. The Mattapony was a meandering watercourse that the Army of the Potomac would bump into again and again, or at least, one of its segments, which were designated the Mat, the Ta, the Po and the Ny. With Sheridan's cavalry still away from the army, the Federals were, once again, advancing blindly, but Meade was able to scrape up a contingent of cavalry to accompany General Hancock. General Torbert, who had been away from his command on sick leave since the Wilderness, had rejoined the army, and he took command of the 2nd Corps' cavalry escort.[1] Grant later observed, "We had neither guides nor maps to tell us where the roads were or where they led to. Engineer and staff officers were put to the dangerous duty of supplying the place of both maps and guides."[2] When Sheridan left on May 9th, he reportedly left only dismounted troopers and 600 wounded. In total, Meade was said to have been able to assemble five regiments of cavalry, which included a contingent that accompanied the Army of the Potomac headquarters.[3] It was a force wholly inadequate to perform the scouting and screening needs of the army.

Lee, upon learning that the Army of the Potomac was leaving Spotsylvania, correctly assumed that Grant was, once again, attempting to get around the Army of Northern Virginia's flank. According to E. Porter Alexander, Longstreet's chief of artillery, Grant may have thought he was laying a clever trap for Lee by isolating Hancock's 2nd Corps as bait, but Lee was not interested. Lee's eyes were focused on interposing his army between the Army of the Potomac and Richmond, and taking up a position that would protect the Virginia Central Railroad at Hanover Junction, the railroad that connected the Confederate capital with the most fertile areas of Virginia. Lee started Ewell's corps off immediately for Hanover Junction with Anderson's corps close behind. By noon on May 22nd, Anderson was on the south side of the North Anna, about 30 miles from his previous camp at Spotsylvania, and about a mile from Hanover Junction. Between his cavalry and the presence of soldiers with local knowledge, Lee could pick and choose the roads he would move over, and he sent Hill on a road parallel to that of his other corps. Lee's cavalry, now under Hampton's command, was actively keeping tabs on Federal movements, and even brought some of Hancock's captured dispatches back to Lee.[4]

As the 5th Corps pressed forward on the morning of May 21st, they were treated to a glimpse of their commanders, Meade and Grant and their staffs, at Massaponax Church, a scene now made famous by the photographs that were taken there that day as they considered reports and their untrustworthy maps. By 5 P.M., the 5th Corps reached Guinea Station with its bridge over the Po, and met surprisingly little resistance in taking that position on the unfordable river. Though Meade had mistakenly assumed that the crossing had been secured, he was fired upon by Confederate pickets when he had ridden ahead with only a small guard. The bridge was subsequently taken by Meade's headquarters cavalry, backed up by Griffin's 1st Division, 5th Corps, which dispersed the enemy cavalry in half an hour.[5] On that rainy night, Warren sent men out on all nearby roads to get their bearings, find the necessary bridges for crossings, and feel for the enemy.[6]

Grant's thoughts were not entirely on the Army of the Potomac, for it was on this day that he sent a telegram to Halleck, pondering what was going wrong in Butler's command at City Point. Grant was wondering whether part of the problem concerned one of Butler's subordinates, Gen. William "Baldy" Smith, who was thought to be one of "Grant's Men." While Smith had solved Grant's supply problems with his "cracker line" at Chattanooga, and he even supplied Grant with a number of ideas for military action in the East, Smith also had the reputation within the army of having no loyalty to his commanders after his outspoken criticism of Burnside's leadership of the Army of the Potomac. While Dana in Washington was pushing for Smith to replace Meade as commander of the Army of the Potomac, perhaps Dana and Wilson were pushing Grant a little too hard.[7] With Grant's description of Smith to Halleck hardly being a recommendation, one wonders if the Grant-Smith relationship was becoming strained, for Grant wrote that Smith, "whilst a very able Officer, is obstinate and is likely to condemn whatever is not suggested by himself." But beyond disparaging Baldy Smith, Grant was pressing for Butler's inactive force at Bermuda Hundred to be reduced to the minimum, sending the rest, including Smith and his corps, to the Army of the Potomac. Was this yet another example of Grant solving a problem with a recalcitrant subordinate by shifting him away from the scene of conflict? Did he think that the solution he had used to defuse Sheridan's conflict with Meade might work with Smith and Butler? It may well be.[8]

But to return to the Army of the Potomac's hard slog to the North Anna, Washington Roebling, Warren's aide, after placing men on all the roads surrounding the 5th Corps on the night of the 21st, didn't return to corps headquarters until 9 P.M. He was, nonetheless, back in the saddle before daylight on May 22nd, checking with the men he had left out on the roads guarding the 5th Corps' perimeter and exploring roads in the area. When Roebling checked on the two companies of cavalry that had been sent down the road to Downer's Bridge, he found them near Lebanon Church, and Roebling could see an enemy wagon train and ambulances moving rapidly south, unaccompanied by any troops. He sent a report back to 5th Corps headquarters, and for the next half hour pleaded in vain with Lt. Col. Edmund Mann Pope to capture the enemy wagons. Pope, who apparently had heard the wagons rumbling through all night without reporting it, refused to make an attack on the unguarded train. Roebling would later comment, "Here was a chance to capture the whole of Lee's wagon train; never was the want of cavalry more painfully felt. Such opportunities are only presented once in a campaign and should not be lost." Pope, who was this cavalry detachment's commander, was the acting assistant inspector general of Custer's 8th New York Cavalry. Pope had been captured in the summer of 1863 and had been exchanged, but did not rejoin the army until May 12th, too late to join Custer on Sheridan's cavalry expedition. Therefore Pope was with the Army of the Potomac instead of with Custer when this sorry event — Pope's failure to report or attack the Rebel train — took place. Though by Roebling's description Pope was a real liability, by 1865, Pope would become a brevet brigadier general of volunteers in the cavalry.[9]

Grant was growing cautious by the morning of May 22nd, and while Hancock was ordered to remain at his current position at Mitford, Warren was warned not to advance until the 6th Corps had come up. It was a plan that by nightfall would bring the Union corps within three or four miles of one another.[10] By the time the 5th Corps was allowed to advance on May 22nd, the enemy's rear guard was estimated to be about three hours ahead of them. As Grant acknowledged in his orders that morning, the Federal maps showed only two roads for the four corps to travel on, but, Grant commented, "No doubt by the use of plantation roads and pressing in guides others can be found to give one for each corps."[11] But lack of roads wasn't their only problem. As the Army of the Potomac passed through this landscape crisscrossed with streams, marshes and drainage ditches, the maps provided were so bad that it left the 5th Corps literally stopping at houses to ask for directions. While their map told them that they should

Spotsylvania to the North Anna (Ned Smith).

"Council of War" at Massaponax Church, Virginia. General Grant (leaning over back of bench) is examining a map held by General Meade (Library of Congress).

soon encounter the Mat River, the locals they encountered claimed to have never heard of it. Before the 5th Corps could find the Mat, hard marching had brought them up to the Confederate 1st Corps' rear guard, a contingent of Rosser's cavalry, John Chambliss's cavalry brigade supported by two guns of James Breathed's horse artillery at a landmark known as Doctor Flippo's house. Though keen to capture the Rebel horsemen's artillery, Griffin's 3rd Brigade succeeded only in driving the Rebels off the road where they had confronted the 5th Corps advance. Rumors and Rebel cavalry had delayed Warren's advance by only one hour, but by the time the 5th Corps reached its goal for the day, Harris Store, Lee's Confederates were already at Hanover Station in force. Grant's caution had prevented the purpose of the exercise, a much desired confrontation with Lee, from happening, and had also allowed the Confederates more than adequate time to place themselves in a another strong defensive position.[12]

On the 23rd, as the full realization that the maps they were trying to follow were useless, with roads and landmarks marked miles away from their true positions, the army was instructed to send out parties to search for bridges or fords by which they could cross the North Anna. When the 5th Corps encountered Torbert's cavalry, the 2nd Corps' cavalry escort, Torbert informed Warren that he was on the road the 2nd Corps needed to reach their assigned position. Warren gave away, and in an attempt to find a river crossing, the 5th Corps was reduced to following the lead of an elderly African American who had not been on the road they were traveling for more than 50 years. But the old man led Warren to a road that led to Jericho Mills, which, though no more than the site of a rowboat ferry, was a place where the river was fordable. While the other Federal corps were having difficulty finding their assigned crossing places and meeting substantial enemy resistance when they reached the North Anna, this little-known crossing, Jericho Mills, was unprotected, with the 5th Corps encountering only a few Rebel deserters and home guards.[13]

Although Warren believed that the enemy did not intend to make a strong stand at the North Anna, he hoped his corps' presence on the south side of the river would uncover all the nearby crossings for the other the Federal Corps. Then, too, there were the tempting sounds of an enemy locomotive just a few miles away. A chance to strike at the Rebel's railroads and rolling stock was not to be missed, and Warren took the initiative to start his corps across in the early afternoon. Warren had little option but to act on his own, for at the time he approached Jericho Mills he had no idea where Meade or Grant were, and when Warren's information on his advantageous position reached Meade, he, in turn, asked Grant what he wanted done. It was hardly a circumstance that lent itself to speedy communication or maneuvers.[14]

With Warren's batteries posted on the south side of the river to cover his corps' crossing, one of Griffin's brigades was the first to wade over armpit deep while a pontoon bridge was started. By the time Warren received Meade's order for the entire 5th Corps to cross, he already had two divisions on the south shore and deployed. Rebel prisoners had informed Warren that Wilcox's division of Hill's corps was waiting for the Federals a mile or two back at the railroad. While Warren apparently contemplated trying to get Pope's cavalry to go have a look, Warren had second thoughts, feeling it was beyond Pope's capabilities.[15]

By 6 P.M., Warren had brought his whole corps over the river, and while his last division was coming into position on the right of his battle line, the 5th Corps was attacked by elements of Gen. A. P. Hill's corps. The position that Warren had chosen was a strong one, but the opportunity to attack an isolated corps, not yet entrenched, looked promising to Hill, who had just returned to command the Army of Northern Virginia's 3rd Corps. Hill had become too ill to continue in command at the Wilderness, and had been replaced by Early. Having lost several weeks, Hill was apparently anxious to make up for lost time, but Hill was not the only Rebel commander feeling aggressive at the North Anna. While Lee's illness would limit his direction on the North Anna, Lee apparently had a strong inclination to find a weakness in the Federal front and attack them here on the river. But the illness that confined Lee to his tent took much of the impetus away from Rebel offensive.[16]

While the division on Warren's right was driven in, his center not only held, but provided reserves to restore order on the right, where well-placed artillery checked the Rebel assault. The enemy repulsed, the 5th Corps alone spent the night on the south bank of the North Anna, busily entrenching and confident that it could hold its own. Lee's hopes for this attack on an enemy corps in such a hazardous position were disappointed.[17] The severity of the 5th Corps' fight could be detected from army headquarters four miles away by the heaviness of the artillery and small-arms fire. Even Dana enthused in his report to Washington about Warren's action and the enemy attack "triumphantly repulsed." Lee, however, when he found out that Hill had only committed one division to attack the enemy, who had the river at their back, took his corps commander to task for failing to put in his whole force. Others told of Lee's great frustration at the North Anna, for he was heard to say, "We must strike them a blow — we must never let them pass us again."[18]

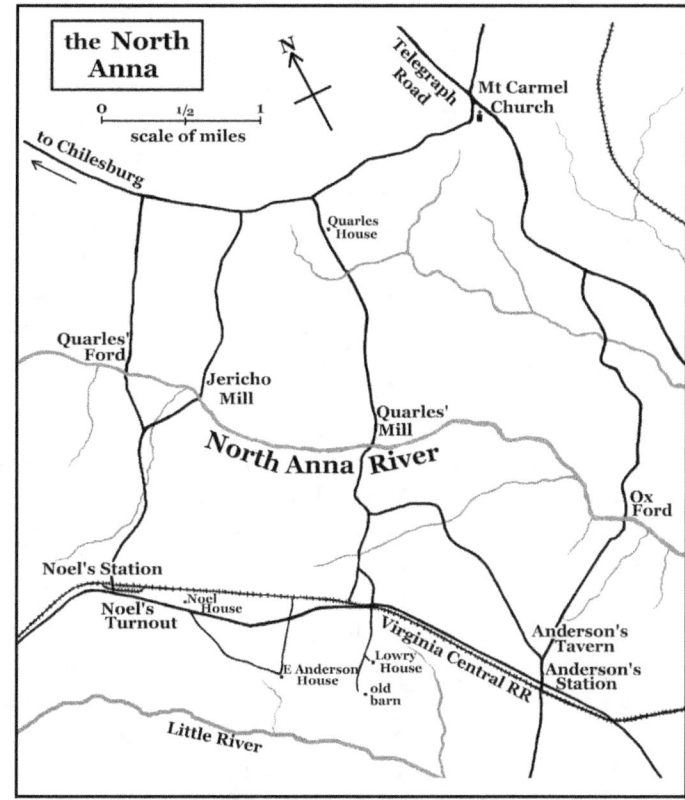

The North Anna area (Ned Smith).

Late that night Warren received congratulations from Meade, along with the news that the 6th Corps would come over the following morning to be positioned on Warren's right, and they would be placed under Warren's command. But the attack that Meade had hoped would be made on May 24th was thwarted by Lee's withdrawal in front of both the right and left of the Army of the Potomac's line. Grant initially misread Lee's movement as a complete withdrawal from the North Anna.[19] The center of Lee's line, however, had remained anchored on the Federal center at the 9th Corps' front, preventing Burnside from crossing the river, while Lee's left and right were thrown back, drawing the Rebel army into a V. With swamps and streams protecting his distant flanks, Lee's remarkable defensive position gave him excellent interior lines, while forcing his enemy to recross the river twice before reinforcements could be sent from one wing to the other. On May 25th, the 2nd, 5th, 6th and 9th corps were given orders to advance to feel for the enemy, and Warren soon sent back word that there was a very strong Confederate position in his front. When Meade endorsed Warren's report with the suggestion that not much could be done on Warren's front, Grant's reply was to let Warren cover his men in their advanced position, letting them rest all he could that day so that they would be "ready for active service." While Meade seemed noncommittal regarding further assaults, for once, Grant was apparently satisfied with Warren's efforts. Meanwhile, Federal reconnaissance soon proved that Lee's position made further Federal assaults on his main lines impossible. Grant had to be satisfied with the 5th and 6th Corps' destruction of part of the Central and Fredericksburg Railroad to the right of the Rebel lines. Of the five miles of railroad destroyed, Roebling cynically pointed out, "A good working party would repair it again in 10 days."[20] It was at the North Anna on this day, May 24th, that Burnside's 9th Corps was put under the command of Meade and went from being an independent command to being one of the corps of the Army of the Potomac. Whether it was Burnside's inability to make a crossing at Ox Ford that was the last straw, or merely the continuing frustration of trying to coordinate movements with Burnside and the rest of the Army of the Potomac, the change finally came about.[21]

While he was at the North Anna, Meade's seemingly mellow mood would be ruined by a dispatch from Sherman to Grant that Dana tactlessly read out loud to Meade. As Meade's aide Theodore Lyman reports, Dana read out that "Sherman, therein told Grant that the Army of the West [Sherman's army], having fought, could now afford to maneuver, and that, if his [Grant's] inspiration could make the Army of the Potomac do its share, success would crown our efforts." As Lyman described it, Meade's eyes bulged out about an inch, and he declared, "Sir! I consider that dispatch an insult to the army I command and to me personally. The Army of the Potomac does not require General Grant's inspiration or anybody's else inspiration to make it fight!" Lyman recorded that Meade fumed for the rest of the day, speaking of the western army as "an armed rabble."[22]

Sheridan returned to the Army of the Potomac on May 24th, and as previously stated, he had destroyed Rebel supplies, railroad tracks, cars, and locomotives. He'd recovered several hundred Federal prisoners, who had been captured at the Wilderness and were on their way to Richmond, and in a fight at Yellow Tavern, Gen. J.E.B. Stuart, the Confederacy's most respected cavalry leader, was mortally wounded. Sheridan had ridden within the inner fortifications of Richmond, an act that surely upset the residents of the city but hardly threatened them, for Sheridan could not take and hold the works through which he rode. While it is likely that Sheridan had been a considerable thorn in the enemy's side, it is debatable whether his weeks away from the Army of the Potomac could be called the sort of success that Sheridan claimed.

As cavalry historian Eric Wittenberg writes in his book *Little Phil*, in a chapter entitled "Sheridan's Mendacity," he is clearly shocked by the claims Sheridan made in the 1866 report of his 1864 exploits. According to Sheridan, the result of his part in the Overland Campaign after leaving the Army of the Potomac at Spotsylvania was "constant success and the almost total annihilation of the Rebel cavalry. We marched when and where we pleased; were always the attacking party, and always successful." After considerable study and consideration, Wittenberg begs to differ, declaring that Sheridan did not always experience success. Nor was he able to go anywhere he cared to unopposed during of his Richmond Campaign. As Sheridan's departure from Spotsylvania became known, Sheridan got into several tight corners that he was lucky to get out of after the Rebel horsemen, despite inferior numbers, trapped the Federals with intentions of destroying them. Sheridan essentially reported to Meade that he could have taken Richmond if he had wanted to, but chose not to.[23] But even if Sheridan's claims came anywhere near the truth, the other side of the story is that, for the Army of the Potomac, one can only guess at the number of lives, and perhaps battles, that were lost because the Federal army had to move blindly through unknown country with the enemy's positions unreported and unchallenged.

On Sheridan's return to the Army of the Potomac at the North Anna, his troopers were soon put to work. General Wilson's division was sent to demonstrate on Lee's left flank, while Meade's army began its withdrawal on the night of the 26th, and Sheridan was sent toward Hanover, where it was intended that the infantry would cross Pamunkey River. Grant commented, "It was a delicate move to get the right wing [5th and 6th Corps] of the Army of the Potomac from its position south of the North Anna in the presence of the enemy." Grant was finally convinced that Lee was not retreating into the Richmond defenses, and called for Smith and the 18th Corps to be sent to join the Army of the Potomac. During the night of May 26th–27th, Lee received reports that Grant was on the move away from the North Anna, and before the last elements of the Federal army were away, Lee put his army in motion. While sending his cavalry to check the Federals, Lee had his eyes on the rabbit warren of roads that led from the Hanover area to Richmond, once again determined to place himself between the Army of the Potomac and the Confederate capital.[24]

On May 28th, as the Army of the Potomac continued their crossing of the Pamunkey, Federal and Confederate cavalry forces, pushed out to ascertain the position of the enemy, met in a sharp fight at a crossroads called Haw's Shop. Though some historians claim this as a victory either for Sheridan or for Wade Hampton, the new commander of the Confederate cavalry, most consider the battle somewhat of a draw, for while Sheridan ultimately took possession of the battlefield at Haw's Shop, Hampton's troopers had held Sheridan back for between five and seven hours on the 28th, time enough for Lee's army, behind their cavalry's screen, to take up a strong position on the Totopotomoy.[25]

In his memoirs, Sheridan would claim that at Haw's Shop, he called upon Meade to send infantry support to the fight he was having against the enemy's cavalry and infantry. While Sheridan admits that Meade was correct in his assessment that there was no Rebel infantry confronting Sheridan at Haw's Shop, Sheridan still criticizes Meade's unwillingness to send nearby infantry to his assistance. No mention of Sheridan's request for support exists in the official record, nor is the matter mentioned in Sheridan's report for Haw's Shop.[26] By the end of the day, Sheridan had added Gregg's division and Custer's brigade to his force to tip the scales at Haw's Shop. But there is no doubt about one issue: Sheridan, who had been sent out to find the position of the Army of Northern Virginia, hadn't fulfilled that mission. The Rebel cavalry had taken up so much of Sheridan's time and attention on May 28th that when the Army of the Potomac was ready to advance on the Army of Northern Virginia on May 29th, they had no idea where it was. It is also of interest that on May 29th, while Sheridan withdrew his cavalry behind the infantry's lines to recover from their fight of the 28th, Rebel cavalry was still in the saddle screening Lee's army. The ever-mistaken Dana, on May 28th, reported to Washington, "Rebel cavalry is exceedingly demoralized, and flees before ours on every occasion."[27]

When darkness fell on May 26th, the 5th Corps began their uneventful withdrawal from the North Anna, beginning their long night by recrossing the river at Quarles Mill and marching on muddy roads toward the Pamunkey. The route they were given was a long one, and once again faced with unscouted and badly mapped roads, the 5th Corps marched on through to the Mangohick Church and the nearby Pamunkey.[28] Early on the morning of May 28th, the 5th Corps crossed the river at Hanovertown and began to reconnoiter and take up their assigned position. They were assigned to hold a mile-long line on the Army of the Potomac's left, forming a line so necessarily thin that Warren, after carefully laying out the line, had unsupported artillery placed in the gap at the center.[29] As the 2nd Corps was crossing the Pamunkey at Nelson's Ford at midday on the 28th, their commanders — Hancock, Meade and Grant — were watching their crossing. While a member of a 2nd Corps battery noted that many were curious to see Grant, he also commented that on May 28th "the men did not evince the slightest enthusiasm. None cheered him, none saluted him." Quite a change from the approval the soldiers had expressed 20 days earlier during the Army of the Potomac's passage from the Wilderness to Spotsylvania. Theodore Lyman, Meade's aide, noted in his diary that Grant suffered from a "sick headache" that day, and Lyman mentioned that Grant treated it by putting chloroform on his head. Chloroform, which came to be widely used as an anesthetic, was invented by an army physician, Dr. Samuel Guthrie, at Madison Barracks, Sackets Harbor, New York, one of Grant's postings early in his military career. It was apparently readily available in all Civil War surgeons' kits.[30]

On the morning of the 29th, Grant ordered three corps, the 5th, 2nd and 6th Corps from left to right, to each send a division forward along different roads to make a reconnaissance in their respective fronts with their entire corps in support, and the 9th Corps in reserve. Following divergent existing roads, the corps drew apart as they advanced. Wright, moving with considerable caution, made little progress with the advance of 6th Corps, while the 2nd Corps was delayed by an engagement with the enemy and Hancock proved unable to push across the Totopotomoy. This left Griffin's division of the 5th Corps, this time on the army's left, in a situation much like that at North Anna, when they were the first and only unit of the Army of the Potomac to make it across the stream. Griffin was ordered to continue up the road to Shady Grove, where, unbeknownst to Grant, Lee's army was concentrated and entrenching, waiting to discover the Army of the Potomac's intentions. Lee was, in fact, in a good position to block Grant wherever he was headed. The Army of Northern Virginia was ready to block a drive on Richmond, or an attempt on the Virginia Central at Mechanicsville. And as one of Lee's officer's described, never in the war was Lee more ready to attack given the slightest opportunity.[31]

With the Federal cavalry having again failed in its mission, and retired to recover from their ordeal at Haw's Shop, even Wilson's division, which had not fought at Haw's Shop, was unavailable, having been assigned to guard the army's slow-moving trains. So, as historian Louis Baltz described it, "Meade's infantry would have to become Grant's eyes."[32] Pushing forward about a mile after crossing the Totopotomoy, Griffin, with the 1st Division of the 5th Corps, first encountered Rebel cavalry, then enemy infantry skirmishers, which he drove a half mile before encountering the enemy's main line of battle. Though Griffin's reports indicated that the enemy was in force on his front, headquarters was apparently optimistic and spoiling for a fight. Griffin was ordered to keep the 1st Division up to the enemy, and while Griffin established his line across the Shady Grove Road, Cutler's division was sent to support him. Having observed the enemy moving in force toward Warren's left during the day, Roebling was sent out to do reconnaissance,

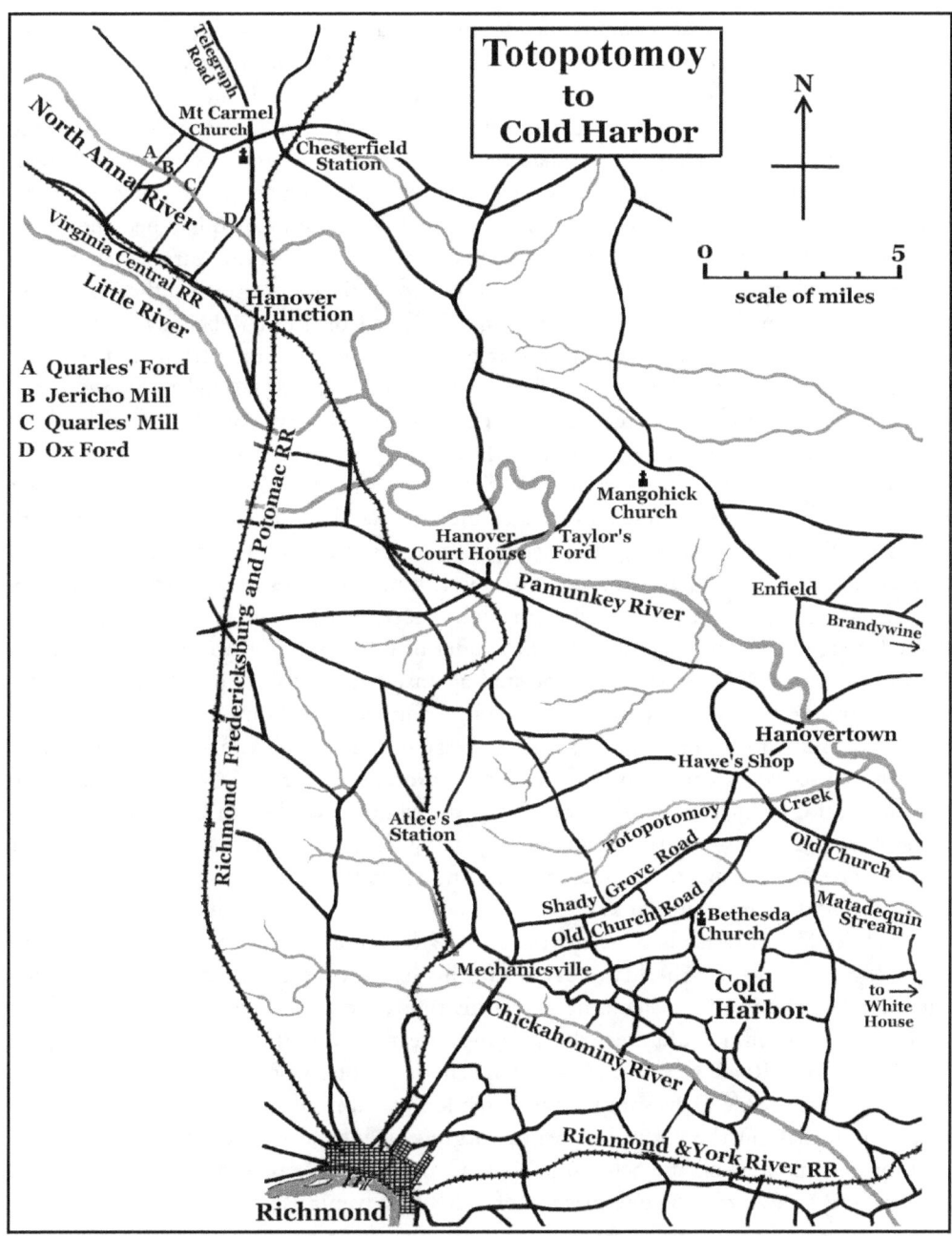

Totopotomoy to Cold Harbor (Ned Smith).

particularly looking for the Federal cavalry that army headquarters had told them was protecting their left. But at some point on the evening of the 29th, Warren received notice from Federal cavalry division commander David Gregg that the cavalry pickets on Warren's left were being withdrawn. And when Roebling was unable to find a single one of Sheridan's troopers nearer than four miles away, Warren sent out an infantry brigade to guard his left flank. Warren also requested on the night of the 29th that Burnside be brought up to fill the gap developing between Griffin and Hancock's 2nd Corps.[33]

On the morning of the 30th, the 5th, 2nd and 6th Corps, from left to right, were again under orders to close in on the enemy. Burnside, now under Meade's command, was ordered to come up and fill the space between the 5th Corps and Hancock.[34] Then, too, while elements of the 5th Corps were still advancing, the position of the 2nd Corps, still unable to cross the Totopotomoy, was static, while the 6th Corps had become mired down in swampland on the right. Early on the morning of May 30th, Warren began making futile requests that Burnside come up and occupy Griffin's position on the 5th Corps' right. Not only had the enemy retired from Griffin's front, but Rebel cavalry was still hovering on the 5th Corps' left, and Warren, expecting an attack from that quarter, wanted to reposition Griffin on the left to meet it. Warren also needed to juggle troops in order to arrange to relieve a brigade of Pennsylvania Reserves on the left of his line, whose terms of service were expiring that day.[35]

While Griffin's 1st Division pushed cautiously forward, two more of Warren's divisions followed in support. But while an initial connection had been made with Burnside's 9th Corps, the 5th Corps, advancing as ordered, soon outdistanced them, and Burnside would later complain that every time he caught up with the 5th Corps they'd move ahead or to the left. Meade apparently accepted Burnside's excuses, for Meade scolded Warren in the day's dispatches for not keeping the commander of the 9th Corps up to date on the 5th Corps' movements. Burnside also protested against relieving Griffin on the 5th Corps' right, claiming it would make his line too long. Hancock's inability to cross the Totopotomoy and Burnside's failure to come up and stay up on the 5th Corps' right meant that Warren had to worry about both of his flanks throughout the day. Warren was right to be worried, for Lee had noted the isolation of the elements of the 5th Corps' alone across the stream, and ordered Early, once again replacing the ailing Ewell as commander of the Confederate 2nd Corps, to make an assault, and three Rebel divisions began their move around the 5th Corps' left flank.[36]

While Warren was alone across the river with the enemy, he was expected to put some degree of trust in Sheridan's cavalry on his left and on the eventuality of General Burnside and the 9th Corps coming up on his right, the latter being expected to relieve Griffin so that Griffin could meet the growing threat on the 5th Corps' left. Moving out the Shady Grove Road, Griffin had found the enemy, strongly posted and ready to receive him on the other side of a swampy ravine, while the sound of skirmishing that had been going on all day on the corps' left began to grow in intensity. Warren had warned his division commander on the 5th Corps' left, Gen. Samuel Crawford, not to rely on the cavalry, and Crawford sent one brigade of his Pennsylvania Reserves, on this, their last day of service, out toward Bethesda Church to investigate the clamor on the left. Here, where there had been only Rebel cavalry, they discovered one of Ewell's division arriving on the 5th Corps flank. The Pennsylvania Reserves, rather understandably reluctant to give their all on this last day of their service, were scattered, but a stubborn, well-placed artillery battery, Lester I. Richardson's Battery D, 1st New York Light Artillery, checked the enemy long enough for the Federals to reform and a second brigade in reserve to come up. Warren, himself, brought soldiers from another division into the fight near Bethesda Church, and the enemy was repulsed. Sheridan, apparently without fear or concern of contradiction, would report that night that he had had cavalry on and connecting with Warren's left all day. The possibility of Sheridan being held accountable for whatever he did or did not do, regardless of orders, was apparently nonexistent.[37]

Shortly after 3 P.M. on May 30th, Warren sent word to Meade of the attack, again asking for reinforcements to come up to Griffin's unprotected right so that the 1st Division could shift to the left. While army headquarters was trying to find Burnside, they promised to send help from the 9th Corps, although at this point Meade rejected the idea of Burnside taking Griffin's position, stating that it was too great a space for the 9th Corps to occupy and still maintain a strong force in reserve. This was rather inexplicable because Warren was asking Burnside with his entire corps to relieve one division. And what was Burnside being held in reserve for, if not to assist in repelling an enemy attack. Burnside had demonstrated many times his inability to follow orders, or if he understood them, to follow them promptly. But forced by headquarters to depend upon the 9th Corps commander, Warren had had to withdraw Griffin's reserve to bolster the 5th Corps' left, and had already wearily sent an aide to find Burnside and lead 9th Corps reinforcements to Griffin. Warren sent back word that he, since he had already asked for Burnside's help, had hopes that by this time the 9th Corps had advanced and was already relieving Griffin's 1st Division. Warren assured Meade that, if Burnside arrived before dark, Warren would counterattack. But a query that arrived from the 9th Corps commander dashed all Warren's hopes for relief from the 9th Corps, for Burnside wrote asking why the 5th Corps line couldn't simply drop back to where Burnside was, rather than having his troops advance. Burnside was not advancing to relieve Griffin. There would be no chance to throw Griffin into the fight, nor would Warren be able to go on the offensive.[38]

While dealing with Burnside's inanity, and headquarters' unwillingness to press the 9th Corps or someone else to move, Warren, meanwhile, was receiving another Confederate attack on his left, and the uproar of the assault was heard at headquarters. Meade's response was to order Hancock, in the center of the Army of the Potomac's line, to attack on his front. A general shelling of Lee's main line and an assault by one of Hancock's divisions on the enemy in their front was all the support, infantry or cavalry, rendered to Warren that day. It is unlikely that the advance near dark by one of the 2nd Corps' divisions, or their capture of the enemy skirmishers' rifle pits on Hancock's front did anything that could be construed as aid to Warren. The 5th Corps repulsed the last Rebel assault, and in the night, Early's force withdrew from its confrontation with Warren. Early leveled criticism at Anderson, declaring that if Anderson had attacked Griffin on the 5th Corps' front while he attacked Crawford on the 5th Corps' left, they might have destroyed Warren's corps. Luckily for Warren, they did not. Seventeen hours after Warren's initial request, Burnside's men relieved Griffin on the right of Warren's line. The 5th Corps lost 500 killed and wounded in the day's action. That night, Sheridan, while reporting that he had driven Rebel cavalry to Cold Harbor in a "very handsome affair," still insisted that he had had troops connected to the 5th Corps' left the entire day.[39]

One perplexing attitude that both Meade and Grant seemed to share was the belief that they had Lee on the run and that his army was demoralized. The basis for this somewhat inexplicable belief was Lee's supposed unwillingness to fight outside his fortifications, staying only on the defensive. As just related, Lee was still willing to go on the offensive, as also evidenced by Gordon's May 6th attack at the Wilderness, Early's May

19th attack at Spotsylvania, and Hill's May 23rd assault at the North Anna. Yet on May 30, 1864, Meade wrote, "They [the Rebels] are now fighting cautiously, but desperately, disputing every inch of ground, but confining themselves exclusively to the defensive."[40] Grant's comments on the subject of Lee's unwillingness to fight were even more emphatic. On May 26th, Grant wrote, "Lees [sic] Army is really whipped. The prisoners we now take show it, and the actions of his Army shows it unmistakeably [sic]. A battle with them outside of entrenchments, cannot be had."[41] Comments such as these leave one to believe that the assaults Lee had made on the Army of the Potomac that May left little or no impression on U.S. Grant. Or was it simply Grant's habit to send reassuring banter to the administration, without regard for what was actually happening in the field? It seems a rather futile charade given that casualties were pouring into Washington's hospitals, and calls for reinforcements for the Army of the Potomac, starting as early as May 10th, were frequent.[42] The number of men actually available for duty was in a state of constant flux, for while reinforcements were arriving by the thousands, the number of casualties and sick was large, and quite a few units were reaching the day when their tours of duty were ending.[43]

The transition from the Army of the Potomac's fighting on the Totopotomoy to the battlefield at Cold Harbor was a somewhat static one for the 5th Corps, as far as movement was concerned, for while the other corps moved toward Cold Harbor, the 5th Corps remained at the same position it had occupied during the fighting on May 30th near Bethesda Church, except much extended.[44] Cold Harbor is best remembered for the costly and utterly futile assaults that the 2nd, 6th and 18th Corps made upon the enemy's earthworks. But the 5th Corps, and their reserve, Burnside's 9th Corps, paid a heavy price as well.

Despite Meade and Grant's insistence that the Army of Northern Virginia was fighting only on the defensive, Lee did, on a number of occasions, come out of the trenches to assume the offense, but only when it seemed that the odds were in his favor. Otherwise, he gave battle from the strength of his own fortifications, canceling the Federals' advantages in numbers and materiel. Regardless of how frustrating Meade and Grant found Lee's strategy, for the smaller and less well-provisioned of the two armies, it only made sense.

NINE

*Cold Harbor—
Another Tragic Muddle*

THE OPENING DAYS OF THE fight for Cold Harbor seemed plagued by confusion, and with little improvement in the planning and implementation of the assaults, it seemed unlikely in the extreme to result in success. When Grant had ordered Butler, still bottled up at Bermuda Hundred, to send him Gen. William (Baldy) Smith's 18th Corps, they came by water, moving up the James River and up the York to the Pamunkey.[1] Smith began arriving with more than 12,000 men at midday on May 30th at White House Landing, the place where the Richmond and York River Railroad crosses the Pamunkey. By 3:15 on the afternoon of the 30th, Lee knew through a Confederate spy, who had heard the news from the overly garrulous Federal cavalry commander, General George A. Custer, that the reinforcements for Grant from Butler were arriving. Though Grant assured Smith that his route to the Army of the Potomac was secure, Meade's chief of staff, Humphreys, heard Grant exclaim at army headquarters that, even though such a move by Lee would endanger Smith, nothing would please Grant more than if Lee tried to make a move around the Army of the Potomac's left flank, creating an opportunity for Grant to attack Lee.[2]

On the night of May 30th, Smith received orders from Grant's Chief of Staff, John Rawlins, ordering him to march to New Castle and await orders. With only about 10,000 of his 16,000 disembarked at White House, and before his wagons and ammunition had arrived, Smith had no idea, considering the orders he'd received, whether speed or numbers were more important. But anxious to please Grant, Smith began marching toward New Castle. While en route, Smith received a second order from Grant, reiterating that Smith's goal was New Castle, and reassuring Smith that his route would be well protected by Sheridan, who would also provide cavalrymen as guides. Smith's men were unused to long treks, and the 18th straggled badly in the heat during their forced march. When it turned out that Grant's headquarters had misdirected them, ultimately taking the 18th Corps several miles away from its goal, it added four or five hours to the corps' ordeal on these sweltering days.[3]

Grant was quite correct to be concerned that Lee might try to interfere with Smith's march to join the Army of the Potomac, for Lee, whose previous requests to Richmond for reinforcements had gone unfulfilled, was obviously distressed that Grant was receiving another infusion of fresh troops. Demanding that Beauregard send troops, Lee declared to him, "If you cannot determine what troops you can spare, the Department cannot. The result of your delay will be disaster. Butler's troops will be with Grant tomorrow." By 11 P.M. that night, Lee learned that Hoke's division was on its way to him from Beauregard. During the night of May 30–31st, Hoke's men left the lines at Bermuda Hundred and were loaded onto trains to make the journey to Lee's army. Meanwhile, Sheridan's orders, to preserve the safety of Smith's route, led to a duel with the Confederate cavalry for possession of Cold Harbor, a village with a valuable intersection of roads. As soon as Hoke's division began to arrive, they were ordered to Old Cold Harbor to support Fitzhugh Lee's cavalry in their fight with Sheridan.[4] On May 31st, Sheridan held Cold Harbor but felt compelled to withdraw at dark, until Meade ordered that the town be held at all costs, and the cavalry returned and dug in. It was almost Spotsylvania all over again, with the Federal cavalry willingly relinquishing and riding away from a key position on the battlefield.[5] While Sheridan was coping with Cold Harbor, the Army of the Potomac's headquarters had ordered James Wilson and his cavalry division to destroy the enemy's railroad bridges on the South Anna and protect the army's right. Wilson soon informed Meade that his orders had been changed by Sheridan to only protecting the army's right. Humphreys, Meade's chief of staff, informed Wilson that his orders had *not* been changed and that he was responsible for destroying the bridges *and* protecting the army's right. Wilson, stating that he didn't have the materials needed to destroy a bridge, requested that Meade's headquarters send him the powder and slow matches he would need. The results of Wilson's expedition were mixed, for while Wilson was able to destroy two railroad bridges, his division was discovered by Hampton's troopers, and one of the Federal cavalry brigades was cut to pieces. Wilson would again find himself cut off and isolated from the Federal forces, and it wasn't until early in the morning of June 3rd that Wilson managed to rejoin the army. Wilson would complain that the assignment to destroy the railroad bridges should have been given to the entire cavalry corps, rather than just his division.[6]

General U.S. Grant, Lieutenant Colonel T.S. Bowers, and General Rawlins at Grant's headquarters, Cold Harbor (Library of Congress).

It was expected that Sheridan's repossession of Cold Harbor would be disputed by the Rebels, and Wright's 6th Corps was ordered to make a night march of 15 miles through the darkness of May 31st–June 1st, with the expectation that Wright would reach Cold Harbor by dawn, in time to support Sheri-

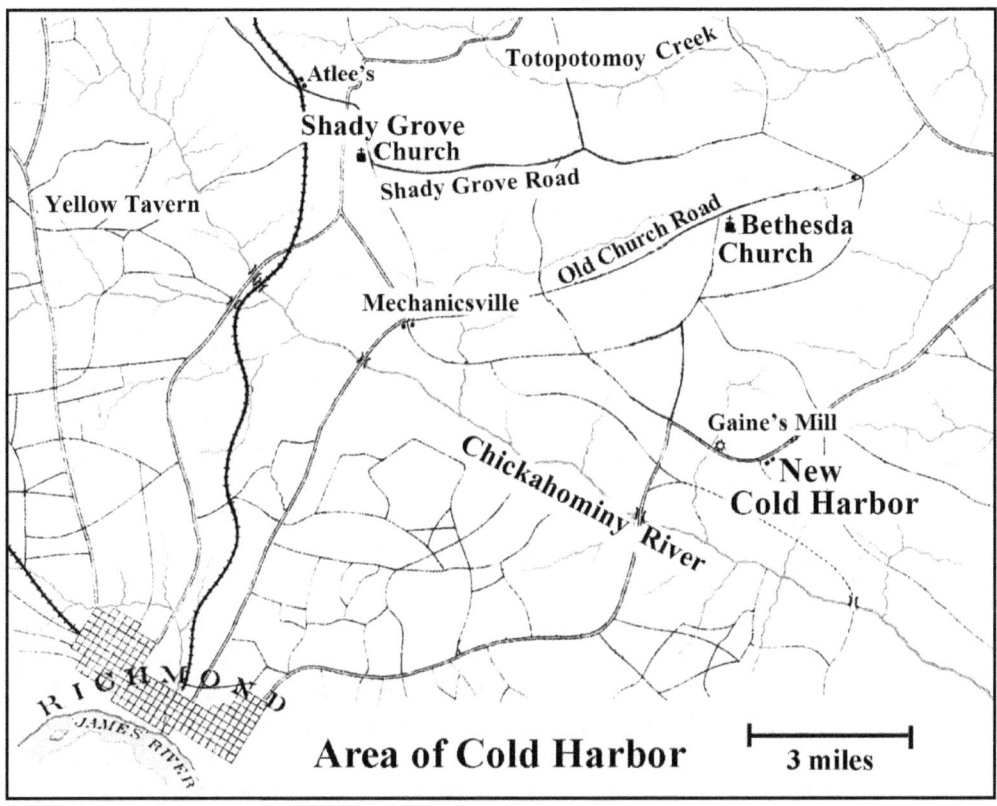

Cold Harbor area. Adapted from Plate LXXXI, #3, *Official Atlas* (Ned Smith).

dan against the expected Rebel attack. While Sheridan had notified headquarters that Hoke's division of Rebel infantry had arrived to support Fitzhugh Lee, he was apparently unaware of Kershaw's presence nearby or that Anderson was to the right of Early between Bethesda Church and Cold Harbor.[7] Traveling on narrow ill-defined roads, the 6th Corps' march was marred by confusion over the best route to Cold Harbor. It seems that Wright didn't choose the most advantageous route, and did not arrive at Cold Harbor until 9 A.M., well after Sheridan's men had already successfully repelled one Confederate attack.[8] Though Dana reported to Washington that Meade and Grant were "intensely disgusted" with Wright's performance, Grant would reserve all his vitriol for failures at Cold Harbor for Warren and the 5th Corps. In his memoirs Grant would comment casually on Wright's late arrival, saying that the 6th Corps "was expected to arrive by daylight or before; but the night was dark and the distance great, so that it was nine o'clock the 1st of June before it reached its destination." Dana did not spare Wright, however, in his report to Washington regarding June 1st. He stated that if Wright had arrived at dawn, as Meade and Grant had desired, Wright and Sheridan could have destroyed Lee's army. Whether this was Dana's fantasy or Grant's is open for conjecture.[9] Instead of uniting with Wright against the enemy, Sheridan, much as he had done on the first day at Spotsylvania at Laurel Hill, didn't join the infantry in their fight as the Confederate cavalry did. Instead, Sheridan took his troopers and rode away. Though headquarters believed that Sheridan was on his way to attack Lee's flank and rear, it was learned on June 2nd that Sheridan had not attacked because "his orders hadn't reached him in time," and he had already dispersed his troops.[10]

Meanwhile, Smith, upon reaching New Castle as he'd been ordered by both Rawlins and Grant, realized there must have been a mistake for, expecting to unite with the 5th and 6th Corps, Smith found no sign of the other corps. The sending of the 18th Corps to New Castle instead of Cold Harbor has always been portrayed as a bureaucratic mistake, but Dana's May 31st report to the administration clearly states that Smith had been sent to New Castle in order to support Warren and Burnside on the Totopotomoy, for Grant at that time, according to Dana's report, believed Lee had fallen back to south of the Chickahominy. Dana later implied to Washington that the time it took Smith to reach Cold Harbor was Smith's fault. Rather than admitting that Grant changed his mind and orders, Dana reported erroneously that Smith had waited for his wagons and supplies at White House. When Grant discovered the realities of Lee's position and intentions, as well as the possible threat the enemy posed to Sheridan, he sent word for Smith's weary men to retrace their steps and then head for Cold Harbor.[11]

While Smith was on the march to Cold Harbor, he was informed that the 18th Corps was expected to form a line between the 6th Corps at Cold Harbor and the 5th Corps on the Totopotomoy, two tasks that Smith, after his arrival, felt were close on to impossible to accomplish at the same time. Connecting the line between Wright and Warren would leave the 18th Corps, Smith believed, with so thin a line that he would not be able to attack. He therefore decided to not even attempt to connect with Warren, but would form in column for an attack, much the same plan that Warren suggested for a proposed assault. Wright, meanwhile, had been feeling his 6th Corps' isolation at Cold Harbor after Sheridan's departure, and had expressed the hope that Smith would arrive quickly. Headquarters did not share Wright's apprehensions and, believing that the Confederates at Cold Harbor had not had time to establish themselves, ordered Wright to attack as soon as his whole corps had arrived. In spite of the fact that most of the 6th Corps was in Cold Harbor by noon, Wright reported that he was still preparing for his attack at 2 P.M., an attack he managed to delay until Smith and the 18th Corps' arrival.[12]

When Smith began arriving at 3 P.M., an assault by the two corps was finally planned for 6 P.M. As daylight was fading, Wright was facing Hoke's division and Fitzhugh Lee's cavalry, while Smith was facing Anderson's corps. Smith was disappointed in his intention to form in column and not worry about his flanks, when he realized his advance was over an open field, leaving the vulnerability of his flanks quite clear to the enemy. And while Wright was facing a division, Smith was facing a corps, yet Wright called upon Smith for assistance, and Smith sent the nervous 6th Corps commander two regiments from the 18th Corps. There were moments of success during the attacks by the 6th and 18th Corps, but the slaughter was terrible, and the effects were not significant or lasting. On the 6th Corps front, Upton, a man known for his aggression, formed his brigade into four lines for the assault, with the newly arrived 2nd Connecticut Heavy Artillery, by far Upton's biggest regiment, making up the first three lines. Their experience was described by Upton as "murderous," and he commented further that "our loss was very heavy, and to no purpose," for it is said that the enemy line bent, but did not break. Only Brewerton Ricketts of the 6th Corps was able to find a weak spot, and there is confusion over whether his men actually occupied a portion of the Confederate defenses, or merely their picket posts, euphemistically called at times the enemy's first line. But regardless of what he took, Ricketts could not retain the position.[13] The first report states that Ricketts carried the enemy's rifle pits, or the skirmish line in advance of the enemy's main works. The second report, by the ever-partisan Dana who was still at Grant's headquarters, suggested to Washington that it was really Smith's 18th Corps' attack on June 1st that had enabled the 6th Corps to temporarily break the Rebel line. But even this was given short shrift, for Dana needed to tell the administration about how Wilson had burned two bridges, then fought his way out of the enemy's encirclement. He reported that Sheridan also had a fight, too, but was unable to force the Rebel cavalry's lines. In the fighting on June 1st, the 2nd Connecticut Heavy Artillery lost 53 killed, 187 wounded and 146 missing; their colonel, Elisha S. Kellogg, was one of those killed. Losses for the 6th Corps were about 1,200, while the 18th Corps lost was about 1,000 killed and wounded.[14]

While Grant's focus was understandably on the 6th and 18th Corps on June 1st, it was left to the Army of the Potomac's infantry remaining on the Totopotomoy — the 2nd, 5th and 9th Corps — to observe any movement of the enemy and occupy the enemy's attention. This was to be accomplished by pressing their men up against the Rebel lines as closely as possible without actually attacking, for the Army of Northern Virginia's positions, naturally strong with well-manned entrenchments, made the success of Federal assault unlikely. Strung out in a very long line in the vicinity of Bethesda Church, Warren was unsure of the 6th Corps' exact position. Nor did Warren know where and when Smith was expected to come into the line. Nonetheless, Warren was expected to extend his line for the five miles from Bethesda Church to Cold Harbor and reach for the new Federal line there. Yet the fact that this stretched the 5th Corps to the consistency of a skirmish line did not excuse Warren from headquarters' expectation that the 5th Corps could be expected to attack.[15]

During the day on June 1st, even though Warren took advantage of entrenchments and relied on seemingly impenetrable swamps to fill gaps in his line, he was nearly without any troops in reserve. Nonetheless, he had orders on the morning of June 1st to send a strong skirmish line forward and push up against the enemy to ascertain their position and strength. The 5th Corps began moving forward at 7 A.M., and as artillery commander Col. Charles Wainwright would later remember, his corps commander, Warren, was in a ugly mood. It is easy to speculate that Warren's anger was produced by being asked to do too many impossible things. He was expected to stretch his force in a line five miles long until finding the 6th Corps, or perhaps the 18th Corps, both at unknown locations. Warren was also expected to advance through the swampy landscape on his front to press up to the Rebel earthworks and report back to headquarters regarding the enemy's strength and movements. While it may have been enough to put any commander in an ugly temper, it is likely that Warren's mood was not sweetened by Wainwright's protests when Warren and Griffin directed his batteries to a place where he thought it was "too hot." The consensus reached at headquarters, that Lee was moving troops to his right toward Cold Harbor, was likely the result of some of Warren's own reports throughout the morning, for as his corps pressed forward against the Rebel lines, Warren sent his observations back to headquarters. Reports of Lee's shift to his right gave Grant and Meade the idea that here was an opportunity to attack the Confederates while they were moving. But

Lee's force was moving to their right in and behind the safety of their own entrenchments, where they'd only have to turn to the left to meet any assault on their lines from the Federals. So although the 5th Corps was facing the same entrenchments that were deemed too strong to assault on May 31st, on June 1st they were ordered to attack.[16]

Warren ordered Cutler's and Lockwood's divisions forward, and by 10:30 A.M. they were within sight of and coming under fire from the Rebel earthworks, but swampy mires that the Totopotomoy and Matadequin streams created in that area stalled their advance. By 11:30 A.M., Warren reported that his advance had been able to stop the Rebel's visible movement to their right, either because the 5th Corps' movement had now fully engaged the Rebels' attention, or because the enemy had merely finished their move to the right. By noon, when the 5th Corps divisions had reached the vast open field in front of the Rebel entrenchment, they came under the destructive fire of a Rebel rifled battery. When Warren reported at 1:30 P.M. that his force had been able to do no more than capture the enemy's picket-line position, he expressed the belief that only a strong column could take the enemy line. He also declared that if the Rebel position could be taken, only a large force, which he did not have, could hold it. Later that same day, when Warren's aide, Roebling, found Lockwood and part of his division lost and rushing through the woods in a belated attempt to obey Warren's order to connect with the 6th Corps line, it was the beginning of the end for Lockwood's field command. Warren was already displeased with Lockwood's performance, and finally, Warren and Grant found one thing they could agree upon. Lockwood would have to be removed from command.[17] In Lockwood's defense, he had been ordered to connect with the 18th Corps' right and advance with them during their 6 P.M. attack. But when Lockwood moved to connect with the 18th Corps, it was not where it was supposed to be.[18] As Roebling reported, the 18th Corps was some distance behind the 5th Corps' position, and there was a half-mile gap between the two corps. So when Dana reported that Lockwood was found lost "two miles in the rear," it was because the unfortunate Lockwood was trying to find Baldy Smith's elusive line. Lockwood's division would be given to Samuel W. Crawford, a favorite of Meade's because of his association with the Pennsylvania Reserves, Meade's old brigade. Crawford, in the coming months, would play his own unique role in fouling up the 5th Corps' performance.[19]

Warren and Grant's agreement on Lockwood would not carry over into Grant's assessment of the movements on June 1st. Among the many things that went wrong that day at and near Cold Harbor, Grant chose to place particular blame in his memoirs on Warren's failure to complete his assault on his front to the lieutenant general's satisfaction. Grant, with obvious disgust, would write, "Warren was ordered to attack him [Anderson] vigorously in flank.... Warren fired his artillery at the enemy; but lost so much time in making ready that the enemy got by, and at three o'clock he reported the enemy was strongly entrenched in his front, and besides his lines were so long that he had no mass of troops to move with. He [Warren] seemed to have forgotten that lines in rear of an army hold themselves while their defenders are fighting in their front." Had Warren been reluctant, once again, to spend the lives of his men to no purpose, or had he simply been asked to do the impossible and been unable to comply? It seems as though Warren made all effort to try to comply with headquarter's orders. It does seem that Grant was seeing what he wanted to see and "remembering" what he wanted to believe. For Hancock, too, experienced many delays in his advance up to the enemy earthworks that day, and had made reports much like Warren's regarding the unlikelihood of an assault having any success. Grant belittled Warren for worrying about the risk of enemy attack, while, interestingly, Hancock did suffer an attack by the enemy on his front that morning. And despite Grant's theory about "lines holding themselves," the 2nd Corps had to fight to get back the picket posts they had lost to the Rebel attack, while they were preparing for their ill-fated assault. While the 5th Corps had been advancing, or attempting to advance all through the morning and afternoon, finally, at around 3 P.M., Hancock made his assault on his front. It was a costly failure.[20]

In Dana's report to Washington regarding June 1st, he stated that Grant and Meade were both "intensely disgusted" by Warren's failure. According to Dana, Meade on this day apparently demonstrated just how ready and willing he was to throw Warren to the wolves, or to "Grant's Men" in this case, for as mentioned previously, there were a number of Grant's cronies who would have liked to acquire command of a corps or an army. Dana reported that "Meade says a radical change must be made, no matter how unpleasant it may be to make it; but I doubt whether he will really attempt to apply so extreme a remedy."[21] How ironic that Meade did not know that while Dana thought Wilson would make a dandy corps commander in place of Warren, he had Baldy Smith or Sheridan in mind to take Meade's command of the Army of the Potomac.

When the 6th and 18th Corps made their 6 P.M. attack on June 1st, Meade questioned Warren as to the practicability of his line going in with the 6th and the 18th. Warren replied that his attempts to discover what Rebel force was on his right were being hindered by swamps and that an advance by the 5th Corps would be improper if he hoped to avoid an enemy attack from that quarter. Nonetheless, he would try to send a division to his left when Wright and Smith's attack began, and demonstrate along his whole front. Warren's attempt to send a division to join Wright and Smith's assault turned into the lost Lockwood's debacle, so the 5th Corps' only contribution in that quarter was skirmishing by Roebling's reconnaissance force on the 5th Corps' left.[22]

Warren's report to headquarters at 4:15 P.M. on June 1st, that he was concerned that while he was trying to advance as ordered, the enemy would attack his right, no doubt annoyed General Meade. But by 7:15 P.M., Warren was reporting that the Rebels had done just that, with a particularly severe assault on the 5th Corps' right by Gordon's division and Ramseur's brigade. While Griffin's division had been able to repulse the attack with significant loss to the enemy, this attempt by Early to probe the Federal right had driven in Burnside's force, causing considerable turmoil in the 9th Corps. Though Dana would later tell the administration about the severity of the enemy's attack on the 5th Corps and Griffin's successful defense, on June 1st as it was happening, Dana had telegraphed Washington that the 5th Corps wasn't doing anything beyond having a "lively skirmish."[23]

That night Warren reported that he was pushed up against the enemy line, as he had been ordered so many times to do. Meade, meanwhile, was described as being "in one of his irascible fits" at headquarters that night. "First he [Meade] blamed Warren for pushing out without orders; then he said each corps ought to act for itself and not always be leaning on him." Meade would also observe that Wright was slow, and then had fits when it was reported that Baldy Smith "had brought little ammunition, no transportation and that 'he considered his position precarious.'" Meade's response to the latter was, "Then, why in Hell did he come at all for?" While Meade's aide, Theodore Lyman, acknowledged that when Meade was in one of these rages that they "were always founded in good reason though they spread themselves over a good deal of ground that is not always in the limits of the question."[24] But it seems that Grant chose to attend particularly to Meade's complaints about Warren. Grant would later observe of the 5th Corps commander's repulse of the enemy that evening at Bethesda Church, in a most backhanded compliment, "There was no officer more capable, nor one more prompt in acting, than Warren when the enemy forced him to it."[25]

During the afternoon of June 1st, Hancock was ordered to withdraw the 2nd Corps from the far right of the Union line after dark, making all efforts to bring his troops to the Federal left between the 6th Corps and the Chickahominy River by early the next morning. Meade, confident that the 2nd Corps would be in position by dawn the next day, urged Grant to schedule an attack for that hour. Meade queried Grant about his plans for the next day, and despite Warren's loss of 200 as he pressed forward and extended to the left, Meade added, "Warren does not seem to have effected anything in his front, except repulsing attacks made on him." Meade suggested to Grant that Warren should be ordered to attack in conjunction with the others. And though Smith had lost roughly 1,000 soldiers in his June 1st assault, Meade commented that he did not believe Smith had been much engaged that day. Grant advised Meade to delay the morning attack until Hancock was actually in supporting distance and, by all means, have Warren attack with the others. While Warren had done all he could to inform Meade of the unpromising conditions on his front, he acknowledged late on the night of the 1st that he would do his best to obey his orders to attack the next morning.[26]

In a letter home this day from Cold Harbor, Meade wrote that the Rebels had again taken up a strong position and entrenched themselves. His mind already moving beyond this confrontation, Meade cooly observed, "This compels us to move around their flank, after trying to find some weak point to attack.... We shall have to do it once more before we get them into their defenses at Richmond." But before any attempt to move around the Army of Northern Virginia would be made, a bloodbath awaited the Army of the Potomac, as they attempted "to find some weak point to attack" at Cold Harbor.[27]

Though Dana had reported that Meade and Grant were disgusted with Wright's slowness, Meade nonetheless consulted Wright on the night of June 1st, asking for his recommendations for the next day. Ironically, though Meade expressed no empathy for the scanty offense or defense that Warren could manage with his five-mile-long line, Meade admitted to Wright, "I do not like extending too much. It is the trouble we have had all along of occupying too long lines and not massing enough." Had Warren heard this, he undoubtedly would have agreed, but Wright responded with a request for reinforcements, stating that his position was not secure. Wright stated that if Hancock would come up on his left and in support of the 6th Corps, "with his aid at daylight I think we might succeed in carrying the rest of the enemy's works, or at any rate extending our line to the Chickahominy.... I shall be ready to renew the attack as soon as he is in position." Though Meade reminded Wright that Hancock would be making the same long march that the 6th Corps had had to make previously, Wright, forgetting his own difficulties and lateness, commented to Meade, "He [Hancock] should get here before daylight, or I may lose what I have gained."[28]

During the night, however, Meade's plan for a dawn attack on June 2nd unraveled. It seems that Meade had all his hopes pinned on Hancock arriving on the army's left early enough on June 2nd to form on Wright's left and rear for a successful attack. Francis Walker, the 2nd Corps historian, noticed the particularly urgent tone of Meade's orders to Hancock, and Hancock's instructions to attack once in position, with or without the 6th Corps. But one of Meade's engineers, William H. Paine, in attempting to lead one of Hancock's 2nd Corps divisions by a short cut, led them into a road too narrow for the corps' artillery, thereby delaying their arrival until 6:30 A.M.[29] While the 2nd Corps arrived in an exhausted condition, Smith's 18th Corps, though more or less already in position, was not ready to make an attack. With the urgency of Grant's orders when they had arrived at White House, the 18th Corps had marched to join the Army of the Potomac before the arrival of their supply trains. By the night of the 1st, when Meade ordered the 18th Corps to be ready for a dawn attack on June 2nd, Smith, having already informed Meade that his men were low on ammunition, with increasing impatience informed headquarters that his troops must be resupplied before he could do anything.[30]

The June 2nd attack was finally postponed until 5 P.M., and Hancock, Wright and Smith were instructed to make use of the intervening time to probe for a suitable weak point for their attacks. Hancock was informed that in his position, now on the far left of the Army of the Potomac, he would be assisted in picketing the gap between his left flank and the Chickahominy, as well as the nearby crossings on that river, by a strong force from Sheridan's cavalry. The rest of Sheridan's force was given permission to leave the front and reprovision. While Sheridan reported late on the morning of June 2nd that he was sending a division to connect with the Army of the Potomac's left, by 5 P.M. on June 2nd, Francis Barlow, Hancock's division commander on the 2nd Corps's left, reported that the cavalry division that had been on his left had been withdrawn, and one regiment of cavalry left in its place. Barlow would report, "I do not think that the cavalry on our left are any protection, and we must rely on ourselves." On the right flank, the situation was similar. Though Wilson had been ordered to connect with the army's right flank as soon as he completed his bridge destruction, Burnside reported that he could find no cavalry on the army's right flank.[31]

Meanwhile, Meade began issuing orders for the 5th and 9th Corps. Warren was instructed to extend his left in order to unite with Smith's 18th Corps line, but that was not all. He must also contract the 5th Corps' right "to such extent as to make one-half his force available for attack." It was expected that this would bring Warren's right to the vicinity of Bethesda Church. But that still was not all. While Warren made these difficult adjustments to his four-to-five mile line in the face of the enemy, Burnside was to simultaneously withdraw from his position on the Army of the Potomac's right, and mass behind the 5th Corps' right where he would assist in protecting the army's flank and supporting Warren's line.[32] If all had worked perfectly, it would still have left Warren with a line three miles long, the left of which would have been chiefly held by artillery. It was a complicated bit of business at best, but when the maneuver had to be coordinated with Burnside, it developed into a disaster. Burnside did not understand his orders, though in this case, it was understandable, and at 2 P.M. on the 2nd, Warren was still waiting for Burnside to move. Meanwhile, though Warren had informed Meade early that morning that he felt he could defend his five-mile-long line against anything the Rebels could

General Gouverneur Warren and his staff (National Archives).

throw at it, he still felt he was too weak on both his flanks to attack. Meade nonetheless sent the order for Warren to attack on his front at 5 P.M., while holding part of his force "ready to cooperate in such a manner as may be required." Nor did Warren's description of swampland — so dire that an aide's horse had drowned in it when he tried to cross — in any way deter Meade from insisting that Warren must establish a picket line that joined Smith's right in the vicinity of the local landmark, Woody's House.[33]

While Warren and Burnside were still contending with Early's Corps on their front and flank, Early had been reinforced by Heth's division. The 9th Corps commander was slow to respond to orders on the best of days, but with orders as confusing as these, neither Burnside nor Warren was confident that they fully understood headquarters' intentions or their own responsibilities. Later in the afternoon, Warren queried Army of the Potomac headquarters as to whether it was his or Burnside's responsibility to hold the army's right. Meade's answer was that the 5th Corps was to hold both its own front and the army's right, while Burnside massed in Warren's rear.[34]

When Burnside finally began his withdrawal at 4 P.M. in the midst of a thunderstorm, within a half hour Warren was surprised by a Rebel attack on his right flank. As Burnside had begun to disengage, the enemy had been quick to follow, and when they struck the 9th Corps during their movement, Burnside's men gave way. Before Warren knew that the 9th Corps had finally begun to retire, the Rebels came in between the 5th Corps' skirmish line and their main line, capturing around 400 of Warren's pickets. Luckily Griffin's 1st Division, massed at Bethesda Church awaiting their own movement, was able to deploy to meet the attack, successfully checking the enemy advance, and then driving the Rebels back. Inexplicably, Grant would express great anger in his memoirs that the 5th Corps had not counterattacked this day. Had Grant not been told at the time that Griffin, though his division was stretched into one line trying to maintain the connection between the two corps, had nonetheless successfully repelled the Rebels, then made an assault on his attackers on June 2nd? Or did Grant merely forget that Griffin's counterattack that day drove Rodes' division all the way back to the Shady Grove Road?[35] The enemy having cut the telegraph wires between the 5th Corps and army headquarters, Warren informed Meade by courier of the attack. At 2 P.M., Grant, citing the "want of preparation for an attack this evening, and the heat and want of energy among the men from moving during the night last night," postponed the assault that had been scheduled for the afternoon of June 2nd at 5 P.M. until 4:30 A.M. on the 3rd. In this case, even the favored Hancock was getting a dose of Grant's disapproval when he did not accomplish the impossible.[36] Besides the delay already mentioned, when the 2nd Corps was misdirected, Hancock patiently reported at 6 A.M. on June 2nd that though he would "admit no unnecessary delay," it would be several hours before he could form up for an attack. He explained that he had just arrived upon ground he didn't know, that the 12 regiments he had left on picket during his withdrawal from in front of the enemy had been unable to leave their position on the army's far right until two that morning, and that his corps was extremely fatigued from the dust and length of the march. While Warren held the army's right opposite an aggressive enemy, he nonetheless received orders late on the night of June 2nd, "The major-general commanding expects you to attack in the morning at the hour appointed," in this case, at 4:30 A.M. [37]

The main attack on the morning of June 3rd was ordered to be made by the 2nd, 6th and 18th Corps on Lee's right, a naturally strong position made stronger by well-manned entrenchments that the enemy had then been working on for 36 hours. And Rebel artillery was in position for direct and flanking fire over the open ground the soldiers would cross. The conditions on the 5th Corps' front promised no more success than those on the Union left, but after the 9th Corps had finally completed its move to the right rear of the 5th Corps, Warren's scout, Roebling, discovered on the night of June 2nd that the Rebels' left flank lay all but unprotected. First going to Burnside, who took no notice, Roebling was then sent by Warren to Meade. The telegraph still down, Roebling was entrusted to not only explain the conditions on the 5th and 9th Corps' front, but to convince Meade that a great opportunity to destroy Early's corps existed there on the Federal right. Warren urged Meade to come the next morning and take command of the attack on the Rebel left flank. Roebling, who was an intelligent, articulate and daring aide and scout to Warren, was, perhaps unfortunately, the same man who had carried Warren's message to Meade at Mine Run, when Warren took it upon himself to call off the scheduled attack. Was it impossible for Meade to trust Warren or Roebling again? Apparently it was, for Meade refused, telling Roebling sarcastically that what he intended to do the next morning after ordering his coffee at 3 AM, "at 4 he was going to mount with his staff and at 6 he would smash the rebel army at Coal [sic] Harbor."[38]

Meade was undoubtedly still smarting from Grant's impatience and criticism expressed regarding the necessary postponements of June 2nd's attack until the next morning, but Meade's reaction was apparently more favorable regarding Warren's request that either Burnside or Warren be put in command of the Union right for an attack on the Rebel left. Meade sent Roebling to see Grant with the proposition. Grant showed scant interest in the dangling Rebel flank within reach of the 9th Corps, commenting only that there was an opportunity there if the Rebels were still there in the morning. But Grant went on to comment that he did not think it proper for Warren to be put in command on the army's right over Burnside, and Meade ultimately sent instructions for Warren and Burnside to cooperate, or as the disgusted Roebling expressed it, to "be good boys and not quarrel." Arriving back at Warren's headquarters at 2 A.M. on a borrowed horse, for his had been stolen at Meade's headquarters, Roebling also brought word that the 5th and 9th Corps were to attack as ordered with the rest of the army at 4:30 A.M.. Furthermore, if the enemy gave way at all, they were to follow closing to the left and south, a "manifest impossibility," as Roebling would later note, "inasmuch as the enemy was due North of us."[39]

Cold Harbor historian Louis Baltz strives to understand, as many have, how the tragic and utterly futile assaults that the 2nd, 6th and 18th Corps were ordered to make on June 3rd could have occurred. Baltz suggests that it was because Meade and Grant both seemed to be convinced that Lee and his army were on their last legs. They drew this conclusion from Lee's perceived unwillingness to fight outside his trenches, and though numerous examples of Lee making offensive moves against the Army of the Potomac can be cited — ample proof of Lee's continued aggression — Grant seems to have been oblivious to them. They did not fit Grant's theories on Lee's growing weakness, so, apparently, they did not need to be considered. So while Grant, having expressed his impatience at the canceled assaults of the day before, had ordered an early morning assault for June 3rd, he left the details of the attacks to Meade. Meade made the unfortunate decision of leaving the details of the assaults up to the commanders of the 2nd, 6th and 18th Corps. While it might be argued that each corps commander could surely make the best decision on where it would be best to attack on his own front, there were issues of coordination. As it turned out, each corps would attack on its own, with no reference to what was going on on their flanks, and they therefore risked being subjected to the enemy's flanking fire, which could only have been avoided by a simultaneous Federal advance.[40]

Washington Roebling (Roebling Collection, Institute Archives and Special Collections, Rensselaer Polytechnic Institute, Troy, New York).

Meanwhile Meade, after having

General U.S. Grant at his Cold Harbor headquarters (Library of Congress).

endured the months of rancorous criticism that had been inflicted on him regarding his own lack of aggression, was not about to let anyone outdo him in demonstrating his willingness to attack, and attack again. As Meade threw his five corps against the enemy, Grant, a mile behind the lines on June 3rd, was contemplating his complicated move across the James River, and hoping that, if nothing else, the Army of the Potomac would keep the Army of Northern Virginia in place in order to ensure the success of Gen. Hunter's expedition outside Richmond.[41] While his engineer, Comstock, suggested that they were wasting time at Cold Harbor, he urged Grant to use the Army of the Potomac to move on and destroy Lee's railroads, while Meade suggested that the cavalry should do it. The thought of sending Sheridan to join Hunter held great promise of success in Grant's imagined plans for upcoming campaigns. How much attention, if any, was Grant giving to the reports Meade was sending back to Grant as he received them from his corps commanders on the morning of June 3rd?[42]

Only the first few reports arriving around 5 A.M. on June 3rd held any good news, and Meade sent a message to Grant at 5:15 A.M., "General Barlow reports that he had enemy's works with colors and guns." But by 6 A.M., the good news had ceased. Though Meade reported to Grant that Barlow had been unable to hold the Rebel works, he commented that, while they were forced to retire a short distance, they were "attacking again. Colors advancing and near the works." Meade would not allow the attacks to stop.[43] The destructive fire and crossfires from Rebel small arms and artillery under which the 2nd, 6th and 18th Corps attacked at 4:30 A.M. allowed only one breach of the Rebel main line in front of the 2nd Corps, and that could not be held. Cold Harbor was yet another battlefield on which the soldiers, having had time to contemplate the assault they would be asked to make, had pinned their names and addresses to their uniforms so that their bodies could be identified.[44]

While some troops advanced as close as 30 yards from the Rebel breastworks, they were unable to carry them, so they dug in. In little more than an hour, the main Federal assault and any forward movement by the 2nd, 6th and 18th Corps were over. When Meade asked Grant at 7 A.M. whether the attacks should continue if they were unsuccessful, Grant advised Meade to suspend the assault the moment it became apparent it could not succeed.[45] Apparently not yet feeling absolved from pushing on, Meade continued to urge further attacks, and it was after noon, on definite orders from Grant, that the assaults were finally, officially suspended. Badeau, Grant's military secretary, asserted that they had heard that the morning's losses were no more than an apparently inconsiderable number of 3,000, while other sources put the losses in the three corps at between 4,000 and 7,000 killed and wounded. Yet Grant would write to Halleck at 2 P.M. that, "our loss was not severe." Perhaps Confederate general Evander Law said it best in his comment on the slaughter: "It was not war; it was murder."[46]

As it has been suggested that the spirit with which the three corps made the main attack on June 3rd may have been lacking, a look at the corps' movements and deployments is of interest. While accounts do contain some incidents of units failing to advance, or even later, refusing to move, it is more a story of grim and violent attacks that eventually all failed. The 2nd Corps, on the army's left, again put soldiers of the newly arrived heavy artillery, in this case the 1,900 men of the 7th New York Heavy Artillery, on the front line for the assault. The theory was that the "heavies" would rush the enemy's rifle pits and trenches while the veterans in the second line would push through and maintain "the momentum of the assault."[47] The whole thing rather smacks of sending sacrificial sheep across a mine field. It was here on Hancock's front that Barlow's troops were lucky enough to find a place in the Rebel line where the trenches had flooded and the enemy troops had withdrawn. But even though the 1st Division, 2nd Corps, commander,

Francis Barlow, was able to break the Confederate line, as Baltz describes it, the "initial penetration was becoming a trap instead of a wedge. The assault was turning from success to disaster as no support was coming up to ensure victory." Ultimately Barlow was driven out, and the loss of men, particularly a proportionately large number of officers, was fearful.[48]

Smith's 18th Corps entered the conflict on June 3rd feeling like they had something to prove. The veterans of the Army of the Potomac had razzed their Army of the James compatriots, calling them "parlor soldiers." And Smith, having tangled with Meade with his unfair criticism, still felt that the urgency of Grant's orders justified his leaving White House without his trains. In short, Smith was in the mood for a fight, but when Smith, on the right of the army's three-corps main attack, asked Wright, in the center and on Smith's left, what the plan of attack was so that he could coordinate his own movements, Smith was startled to receive the reply. Wright told him that he was "going to pitch in." At this point, Smith realized that he was on his own. Smith's attack in column was heavy and determined, an assault the enemy described as "ten lines deep" and enough to "sweep our thin lines from the face of the earth." But when the Confederates opened on Smith's advance with double charges of canister, it destroyed any hope of success. And at close quarters to the Rebel small arms, one soldier noticed how much more vicious a ball was at close range as compared to one half-spent fired from a distance. Though failure was plain, Smith was not willing to admit defeat after only one assault, but he admitted to Meade that his men were "much cut up" and that there was no chance he could succeed on his front unless the 6th Corps attacked with them. It was a theme that Hancock would also dwell upon, as fire from both his own front and from the 6th Corps' front hammered his men. Meanwhile on Smith's front, Law's comment on the murderous nature of the day's fighting was made while watching the 18th Corps' assault, and another Rebel commented, "It was one of the bravest and most useless charges I witnessed."[49]

The actions or inaction of Wright and his 6th Corps in the Federal center did indeed impact greatly on the progress that Hancock's and Baldy Smith's attacks could make on the left and right, respectively. As Baltz observes, apparently a lot of the fight had gone out of Wright and the 6th Corps after their June 1st attack. In fact, while the Rebels on Wright's front witnessed the storms that were breaking on their left and right on Hancock's and Smith's fronts, they waited, ready for the attack on their own front that did not come. Wright insisted to Meade that the 6th Corps was in a position in advance of the other two corps, and he must therefore wait for them to come up before making his own assault. By 7 A.M. Wright had nonetheless reported to Meade that his troops had captured enemy rifle pits, and while the 18th Corps had done so also, Wright claimed that Smith was falling back, while he was pushing on.[50] In reality, even the aggressive Upton admitted that his men simply did not move, and it is estimated that roughly 40 percent of the 6th Corps did not advance on June 3rd. As Johnson Hagood, the Rebel commander of the South Carolinians on Wright's front later said, he wasn't even aware there had been any serious assault on his line. Baltz further observes that with Wright's lapse, "the assaults of Hancock and Smith were doomed to failure." As the dreadful morning wore on, it was Hancock, and Hancock alone, who ultimately was given any discretion as to when to halt the fighting on his front. And as Baltz points out, "Lacking the discretion that Hancock enjoyed, Wright and Smith were forced to act out a farce." Swinton, a correspondent for the *New York Times* reported a number of troops in the two other corps, who, when ordered to advance, refused.[51]

To return to the theme of whether or not Federal bravery displayed itself on the field at Cold Harbor, perhaps the most poignant, if terrible, tribute to Federal valor on June 3rd was offered by a Confederate officer, Lt. Col. Charles S. Venable, on Lee's staff. He said of the Federal casualties, "The dead and dying lay in front of the Confederate lines in triangles, of which the apexes were the bravest men who came nearest to the breastworks under the withering, deadly fire. The battle lasted little more than one brief hour, beginning between 5 and 6 A.M."[52] It is also sad to contemplate that those who gave so much on that field would be left there to die without aid from those who sent them there, as was the case in the coming days. Wounded and dying had lain on the field for two days, or until June 5th, when Grant proposed to Lee that both sides go out and pick up their wounded and dead. Lee responded with a demand for Grant to request a formal flag of truce, which was considered the responsibility of the defeated party. More wrangling ended in several more days being lost, and finally, on June 7th, the few survivors on the field were rescued. As historian Ethan Rafuse points out, it had to have been embarrassing for Grant to have, finally, asked for a truce, a public admittance that the Rebels he had reported to Washington as being "whipped" still had plenty of fight in them.[53]

On the Federal right, though the 5th Corps line had been compressed to cover a mere two plus miles, Warren was still in a single line with no reserve, nor had Warren been able to stretch far enough to connect with the 18th Corps on his left. The 5th Corps on their long front were taking prisoners from both Anderson's and Ewell's corps, and Burnside, on the 5th Corps' right and rear, was taking prisoners from Hill's corps. While Warren realized that it was likely they were facing elements of those corps rather than the entire complements of the three enemy corps, he still stated that he could not fight under those conditions the whole day without receiving reinforcements. Yet Warren, nonetheless, advanced the right of his line at least twice on the morning of June 3rd, sending Griffin's 1st Division, which faced the enemy to the north, forward in an attack along with two divisions of the 9th Corps.[54]

By 9 A.M., the Federals were pushing Early's troops back, and Roebling went off in search of the missing cavalry of James Wilson, which he found at Linney's Corner with 2,000 convalescent recruits who were being sent to the army. Roebling led the recruits to the 9th Corps' right where they were added to Burnside's line, thereby freeing up all of Wilson's cavalry to act on the army's flank. While Wilson had seemingly been in no hurry to return to the Army of the Potomac, he was willing to take credit at headquarters for posting the new infantry with Burnside. It was Roebling who instigated Wilson's attack on the Rebel left. While Wilson said he had captured and held Rebel cavalryman William H. F. Lee's rifle pits for an hour or more, viewed from the other side, Lee's reports indicate that Hampton's cavalry did indeed find Federal cavalry on their left and that W.H.F. Lee was sent to drive them off. It's always interesting, and often startling, to have Dana's version of what Wilson had been up to. While Grant's headquarters ignored the repeated attacks Griffin made on Heth's division on the 5th Corps' front that day, Dana sent this report to Washington regarding Wilson's June 3rd exploits. "At 6 P.M., Wilson with his cavalry fell upon the rear of a brigade of Heth's division, which Lee had

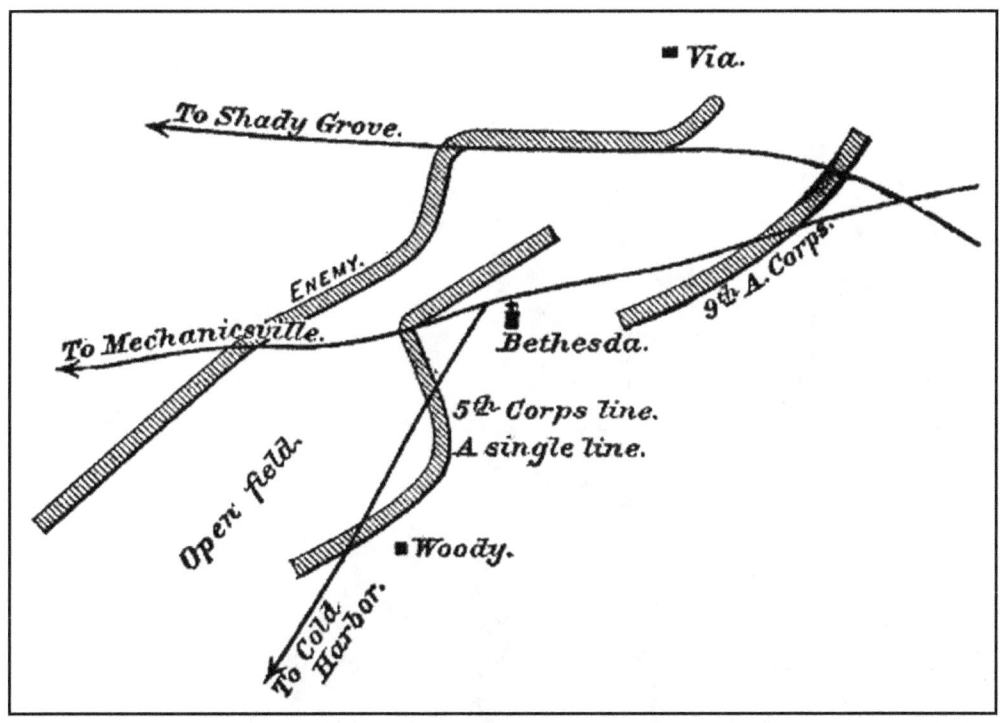

Map accompanying General Gouverneur K. Warren's report of June 3, 1864 (*Official Records*, Ser. 1, Vol. XXXVI, Pat. 3, 536).

thrown far around to his left, apparently with the intention of enveloping Burnside. After a sharp but short conflict Wilson drove them from their rifle-pits in confusion.... He [Wilson] had previously fought with and routed Gordon's brigade of rebel cavalry." (A Rebel cavalry commander named Gordon could not be found in the eastern theater, other than James B. Gordon, who died in May of 1864, the month before Wilson's alleged encounter.) Meanwhile, as Humphreys's history observed, Early reported that Federal cavalry had shown up on the Confederate left flank and were repulsed.[55]

Neither Dana nor Grant reported Warren and Griffin's June 3rd attacks, but at 9:30 A.M., the enemy attacked on Warren's center right, which he reported to Meade's headquarters, though it would take a very long time for the word to get to Meade by Warren's courier. About the same time, Warren sent Griffin on an attack against the Rebel line in his front. Griffin was ordered to advance again on his front, where he was facing Heth's division, Warren had Griffin advance again at 6 P.M., and in all three assaults, Griffin's division suffered a bloody repulse. Lee would report that the attack on Heth had been particularly heavy but had been resisted.[56]

With the telegraph on the Federal right still down, two hours after Warren requested reinforcement, Meade sent a courier with his response: there would be none. Nor would Meade allow Warren to withdraw his left to consolidate his troops. Meade again instructed Warren to move toward the left and southeast, and make a connection with Smith's 18th Corps to support Smith's attacks. Not until Meade finally heard about the attack upon Warren, did he send Birney's division from the battered but now idle 2nd Corps to fill

Assistant Secretary of War Charles A. Dana in front of his tent at Cold Harbor (Library of Congress).

the gap between the 5th and 18th Corps. It would be hours before Birney came up on Warren's left, his arrival occurring at about the same time Warren was repulsing another attack on his right. Birney had been in position no more than an hour or two when headquarters decided that Birney must return to the 2nd Corps and that the 9th Corps should be completely withdrawn from the 5th Corps' right and rear to be placed between Smith and Warren. Surprisingly, Meade asked that the matter of moving Burnside be "submitted" to Warren before Meade gave the order. Warren undoubtedly reported that there was a gap of at least three-fourths of a mile existing between Smith's right flank and the 5th Corps' left. Thus, Birney stayed, plugging the gap before returning to the 2nd Corps on June 5th.[57]

At midday on June 3rd, though Warren had plenty to worry about, he hadn't forgotten Early's vulnerable left flank, and, wonder of wonders, Early was still there. So Warren and Roebling were still hopeful that Burnside might take advantage of the situation with Warren's support. Burnside scheduled an attack for 2 P.M. Roebling continued to labor to make it happen, trying to get Wilson's cavalry to join in the attack on Heth's flank and rear, but there is no evidence in Confederate reports that he did that. As the time for the attack approached, literally as the 9th Corps skirmishers began to move forward, orders from Army of the Potomac headquarters canceled the assault. In agony at this lost opportunity, the scout Roebling would bitterly declare of the canceled assault, "It was countermanded for some unknown reason, perhaps because there was a prospect of success." That night Early acknowledged that his left flank was very much exposed, and he withdrew. The day's fighting, except for Griffin's afternoon assaults, was, for the most part, over for the 5th and 9th Corps. But the 5th and 9th Corps added their own 1,600 killed and wounded to the day's terrible toll.[58]

Though Meade claimed he had been in full command of the field at Cold Harbor on June 3rd, Grant apparently had a hand in operations throughout the day. As mentioned, Grant suggested at 7 A.M. that day that Meade suspend attacks when they proved unsuccessful, and Meade did have a visit from Grant at his headquarters about midday. Then there is also Grant's later well-known expression of his regret about the last charge made at Cold Harbor this day, as testimony that he had some measure of responsibility for it.[59] It is also clear that Grant, the man who claimed never to consult with his subordinates in a council of war, did something very like it this day, for he apparently considered the opinions of the corps commanders regarding another assault. Grant wrote to Meade at 12:30 P.M. on June 3rd, "The opinion of corps commander not being sanguine of success in case an assault is ordered, you may direct a suspension of farther advance for the present." Grant's orders halting any further attacks on this day was accompanied by the rather startling, if not absurd, observation that it was just as well if they didn't drive Lee's army away from Cold Harbor and into the Richmond entrenchments at this time. After all, they didn't want Lee's army interfering with David Hunter's expedition until that cavalry commander's raid was well on its way to Lynchburg. It seems a bizarre assessment and commentary on the day's overwhelming and sanguinary failures. While it suggests a mind-boggling attempt at face saving and self-justification in the face of conspicuous defeat, perhaps it was nothing more than Grant having paid little attention to what was going on at Cold Harbor. The final bit of insanity is found in the diary of Cyrus Comstock, Grant's engineer. Whatever Grant's "regrets" were regarding June 3rd, Comstock recorded that Grant was considering ordering assaults at Cold Harbor on June 4th. Rawlins, Grant's military right-hand man, would, according to Wilson, lay the blame for the continuing assaults against the enemy fortifications on Comstock, declaring it was impossible for him and Wilson to neutralize Comstock's influence on Grant. In his 1912 memoir, Wilson went on to describe how at that time Dana and Rawlins begged Wilson to come back to Grant's staff, for "there was no one in whose judgment Grant had so much confidence as he had in mine."[60]

Meade, inexplicably feeling some sense of vindication from the bloodletting on June 3rd, would write several days later, "I feel a satisfaction in knowing that my record is clear, and that the results of this campaign are the clearest indications I could wish of my sound judgment, both at Williamsport and Mine Run. In every instance that we have attacked the enemy in an entrenched position we have failed, except in the case of Hancock's attack at Spottsylvania, [sic] which was a surprise discreditable to the enemy.... I think Grant has had his eyes opened, and is willing to admit now that Virginia and Lee's army is not Tennessee and Bragg's army." It was also here, at Cold Harbor, that one of Meade's aides, Col. Theodore Lyman, while noting that Warren looked careworn, commented, "Some people say he [Warren] is a selfish man, but he is certainly the most tenderhearted of our commanders. Almost all officers grow soon callous in the service; not unfeeling, only accustomed, and unaffected by the suffering they see. But Warren feels it a great deal, and that and the responsibility, and many things of course not going to suit him, all tend to make him haggard." Lyman added that Warren had said, "For thirty days now, it has been one funeral procession, past me; and it is too much!"[61]

The lines of the opposing forces in front of the 2nd, 6th and 18th Corps at Cold Harbor on June 4th remained so close and sniper fire so hot that any attempts to establish picket lines brought on sharp contests, each side thinking they were being attacked. Grant also ordered that the men at the front "advance by 'regular approaches,'" work that had to be done in the dark, running forward several yards and digging in. It was a tribute, Cold Harbor historian Baltz comments, to Grant's stubbornness. But there was another indication of Grant's stubbornness. Between the lines was a nightmare of Federal dead and wounded, where there was little or no opportunity to remove or succor those who were still alive. As related above, it would be June 7th before Grant would agree to Lee's terms for a cease-fire. By then, many of the wounded were dead.[62]

On the morning of June 4th, it was discovered that the Rebels had disappeared from Burnside's and most of Warren's fronts, though they had not retired very far. The enemy still confronted Warren's left front but apparently had withdrawn from Warren's right and the 9th Corps' front. Since there was no cavalry on the army's flank, Warren pressed forward and sent Roebling out to discover that most of the Rebels who had withdrawn were massed just west of the Shady Grove Road. In response to the enemy having fallen back from the Federal right, Meade, anticipating that Lee was either forming to attack or beginning a movement, ordered the withdrawal of the 9th and 5th Corps, rearranging them on the army's right and rear, with Burnside to take up the protection of the Army of the Potomac's right flank and the 5th Corps to be in reserve. In the same circular that directed this movement, Sheridan was ordered to have one division of his calvary on each of the army's flanks and one in reserve. At noon, the 9th Corps was ordered to begin a withdrawal, and by nightfall, the 5th Corps alone held the Federal Army's right. Late in the evening, orders came for the 5th Corps to push out as close to the enemy as possible. Roebling observed that since no preparations for this unexpected order had been made and the arrangements would have to be "well-digested" ones, no movement was made that night.[63]

On the night of June 4th, an odd exchange took place between Grant and Meade. Shortly after 8 P.M., Grant suggested that Meade "answer" what Grant described as "annoying" enemy artillery fire. Grant suggested that Meade at midnight or 1 A.M. should open on the Rebels with "every battery that bears upon them." Meade, ten minutes later, reminded Grant that any shelling they did on the enemy in the middle of the night, would undoubtedly be answered, and would result in keeping their own army awake. Meade pointed out that it would also keep the enemy awake and alert, while Meade's soldiers were trying to dig the approaches toward the enemy lines that Grant had ordered. Grant responded shortly that he had "only a desire to retaliate for annoyances," and he suggested that if they were going to interfere with Meade's operations, he need not direct the artillery attack. It is indicative of Meade's state of mind and his responsiveness to every suggestion by Grant that at 9:40, Meade ordered his corps commanders to open on the enemy at midnight or 1 A.M. with every gun that bears on the enemy, and to keep up the fire until daylight. Meade added that each commander must judge for himself whether the bombardment will cause "annoyance or loss to their own troops, or interfere with their advances of position by regular approaches."[64]

As Warren prepared to obey his orders for the morning of June 5th, at 1 A.M. that morning, Warren was informed that no cavalry could be found closer that 2 miles from the 5th Corps right flank. Warren informed army headquarters, and stated "I am not capable of maintaining any position whatever, if that is all the cooperation I am to have. Officers being informed that two divisions of cavalry are on my right flank, it but gives me false assurances of being timely warned of the enemy's flank movements."[65] Meanwhile, Warren sent the following to the cavalry commander whose obligation it was to connect with the 5th Corps, Gen. James H. Wilson. Having suffered throughout the campaign from Wilson's mistakes and derelictions, Warren wrote to Wilson, "I understand from headquarters Army of the Potomac that you are to watch my right flank and give me notice of any efforts to turn it. Your nearest pickets are 2 miles off from my flank. On May 30 I was told that the cavalry would guard my flank, and they did not, so that the enemy attacked me from where they [Federal cavalry] should have been. If your instructions do not require you to connect with me, then I am misinformed by high authority."[66]

Wilson answered the Army of the Potomac headquarters quite politely, stating that it was difficult to maintain communications at night, that the line his division must guard was too long and he implied that he had not been kept informed of movements on the infantry's line. Humphreys, at Meade's headquarters, therefore reminded Wilson that the right flank of the 5th Corps had been in the vicinity of Bethesda Church for days, making it hard to swallow that some unknown movement by the army had made it hard for Wilson to find Warren's flank. Humphreys then forwarded Warren's and Meade's messages to Sheridan.[67] While Wilson's message to Meade had been relatively subdued, Wilson's reply to Warren had quite a different tone. Wilson wrote to Warren, "My instructions are to cover the right flank of the army from the incursions of the enemy. This duty requires me to watch a line at least 4 miles in length. I don't understand that I am to place my command in your front, or to dispose it specially to take care of your flank..." Wilson went on to say that he had had no idea that Warren was on the right of the army, and though his pickets and patrols were directed to connect and keep up communication with the army's right flank, and he would do so as long as possible, the infantry "should not rely too much upon me for close connections, since I have so much country not only to watch but to guard from attacks of cavalry." Wilson closed by suggesting Warren try to contact General Torbert's division on the road somewhere near Cold Harbor.[68]

If Wilson's reply to Warren was surly, it was nothing compared to Sheridan's when he decided to weigh in. Sheridan wrote to Humphreys, Meade's chief of staff at Army of the Potomac headquarters, "General Wilson reports the connections with General Warren complete since some time last night, and the reason why the connection was broken was the withdrawal of some army corps without any notification to the cavalry. Infantry commanders are very quick to give the alarm when their flanks are uncovered, but manifest inexcusable stupidity about the safety of cavalry flanks."[69] Once again, Sheridan expressed his utter disregard for Meade's or anyone else's rank, displaying his complete confidence that there would be no reprisals for his disobedience or insubordination.

While Humphreys reiterated Meade's protest that the right of the army, regardless of which corps was holding it, was, and had been, at Bethesda Church, he also pointed out that while infantry commanders were instructed to keep in communication with the cavalry commanders on their flanks, they often were unable, with the means at their disposal, to find either the cavalry pickets or their commanders. Within hours of this confrontation between Meade, Sheridan and Warren, Grant offered the same solution for Sheridan's bad behavior that he had given at Spotsylvania. Again, Grant gave orders for Sheridan to leave the army on June 7th, this time with two of his divisions, with the objectives of destroying the enemy's railroad lines and a canal, and potentially to unite with Gen. David Hunter's expedition. The division that would be left behind to protect the Army of the Potomac was James Wilson's.[70]

The 5th Corps withdrew as ordered from the front line at Cold Harbor on the night of June 5th and 6th. Though the withdrawal began at sunset on the 5th, due to the darkness of the night and the muddiness of the roads, it was almost dawn before the last pickets of the 5th Corps left the line. The exhausted 5th Corps men were grateful that the enemy, apparently unaware of their movement, did not follow or respond. The 9th Corps was now in position to hold the right flank of the army.[71] Once away from the front lines, Warren on June 6th hoped for an opportunity to bring up the 5th Corps' baggage trains for the first time since his men had crossed the Rapidan. His officers and men were unavoidably filthy and lice ridden, and Warren asked if they were to remain in their position in the rear long enough for him to bring up the trains. Humphreys, in Meade's absence, could offer no guarantees, but agreed it was worth attempting. But when Meade returned to his headquarters, he refused permission, and the 5th Corps' wagons were sent away.[72]

The likely reason why Meade refused permission for Warren's trains was Burnside, for as soon as he had assumed responsibility for holding the Army of the Potomac's right, Burnside became uneasy. It was true that the enemy was seeking the Army of the Potomac's right flank, but as Warren pointed out, Burnside's right and rear were presently protected by impenetrable swampland. In fact, when Early tried to gain access to Burnside's position, he failed, as Warren predicted he would. But Warren's soldiers would be held under arms in readiness for the enemy breakthrough that didn't come. A frustrated Warren pointed out that "to be always ready is to be never ready, for men cannot stand with belts, knapsacks, &c., on all the time without becoming broken down." Finally, the next day, Army of the Potomac headquarters acknowledged that it was unlikely the 5th Corps would be called on to support the 9th Corps, but by that time. two of Warren's divisions had been sent to connect with the cavalry on the 2nd Corps' left flank at the Chickahominy.[73]

Though the Army of the Potomac remained at Cold Harbor, Grant was far from idle as the first week of June ended. On June 6th, Baldy Smith and the 18th Corps marched to White House in preparation for their passage to City Point, to be ready for the assault on Petersburg that Grant contemplated. Before Smith's return, Butler had attempted an assault on Petersburg on June 8th and 9th. One historian, William Glenn Robertson, infers Butler was anxious to make the assault before Grant and the Army of the Potomac showed up to steal his thunder. Quincy Gillmore, commander of the 10th Corps, because of his seniority, demanded and got command of the expedition, with Edward Hinks's Colored Troops and August Kautz's cavalry under Gillmore's orders. It became an attack, that wasn't an attack. While Kautz was able to ride into the undefended far right of the Confederate bastion, Kautz waited in vain for Gillmore's attack to begin on the Rebel center, and finally had to withdraw. Gillmore, intimidated by the strength of the Petersburg fortifications, did little more than demonstrate before he turned around and went back to Bermuda Hundred. Hinks's had apparently clamored to be allowed to attack, and William Glenn Robertson observes that, perhaps, if Hink's had been in command, rather than Gillmore, the Federals might have taken the city on that day.[74]

On June 7th, Sheridan moved out with his two divisions to begin his raid. On that same evening, Meade's headquarters was in an uproar. Surely it was because they realized this day, during the truce that had finally been arranged, that of the 434 Federal casualties taken off the field at Cold Harbor, only two were still alive.[75] But no, the hubbub at Meade's headquarters was caused by a copy of an article written by a journalist with the improbable name of Edward Crapsey that had come into Meade's hands. Crapsey's article accused Meade of wanting the Army of the Potomac to retire back across the river after the Battle of the Wilderness and stated that it was only Grant's intercession that had saved the army and the nation. Meade was furious and, with Grant's approval, put Crapsey under arrest, had the journalist drummed through the Federal camps wearing a sign "libeler of the press," and had him expelled from the army.[76] It did not endear Meade to the gentlemen of the Fourth estate. Nor was this Meade's only complaint. Meade also confronted Grant at this time regarding what Meade assumed was Grant's neglect to mention Meade in his reports to Secretary of War Stanton. Meade thought Stanton's failure to ever speak of Meade was attributable to Grant's purposely avoiding mentioning him to the secretary. Grant patiently explained to Meade that he did not write directly to Stanton, but directed all his reports to Halleck. Meade was appeased.[77]

In the midst of Meade's turmoils, Grant was planning one of the best-known, and perhaps, best-planned movements of his career. On June 8th, Grant, Meade and Warren met outdoors under an apple tree and studied a map together for some time. It could only have pleased Warren to be privy to Grant's plans and considerations, but his involvement may also have occurred because Warren had also been chosen to play an important role in the Army of the Potomac's upcoming move. Grant had designed an audacious plan to not only take his army across the Chickahominy, but across the James River as well, in order to assist in an investment of Petersburg, the transportation hub on the very doorstep of Richmond. The plan demanded secrecy and speed. Warren's 5th Corps would be charged with keeping Lee and his army in the dark and in place, while the rest of the Army of the Potomac moved south of Richmond before the Army of Northern Virginia could react. On this day Grant's aide, Comstock, traveled to the James to choose an advantageous crossing for the Army of the Potomac, even as Gillmore was beginning his ineffective attempt on Petersburg. The plan was that the Army of the Potomac would withdraw from Cold Harbor, and the 5th Corps would cross the Chickahominy at Long Bridge, followed by the 2nd Corps. The 6th and 9th Corps would cross the river lower down at Jones Bridge, and while the 5th Corps remained behind to screen and protect the army's movement, the 2nd, 6th and 9th Corps would march to Fort Powhatan to cross the James. Meanwhile, Smith's 18th Corps was returning to the Army of the James by water.[78]

Nor was Lee resting on his laurels. Upon Burnside's and Warren's withdrawal from the Federal right, it was Early's turn to discover where the Yankees had gone. Lee was also faced with the necessity of sending troops to deal with Hunter's incursion, and he was contemplating just who to send. Lee also had to deal with the awkward situation of explaining to Ewell, who argued that his health had improved enough to allow him to come back to the army, that Lee thought it best that Early retain command of the corps formally known as Ewell's corps. By June 8th, Lee also received word from his cavalry commander, Hampton, that Sheridan had crossed the Pamunkey, and Lee sent Hampton and Fitzhugh Lee in pursuit of the Federal horsemen.[79]

On the night of June 12th–13th, the 5th Corps moved the last two of its divisions toward the Chickahominy in preparation for crossing. Warren gave considerable attention to seeing that his advance to the river was not observed by the enemy, and even within their own army, secrecy was so stringent that pickets were posted to keep in stragglers and prevent any movement in or out of the corps. Dana's report to Washington that day told that Wilson's cavalry had crossed the Chickahominy without opposition, that the bridge had been laid at once, and the advance made without delay. In reality, things did not go at all well[80] As Roebling reported it, when the vanguard of the 5th Corps reached the river at 10 P.M. on the 12th, they found Wilson just arriving. Another hour was spent clearing the river of enemy pickets, so work on the pontoon bridge could begin. At 1:00 A.M. on the 13th, the 5th Corps began to cross. It is interesting to compare Roebling's account and Wilson's account of the same event. Wilson's account follows.[81]

Wilson, in his usual form, told a much different story regarding the Chickahominy crossing in his 1912 memoir, long after Warren was dead. Wilson offers that it was the 5th Corps who was supposed to lay the pontoon bridge on the night of June 12th–13th, and after sending two requests to Warren, Wilson had a young aide return to him in tears after Warren cursed at him and said to "tell General Wilson if he can't lay that bridge to get out of the way with his damned cavalry and I'll lay it." When he met Warren the next day, Wilson records that he refused to shake Warren's hand and demanded an apology for the way his aide had been treated. According to Wilson, Warren didn't remember the incident but apologized anyway. But Wilson wasn't finished insulting Warren. He went on to tell what, no doubt, he considered an amusing anecdote.

A few days later, Wilson found himself in Grant's company, and while the Army of the Potomac's progress toward Petersburg wasn't going exactly as planned, Grant, according to Wilson, asked, "Wilson, what is the matter with this army?"

"General, there is a great deal the matter with it, but I can tell you much more easily how to cure it."

"How?"

"Send for Parker, the Indian chief, and, after giving him a tomahawk, a scalping knife and a gallon of the worst whiskey the Commissary Department can supply, send him out with orders to bring in the scalps of major generals."

Wilson reports that this brought a smile to Grant's face, and Grant asked, "Whose?"

and Grant added, "But where shall we get generals to fill their places?" At which point Brigadier General Wilson suggested that there were plenty of brigadiers who would gladly accept a higher grade.

Wilson goes on to say that Grant, becoming serious, asked Wilson if he had anyone in mind who he felt should be replaced, and it was at this point that Wilson told Gen. Grant all about Warren's abusive treatment of his young aide. Grant's response, according to Wilson, was, "Well, I'll take care of Warren anyhow." Wilson, if one's follows his career and considers the archival material, is an inveterate liar, but one wonders if, in this case, that perhaps that is just what Gen. Grant said that night.[82]

It was hardly an auspicious start to what could only have been a daunting assignment, the 5th Corps being left on its own to cope with the entire Army of Northern Virginia and its cavalry, while the only force they had to call on was commanded by James Wilson. It was nearly daylight before the lead elements of Warren's corps were able to follow Wilson's Cavalry across the pontoon bridge, and because of obstructions on the Long Bridge Road, progress was slow. With the cavalry skirmishing in the lead, two miles from the crossing, the 5th Corps deployed in a line of battle, covering the river crossings and roads. Though the cavalry broke once, and ran back through the infantry, Crawford's infantry maintained their line. Once again, the maps were inaccurate, and Roebling was sent out to find a road upon which the 5th Corps could later follow the Army of the Potomac to the James when their screening duties were over. As Wilson skirmished with Rebel cavalry, Warren pushed his force up to White Oak Swamp Bridge and dug in. It was a position well chosen, for when Lee discovered that the Army of the Potomac had withdrawn from Cold Harbor and crossed the Chickahominy, he brought Anderson's and Hill's corps up late in the day to confront the 5th Corps, whose five-mile-long defensive position ran from White Oak Swamp to Malvern Hill.[83] Though the Rebels plied Warren with artillery, his position was strong and secure. Lee, meanwhile, pondered whether Warren presented a screen behind which the Federals were moving, or was the vanguard of a march on Richmond. Regardless, as the day closed Lee determined to attack Warren in the morning, but in the night, Warren safely withdrew his corps, followed by Wilson. The troopers, although they were supposedly the force's rear guard, pushed ahead of the infantry during the night, and the 5th Corps eventually made an unexpected stop at St. Mary's Church when Wilson's horsemen blocked the road and refused to give way. The arrogance of the commander seems to have been contagious, for the Federal horsemen found it highly amusing to throw cartridges into their fire to watch and laugh as the infantrymen who were trudging by, thinking they were under attack, were ordered to deploy.[84]

After Cold Harbor, Lee felt confident enough to send part of his force to confront Hunter's raid. On June 13th, he chose Early's corps, some 8,000 men, the Confederate corps that had been most depleted in the fighting during these days that would become known as the Overland Campaign. Lee also sent Hoke back to Beauregard, whose return was much welcomed by the commander charged with defending Petersburg. That June, Breckinridge was also sent back to the Shenandoah Valley.[85] These assignments are an interesting commentary on Lee's perception of the threat or threats that various Federal forces did or did not pose.

Ten

Petersburg

AT DAYBREAK ON JUNE 14TH, with the cavalry finally gotten out of the way, Warren and the 5th Corps marched on to Charles City Court House, near to, but not on, the James. They arrived at noon and elements of the corps occupied the trenches that the 2nd Corps had erected as they passed through. The 6th and 9th Corps began to arrive at Charles City as well, massing around the picturesque little town. So far, Grant's movement had gone rather well, but that didn't last. Roebling was astounded that at first he could find no one at Charles City who seemed to know how to get down to where the army was to cross the James. The plan was that the entire army would cross on the pontoon bridge, but with the delay of the bridge's completion, much of army's infantry would cross by boat. It took approximately 12 hours to cross an entire infantry corps by boat, four times longer than it would have taken them if they could have marched across the long pontoon bridge.[1] While the bridge was an engineering marvel, it was not completed until near midnight on the day it was needed. Yet another delay had occurred when one of the pontoon bridges back on the Chickahominy, one over which the army's wagons were to have crossed, proved too short. Once again, Roebling was astonished that, rather than risk a wagon train, the whole army stopped and waited, thereby risking their best chance of getting to and taking Petersburg before Lee could intervene. Roebling was not the only one who fretted throughout the day of June 14th that they would lose the race to Petersburg as the advantages that speed and surprise had earned them were continuing to slip through their fingers. Roebling reported that as they waited to cross the James, Baldy Smith's fleet passed on the river. This added to the delay in building the bridge, for Smith's boats had to be allowed to pass before the final pontoons could be put in place. Grant chose to go by water to his new headquarters at City Point, while his engineer, Comstock, stayed behind and "hurried things up a little."[2]

If things were rocky on the James, they were much worse for Philip H. Sheridan and his expedition. On June 11th, he met Rebel cavalry commanders Wade Hampton's and Fitzhugh Lee's divisions at Trevilian Station, and although Custer got himself into such a tight spot that one historian describes it as a dress rehearsal for the Little Big Horn, the day ended with victory seemingly within the Federal cavalry's grasp. But by the next day, June 12th, Hampton and Lee had Sheridan on the run. Abandoning any thought of being able to unite with David Hunter's Federal raid, Sheridan began his days-long struggle

Cold Harbor to Petersburg (Ned Smith).

back to the Army of the Potomac, his every step dogged by the Rebel horsemen. When Sheridan finally reached the former supply base at White House, he found, to his disgust, that he was expected to escort a supply train to the Army of the Potomac's new position, and all the while Hampton was still snapping at his flanks and his heels. After leaving White House with a long train, Sheridan finally decided to leave, or perhaps a better word for it was sacrifice, David Gregg's division, so that he and Torbert could ride on to the army in peace. Greatly outnumbered, five Rebel brigades to his two, Gregg's horsemen were left at St. Mary's Church (also known as Samaria Church or Nance's Shop), where they lost heavily, and were nearly captured en masse. While Gregg fought off the Rebel cavalry, Sheridan and Torbert rode on unmolested. After being away from the army for 21 days, Sheridan had accomplished almost nothing, for what little damage he had managed to do to Confederate infrastructure was quickly repaired. Comstock expressed his disgust in his diary, recording that he had urged Grant to send Sheridan back out to finish the job of destroying the railroads. But it would not be done, for the appalling number of men and horses lost during the raid would impair the Federal cavalry's usefulness for weeks to come. While Dana could always be relied upon to send positive news to Washington regarding Wilson's exploits, Dana did not afford Sheridan the same courtesy. On June 16th, Dana would write to the administration, "A dispatch from the same paper[3] General Lee reports that Hampton and Fitzhugh Lee have routed Sheridan at Trevilian Station, capturing 500 prisoners and 6 guns, and Sheridan is said to have left his dead and wounded on the field."[4]

To add to Sheridan's less than admirable actions during this period, after the Army of the Potomac reached Petersburg, Wilson was sent on an expedition that would be the worst disaster of his military career, a career that one could say should be known for its disasters. Sheridan, making his way from White House to City Point, ignored all Meade's orders to send help to Wilson. One can't help but, at this particular time, remember Sheridan's postwar boasting in his report on his role in the Overland Campaign, describing how he and his cavalry could ride wherever they liked and always defeated the Rebel cavalry. It's indefinite exactly when Grant received news of Sheridan's failure, though it is known that by June 12th, the day the Army of the Potomac left Cold Harbor, Grant still believed that Sheridan would unite with Hunter.[5] But with Sheridan returning without having completed his assignment, and

General David M. Gregg (Library of Congress).

"General Grant's Campaign — Transportation of Hancock's Corps Across the James at Wilcox's Landing" (sketch by William Waud, *Harper's Weekly*, July 9, 1864).

Hunter defeated at Lynchburg and moving off through West Virginia, it left Grant in a spot. It was essential that the enemy's all important railroads and transportation canal be destroyed, for it seemed that the only way to defeat Lee's army was to deny them their supplies. But who was to do it?

To return to the crossing of the James on June 15th, as boats became available, the 2nd Corps began ferrying across the James, and by 4 A.M., Hancock had all his infantry and four batteries of his artillery across the river. Though the corduroy roads to the river and the landings were incomplete for Hancock, Roebling was relieved to see that a good road and wharves were being made for the troops' passage down to the river. Hancock crossed under Meade's orders from the previous night, and while Meade had directed him to be prepared once he reached the other side to march to Petersburg, he was also told to await rations that were to arrive at the river crossing. Confusion reigned, but when the rations still had not arrived by 10:30 on the morning of the 15th, Hancock marched without them.[6] One substantial piece of evidence: Grant may have suspected that he had made a serious mistake regarding Hancock's orders, for at noon on June 15th, Grant tried to cancel the order sending rations to Hancock at the James River crossing. He ordered that the rations instead be sent to the illusive Harrison's Creek near Petersburg that Hancock would later claim was not where Grant or his staff thought it was.[7]

Grant, who had returned from City Point to watch the Army of the Potomac's crossing at Wilcox Landing, surveyed the bridge and the 2nd Corps' crossing, and was well satisfied. "All effect of the battle of Cold Harbor seemed to have disappeared," he is said to have remarked. One of Meade's aides reported that Grant then broke into a smile and commented, "I think it is pretty well to get across a great river, and come up here and attack Lee in his rear before he is ready for us."[8] Grant states that he informed Meade, as he had Butler, that Hancock must proceed to Petersburg first thing in the morning. While Grant acknowledges that Hancock had been ordered to await rations when he reached the other side of the James, Grant does not explain why neither Meade nor Hancock knew what else Grant expected of them.[9] One begins to suspect that Grant was so confident that Smith and the force given him would take Petersburg without difficulty, that he chose not to share his plans with Meade and Hancock. Smith's 18th Corps was supported by Edward W. Hinks's division of U.S. Colored Troops and General August Kautz's cavalry division,[10] in all, a force of between 14,000–18,000 men. They would be investing the formidable fortifications at Petersburg, which, while they were well planned and strongly built, were seven and a half miles in length at that time, and were defended by a small Confederate force of between 2,200–4,200 men under the command of General Beauregard.[11]

There is no question that things went badly wrong with Smith's attack. Uninformed that he was to assault Petersburg on his arrival, after delay for a lengthy reconnaissance, Smith began his assault on the city late in the afternoon of June 15th, and seized a mile of Petersburg's fortifications with its eight batteries. But inexplicably, Smith then stopped. It seemed apparent to everyone but Smith that Petersburg lay at his mercy, but if 2nd Corps historian Francis Walker's claim is accurate, it was not only Meade and Hancock who were ignorant of Grant's plans. Baldy Smith was also unaware of Grant's intention that the 2nd Corps would support his attack.[12] Did believing that he was acting alone increase Smith's caution? In all likelihood, it did. Walker also described Hancock's growing physical disability, which involved fragments of the badly splintered bone from his Gettysburg wound, dislodged by constant time in the saddle, working their way out through Hancock's inflamed flesh. It was yet another factor that was putting the possibility of success beyond the reach of the Federals. Lastly, Walker tells us that at Hancock's arrival in the last light of day on June 15th, it should be known that topographical insight, perhaps best described as a quick assessment of a military landscape, was not one of Hancock's strong points. All of these factors contributed to the mistakes and misunderstandings at Petersburg on June 16th that spelled failure in those first days of uniting the Army of the Potomac and the Army of the James.[13]

As stated, it wasn't until after dark that the first elements of Hancock's force began arriving in front of the city's fortifications, and by that time, Smith was not inclined to attack. On new ground, in the dark, it was impossible for Hancock to get a good idea of what he and Smith were facing at Petersburg.[14] Meanwhile, a message arrived from Grant that had been sent to Hancock at 8:30 P.M., but hadn't caught up with him until two hours later. In it, Grant gave Hancock the unwelcome news that Rebel reinforcements were beginning to arrive at Petersburg. Grant also reminded Hancock to collect the rations that had caused such delay on the James. Having failed to arrive at Hancock's crossing point, the needed rations were being redirected to the 2nd Corps' new position at Petersburg. If there was any further question about the reasonableness of an attack on the night of June 15th, it seems that Grant was also seemingly dismayed by the failures of the day, and he, too, deemed it wise for the 2nd and 18th Corps to wait until more of the Army of the Potomac arrived. That night, Grant sent orders to hurry the rest of the Army of the Potomac to Petersburg, and by 9:30 P.M. Meade started Burnside on a night march while the rest of the army continued to cross the James.[15]

Within days after the Battle of Petersburg, Hancock would demand a court of inquiry to clear him of implied criticism that it was somehow his fault that the Federals failed to take Petersburg in June of 1864. Meade forwarded Hancock's angry complaints to Grant, who turned away the 2nd Corps commander's wrath by declaring that no one who mattered blamed Hancock for the Army of the Potomac's failure to take Petersburg. Grant would, in fact, declare in his memoirs that if General Hancock's orders of the 15th had been communicated to him, "that officer, with his usual promptness, would undoubtedly have been upon the ground around Petersburg as early as four o'clock in the afternoon of the 15th," at which time, Grant asserted, Petersburg would then have been taken. But who does Grant blame for the fact that Hancock did not receive his orders? Does Grant blame his own staff? Does he blame Meade? Is it possible that Grant simply forgot to give Meade the all important instructions for the investment of Petersburg? What Meade and Hancock did not know on June 15th, Dana apparently was aware of, for he reported to Washington at 8 A.M. on the 15th that Hancock's corps was crossing the James, and by 10 A.M., "Hancock moves out instantly for Petersburg to support Smith's attack on that place." It didn't work out that way, and the reason for this costly failure in communication has never been resolved.[16]

One of Grant's traits that offers itself as a possible explanation of what happened, is suggested by a statement that Grant made after the war. He declared, "I never held a council of war in my life.... I always made up my mind to act, and the first that even my staff knew of any movement was when I wrote it out in rough and gave it to be copied off." Did Grant simply forget to give the orders he intended, or did he fail to fully spell out his requirements? In the end, it would be Gillmore and Smith who would come in for most of the blame for this disappointing conclusion of the Overland Campaign. Instead of a victorious conclusion to the campaign, the war continued for months, with the Armies of the Potomac and the James laying siege to the Army of the Northern Virginia in the trenches at Petersburg.[17] Though the reasons for the confusion of orders at Petersburg may always remain obscure, as Grant biographer William McFeely points out, Grant's failure to take Smith, Hancock and Meade into his confidence regarding his intention to attack the fortifications at Petersburg with the support of one or more of the Army of the Potomac's corps had resounding repercussions, and could easily be pointed to as the one factor that caused a magnificent move by the Army of the Potomac to end in abject failure. The Battle of Petersburg would become another terrible and, as it turned out, pointless bloodletting in a campaign that became known for its high casualties and questionable assaults.[18]

Many years later, when Grant wrote about it, he still seemed baffled by Smith's failure to take Petersburg. "I believed then, and still believe, that Petersburg could have been easily captured at that time."[19] The pity of it is that Grant had seemingly flummoxed Lee, who, because he could not be sure of Grant's goal, had continued to hesitate before he committed the bulk of his troops. Though Lee did send some assistance to Beauregard when Smith attacked Petersburg, being unable to convince Lee that Petersburg was the Army of the Potomac's destination gave Beauregard fits. In desperation, on June 16th Beauregard stripped his troops, some 4,500 men, from the line where they had been confronting Butler at Bermuda Hundred in order to put them in the Petersburg fortifications. Becoming aware of the enemy's disappearance, Butler rather sluggishly came out and began destroying nearby railroads.[20] Only then did Lee take action, throwing Pickett's division forward to retake the trenches confronting Butler, while preparing the rest of his army to move toward Petersburg. By 3 P.M. on June 16th, Pickett would be threatening Butler's force and forcing it back to their lines. Though Grant expressed his willingness to bring elements of the 6th Corps — the last infantry corps to leave the James River crossing — directly by water to assist Butler, it would have been too little, too late. At 7 P.M. on June 16th, Grant also received word from the navy that 40,000 to 50,000 Confederate soldiers had been seen passing Deep Bottom from Malvern Hill that afternoon. This news of Lee's imminent arrival did not seem to unduly worry Grant, but it worried Meade, who passed on word of it to Hancock and Burnside as an inducement to push hard in their coming attacks.[21]

For once, Wilson's cavalry was keeping Meade apprised of at least some of the Army of Northern Virginia's movements, but he rather spoiled this bit of efficiency by complaints that his men and their mounts were "suffering," and he wanted to withdraw them for a day's rest before they crossed the James. It's hard to imagine McIntosh's brigade being too exhausted, for they were still at St. Mary's Church, the same place where they had earlier blocked the 5th Corps during their night march to the James, and where they threw cartridges in their campfires for a joke.[22]

As already stated, according to historian Francis Walker, General Smith had not known that Grant expected Hancock to join Smith's attack on the Petersburg fortifications; he first learned of it about 4 P.M. on the 15th. It was not until 5:30 that evening, that Hancock, still about four miles from Smith, heard that he had been expected to hurry to Petersburg to join Smith's assault.[23] Hancock, who had expended time trying to locate his originally assigned position at Harrison's Creek, abandoned that search and took his corps in hand to move as soon as possible to Petersburg. Hancock sent a staff officer ahead to inform Smith of the 2nd Corps' position and projected time of arrival, but when Hancock's aide approached Smith at Petersburg at about 6:30 P.M. to find out where Smith wanted the 2nd Corps, Smith told him merely they should form on his left. Smith failed to impart the vital information of where his left was, but instead referred Hancock's man to Gen. Edward W. Hinks, commander of the

General Cyrus B. Comstock (Library of Congress).

U.S. Colored Troops division with Smith, for further information. Around 7 P.M., Hancock came up to tell Smith that two of his divisions were at hand, and Smith, with no apparent intention of making an assault that night, requested that Hancock relieve Smith's troops in the captured works. It was already dark when Hancock's first division came up by 8 P.M., and by the time they relieved Smith's troops it was 11:00 P.M.[24]

It seems that some responsibility for the confusion that took hold before the Battle of Petersburg should be attributed to Comstock, the engineering officer who had chosen and laid out where the army would cross the river and, presumably, their route to and destinations at Petersburg. Comstock provides a less than impressive example of his abilities on June 15th, for as he rode ahead of the 2nd Corps that day with Charles Dana, on approaching Petersburg and City Point, Comstock and Dana got lost. While this was not an unusual thing for Comstock (see reconnaissance on June 11th in preparation for the second Federal attack on the Bloody Angle at Spotsylvania), Comstock and Dana added to the confusion at Grant's headquarters at City Point by apparently reporting that they couldn't understand why they hadn't seen the 2nd Corps marching to Petersburg along their route. Meanwhile, back at the James River Crossing, at 6 P.M. on June 15th, Burnside and his corps were ordered to cross the river and march to Petersburg, while at 8:40 P.M., the 5th Corps was ordered to be ready to be ferried across the James at daylight the next day.[25]

At Petersburg, Grant was apparently so confident that Smith would succeed in taking the city, that he seemingly could not or would not accept that Smith's assault had failed. Yet in the hours before hearing of Smith's results, there were signs that Grant was apprehensive, for his calls for the Army of the Potomac to hurry to Petersburg began well before Grant received word from Smith at 9 P.M. on the 15th.[26] The news initially seemed good, and perhaps that is why it would later be such a shock when Grant finally came to realize that Smith had accomplished very little. Smith, shortly before 9 P.M., reported that he had taken the works that Gillmore had previously failed to attack and that there were no other defenses between Smith and the town of Petersburg. Smith later reported that there *was* another fortification between his force and the city, but this may have referred to the earthworks that the enemy threw up the Hagood Line when they fell back from their major fortification, the Dimmock Line (see map page 203).[27]

By 10:00 A.M. the next day, June 16th, Grant had reported that Smith had taken the strongly constructed works at Petersburg and 16 pieces of artillery. Dana, meanwhile, wrote to Stanton that Smith had taken a first line of works, then that Smith had taken the main works. Dana also suggested in his report that it looked like the enemy was retreating across the Appomattox. The next day, Dana was still praising Smith's accomplishment, stating that "the success of Smith last night was of the most important character. He carried these heights, which were defended by works of the most formidable character, and this gives us perfect command of the city and railroad. The enemy still hold south of the city and west of the river, but their position of little comparative value." Was this the perception of things at this time at Grant's headquarters? Considering the misery the Army of the Potomac would go through in the coming months, let alone the next few days, before they would take the city of Petersburg, one wonders who was feeding Dana such startling misinformation.[28]

But beyond the hopeful, and in most cases wishful, observations of Dana, Grant was realistic enough to be urging Meade to hurry the 5th Corps from their crossing place on the James to a position near Petersburg on the Jerusalem Plank Road. He also wanted Meade to come to Petersburg to take command of the continuing assault.[29] Although Grant came over from City Point to Petersburg to consider the attack that he had ordered for Baldy Smith, Hancock, and Burnside to make at 6 P.M. on the 16th, Grant returned to City Point, leaving Comstock to stay with the ailing Hancock, who would relinquish command completely two days later.[30] Though it was understood that Meade was on his way to take command, it seems a remarkable abdication of responsibility on Grant's part to leave the field in the face of Hancock being unwell and the great importance of the assault. The fact that the less than reliable Comstock was Meade's advisor at a time when Meade was faced with arriving on unknown ground to take immediate command of an assault, would seem to provide two more reasons why Grant should have considered staying on the field.[31]

By 2 P.M. on June 16th, Meade had arrived by water to take command at Petersburg, and surprisingly, he came with only three members of his staff, leaving him dependent on the corps commanders' aides for communication.[32] Meade was also, to some extent, dependent on the advice of Grant's engineers, Comstock and John Barnard (General John Gross Barnard, USMA, 1833). When Grant became lieutenant general, he selected Barnard as his chief engineer of the armies in the field. Having served as McClellan's engineer during his peninsula campaign, it was Barnard who reconnoitered and selected the site at which the Battle of Gaines' Mill was fought, and as to where and when the assault should be made to advantage.[33] Meade had the 2nd Corps, the 18th Corps, and part of Butler's force at his command, as well as Burnside's 9th Corps, which had marched through the night and was up to the 2nd Corps' position by 10:00 A.M. on the 16th. While Beauregard had augmented his skeleton force in the Petersburg fortifications with men from the Bermuda Hundred line, Meade's Federals numbered near 35,000, while Beauregard had to make do with around 7,000.[34] But nonetheless, there was considerable evidence that Lee's army was on the move and this was worrying Federal commanders.[35] Yet nothing was done during the day on June 16th, and the attack remained scheduled for 6 P.M., after Meade's arrival. The attack, as it was planned by Grant and his engineers, would be made by Hancock's 2nd Corps, with Burnside in support. Smith's 18th Corps had withdrawn from the line they had taken the previous day, and by the 16th, Smith had changed his mind that the works could easily be retaken.[36] The 18th Corps, therefore, would only demonstrate, threatening and holding the attention of the enemy on their front but not attacking. Smith would also stand ready to exploit any advantage the 2nd Corps might develop, or be ready to go to the 2nd Corps' assistance, as the case might be. To put it another way, though three Federal corps, plus the soldiers of Butler's Army of the James, were at Petersburg, the attack on June 16th was to be made, according to Grant's plan, by one corps, Hancock's 2nd Corps. Meade soon arranged to have Burnside come up on Hancock's left, and have the 9th Corps prepare to attack with the 2nd Corps.[37]

When Hancock sent orders at midnight on the night of June 15th–16th for the next day, June 16th, he left a good deal of the responsibilities for reconnaissance to his division commanders, directing them to identify points on the enemy's line that commanded their own positions. Hancock's orders reflected his expectation that, once these threatening points had been identified, each officer would attack and take that enemy position at or before daylight, an expectation rather difficult to fulfill. Birney, in particular, fell under criticism for failing to rid his section of a line of commanding Rebel positions. Whatever Birney's failures may have been, it was his division that paid the price, for the heaviest burden of the 6 P.M. assault on June 16th was given to Birney's and Barlow's divisions. Though the Petersburg fortifications were still held by Beauregard's force alone, the 2nd Corps was unable to break the Confederate line, though several redoubts and their connecting works were captured. The 2nd Corps again suffered heavy losses.[38]

Having assembled to cross the James at dawn on June 16th, the 5th Corps began crossing the river at 4 A.M. on small boats, and by 1 P.M., shortly after marching away from the river crossing, Warren received a puzzling, erroneous message from Grant that Petersburg had been captured. It is one more indication that Grant was still convinced that the city must fall, or perhaps more evidence that Grant was still in denial that the initial assault had failed to take the inadequately defended city. Nonetheless, Warren's corps continued marching down the road to Petersburg under a scorching sun. They discovered, as the other corps had, that there was no water along their route, a situation exacerbated by the choking dust kicked up by their passage.[39] At 2 P.M. on the 16th, Warren received orders urging speed, and he responded that, while he could not be in Petersburg by dark, he would certainly be there by the morning of June 17th. During their march, the only Federal cavalry at Petersburg, Butler's cavalry under General Kautz's command, reported to Warren that his route might not be secure. Warning Warren that he might very well meet a Rebel force if he took the route Burnside had taken, Warren shifted to roads leading through Sycamore Church and Prince George Court House. Unfortunately, the vigilant Kautz, who was picketing the roadways on the Federal left, was ordered back to the Army of the James during the night by Butler. But Comstock also expressed some anxiety that Warren might be marching into difficulty. According to Comstock, who took it upon himself to change Grant's orders since Grant was away with Butler, if Warren went to the Jerusalem Plank Road as Grant had ordered, he would be separated from the rest of the army by a swamp.[40]

During the night, while the 5th Corps was allowed time enough to stop and eat, the bugles signaled for them to once again take up the march with a changed route that took heed of Comstock's warning. As they approached Petersburg, the men of the 5th Corps could hear the uproar of the 2nd Corps' continuing attack on the Petersburg fortifications, a strong indication of the falsity of the report that the city had fallen. The 2nd Corps' assault had driven the enemy some distance, and though Birney and others "carried the enemy's first line," the gains made did not meet Meade's expectations. Though the Rebels continued to attack throughout the night in futile attempts to retake their lost positions, the Federals held the gains they had made. Meade was encouraged by the 2nd Corps' limited success, and reports that Lee was not yet at Petersburg raised his expectations. Meade therefore ordered the 5,000 men of the 9th Corps, on the 2nd Corps left, to attack in column across the now moonlit landscape on the 16th, though it would be near daybreak before Burnside's assault got underway. Late on the night of June 16th, Meade reported from Petersburg, asking Grant at City Point for instructions for the next day. Grant begged off, pleading ignorance of conditions on the front, and Grant deferred to Meade as the officer on the field. That night of the 16th, Meade's aide Lyman arrived at Grant's headquarters at City Point just as the lieutenant general was going to bed.

Grant again expressed glee at having crossed the James and outfoxed Lee. At midnight on the night of June 16th–17th, the 5th Corps reached a position in rear of the 9th Corps, and, as Grant slept, Warren went out to look over the new field and meet with the Army of the Potomac's other commanders.[41]

Before dawn on June 17th, the 2nd Corps and 9th Corps attacked the fortifications on their fronts, surprising the sleepy defenders of Petersburg, and taking another portion of the enemy's fortifications, up to where the Rebel works met the Norfolk Pike (also known as the Sussex or Baxter Road). The enemy, in the same way that they had responded to Smith's taking of a portion of the original Petersburg fortification on June 15th, had again fallen back, and hastily prepared a new line of earthworks (the Harris Line). At daybreak, the 5th Corps was ordered to continue to act as reserve for the 2nd and 9th Corps, and to protect the army's left flank. Meanwhile, Grant's attention was seemingly focused on Butler and Bermuda Hundred, where the Army of the James was being forced back to its original position by Lee's forces. It was a loss of ground that meant loss of the opportunity to drive a permanent wedge between the Rebel forces at Petersburg and those at or coming from Richmond, and it is not surprising that Grant was concerned about it. But it is striking that he did not leave City Point to go either to Butler or to Meade. Grant instead sent his aide Lt. Col. Orville Babcock (USMA, 1861) to Butler. Grant also diverted elements of the 6th Corps away from Petersburg to assist Butler at Bermuda Hundred, and he began requesting that Meade return Smith's 18th Corps to the Army of the James. Babcock and Godfrey Weitzel, another of Grant's engineers, agreed that Butler could and should retake the ground he had just lost. But while the two engineers were conferring on where to attack, the Rebels took the initiative, and in a smashing attack regained and retained their former line at Bermuda Hundred. Butler then ordered Terry's 10th Corps and Wright's 6th Corps to counterattack, but both commanders declared that, though they might be able to retake the Rebel line, they could not hold it. Butler renewed his orders for an attack and was ignored.[42]

During the afternoon of June 17th at Petersburg, when an advance by elements of the 2nd and 9th Corps succeeded in taking some of the line that the enemy had thrown up during the night, two 5th Corps divisions, Crawford's and Griffin's, were advanced to occupy that portion of the Rebel fortification that Burnside had taken the previous night. Lysander Cutler's division was sent in to confront Rebel sharpshooters holed up in the Avery House and to extend the Federal left to the Norfolk Pike. Cutler's failure to take the Avery House, lightly defended at that point, puzzled Roebling, who spent the afternoon exploring beyond the infantry's left, circling around and moving up the Jerusalem Pike before running into Rebel cavalry.[43]

On returning around 4 P.M. to the 5th Corps, still positioned in reserve for the 9th Corps, Roebling witnessed the three assaults Burnside made on his front, and while the first two failed, one made just before dark with heavy fighting pushed back a portion of the enemy's new line. Though it was now dark, Crawford, Meade's protégé and the new commander of the 5th Corps' 3rd Division, was ordered to advance with the 9th Corps when they went in for yet another attack. As Roebling describes, Crawford's division started out well, and although ravines and a house broke their line as they advanced, they were able to restore their line and again went forward. Crawford had quite a night for himself, his division capturing about 60 of the enemy's men and a flag from one of Pickett's

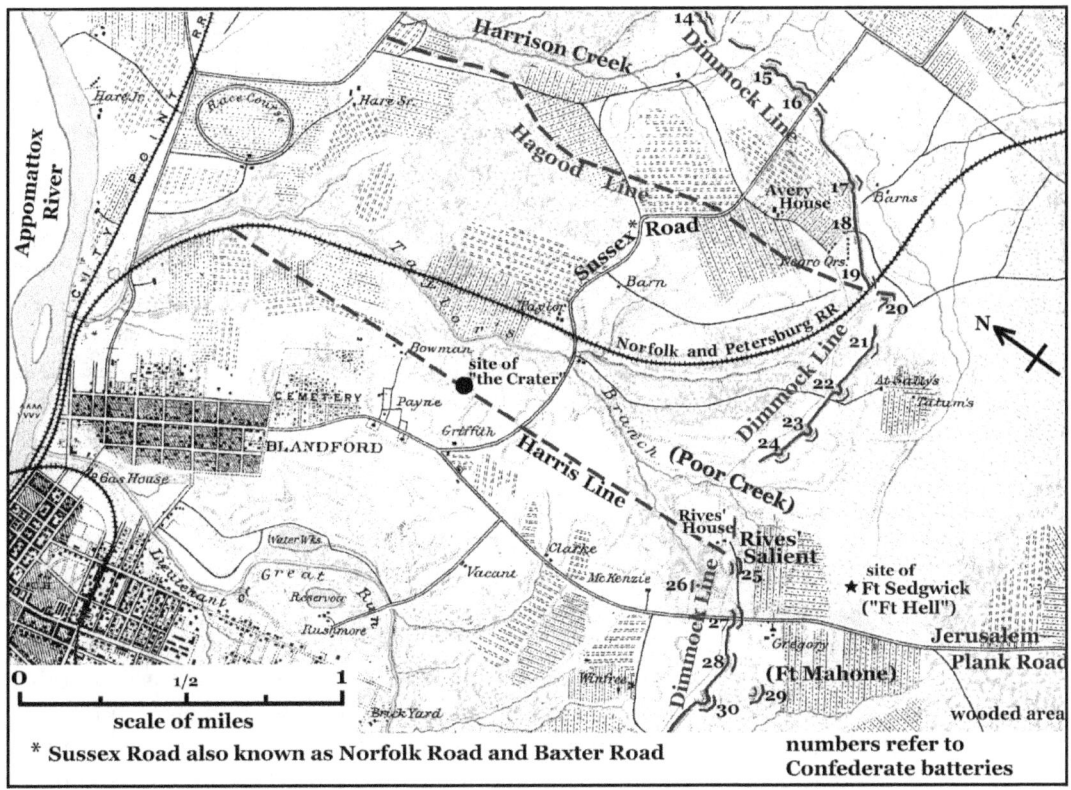

A portion of the Petersburg battlefield. Based in part on Plate XL, #1, *Official Atlas* (Ned Smith).

regiments. However, at that point, success turned to failure. Crawford's men became hopelessly mixed up with the 9th Corps, and presently everybody fell back, so that no part of the enemy's line remained in Federal possession that night.[44]

It is likely that Meade did not learn until very late in the day that none of the ground taken that day had been retained. Before the bad news arrived, Meade wrote a very upbeat letter to his wife. The general teased Mrs. Meade, who was involved with such organizations as the Sanitary Commission and the fairs being held to raise money to support wounded soldiers. Meade asked her if she was going to let the New York fair raise more money than her fair in Philadelphia. Meade also told of joking with Hancock about which of them would be selected by the fairgoers to receive a presentation sword in another fundraiser, in which those who donated could vote for their favorite general.[45]

Before Meade received the bad news at the end of the day, he ordered Warren to take advantage of any gain that the 9th Corps or Crawford's division might make. But he also urged caution. Warren was not to take any risks that would jeopardize what had already been gained, and Meade encouraged Warren to let his tired men rest up for the attack contemplated for early on June 18th. But at the end of the day, Meade finally learned that all the ground that had been dearly bought during the day had been relinquished, with the whole Union advance falling back through the darkness. At that point, for Meade, all seemed to depend on the dawn attack the next morning. And on June 18th, the 5th Corps wouldn't be waiting in reserve; they would be joining the Federal attack on Petersburg. During the night, Beauregard left a strong picket line and fires burning on his front line in hopes of deceiving the enemy, while the rest of the battered Rebel defenders dropped back one last time, to throw up another makeshift line of earthworks to resist the Federal attack that was sure to come the next day. The Federal pickets on the 2nd and 9th Corps fronts did not detect the Rebel withdrawal. The new line that Beauregard created during the night joined on to the formidable original fortifications at a place called Rives' Salient, for its proximity to the nearby Rives farm. Yet however impressive those original works on the Dimmock Line may have been, the fact was that on June 15, 16 and 17, while the men of the 2nd, 9th and 18th Corps had thrown themselves against the fortifications of Petersburg that Beauregard had manned, there were no Confederates in those earthworks confronting the Jerusalem Plank Road., nor men to man the batteries. The Rebel right had been empty and undefended since June 15th, but that was about to change.[46]

For the 5th Corps, the timing couldn't have be worse, for while the city had been defended by the small force that Beauregard had been able to throw together, on the night of June 17–18th, Lee was finally convinced that Grant had indeed brought the entire Army of the Potomac to Petersburg. Not until that night did the Rebel commander commit to bringing the Army of Northern Virginia to Beauregard's aid in the besieged city. Two divisions of Anderson's 1st Corps, near 10,000 soldiers, led the advance of Lee's army to Petersburg, in a night that one participant described as starting out as a forced march, but ending up on the run. But by 7:30 A.M. on June 18th, Kershaw's division of Anderson's corps arrived at Petersburg. Kershaw's men were placed in the fortifications at Rives' Salient, their line reaching to the Jerusalem Plank Road. Two hours later, another of Anderson's divisions arrived, and by noon Field's division was placed in the fortifications to Kershaw's right. Was Federal cavalry ever more needed, for Meade had no knowledge of these Confederate arrivals. In fact, Meade still believed that no enemy reinforcements had arrived. With the setbacks that his army had experienced on June 17th, Meade was described as in a "tearing humor," one that seemed to make him oblivious to distances or obstacles. Meade ordered a simultaneous assault by all corps to be made at dawn the next day. It was an order that his corps commanders would try to obey, but would find impossible.[47]

When the Federal advance began on the foggy morning of June 18th, it did not take long for the men of the 2nd, 9th and 5th Corps to realize that a good portion of the enemy had withdrawn from the line they had occupied the previous night.[48] While the 2nd and 9th Corps continued their advance in search of the elusive Rebel line, elements of the 5th Corps started their advance at 4:30 A.M. to discover that the enemy had taken precautions that would slow down any Federal advance against their right flank. The 5th Corps encountered an advanced Confederate rifled battery, accompanied by a skirmish line, in turn supported by an entrenched line with earthworks formidable enough for the Rebels to be standing on its parapet, surveying the Federal advance. Attempts to move forward also revealed that a deep and curving railroad cut blocked the entire 5th Corps line's progress, with the one bridge that had been available for crossing the ravine still in flames. The Rebel contingent did their work well, and there was considerable delay in forcing back the enemy's skirmishers, and the men of the 5th Corps faced a real challenge in getting in and out of the deep railroad cut while under enemy fire. Sniper and artillery fire from Rives' Salient, where the enemy's new line joined the old, was "doing considerable execution," as Roebling commented.[49]

Denied cavalry reconnaissance, the 5th Corps was on its own trying to feel their way across a landscape of barriers, natural and manmade, to reach the enemy's main line. By 10 A.M., Meade pressed Warren as to whether he could be ready to make a simultaneous attack with the corps at noon, and Roebling describes every energy being bent to accomplishing that task. But as Warren explained, though he was in sight of the enemy's lines, they were still fighting the enemy's skirmishers for the ravine in their front. Ignoring Warren's response, Meade ordered Warren to attack at noon.[50]

Warren's intrepid scout, Roebling, found that as the 5th Corps' advance slowly pressed the enemy back, beyond all the obstacles already mentioned and the enemy's determined resistance, the 5th Corps began encountering a series of ravines that were the headwaters of Poor Creek, mistakenly labeled as "Poo Creek" on Federal maps, and therefore referred to as such in reports. It would be an amusing mistake, if Poo Creek hadn't become the scene of so much death. The Petersburg fortification had a clear field of fire over that area, and the creek created swampy areas that could mire the troops under that deadly storm of lead. The many ravines made it impossible for one commander to know what those on his left and right were doing. Nonetheless, Griffin, having placed Federal batteries that silenced some of the enemy's guns, allowed Warren to renew his advance, and he notified Meade that the corps would be able to reach the enemy in time to assault by 1 P.M. Meade informed Warren that he would not change the hour of the assault and that "everyone else was ready" for the noon attack.[51]

While the 5th Corps was striking out over the previously untried ground on the Federal left, the corps on Warren's right, Burnside's 9th and Hancock's 2nd, had discovered when they made their early morning advance that the enemy had withdrawn from their front. Though they met Rebel resistance, they had to push the enemy defenders only a short distance before confronting the enemy's new main line. Most significantly, the 9th and 2nd Corps were then confronting that third and last line that the Confederates had thrown together in the night, really no more than a occupied trench. Most of the 5th Corps had a much greater distance to advance before approaching the enemy's main line, in some cases as much as a mile and a half. When they got there, the men on the left and center of Warren's line found themselves confronting the original Petersburg's fortifications, the formidable Dimmock Line. And as previously stated, while these works had lain empty on June 15th, 16th and 17th, as the men of the 5th Corps prepared for their attack on June 18th, Lee's men were pouring into Petersburg's fortifications.[52]

Still believing that only Beauregard's skeleton force was in the Petersburg fortifications, and surmising that the Rebels had not had time to throw up anything substantial on their new line, Meade's orders were for all the corps to attack at noon at all hazards.[53] Walker describes Meade's mood as one in which he wanted the enemy's lines at Petersburg taken, no matter what the cost. Hancock would not have to deal with Meade's demands this day, as he became completely incapacitated because of his old wound and turned command over to David Bell Birney.[54] Roebling observes that Meade's orders were given "no matter whether we understood the ground or not, or were prepared any how." Roebling states that the left of the 5th Corps did not attack at noon, as they had not been able to form a line by then. And contrary to Meade's assertion about makeshift trenches, Roebling reported that the enemy fortification that the 5th Corps' center and left was fighting it's way toward was formidable. The 2nd Corps attacked on its front and was repulsed. At noon, only elements of the division on the right of the 5th Corps line were reported as advancing on the enemy defenses. At about 1 P.M., when Warren had been able to bring most of his corps up into something resembling a line for the assault, Warren suggested a 3 P.M. attack to be made simultaneously by all corps.[55]

Roebling comments that the 5th Corps' three o'clock assault resulted in a repulse along the whole line, with an estimated loss of 1,600 men. The nearest anyone got to the enemy's line was on Griffin's front, where members of Chamberlain's 1st Brigade came within 20 feet of the fortification. Chamberlain was believed to be mortally wounded, and a second attack ordered for later that afternoon was finally called off. Dead and wounded were brought off during the night, and elements of the 5th Corps, some taking up a position as close as 150 yards from the Rebel fortifications, dug in to be ready to resist a counterattack. Roebling commented that the attacks by the other corps to their right were less successful than those of the 5th Corps. Meade's aid Lyman, who had been with the 5th Corps the entire day, described the attacks as costly, with many dead on the field; he also described some of the attacks as "sullen," as if the men were saying, "We can't assault but we won't run." After returning to Meade's headquarters that night, Lyman observed regarding the failure of the army to make a breakthrough, "The whole thing resulted just as I expected. You can't strike a full blow with a wounded hand."[56]

As the day went on, Meade's orders to his corps commanders grew more strident, and when Warren reported that only the right of his corps had been able to make the noon assault with the 9th Corps, something in Meade snapped. Perhaps it was Warren's additional comment that he had kept pace with Burnside until the 9th Corps stopped. Burnside had stopped because the 2nd Corps on his right had stopped advancing. Furiously, Meade complained that it was "useless to appoint an hour to effect cooperation," and he fired off orders that all the corps were to attack immediately at all hazards with their whole corps.[57] In the 3 P.M. assaults on the Petersburg defenses on June 18th, Chamberlain wasn't the only son of Maine to pay the price for Meade's folly.[58] Serving with the 2nd Corps, the 1st Maine Heavy Artillery, which had served previously in the defenses of Washington, was ordered to attack the Rebel earthworks across an open field on the 2nd Corps' front late in the day on June 18th. The First Maine "Heavies" were put in the first line of the 2nd Corps attack, followed by what were perhaps more experienced, and thus more reluctant veterans. Col. Daniel Chaplin's "Heavies" advanced for 350 yards over open ground swept by musketry and artillery, and lost more than 600 out of the 900 who made the assault. The Heavies' historian estimates that it took a mere ten minutes for this slaughter to take place. It earned the Maine men the dubious distinction of being the regiment with the heaviest loss in a single battle throughout the war.[59]

After June 18th, the assaults by the entire Army of the Potomac against the Petersburg fortifications were for the most part over. Several days later, Meade suggested that since they had been fighting and marching for 49 days, the army should rest in order to prevent its morale from being impaired. Fighting was minimal on June 19th, although the 5th Corps lost an additional 800 men, some of whom were shot by enemy snipers. Apparently "limited fighting" resulted in casualties in the hundreds, as opposed to losses in the thou-

General Charles Griffin and staff (Library of Congress).

sands as in the previous days.[60] On the 21st, Griffin's men were withdrawn from the front line to take part in an extension to the left across the Jerusalem Plank Road. A former artillery commander, Griffin noted the lack of artillery on the 5th Corps front, but when Meade came by on the 21st, he fussed at Griffin for not moving promptly from the 5th Corps front to its left. When the 2nd Corps was brought to the Army of the Potomac's left, a gap between the 5th and 2nd Corps provided an opportunity for the Confederates to come out of their fortifications and attack the 2nd Corps. They did it so suddenly, that Birney, now commanding the 2nd Corps in Hancock's absence, lost 2,300 of his men captured and lost four of his guns. As Roebling stated, if they could have taken the time to place a battery on the 5th Corps front, it would have covered Birney's advance, and prevented the whole unhappy affair.[61]

There is no question that on the night of June 19th, Meade and Warren had a heated argument, one witnessed by General Crawford. The rumor that circulated around Gen. Grant's headquarters was that Meade had given Warren an ultimatum. It is not hard to guess that the delays Warren and his corps had encountered while trying to reach the enemy fortification during the day on June 18th infuriated Meade. Did it become easy for Meade to blame Warren for the failure of all the corps to attack at the same time, and for the lack of success they had all experienced? Others offered reasons why the army's assaults on Petersburg failed. Dana, who explained that he had not been able to witness the fighting since he had remained at City Point because he was sick, reported that Grant's engineer, Comstock, had said that the fighting "hadn't been equal to our previous fighting, owing to our heavy loss in superior officers. The men fight as well, but are not directed with the same skill and enthusiasm." Without missing a beat, Dana that same day reported that casualties for June 16th, 17th and 18th were about 7,000, although that number was later amended to 9,500 casualties for the three days.[62]

But the hottest news from the front went to the administration when Dana, who had apparently been basing at least some of his news on nothing more than overheard gossip at Grant's headquarters, wrote to Washington on June 19th, "General Meade notified Warren this morning that he must either ask to be relieved, or else he (Meade) would prefer charges against him."[63] As it turned out, though Meade and Warren had argued on June 19th, Meade had not demanded Warren's resignation, but Warren had heard of the rumors circulating among Grant's staff at the time. But weeks later, on July 22nd, when that same rumor was being published in a Pennsylvania newspaper, Warren asked Meade for an explanation.

> Major General Meade:
> Dear General:
> I send you herewith the *Pittsburgh Commercial* of July 14th, which has an allusion to you and myself, which I have marked. Seeing this in the papers, I thought it best to indicate at least one way which it may have started.
> About two weeks ago, General Smith [William F. "Baldy"] told me that it was common talk at General Grant's headquarters that you had threatened me with a court-marital, if I did not resign. As you had never done so, I could not believe that you had ever said so to General Grant; and yet I believe the story circulates as coming from the highest authority.[64]

When Warren asked that Meade assist him in making a public denial, Meade replied to Warren,

> General:
> Although I cannot be held responsible for the newspaper correspondents, or the talk of staff officers, I have enclosed a note denying the statement in the *Pittsburgh Commercial* which you can make any use of you think proper. I could not deny the existence of a disagreement, because there was a serious one between us on the 19th instant, and I don't think you ought to be surprised at its publicity, as your conversation in the presence of General Crawford, and within the hearing of several officers outside your tent, precluded the possibility of its being kept private. I frankly confess to you that I was very much irritated, and felt deeply wounded by the tone and tenor of your conversation on that occasion, and fully determined, on leaving you, to apply to have you relieved. I did speak to General Grant upon the subject, with whom I have frequently spoken about you, and I even went so far as to write an official letter giving my reasons for desiring you to be relieved. But, upon further reflection, in view of the injury to you, and in the hope the cause of the disagreement would not occur in the future, I withheld the letter and have taken no official action.[65]

Meade went on to exclaim that he didn't want any of this hidden from Warren, and was, in fact, glad of an opportunity to discuss it. He said that he felt that on June 19th Warren had "exhibited a great deal of temper and positive ill-feeling against me, not justified, as I think, by anything I have ever said or done." Reminding Warren that, while he wanted harmony and cooperation among his officers, "I cannot always yield my judgment to theirs." Meade declared that if the relations necessary for harmony weren't in evidence "a separation is inevitable. I do not make these remarks for any other purpose than to explain the reason I felt called upon to speak to General Grant about you."[66]

A week and a half after Dana had written about Meade's threat to court-martial Warren, Dana reported to Washington that the matter had been settled without having to resort to Meade's "extreme remedy."[67] Though Warren continued to serve with considerable success as commander of the 5th Corps through the months of the siege at Petersburg, relations between Meade and Warren continued to deteriorate. Warren put the major difficulty of serving as a corps commander in the Army of the Potomac under Meade and Grant quite succinctly when he declared that when operations were being considered, he wished "the matter would be taken up by competent staff officers, so that opinion can rest on mere military grounds and not hereafter be a question of individual willingness, ability or boldness." Put more simply, Warren wished, though likely in vain, that the advisability of the movement would be paramount, without letting the consideration degenerate into a mere test of a commander's aggression and willingness to expend his men.[68] Warren would write to his wife that summer regarding his frustrations and feelings, ones that warred between a desire to resign and be out from under the strain, and Warren's own determined feelings of patriotism that would not permit his leaving the field. By the end of July, Warren commented that he did not think it possible that he and Meade could ever be on a friendly basis again. Warren declared that he had lost confidence in his chief's abilities, as had a number of Meade's staff, for he felt that Meade had lost the ability to act with patience and judgment.[69] And there were still months of conflict ahead for the soldiers and commanders of the Army of the Potomac.

Appendix

Federal Overland Campaign Commanders After the War

THE EVENTS OF THE SPRING OF 1864 had lasting repercussions for the Army of the Potomac, but the men who grasped power that year were to attain status well beyond the country's battlefields or its military establishment. They would gain, through their authority in Washington and the country's policies in the West, far-reaching influence over our nation and its destiny. One likes to think that those who lead our country are the best and the brightest, but is that always the case? Under the leadership of Grant and Sheridan during the Overland Campaign, it seems that blind obedience became more important than intelligent cooperation. Unwavering compliance to orders was seemingly even more important than success or failure, and when that success or failure means the lives of thousands of men, perhaps one should give it some thought. It also seems that any hesitancy to spend the lives of one's troops, perhaps wantonly, was considered a weakness. Consider the attitudes displayed by Grant and Sheridan toward Warren and Hancock. Warren was pilloried for wanting to maneuver, while Hancock was considered the fair-haired boy because he would obey orders to make those frontal attacks quickly and often without question. Were there different standards for "Grant's men" than there were for the original Army of the Potomac commanders?

It is true that Grant, in 1864, made no changes in the commanders of the Army of the Potomac's infantry corps when he became lieutenant general, leaving the reorganization that occurred in that army's infantry just before the Overland Campaign in the hands of Meade. But it is also true, that by the war's end, in April of 1865, not a single one of the corps commanders who began the Overland Campaign with Meade and Grant remained. Hancock, Sedgwick, Warren and Burnside would all be gone. Only Meade would remain, and his role had been marginalized.

An indication of just what the stakes were and just how startlingly high they could be gives us more insight into what some of the more ambitious and unscrupulous of those who became known as "Grant's Men" had in their sights. Here then is a consideration of where a number of the major players of the Overland Campaign landed in later years. For ease, they are listed alphabetically.

Badeau, Adam. Badeau would write of Edwin Booth's infamous brother, John Wilkes, after Lincoln's assassination, "It was exactly what a man brought up in a theater might have been expected to conceive.... A man, too, of his peculiar family, the son of Junius Brutus Booth, used all his life to acting tragedies."[1] During Grant's presidency, Badeau was appointed consul-general at the American Embassy in London, serving there from 1870–1881, and at Havana from 1882–1884. Badeau, according to fellow lodger and writer Henry Adams, benefited especially from Mrs. Grant's patronage. Badeau, often in his cups with Adams, told that he and Grant's staff would influence the general by discussing things in his presence, and eventually Grant would announce the idea as if it had been his own. Adams assumed that Badeau was treading water in Washington until Mrs. Grant used her own powers of suggestion with her husband to get Badeau an appointment to a consulate or legation, which, of course, she did.[2] Badeau would later repay Mrs. Grant's kindness to him by trying to claim authorship of Grant's memoirs, later suing the Widow Grant in 1887 for part of the profits from the sale of the book.[3] Badeau fell on hard times at the end of his life, and signed a note acknowledging that his debts to Edwin Booth amounted to $10,000. Badeau wrote an article after Edwin Booth's death telling that he would attend Booth's performances and take notes, and Booth would adapt his performances accordingly the next night. Badeau died in 1895 of a stroke.[4]

Bierce, Ambrose. Ambrose Bierce continued to serve with General Hazen and became a famed journalist after the war. His sarcasm was legendary, and he irritated some people to the point that he found it necessary to keep a pistol on his desk at the newspaper office. Bierce wrote a piece in response to one James Wilson wrote for the *Century Magazine* entitled "The Death of General Grant." It is so scathingly condemning and sarcastic that some modern-day readers have mistaken it as being complimentary to Wilson, but Bierce's description of Wilson as "a man with gentleman's eyes in his head, ('the better to see you with')" should have given them some warning. Bierce mentions Wilson's criticism of Grant "as a poor tactician," as an example of "what every man having knowledge of the matter and brains to digest the knowledge" already knew. But Bierce observes that "the superpatriotic person" will be outraged, while "the moral monster for whom the truth as an ingredient of history isn't good enough" will be among those who mistake distinction "for perfection of character and a flawless life." Bierce also takes notice of Wilson's testimony that "Grant cherished personal resentments and 'lay for' his private enemies till he got opportunity to pay them off," and here Bierce's sarcasm is unmistakable, for after this example of Wilson's pettiness, Bierce offers, "What a miserable business it is, this deification of the eminent." Bierce goes on to question who would want to be famous or give public service? He comments, "The animosities, intrigues, envy, obloquy and falsehoods alurk along the paths of renown like rattlesnakes infesting a mountain trail.... None but the maddest ambitionist, the hardiest philanthroper or the most insensible blockhead will incur public admiration and surrender himself naked to his eulogists. I would rather be a dead dog among buzzards than a dead hero among admirers."[5] The author recommends all of Bierce's writings on the Civil War, both memoirs and fiction. Bierce's "Four Days in Dixie" is a personal favorite. The actual date of Bierce's death is unknown, but believed to be at the end of 1913 or during the first few days of 1914. Though historians are still arguing over the details, the story most accepted is that Bierce traveled into Mexico with the alleged intention of reporting on Pancho Villa's battles, and after reaching the scenes of the conflict and beginning to write his reports, Bierce was never heard from again.[6]

Burnside, Ambrose. Grant relieved Burnside from command of the 9th Corps after the debacle of the Battle of the Crater at Petersburg in July 1864. Burnside was sent home to await orders that never came, and he finally resigned on April 15, 1865. Burnside went on to serve as Rhode Island's governor for three years, and he was one of that state's senators at the time of his death in 1881.[7]

Chamberlain, Joshua. Though the wound Chamberlain received at Petersburg on June 18, 1864, was considered mortal, he recovered and returned to the army in time to be with the 5th Corps in the last days of the war. After the war, Chamberlain served four one-year terms as Republican governor of Maine, and 12 years as president of his alma mater, Bowdoin College. He wished to serve as his state's senator, but having gotten on the wrong side of the powerful Republican James G. Blaine, who controlled Maine politics and the choice of senators, he would never hold that post. Chamberlain went on to fail in a number of business ventures, and ended his days serving in a secondary position, as surveyor of the port in the U.S. Customs House in Portland, Maine. Although he suffered reoccurring infections of his Petersburg wound for the rest of his life, he lived until 1914, when a final infection of his wound carried him off. Though Chamberlain is remembered for many of the speeches he made, he wrote only one book, and that was published posthumously in 1915.[8] The author recommends Chamberlain's *The Passing of the Armies* as an admirable account of the last days of the war, and the roles that the 5th Corps and the Army of the Potomac and its commanders played. Having done considerable research on Chamberlain and his service with the army, I have found him to be a careful and honest historian, who often consulted his Confederate counterparts.

Crawford, Samuel Wylie. One could say that General Meade sealed Warren's fate in a number of ways, and one of them was when he urged Warren to appoint one of his favorites, Samuel Wylie Crawford, to command one of the 5th Corps' divisions. For it was General Crawford who, at the Battle of Five Forks in 1865, because of Sheridan's staff's faulty reconnaissance work and Crawford's own ineptitude, began to march away from the battle, rather than toward it. It was when Warren rode to retrieve the errant Crawford and turn his division to attack the Rebels' left flank and rear that the Confederate defense at Five Forks crumbled. For his troubles, Sheridan accused Warren of having not been in the battle, and he removed Warren from command of the 5th Corps. Crawford continued in the army after the war, retiring in 1873 as a brigadier general, R.A.[9]

Dana, Charles. After the war, Dana became owner and editor of the influential New York newspaper, the *Sun*. Dana had mentioned Grant's potential as a presidential candidate very early in his assignment to Grant's headquarters as the administration's eyes and ears on that general's character and performance. Dana, whose steady stream of positive reports to the administration assured Grant's rise to lieutenant general, would co-write, with James H. Wilson, Grant's campaign biography in preparation for the general's 1868 run for the presidency. Dana expected no less than an appointment to the lucrative position of collector of the port for the City of New York. When the position was not awarded to Dana after Grant became president, Dana turned from Grant's unfailing advocate to one of his most vocal political enemies, accusing him of all manner of discreditable weaknesses and of dishonesty in the pages of his powerful newspaper. Despite the fact that Grant was old and insolvent in his last days, in Wilson's biography of Dana, he chronicles that publisher's opposition to a government pension for Grant.[10]

Grant, Ulysses S. During or immediately after the war, Grant took $100,000 from the grateful people of New York, and he accepted two houses. One, fully furnished, was in Philadelphia at 2009 Chestnut Street. The other, described by Mrs. Grant as "a lovely villa exquisitely furnished with everything good taste could desire," was at 500 Bouthillier Street, in Galena, a gift to Grant from several Galena Republicans.[11] Grant was President of the United States from 1869 to 1877, two terms not known for excellence or honesty. After his presidency, Grant embarked on a "Round the World Tour," and it seems that the usually taciturn Galenian became very talkative. Whether it was the sheer relief of being out from under years and years of pressure and responsibility, or the effect of his being feted as the former president and victorious General everywhere he went, a circumstance designed to leave one feeling rather full of oneself, Grant had many startling conversations with his traveling companion John Russell Young. There are many mind-boggling revelations in Young's book, *Around the World with General Grant*, and perhaps the most startling of all is Young's assurance that all the quotations in the book were looked over and approved by Grant. Therefore, when Grant declares that he sent Sheridan south after

Appomattox to provoke a war with France, that's just what Grant had intended to do, despite his knowledge of Seward's opposition. But the *reason* Grant offers as to why he did this is, perhaps, what's most disturbing. While commenting that the French had been supportive toward the Confederates in some way during the war, Grant asserts that a conflict with Mexico was just what was needed. It would unite all those warring Federals and Rebels in a common cause, and sending the Confederates to Mexico, now that their livelihoods in the South were destroyed, would give the Rebels something to do. Grant did add that he hadn't, at the time, thought out the part of it about the Rebels carrying slavery into Mexico with them. Grant also had something to say about how the United States needn't have feared Great Britain's interference during the war. A little bombardment of American cities by the British navy wouldn't have amounted to much or had much effect, as he had learned while bombarding Vicksburg. And the United States would have benefited from a British blockade. Just think, Grant mused, what it would have done for promoting American industries! Grant asserted that the United States could have taken Canada from Great Britain, if they had wanted to, because America, at the end of the war, could have thrown half a million soldiers, veterans not militia, into Canada. And besides, the British soldier lacked training. Grant also offered that Sheridan could have taken Canada in 30 days.[12] Grant lost everything in unwise business dealings, and ended up insisting that William Henry Vanderbilt take all of his property, including presentation swords and the many gifts from this European tour as security for a $150,000 loan from Vanderbilt, who was the world's richest man at the time of his death. Grant was finally put on the retired list with a pension in 1885, the year he died, but he managed, despite the fact that he was dying of throat cancer, to finish his highly successful memoirs.[13]

Gregg, David McMurtrie. Sheridan amply demonstrated his willingness to sacrifice David Gregg, one of the few experienced and efficient commanders in his cavalry, in the Battle of St. Mary's Church (also called Samaria Church in the South, or Nance's Shop). After Sheridan's abortive expedition to meet Hunter, cut short by his defeat at Trevilian Station, Sheridan finally reached some semblance of safety when he and the tired remnants of his cavalry force reached White House. There, he found himself responsible for the safe passage of the Army of the Potomac's immense wagon train. Hampton's cavalry, which had been nipping at Sheridan's flanks and rear all the way, was waiting for Sheridan to move. Sheridan ordered David Gregg with two brigades to stand up to Hampton's five, to act as Sheridan's rear guard, while Sheridan and Torbert continued on. Gregg suffered heavy losses and was almost captured, while Sheridan and Torbert rode on unmolested and unconcerned.[14] Later in 1864, Gregg remained with the Army of the Potomac while Sheridan went to confront Early in the Shenandoah Valley. Gregg resigned his commission on February 3, 1865. Edward Longacre, in his biography *General John Buford*, makes the outlandish assertion that Gregg resigned from the military because he had lost his nerve. Longacre based this on a conversation that Gregg had with Dr. Alonzo Rockwell of the 6th Ohio Cavalry, where the self-effacing Gregg admitted that he was not immune to being afraid. While Longacre interpreted this as proof of Gregg's cowardice,[15] Eric Wittenberg makes the more sensible suggestion that Gregg resigned when it became inevitable that Sheridan would return to the Army of the Potomac. It would make sense that Gregg was reluctant to serve again under Sheridan, making that an adequate enough reason to quit. Sheridan had already demonstrated his willingness to sacrifice Gregg and his men on the movement from White House to City Point on the cavalry's return from the Trevilian raid. And if Gregg needed any further proof as to Sheridan's reliability or character, he had only to look at what Sheridan did to Gregg's friends and classmates, Torbert and Averell.[16]

Griffin, Charles. Griffin continued to fight as the 5th Corps' 1st Division commander, after the Battle of Petersburg, serving with distinction at Weldon Railroad, Peebles Farm and Hatcher's Run. At the Battle of Five Forks in April of 1865, when Sheridan removed Warren from command of the 5th Corps, Sheridan replaced Warren with General Griffin. With numerous brevets, Griffin became a major general in the regular army in August of 1864. Assigned to Texas after the war on occupation duty, Griffin died of yellow fever in Galveston in 1867. After Griffin's death, his family sent a number of war-years' momentoes to Griffin's friend from the 5th Corps, Joshua Chamberlain. They sent the kepi Griffin had worn during the war, and a bugle and division flag that had been used at Appomattox. They also returned a sword to Chamberlain that he had loaned to Griffin when his own had been lost.[17]

Halleck, Henry. With Grant in the field, all the responsibility of supplying and keeping Grant's far-flung endeavors in 1864 and early 1865 fell on Chief of Staff Halleck's shoulders, but it was a role that seemed to suit him. Although the relationship between Grant and Halleck throughout this period was quite cordial, there were times when Grant asserted his authority and disregarded Halleck's advice. Halleck biographer John F. Marszalek offers the example of Halleck, against his better judgment, stripping the defenses of Washington when Grant demanded reinforcements in 1864. As Grant declared at the time, "We can defend Washington best by keeping Lee so occupied that he cannot detach enough troops to capture it."[18] But when Early and his army of Confederates were on the doorstep of a barely defended Washington, Halleck must have at least been thinking, "I told you so," although Marszalek lays some of the blame for the crisis on Halleck's refusal to take up a leadership role.[19] By September of 1864, after Sherman took Atlanta, Halleck's anger toward the enemy seemingly reached the boiling point, pushing the transformation from limited warfare to what came to be known as total war. Halleck wrote to Sherman expressing his approval of his destruction in Atlanta, commenting, "I have endeavored to impress these views upon our commanders for the last two years. You are almost the only one who has properly applied them." Halleck went on to tell his protégé, "I would destroy every mill and factory within my reach which I did not want for my own use," though Halleck inexplicably demurred at "uselessly destroying private property—that is barbarous."[20] Meanwhile Halleck reveled in his favorites' successes. He told a friend, "Nearly all the western Generals that I selected & put forward ... have turned out Trumps."[21] A complete break in relations between Halleck and Sherman occurred when Halleck accepted Congress's condemnation of Sherman's peace terms with Johnston. Within weeks after the fall of Richmond, Halleck was assigned to command in the devastated city, and despite his harsh attitude toward the Rebels in the last months of the war, he is reputed to have been a compassionate commander toward the residents and refugees of Richmond, though much less so to the former slaves. In 1865, Halleck was sent to command the Department of the Pacific. Here Halleck let the cat out of the bag that he, Halleck, had delayed sending Grant's orders to Thomas that would have put Schofield in Thomas's place as commander of the Army of the Cumberland at Nashville in late 1864. By 1869, Halleck was serving as commander of the Division of the South, with headquarters in Louisville, where he died in January 1872. He left an estate of more than $400,000.[22]

Hancock, Winfield Scott. A successful and charismatic leader, Hancock was forced to leave the army during the Battle of Petersburg to recuperate from the aggravation that campaigning had caused to his Gettysburg wound. Within days of Hancock's departure, the 2nd Corps suffered a defeat while attempting to extend the army's left, which began a downhill slide in that corps' much vaunted reputation. Hancock rejoined his corps in time for their poor performance at Ream's Station, and neither the corps' nor Hancock's military reputation was ever quite the same. Nonetheless, Hancock remained a popular leader and he was the Democratic candidate for president in 1880, but he was defeated by the Republican candidate, veteran James Garfield. Hancock died while still on active duty in 1888.[23]

Hazen, William Babcock. Sheridan never forgave Hazen for his insistence that his men, not Sheridan's, took the summit and the guns on Missionary Ridge during the fight for Chattanooga. Hazen continued in the regular army and came into conflict with Sheridan again over the army's Indian policies. Hazen was no admirer of Native Americans, whom he referred to as dirty beggars who murdered the weak and unprotected, but Hazen also believed the American government should keep the agreements it made. If the Indians were doing what they said they would do, then the government should do so too. Hazen was also outspoken in his protests against the slaughter of the buffalo.[24] As for Sheridan's feelings about Hazen, Sheridan biographer Paul Hutton wrote, "Sheridan was a good hater, especially if someone was beyond his power to punish. His contempt for Meade was notorious, but his persecution of General William B. Hazen displayed even more glaringly a cruel pettiness."[25]

Howard, Oliver Otis. General Howard was a Maine man and a graduate of Bowdoin College, as well as West Point's class of 1854. He had a somewhat checkered reputation in the war before 1864, and some of the soldiers serving under O.O. Howard in Sherman's army referred to their commander as "Uh-Oh" Howard. When James McPherson was killed in 1864, John Logan, though one of the political generals, was acknowledged as a successful commander, and he expected to replace McPherson as commander of the Army of the Tennessee. Logan never quite got over Sherman instead giving the command to Howard. Immediately after the war, Sherman was smart enough to realize that he had made an adversary of the politically powerful Logan. Sherman therefore asked Howard to ride with him in the Grand Review, asking Howard to step aside and let John Logan ride at the head of the Army of the Tennessee down Pennsylvania Avenue. Howard reluctantly agreed. After the war, Howard was a commissioner of the Freedmen's Bureau and the founder and president of Howard University. Howard fought in the Indian Wars and became superintendent of West Point in the 1880s. Congressman Logan was surprisingly supportive of Howard at the time, though Logan declared that if West Point didn't change its ways, training its graduates in "aristocratic snobbery," its days were numbered. Logan applauded Howard's institution of an oath of allegiance to the United States, as opposed to any further misapprehensions of allegiance to one's state. Howard retired from the military in 1894 as a major general, USA, and he was one of the few Civil War commanders who did not write about the war.[26]

Logan, John. John Logan was an Illinois politician who, like McClernand, influenced the people of "Egypt," as Southern Illinois was known, to remain loyal to the Union. Logan became a great favorite of Grant's; perhaps there is some significance that two of Grant's favorites, Sheridan and Logan, were the only two major generals in the army shorter than Grant. It was Logan whom Grant sent west when Grant intended to replace George Thomas in late 1864. There is still some question as to whether Grant intended Logan or John Schofield to replace Thomas as commander of the Army of the Cumberland at Nashville.[27] But when Logan served with Sherman in 1864, Logan never quite forgave Sherman for failing to appoint him to replace the fallen hero, McPherson, as commander of the Army of the Tennessee. And although Sherman tried to make up for it by appointing Logan to command that Army in time for Logan to lead it down Pennsylvania Avenue in the Grand Review after the war, it apparently didn't work. Logan would have much to say in Congress about curbing the arrogant ways of West Pointers, downsizing the army and curtailing their wasteful ways. In 1869, Congressman Logan pointed out that while Congress had just reduced the number of infantry regiments in the army from 45 to 24, they'd done nothing about the 509 officers now left without commands. Declaring that they should be dismissed, Logan publicized the sort of salaries the heads of the army, with food, clothing and housing allowances, were receiving: Sherman, more than $18,000 a year; Sheridan nearly $15,000; and major generals, $8,000. Logan pointed out that the latter amount was what the Speaker of the House and the Vice President received as an annual salary.[28]

McClernand, John. John McClernand might be considered the perfect prototype of a political general. A friend of Lincoln's and an influential Illinois Democrat who supported the war, McClernand's rise in the volunteer military was fast and, according to Grant's and his supporters' later assessment, undeserved. But it seems that McClernand did rather well in the battles in which he fought, and did not deserve the treatment he received. Charles Dana certainly played a considerable role in McClernand's removal from command, with his constant stream of negativity in the reports he sent to Washington. When McClernand was sent away from Grant's army, he next served in the Red River Campaign, then resigned in November of 1864 because of ill health. Unlike Logan, who became a Republican, McClernand remained in the Democratic Party, and never regained the political prominence he had had before and during the war. He became a judge after the war and died in 1890.[29] The author recommends Richard L. Kiper's book, *Major General John Alexander McClernand*, for a thoughtful exploration of McClernand's military career. Kiper is one of the few authors to consider that McClernand, while he had his faults, might not have been such a bad commander after all.

Meade, George Gordon. During the Overland Campaign, friends of Meade contributed to a fund to buy the house Mrs. Meade was living in for him and his family. He turned it down, declaring "that a public man makes a mistake when he allows his generous friends to reward him with gifts." Meade expressed his wish to remain independent, but it seems that his family had already, irrevocably, accepted the house as a gift, and Meade acquiesced. It is interesting, however, to note the great difference in attitude between Meade and Grant as far as gifts of great value were concerned.[30] Meade completed the war as commander of the Army of the Potomac, but nothing could be more eloquent of his standing in Grant's estimation than a consideration of the Federal officers who were conspicuous by their presence or absence when Grant accepted Lee's surrender at Appomattox. Other than Rawlins and the other members of Grant's staff, General Sheridan and General Ord, who had recently brought the 14th Corps from the Gulf to fight in the East, were present at the McLean House. Gen. Meade, though he was a mere three miles from Appomattox, was not there. After the war, Meade served as commander of Departments of the East and South, and the Division of the Atlantic. He died in 1872 at the age of 57 of pneumonia. He is buried beneath a modest gravestone in Laurel Hill Cemetery, Philadelphia.[31]

Rawlins, John Aaron. Grant saw to it that a new office was created especially for Rawlins when he was appointed as brigadier general and chief of staff in the United States Army on March 3, 1865. Also, Rawlins received what was the last brigadier's star awarded during the war. He was also brevetted a major general of volunteers in February of that year, and on April 9, 1865, Rawlins was appointed a major general in the regular army for the Appomattox campaign. It is said that Grant, since Rawlins was suffering from tuberculosis, had intended to send Rawlins to command the Department of Arizona, but Rawlins indicated that he preferred to be secretary of war. When Grant agreed, Rawlins resigned his commission in 1869 to serve as President Grant's secretary of war. He died five months later and was buried at Arlington National Cemetery.[32]

Roebling, Washington. Roebling served as Gen. Gouverneur Warren's aide and engineer at Gettysburg and after, until the final days of the war, when he resigned. Roebling married his sweetheart, Emily Warren, General Warren's sister, and Roebling continued to work as a civil engineer with his father, their most important project being the Brooklyn Bridge. Its new, radical design was the work of John Roebling, and when he died in 1869, Washington became chief engineer of the project. Unwilling to send any man where he would not go himself, Roebling made numerous trips down into the caissons in the bridges foundation, endured severe bouts of caisson disease, also known as the bends, and became completely disabled. The bright and capable Mrs. Roebling became Washington's "Aide de Camp," as Roebling's alma mater, Rensselaer Polytech, describes it in their alumni "Hall of Fame." Emily Roebling, with a firm grasp of the engineering details, and bearing many messages back and forth between her husband and the builders, managed and directed the last days of construction of the bridge. When completed, it was the longest suspension bridge in the world. Roebling, despite precarious health, lived until 1926.[33] Roebling was a bright and articulate witness to the Overland Campaign, who took many risks and delivered many valuable scouting reports to Warren and to Meade and Grant, if they'd listen. Roebling who may have decided he had pushed his luck dodging his Rebel counterparts long enough, resigned and left the army in the spring of 1865, just before the last days of the war. Although he was not with Warren at the Battle of Five Forks, Roebling leaves us in little doubt of how he felt about the treatment his commander, Warren, suffered at the hands of Sheridan. Roebling's comments, given below, indicate that he still wished he had been with Warren, thinking that he somehow could have prevented what happened. But however much Roebling may have wished it, it is hard to imagine how he might have prevented the injustice meted out to Warren by Sheridan and Grant at Five Forks. The following is taken from Roebling's correspondence with a friend, who in 1916 had inquired about the Overland Campaign. Roebling wrote,

> This campaign has never been written up properly — the underlying motives that prompted action were known to few — strict army etiquette prevented army officers from ventilating the gross blunders and mistakes that were made — Grant, swollen by the fulsome praise of his personal staff, tacitly accepted the honors belonging to other and better men — I left the army shortly before the victory at Five Forks, won by Warren and not by Sheridan and the only victory won by Grant's army in this campaign up to that time — I have always felt that if I had been there the outrage perpetrated by Sheridan could have been forestalled as I was well aware of the jealous motives that governed [Washington Roebling to Gen. James Rusling, February 18, 1916].[34]

Schofield, John Mcallister (USMA, 1853). Schofield served under George Thomas, and, according to Halleck, intrigued to get Thomas's command at Nashville in late 1864, and came close to doing it.[35] After the war, Schofield served as Andrew Johnson's secretary of war during Johnson's impeachment and the controversial removal of Stanton as Secretary of War. Grant honored Schofield by allowing him to remain as secretary of war in the early days of Grant's presidency, before Grant appointed his friend John Rawlins to that cabinet seat, at which point Schofield became superintendent of West Point. Just before Thomas's death in California, letters appeared in the *New York Tribune* claiming that Schofield, not Thomas, should be credited with winning the Battle of Nashville in late 1864. Though the letter was sent anonymously, it was known to have been written by Jacob Cox, who served under Schofield in the war and, it is said, wrote the letter with Schofield's knowledge. At the time Cox wrote his controversial Thomas vs. Schofield letter, Cox was serving as Grant's secretary of the interior.[36] While he was serving as Johnson's secretary of war, Schofield wrote his own recommendation that he be awarded the Medal of Honor, and in 1892 Schofield received it for Wilson's Creek. The citation, remarkable for its lack of detail, read: "Was conspicuously gallant in leading a regiment in a successful charge against the enemy." Historian Benson Bobrick found the citation outrageously vague and undocumented.[37] Schofield became Commander in Chief of the Armies at Sheridan's death, serving from 1888 to 1895, as well as achieving the rank of lieutenant general. He retired in 1895, and in 1897, wrote his memoirs, *Forty-six Years in the Army*, a version of his service that did not go unchallenged. Schofield died in 1906 and was buried at West Point.[38]

Sheridan, Philip Henry. In John Russell Young's *Around the World with General Grant*, Grant displayed, as Young reported from their conversations, what seems more like an irrational infatuation, rather than a friendship, with Philip Sheridan. One has to question Grant's reasoning when he made the declaration that West Point had treated "poor Sheridan" unfairly when he was suspended after attacking a cadet sergeant acting as file-closer because Sheridan didn't like his tone of voice. For Sheridan had gone after William R. Terrill with a lowered bayonet, and later with his fists because the senior cadet had reported him for infractions. It is often suggested that Sheridan didn't like Terrill because he was a southerner. What those Sheridan apologists fail to acknowledge is that Terrill was one of those Virginians who remained loyal to and fought in the Federal army. Terrill died in the Battle of Perryville in 1862 wearing a blue uniform. Then too, Grant didn't seem able to come up with enough superlatives for Sheridan. While describing Sheridan's genius, Grant stated that Sheridan was "one of the greatest soldiers of the world, worthy to stand in the very highest rank," to be considered with "Napoleon and Frederick and the great commanders in history."[39] Grant also said that if Sheridan had been in command at Gettysburg instead of Meade, Sheridan would have destroyed Lee's Army. Grant also insisted that either Sheridan or Sherman would have made short work of Stonewall Jackson. After Appomattox Grant sent Sheridan to the Texas-Mexican border for a show of force with 50,000 men. In 1867, Sheridan was appointed military governor of Texas and Louisiana, but his administration was so harsh that he was recalled within six months.[40] Sheridan was sent by the United States as an observer during the Franco-Prussian War, 1870–1871. It seems that he thought of himself as more of an advisor than an observer, however, and is quoted as saying of the Prussians, "They had yet to understand the nature of modern war." Sheridan declared that he wanted to see "more smoke from burning villages" and suggested that there should be so much French suffering that "the people must be left nothing but their eyes to weep with after the war."[41] Sheridan married Irene Rucker, 24 years his junior, on June 3, 1875. She would outlive him by nearly half a century. They lived in Washington, D.C., in a large house at Rhode Island Avenue and 17th Street North, which was bought for Sheridan by the city of Chicago in gratitude for his work following the great Chicago Fire of 1871.[42] As David Coffey points out in *Sheridan's Lieutenants*, regarding the influence Sheridan had on our country, "For twenty years, as a regional commander and as commanding general, he was the chief prosecutor of the Indian Wars in the West. Among the five most prominent instruments of that prosecution, four — Crook, Custer, Mackenzie and Merritt (Nelson Miles being the fifth) — owed their postwar careers, in large measure, to service under Sheridan in 1864 and 1865." Sheridan died at the age of 57, but his influence and the impact he had upon military policy continued after his death in 1888. In 1890 his Civil War chief of staff, James Forsyth commanded the 7th Cavalry in the now infamous Battle of Wounded Knee, and in 1898, Wesley Merritt led the ground troops that took Manila during the Spanish American War. It is, therefore, useful to examine the genesis of the martial brotherhood that dominated the American military establishment for almost 40 years. Sheridan, whose fondness for food and drink was legendary, died at 57 of a heart attack. Just weeks before his death, Congress awarded him a fourth star making him a full general, only the fourth man in American history to have that rank. It pleased the ailing Sheridan that he had finally joined Washington, Sherman, and Grant in that high achievement.[43] Once again, let us leave it to one of Sheridan's subordinates to have the last word on Philip H. Sheridan. George Crook, one of Sheridan's commanders in the 1864 Valley Campaign, had continued to serve under Sheridan in the Indian Wars. Though they had been friends since childhood and he was Sheridan's roommate at West Point, Crook's success in the West drew Sheridan's negative attention. As Sheridan biographer Paul Hutton points out, Sheridan grew distrustful of anyone who seemed to be getting any of the fame and glory that he wanted for himself. Crook's growing sympathy for the Native Americans' plight also put him at odds with Sheridan. Crook is described as a reticent man, but rarely has there been a more scathing indictment given than Crook's appraisal of Sheridan. Several months after Sheridan's death at 57 years of age in 1888, Crook revisited the battlefields in the Shenandoah Valley, and wrote in his diary,

> After examining the grounds and the position of the troops after twenty five years which have elapsed and in the light of subsequent events, it renders General Sheridan's claims and his subsequent actions in allowing the general public to remain under the impressions regarding his part in these battles [Fisher's Hill and Cedar Creek], when he knew they were fiction, all the more contemptible. The adulation heaped on him by a grateful nation for his supposed genius turned his head, which, added to his natural disposition, caused him to bloat his little carcass with debauchery and dissipation, which carried him off prematurely.[44]

Sherman, William Tecumseh. In 1864, Sherman, for the most part, avoided the bloodbaths that Grant was creating with the Army of the Potomac, but as historian John Marszalek observes, Sherman also "seemed unable to flank Johnston successfully, no matter what he tried." In June of 1864, when Sherman had once again been stymied by the Rebel general, he explained it away by writing to Halleck, "One of my chief objects being to give full employment to Johnston, it makes but little difference where he is, so he is not on his way to Virginia."[45] When Hood replaced Johnston, Sherman was able to force the Rebels out of Atlanta, and Sherman's exultant message to Halleck was, "I confess I owe you all I now enjoy of fame." Sherman believed that it was Halleck who had saved him back in 1861, and Halleck rejoiced in Sherman's success, calling his campaign "the most brilliant of the war." Goodwin in her *Team of Rivals* points out that though supporters of Grant and Sheridan like to credit them with Lincoln's nomination and election to a second term because of their victories on the battlefields, since there weren't any unequivocal victories in 1864, maybe there was something else going on.[46] Halleck, for one, was convinced that victories or seeming victories on the battlefield had a very direct impact on Lincoln's election. Interestingly, Halleck, a lifelong Democrat, abhorred that party's Copperhead or pro–Southern inclinations and their candidate of choice, George B. McClellan. So Halleck supported Lincoln, although he commented of the President, "Mr. Lincoln has not the qualities suited to times like the present." Goodwin therefore suggests that a more likely reason for Lincoln's success was the Democrats' having so splintered their party by choosing McClellan as their candidate. With neither the War Dems (peace with a military solution) or Peace Dems (peace at all costs) liking McClellan, that's what made Lincoln's election to a second term possible.[47] Meanwhile, did Sherman's taking of Atlanta earn Lincoln votes? Perhaps a better case for that could be made than citing Grant and Sheridan "victories." After taking the Georgia capital, Sherman left Atlanta on November 16th, 1864, to begin that for which he is best remembered, his march to the sea. He left George Thomas with the not inconsiderable job of coping with Hood and his army. The end of Sherman's war was marred by the controversy over the terms of surrender he had offered to Joseph Johnston, which many in Washington felt were too lenient and a case of Sherman having exceeded his authority. While Grant stuck by his friend, and traveled south to help Sherman repair the damage, stories would abound that Sherman, furious over the criticism he received in Washington, refused to shake Stanton's hand when they met in the reviewing stand at the Grand Review. Nonetheless, Sherman was appointed lieutenant general on July 25, 1866, and full general in March of 1869, when he then became commander in chief of the armies, a position in which he served until he retired in 1884.

Sherman and Grant did not always agree. In fact, when Grant made Sherman a lieutenant general, Sherman had felt that the appointment should have gone to Meade or Thomas. There were other differences of opinion during Sherman's term as the army's commander, and undoubtedly the most serious was the conflict that developed among Sherman, President Grant, and his secretary of war, William W. Belknap. Ironically, it was Sherman, who had recommended Belknap to replace Secretary Rawlins at the time of his death. Belknap had served under Sherman at Shiloh and during the March to the Sea.[48] That in no way deterred Belknap from stripping Sherman of his authority to control the appointment or dismissal of post traders who were allegedly giving bribes to Belknap. When in 1876 Congress would consider evidence that Belknap was receiving $80,000 a year in bribes from the post traders, Congress could not muster the two-thirds vote necessary for conviction, and Belknap resigned.[49] But to return to Grant and Belknap's refusal to acknowledge Sherman's previous authority over post traders, when it seemed there could be no resolution, Sherman asked permission to move his headquarters from Washington, D.C., to St. Louis, a jaw-dropping withdrawal from the halls of power. Equally astonishing is Belknap's notification to Sherman that Grant had approved the move, an indication that Grant was apparently complacent about Sherman's great dissatisfaction. Regardless of this standoff, Sherman continued as chief of the army until he retired in 1884, to be succeeded by Philip H. Sheridan.[50] Sherman died in February of 1891 and was buried in Calvary Cemetery in St. Louis. The 1875 publication of Sherman's memoirs had caused some friction between Sherman and Grant, but disagreements were smoothed over, and their friendship apparently resumed.[51]

Thomas, George Henry. In 1864, George Thomas was one of General Sherman's commanders, but on November 16th, when Sherman left Atlanta to start his march to the sea, he left George Thomas with the responsibility of handling General John Bell Hood's Confederate army. It is interesting that Sherman, pressing his case to Grant that his march through Georgia would accomplish more than a pursuit of Hood, made light of Hood's capacity to threaten Federally held territory or cities. It was a point of view that Grant apparently held, too, until, as Thomas biographer Benson Bobrick points out, Sherman and his 60,000 soldiers disappeared into Georgia. Then Grant began declaring that Hood constituted a real threat that General Thomas was not dealing with adequately, in Grant's eyes anyway. Never mind that Sherman left Thomas with only 22,000 men and 5,000 cavalrymen without mounts, or that Thomas was left in command of a military division that extended from the Ohio River to the Gulf, and from the Mississippi to the mountains. With the responsibility of maintaining a garrison in a dozen or so cities, a number of Thomas's troops on paper had to remain where they were posted. Sherman also left Thomas with all the "trash," as Sherman called it, "the convalescents, the injured, and an estimated 15,000 soldiers whose terms of service were about to expire."[52] It's little wonder that Thomas felt he must prepare and get this patchwork force in hand before advancing on the ever-aggressive Hood, who was leading an army of between 40,000 and 45,000 veteran infantrymen, and a Rebel cavalry corps of 10,000–15,000 horsemen. Just before the confrontation between Thomas and Hood culminated in the Battle of Nashville in December of 1864, Grant had arranged to hand Thomas's army over to one of his cronies, either Logan or Schofield. Only Thomas's winning one of the most decisive victories of the war, one that left Hood no longer a threat, forestalled Thomas's being removed from command. During Reconstruction, Thomas would be the only major general in the regular army *not* assigned to command a military division. He was assigned to remain in command in Tennessee until 1867,[53] when Grant sent Thomas to the West Coast. It seems impossible to frame a better example of the cruelty and ignoble treatment that Grant and his men subjected Thomas to than by quoting Grant's own words to journalist John Russell Young, who recorded it for posterity in *Around the World with General Grant*. Once again, we are assured that Young made certain that Grant saw and approved all of his quotations before publication. It is hard to recognize Thomas, the loyal and capable general who never lost a battle, in Grant's disparaging descriptions of him, some that even recall the doubt some had about Thomas's faithfulness to the Union cause. Grant describes Thomas in terms that would lead one unfamiliar with him and his career to deduce that Thomas was either slow-witted or an invalid, when, in fact, he was quite clearly neither. In December 1864, while Grant himself was still besieging Lee's army in the trenches at Petersburg, the lieutenant general became impatient with Thomas's delay in attacking Hood, and Grant sent Gen. John Logan to Nashville to replace Thomas as commander of the Army of the Cumberland. Grant claimed at the time that Thomas's unwillingness to attack Hood until he felt he was ready was endangering the prosecution of the war in the West, with Grant alleging that Thomas was allowing Hood the option to strike other vulnerable Federal targets. While Grant insisted that Hood was liable to push north and perhaps strike northern cities, there was evidence that Hood was in no shape to take his ragtag army anywhere.[54] During his trip around the world with Young, Grant said of Thomas,

> It was a severe trial for me even to think of removing him. I mention that fact to show the extent of my own anxiety about Sherman and Hood. But Thomas was an inert man. It was this slowness that led to the stories that he meant in the beginning to go with the South. When the war was coming, Thomas felt like a Virginian, and talked like one, and had all the sentiment then so prevalent about the rights of slavery and sovereign States and so on. But the more Thomas thought it over, the more he saw the crime of treason behind it all. And to a mind as honest as that of Thomas the crime of treason would soon appear. So by the time Thomas thought it all out, he was as passionate and angry in his love for the Union as any one. So he continued during the war. As a commander he was slow. We used to say laughingly, "Thomas is too slow to move, and too brave to run away."[55]

Grant went on to comment, "The success of his [Thomas's] campaign will be his vindication even against my criticisms," even so referring to Thomas's death at a young age in a patronizing, disparaging way. Noting that it was found that Thomas had had "fatty degeneration of the heart," Grant commented, "I have often thought that this disease, with him long-seated, may have led to the inertness which affected him as a commander. At West Point, when he was commanding cadets in cavalry drill, he would never go beyond a slow trot. The boys used to call him 'Slow Trot Thomas.' I have no doubt ... the disease from which Thomas died demanded from him constant fortitude, and affected his actions in the field."

Thomas biographer Thomas Van Horne suggests one strong reason Grant and his supporters were so willing to disparage Thomas, was to prevent this winning general from gaining any more public favor. Though Thomas declared he wanted nothing to do with politics, his popularity had led to his being considered as a possible presidential candidate in 1864, and another victorious battle in the West, another Chickamauga so to speak, might make Thomas an invincible political opponent.[56] Other than an unlimited supply of cussedness, it is less easy to fathom why Grant continued to defame Thomas, even after Thomas's death, but it seems likely that Grant continued to feel the need to justify his ill treatment of the still highly regarded Thomas.[57] When Grant became president elect, he called Thomas to come to him, saying that either Thomas or Sheridan would be assigned to California, and he asked Thomas how he would feel about going west. Thomas, who had been hoping for a posting in the East, suggested that he didn't mind, but that Mrs. Thomas would prefer to stay where her friends were. Mrs. Grant joked that that was all the more reason for Thomas to go, so that Sheridan could stay in the East and find a wife. Grant then, laughingly, changed the subject, but Thomas suspected at the time that his fate was sealed. In March of 1869, Grant then sent Thomas to serve as commander of the Military Division of the Pacific in California in place of Henry Halleck, an assignment that saw Thomas travel 14,000 miles in one year inspecting the posts under his command. It was in California that Thomas learned about Schofield's ambitions and machinations regarding the Army of the Cumberland, and Thomas heard of another of Grant's orders that would have given Schofield Thomas's command at Nashville. Thomas died of a heart attack at age 54 while he was writing a response to a letter in the *New York Tribune* that claimed that Schofield was the one who should have the credit for Thomas's victory at Nashville in 1864. The author of the letter was one Jacob Cox, who had served as one of Schofield's division commanders and was currently serving as President Grant's secretary of the interior.[58] General Sherman gave Thomas a sublime tribute. He described Thomas as, "The very impersonation of honesty, integrity, and honor ... the *beau ideal* of the soldier and gentleman. Though he leaves no child to bear his name, the old Army of the Cumberland, numbered by tens of thousands, called him father, and will weep for him many tears of grief." It is a touching tribute, but one that makes the adherence that Sherman adopted in his own memoirs to supporting Grant's denigration of Thomas all the more inexplicable. Schofield, in his own 1897 memoirs, would contribute his own denials of Thomas's achievements and support Sherman and Grant's continuing defamation of Thomas.[59]

Warren, Gouverneur K. Warren, after winning the battle of Five Forks for Sheridan, was relieved of command of the 5th Corps by Sheridan, and when the Army of the Potomac continued its pursuit of Lee and the Army of Northern Virginia to Appomattox, Warren was left behind as commander of the occupation force at Petersburg by Grant's orders. Warren asked for a court of inquiry for years, and was denied. And beyond that, with Grant and Sheridan in positions of such authority, who among the army's commanders was going to testify on Warren's behalf in defiance of the president or the commander of the armies?[60] Grant was so irrational about the subject of Warren that, as cited in Young's *Around the World with General Grant*, in conversation Grant even blamed Warren for the failure of the assault at the Crater at Petersburg in 1864. Though Warren and the 5th Corps weren't involved in the assault, except as standing in reserve if needed, Grant declared that Warren had failed in some way and precipitated the sad Federal disaster that, in fact, had been under Burnside's direction, and had led to Burnside's being relieved from command for the costly calamity. In December of 1879, President Rutherford B. Hayes finally gave Warren his court of inquiry, but before the court exonerated him, Warren died in 1882. Though he had continued to serve in the Army, his career had been destroyed. At the time of his death, Warren was serving as a lieutenant colonel of engineers, but Warren requested that he not be buried in his uniform and that there be no symbols of his service at the funeral. He was buried at the Island Cemetery in Newport, Rhode Island.[61]

Washburne, Elihu. Though Washburne wished to be President Grant's secretary of the treasury, Grant had already promised that post to another. Grant offered Washburne the Interior Department, but Washburne then asked to be appointed minister to France, while also requesting that he first be allowed to serve as secretary of state for a few days before he went, so he could include a cabinet post in his resume, so to speak. And that is just what happened. Washburne's name was submitted for secretary of state, was approved in early March, and he resigned on March 10th. Then, Grant appointed him minister to France. Grant biographer Jean Smith comments that Washburne could only have been disappointed at not receiving the expected appointment as secretary of the treasury from the General he had championed all through the war, but Grant had already promised that position to George Sewall Boutwell, a Republican Representative from Massachusetts instrumental in prosecuting Johnson's impeachment.[62]

Wilson, James Harrison. Shortly after the army's role at Petersburg changed from battle to siege, Wilson was sent on a cavalry expedition that failed utterly. He lost a substantial number of his men and much of his equipment. When the Rebel cavalry continued to prevent Wilson from returning to the Army of the Potomac, Meade called upon Sheridan to rescue Wilson and what was left of his beleaguered division. But Sheridan, still licking his own wounds from his confrontation with the Confederate cavalry at Trevilian Station, failed to obey Meade's orders to send help to Wilson, who eventually limped back on his own. After the raid, Southern newspapers reported that plunder, such as wine and silver, was found in Wilson's captured headquarters wagon. When Meade questioned Wilson about it, Grant and Wilson were outraged, and no more questions were asked.[63] Wilson did accompany Sheridan on his assignment to drive Early out of the Shenandoah Valley and, seemingly having worn out his welcome with Sheridan, was sent to lead Thomas's cavalry in the West. Spending months putting together a well-equipped cavalry force that could overwhelm anything that the Rebels could throw at him, Wilson ended the war, perhaps best known for his cavalry's capture of the Confederate president, Jefferson Davis. Wilson applied for the $100,000 reward for Davis's capture, getting the "admiral's share," as he called it, of 5.25 percent or $5,250. Though Wilson would at times tell a truthful version of what happened when he made Davis a prisoner, he would return, again and again, to the spiteful, though erroneous version that he most enjoyed putting about that Davis had been captured wearing his wife's dress. After the war, Wilson was awarded a second star, and he served as a general officer of volunteers in the Spanish-American War and during the Boxer Rebellion. Wilson, who lived until 1925, managed to be around longer than any of his fellow commanders, or, as Wilson put it himself in 1906, when asked if any of the prominent cavalrymen were left, Wilson replied, "None but Merritt and myself." And by the time Wilson wrote his memoirs in 1912, there was no one left among his fellow cavalry commanders to contradict him.[64]

Wright, Horatio Gouverneur. After the Overland Campaign, Wright and the 6th Corps were sent to confront Early's advance on Washington, and he and his corps served with Sheridan in the Shenandoah Valley. Wright's initial movements in defense of Washington and in the valley were undistinguished. But at Cedar Creek in October of 1864, the 6th Corps, though they were at first routed, had regrouped and gained the upper hand on the battlefield, when the Rebels stopped to plunder the Yankee camps. But Wright would placidly accept Sheridan's version of how he, Sheridan, had saved the 6th Corps from defeat at Cedar Creek. For his complacency, Wright would end his army career as a brigadier general, regular army, and chief engineer of the army. He died in 1899 and is buried at Arlington National Cemetery.[65]

Chapter Notes

Preface

1. Donald, *Lincoln*, 491.
2. Waugh, *Class of 1846*, 68, 73. Waugh cites tongue-in-cheek descriptions of the engineers as gods, topographical engineers as demigods, and the rest as lesser mortals. Winfield Scott in the Mexican War surrounded himself with the engineering elite, including Lee, Beauregard and McClellan. Morrison, "Educating," 108–111. Morrison points out that the West Pointers were really educated as engineers who could serve as soldiers, as opposed to soldiers who could serve as engineers. Of the Military Academy men who served in the war, "In all 359 Confederates and 638 Union officers — more than three-quarters of all the West Pointers who fought in the war graduated between 1833 and 1861." Classes in engineering, mathematics and Natural Philosophy (physics) dominated the curriculum. Though it has been suggested that it was difficult to get into West Point, statistics indicate otherwise. After passing the physical, 93.1% of those who took the examination to enter, passed, though one quarter of those would not graduate from West Point because of academic shortcomings.
3. Shanks, *Personal Recollections*, 126.

Chapter One

1. Norlands Living History Center, http://www.norlands.org/.
2. Hughes, *Belmont*, 18–19.
3. Warner, *Generals*, 184. Grant's Brigadier General of Volunteers dated from May 17, 1861.
4. Simpson, *Grant* 96.
5. Donald, *Lincoln*, 181, 278, 469, 474.
6. Tarbell, 188.
7. Waugh, *Class of 1846*, 188–190.
8. Boatner, *Civil War*, 15; Simpson, *Grant*, 80–81; W.T. Sherman, *Memoirs*, I, 220. The fourth promotion was given to Ambrose Burnside, who was shortly replaced by O.M. Mitchel.
9. George B. McClellan, *Diary*, 180.
10. Goodwin, *Team*, 428.
11. Marszalek, *Commander*, 132–171.
12. John Sherman, *John*, 250.
13. Bearss, *Receding Tide*, 51.
14. W.T. Sherman, *Memoirs*, 215–217.
15. Kennett, *Sherman*, 116–126; Meagher "Last Days"; John Sherman 261, 165.
16. John Sherman, *John*, 265; Sifakis, *Who*, 249–250; Waugh, *Class of 1846*, 341–376, 393–403.
17. Bobrick, *Master*, 81–82; W.T. Sherman, *Memoirs*, I, 221, 227.
18. John Sherman, *John*, 243.
19. W.T. Sherman, *Memoirs*, 194; Kennett, *Sherman*, 112–113; John Sherman, *John*, 244.
20. Bobrick, *Master*, 85–87.
21. Engle, *Buell*, 86–87; Noe, *Perryville*, 10.
22. Hoppin, *Foote*, 185.
23. Simpson, *Grant*, 103–104; Ambrose, *Halleck*, 11–13.
24. Kennett, *Sherman*, 130–149; Bobrick, *Master*, 92–93; Ambrose, *Halleck*, 15–17.
25. Simon, *Papers*, v. 4, 116–119; Boatner, *Civil War*, 287.
26. Geare, "Swords," 629. Belmont, Donelson, Shiloh, Vicksburg, Mission Ridge, Spottsylvania and Richmond were inscribed on the sword.
27. Hughes, *Belmont*, 56; Simpson, *Grant*, 92.
28. Hughes, *Belmont*, 36–37, 191. The Whitworth, nicknamed "Lady Polk," later exploded, killing its whole crew and nearly doing in Columbus's stunned commander, Leonidas Polk.
29. Force, *Fort Henry*, 20–21; Hughes, *Belmont*, xiii, 4–5, 29–30, 82–3; Simpson, *Grant*, 92.
30. Hughes, *Belmont*, 45–56, 193. While a warning message from W.H.L. Wallace is offered as the impetus behind Grant's decision to attack Belmont, Grant historian John Simon points out that there is no record of such a message, and the supposed author of it, Wallace, told his wife that the alleged notice of Polk advancing into Missouri was "just Grant blowing smoke." Grant's report on Belmont in the Official Record is not the report Grant wrote in 1861, but one he wrote in 1864, and it is this revised report that contains Grant's claim that it was Wallace's message that influenced him to attack at Belmont.
31. Hughes, *Belmont*, 7, 45–51, 55–56.
32. Ibid, 50–53.
33. Ibid, 56–63. While ironclads were under construction, the Mississippi flotilla consisted of 3 timberclad steamers to cope with Confederate batteries. Sheathed with oak five inches thick, coal bunkers were relocated to protect the boat's boilers.
34. Ibid, 31–35, 67–69, 71–74, 77.
35. Ibid, 79, 84–86, 88–92.

36. Force, *Fort Henry*, 22–23; Hughes, *Belmont*, 94–121.
37. Brinton, *Memoirs*, 77; Hughes, *Belmont*, 126–134, 147–148, 184.
38. Force, *Fort Henry*, 22–23; Hoppin, *Foote*, 187; Hughes, *Belmont*, 148–158, 161–165, 170–175, 192, 195–196, 202–203, 205.
39. Hughes, *Belmont*, 182, 184, 186, 188. Hughes believes the Rebels had slightly more casualties than the Federals at Belmont. The author recommends Hughes' battle summary of Belmont, pp. 198–208.
40. Simpson, *Grant,* 96–97; Boatner, *Civil War,* 58.
41. Simpson, *Civil War,* 590–591.
42. Simpson, *Grant,* 106.
43. Hughes, *Belmont*, 207.
44. Grant, *Memoirs*, 160–168.
45. Hughes, *Belmont*, 195–6.
46. Hoppin, *Foote*, 185–188.
47. Hughes, *Belmont*, 45–56.
48. Simpson, *Grant,* 103.
49. Force, *Fort Henry*, 26–27.
50. Cooling, *Forts,* 29, 37, 43–44.
51. Daniel, *Shiloh*, 15–19; Kiper, *McClernand,* 59; Cooling, *Forts,* xii.
52. Simpson, *Grant,* 108–109; Ambrose, *Halleck,* 18.
53. Bobrick, *Master,* 93–95; Shanks, *Recollections,* 63.
54. Bobrick, *Master,* 94–99; Van Horne, *Life,* 41–57; McKinney, *Education,* 125–131.
55. Daniel, *Shiloh,* 21.
56. Shanks, *Recollections,* 71, 252–267.
57. Cooling, *Forts,* 73. Cooling inexplicably blames Thomas, as if he chose not to advance into East Tennessee.
58. Engle, *Buell,* 100–107; Noe, *Perryville,* 11–12, 14; OR VII, 443–444.
59. Bobrick, *Master,* 99–100; Van Horne, *Life,* 57–62; McKinney, *Education,* 132–33; Daniel, *Shiloh,* 24; Ambrose, *Halleck,* 20–22; Kiper, *McClernand,* 65.

Chapter Two

1. Hughes, *Belmont,* 196–197, 208.
2. Simpson, *Grant,* 109.
3. Simon, *Papers,* 99–100.
4. Kiper, *McClernand,* 59–65.
5. Boatner, *Civil War,* 287. Henry Foote was the son of a Connecticut politician, whose mother was the daughter of an U.S. Army general. In his youth, Foote was enrolled at West Point but insisted on going into the U.S. Naval Academy.
6. Simon, *Papers,* 4: 103–104, 122; Cooling, *Forts,* 78–79.
7. Cooling, *Forts,* 88–89; Kiper, *McClernand,* 65–66; Simpson, *Grant,* 110–111; Boatner, *Civil War,* 538; Cooling, *Forts,* 65–67, 72. Many would take credit for developing the idea to attack Forts Henry and Donelson: Grant, Halleck, Foote, Sherman, McClernand, Buell and C.F. Smith to name a few.
8. Cooling, *Forts,* 46–57.
9. Cooling, *Forts,* 72; Simon, *Papers,* 4: 91.
10. Simon, *Papers,* 4: 90–91, 122–123.
11. Boatner, *Civil War,* 394.
12. Kiper, *McClernand,* 71.
13. Simon, *Papers,* 4: 169.
14. Ibid., 157.
15. Cooling, *Forts,* 92.
16. Ibid., 79; Brinton, *Personal Memoirs,* 130–131.
17. Cooling, *Forts,* 98; Simon, *Papers,* 4: 145–154.
18. Cooling, *Forts,* 92–93.
19. Simon, *Papers,* 4: 154; Cooling, *Forts,* 88, 90, 93–100–109.
20. Simon, *Papers,* 4: 160; Hoppin, *Foote,* 205.
21. *OR*, Ser. 1, Vol. VII, 122–124; Cooling, *Forts,* 85–86, 109–111.
22. Hoppin, *Foote,* 205; Cooling, *Forts,* 112, 237.
23. *OR*, Ser. 1, Vol. VII, 124–125; Simon, *Papers,* 4: 158–160, 163, 167–168; Cooling, *Forts,* 109–110.
24. Simon, *Papers,* 4: 131–132.
25. *OR*, Ser. 1, Vol. VII, 609; Ambrose, *Halleck,* 32.
26. Simpson *Grant,* 12; Cooling, *Forts,* 115.
27. Simon, *Papers,* 4: 171; Cooling, *Forts,* 115.
28. Simon, *Papers,* 4: 209–210; *OR*, Ser.1, Vol. VII, 162; Cooling, *Forts,* 136–138.
29. Cooling, *Forts,* 117–119, 139; Simon, *Papers,* 4: 215–216.
30. Simon, *Papers,* 4: 216, 249.
31. Simon, *Papers,* 4: 172, 175, 184; Young, *Around the World,* 306; Simon, *Papers,* 4: 184. Though Grant, in later years, claimed he *never* called a council of war, he had one with Gens. Lewis Wallace, Charles F. Smith and John McClernand on Feb. 10th to decide whether or not to march on Donelson before the gunboats returned. According to Wallace, they agreed to move forward at once, but were annoyed by McClernand reading a long proposal on how to invest the fort. While it was no doubt presumptuous of Grant's subordinate to second-guess his West Point–educated commander and colleague, McClernand had, after all, taken the time to conduct considerable reconnaissance of the area around Donelson beyond that which had been done by Grant.
32. Simon, *Papers,* 4: xxiii, 180.
33. Cooling, *Forts,* 140–142.
34. Ibid., 142–143.
35. Ibid., 143–145, 147–148.
36. Ibid., 121–122, 151–167; OR, Ser. 1, Vol. VII, 166–167; Hoppin, *Foote,* 226–232; Simon, *Papers,* 4: 160, 215.
37. Cooling, *Forts,* 166–170; Simon, *Papers,* 4: 90–91, 164–165, 216.
38. Cooling, *Forts,* 168.
39. Ibid., 149, 168.
40. Ibid., 167–177; Simpson, *Grant,* 114–115; Kiper, *McClernand,* 79–84.
41. Cooling, *Forts,* 177–183.
42. *OR*, Ser. 1, Vol. VII, 618.
43. Cooling, *Forts,* 183–189.
44. Ibid, 177–194. It is estimated that each side lost approximately 3,000 combatants on this day, a full one-half of the Federal causalities were incurred by McClernand. Kiper, *McClernand,* 81–87; Simpson, *Grant,* 115–116.
45. Cooling, *Forts,* 174–175, 181–183, 200–208, 213; Stickles, *Buckner,* 151–173; Noe, *Perryville,* 5. Buckner taught philosophy at West Point, and formed the pro-secession Kentucky state guard while Kentucky was still neutral.
46. Cooling, *Forts,* 212–223.
47. Ibid., 183; Boatner, *Civil War,* 769.
48. Jean Edward Smith, *Grant,* 163. Mrs. Delia Buckner, who visited Grant on his deathbed with her husband, states that Grant told Buckner that he had thought Buckner was acting as an agent for Pillow, and if he had known Buckner was in command, "the articles of surrender would have been different." Stickles, *Buckner,* 172; Cooling, *Forts,* 208–213; Kiper, *McClernand* 84–87; Simpson, *Grant,* 115–117; Grant, *Memoir*s, 1: 183. Grant's statement that he would have acted differently if he had known that Buckner was in command is puzzling, for Grant in his own memoirs gives a transcription of Buckner's letter in which Buckner is asking for terms and declares that he, Buckner, was in command of Fort Donelson. *OR*, Ser.1, Vol. VII, 161.
49. *OR*, Ser. 1, Vol. LII, Pt. 1, 7, 9, 177, 179–180. Smith's unfinished

report was written up by an unknown colleague working from a first draft found after Smith's death from injury on April 25, 1862.
50. Simon, *Papers*, 4: 216, 263–264; *OR*, Ser. 1, Vol. VII, 170–182.
51. *OR*, Ser. 1, Vol. VII, 163.
52. *OR*, Ser. 1, Vol. VII, 170–182; Simon, *Papers*, 4: 272.
53. Simon, *Papers*, 4: 29–30, 286.
54. Daniel, *Shiloh*, 29; Simon, *Papers*, 4: 226, 267, 274–276. Logan received three wounds at Fort Donelson on Feb. 15th, in the shoulder, the side and the thigh.
55. Simon, *Papers*, 4: 274–276.
56. Daniel, *Shiloh*, 29; Cooling, *Forts*, 44–46.
57. Cooling, *Forts*, 126–135, 138–139.
58. Daniel, *Shiloh*, 29.
59. Simon, *Papers*, 4: 218, 222.
60. Warner, *Generals*, 230–231.
61. *OR*, Ser. 1, Vol. VII, 595, 636.
62. Simon, *Papers*, 4: 196–7; Ambrose, *Halleck*, 29.
63. Daniel *Shiloh*, 30; Ambrose, *Halleck*, 33; Cooling, *Forts*, 224–225.
64. *OR*, Ser. 1, Vol. VII, 628.
65. Ibid., 632, 635.
66. Simon, *Papers*, 4: 272.
67. *OR*, Ser. 1, Vol. VII, 636; Simon, *Papers*, 4: 231.
68. Donald, *Lincoln*, 336–338; Cooling, *Forts*, 225–228.
69. Simon, *Papers*, 4: 257–262, 267; Cooling, *Forts*, 224–228.
70. Simon, *Papers*, 4: 263–4; Warner, *Generals*, 542–543.
71. Simon, *Papers*, 4: xxiv, 279–280, 286, 288. Johnston's troops remained at Murfreesboro until February 28th.
72. Battle of Pea Ridge Summary and Facts, http:www.civilwar.org/battlefields/pea-ridge.html; Simon, *Papers*, 4: xxiv, 287, 341.
73. *OR*, Ser. 1, Vol. VII, 628, 636, 645; Daniel, *Shiloh*, 26–27.
74. *OR*, Ser. 1, Vol. VII, 655.
75. Simon, *Papers*, 4: xxiv; Simpson, *Grant*, 121.
76. Ambrose, *Halleck*, 35.
77. Simon, *Papers*, 4: 265–266.
78. Ibid., 235–242, 246–247, 250–251, 256–257, 267–268, 285.
79. Ibid., 277–278, 292, 301–305, 445; Cooling, *Forts*, 251–252.
80. Simon, *Papers*, 4: 284, 305, 327, 406.
81. Cooling, *Forts*, 217–223, 255–263.
82. Simon, *Papers*, 4: 286, 288–289, 297, 305–306.

83. Ibid., 292–294.
84. Ibid., 293–294, 297, 299–300; Grant, *Memoirs*, 1: 188–191.
85. Cooling, *Forts*, 230.
86. Simon, *Papers*, 4: 286–287; Cooling, *Forts*, 249–250.
87. Simpson, *Grant*, 120–122; *OR*, Ser. 1, Vol. VII, 682–683; Ambrose, *Halleck*, 37; Cooling, *Forts*, 249; Grant, *Memoirs*, 1: 193–195. Grant wrote in his memoirs, just before his death in 1885, that after Fort Donelson, McClellan and Halleck conspired to get rid of him.
88. Simon, *Papers*, 4: xxiv, 319–320, 344.
89. Ibid., 271, 284, 292; Simpson, *Grant*, 122.
90. Ambrose, *Halleck*, 36–37.
91. Simon, *Papers*, 4: 111–116, 295.
92. Ambrose, *Halleck*, 37; Simon, *Papers*, 4: 317–320, 331.
93. Simpson, *Grant*, 123–125; Brinton, *Personal Memoirs*, 145–150. While Grant apparently believed Halleck, at least one of his inner circle, Dr. John Brinton, wrote that Halleck's chief of staff, George Washington Cullum, and General Buell and General McClellan were all suspected of having caused Grant's troubles.
94. Ambrose, *Halleck*, 39–40; Simon, *Papers*, 4: xxv.
95. Simon, *Papers*, 5: 20.
96. Ambrose, *Halleck*, 38–39; Hoppin, *Foote*, 258–293; Cooling, *Forts*, 228–229.
97. Simon, *Papers*, 4: 313, 327, 406.
98. Cooling, *Forts*, 230–233, 239–245.
99. Simon, *Papers*, 4: 331, 334, 353.
100. Ibid., 408–409.
101. Grant, *Memoirs*, 1: 194–195.
102. Simon, *Papers*, 4: 412–413.
103. Ibid., xxiv–xxv, 321–324, 331, 335, 343, 348–349, 353–355, 358; Simpson, *Grant*, 124–125; Ambrose, *Halleck*, 37.
104. Simon, *Papers*, 4: 405, 414–415.
105. Ibid., 310, 325, 360, 367, 369.
106. Sifakis, 375; Warner, *Generals*, 455–456.
107. Simon, *Papers*, 4: 287–288.
108. Ibid., 364, 375–378, 404; Brinton, *Personal Memoirs*, 148–149.
109. Simon, *Papers*, 4: 394, 423.
110. Ibid., 396–397; Simpson, *Grant*, 129–131.
111. Joshi and Schultz, *Sole Survivor*, 12–14.
112. Ibid., 25–26.

113. Simon, *Papers*, 4: 409.
114. Ibid., 386–389, 400–401, 405–406, 412–416, 426; Cooling, *Forts*, 253–255. Grant's medical advisor, Surgeon Brinton, blamed the Cairo quartermaster for much of Grant's army's troubles, but historian Cooling believes that inadequate transport and lack of supplies, including lack of ambulances and hospital tents, and overcrowded steamboats, were the real problems.
115. Simon, *Papers*, 4: 433–434, 438–443.
116. Ibid., 422, 428–431.
117. Daniel, *Shiloh*, 21–24.
118. McDonough, *Shiloh*, 65–69, 98.
119. Simon, *Papers*, 4: 447–479; 5: 3–7, 13–16.
120. McDonough, *Shiloh*, 52, 57.
121. Ibid., 45–46, 56.
122. Mahan, *Advanced-Guard*, 200.
123. Ibid., 199.
124. Waugh, *Class*, 65. Dennis Mahan was such a brilliant student at West Point that the Army paid for him to study in France with Lafayette, himself, as Mahan's patron.
125. McDonough, *Shiloh*, 73–85, 98–99 105–107, 132–133; Simon, *Papers*, 5: 17.
126. Noe, *Perryville*, 20; McDonough, *War*, 1–2, 6. Braxton Bragg, who graduated from USMA in 1837, replaced Beauregard in June of 1862 as commander of the Army of the Mississippi, known as the Army of the Tennessee for much of the war.
127. McDonough, *Shiloh*, 91–92, 103, 182, 221–225.
128. Simon, *Papers*, 5: 18–19.
129. McDonough, *Shiloh*, 156–161; Simon, *Papers*, 5: 69.
130. Ibid., 19.
131. Ibid., 20–25, 33.
132. Ibid., 27–28. Union casualties were 1,754 killed, 8,408 wounded, and 2,885 missing. Rebel casualties were 1,723 killed, 8,012 wounded, and 959 missing. The number of missing Federals is of interest.
133. Ibid., 32–35; McDonough, *Shiloh*, 162–167; Boatner, *Civil War*, 667–668; Bearss, *Receding Tide*, 51–52. Historian Ed Bearss suggests that McPherson was promoted too fast, for being inexperienced, he was overly cautious. Boatner, *Civil War*, 538; Warner, *Generals*, 385–386.
134. McDonough, *Shiloh*, 171, 178–183, 190–191.
135. Ibid., 196–210.
136. Simon, *Papers*, 5: 21–22;

McDonough, *Shiloh*, 103–104, 114–116, 219–220.

137. Simon, *Papers*, 5: 28–31.
138. Ibid., 47–49, 52.
139. Ibid., 57–58.
140. Brinton, *Personal Memoirs*, 162–165; Shanks, *Personal Recollections*, 141–142. It was not the first time that Halleck had overlooked Sheridan's shortcomings. When charges were brought against Sheridan by Gen. James Gilpatrick Blunt for refusing to obey orders to take possession of local Rebel-supporters' provender in May of 1862 (a surprising action for the soon-to-be enthusiastic "burn-'em out" commander of 1864 in the Shenandoah Valley), Halleck had the charges dismissed and appointed Sheridan to his staff as acting chief quartermaster. As historian Shanks points out, threat of arrest for most officers is not a good career move, but for Sheridan it began his rise from captain to a major generalcy in three short years. Boatner, *Civil War*, 71. General Blunt was a self-made Maine man who, after going to sea at 15, put himself through medical school, and followed his abolitionist beliefs by going to Kansas before the war and helping escaped slaves make their way to freedom.
141. Young, *Around the World*, 297, 450. The journalist who wrote *Around the World with General Grant* traveled with Grant on his world tour in the late 1870s. It is important to observe that Young submitted all of Grant's quotations in his manuscript to Grant for his approval before publication.
142. Simon, *Papers*, 5: 50.
143. McDonough, *Shiloh*, 77–80. McDonough notes that the 19,897 casualties at Shiloh were more than at Manassas, Wilson's Creek, Donelson and Pea Ridge put together.
144. Simon, *Papers*, 5: 50–51; Howe, *Home*, 222–223.
145. Simon, *Papers*, 5: 50.
146. Ibid., 53.
147. Ibid., 68–70.
148. Ibid., 49.
149. Ibid., 70–74, 89.
150. McDonough, *Shiloh*, 220–221.
151. Simon, *Papers*, 5: 108–109.
152. Ibid, 102, 111.
153. Ibid, 105.
154. Simpson, *Grant*, 143.
155. Simon, *Papers*, 5: 114–118, 129–130, 134, 136–137.
156. Ibid., 137; Simpson, *Grant*, 142–147.
157. Simon, *Papers*, 5: 118, 140.
158. Cooling, *Forts*, 251.
159. Simpson, *Grant*, 143.
160. Simon, *Papers*, 5: 140–141.
161. Ibid., 200–201.
162. Tucker, "Chattanooga," 37.
163. Simon, *Papers*, 5: 120, 145–146.
164. Ibid., 199; Marszalek, *Commander*, 127–128.
165. Simon, *Papers*, 5: 206–207; *OR*, Ser. 1, Vol. XVII, Pt. 2, 90–91.
166. *OR*, Ser. 1, Vol. XVII, Pt. 2, 45–47, 67–68.
167. Emerson, "Grant's Life"; Marszalek, *Commander*, 128.
168. Marszalek, *Commander*, 135.
169. Woodworth, *Victory*, 210.
170. Simpson, *Grant*, 147–148; Marszalek, *Commander*, 126–130.
171. Marszalek, *Commander*, 131–132, 134, 136–139.
172. Ibid., 140–141.
173. Ibid., 141–144.
174. Ibid., 146–147, 150, 152, 173; Anders, *Halleck's War*, 206–247. Halleck biographer Anders defends Halleck, denies that he had a breakdown, and gives a detailed alternative interpretation of Halleck's actions after Second Bull Run and the reappointment of McClellan to defend Washington.
175. Marszalek, *Commander*, 147–148.
176. Ibid., 150–151.

Chapter Three

1. Marszalek, *Commander*, 150–151; Noe, *Perryville*, 24–28, 47.
2. Noe, *Perryville*, 28–41; McDonough, *Kentucky*, 70.
3. Noe, *Perryville*, 47–50; McDonough, *Kentucky*, 70.
4. Noe, *Perryville*, 50–53, 58–61; *OR*, Ser. 1, Vol. XVI, Pt. 2, 470–471.
5. Noe, *Perryville*, 50–53, 57–58, 61–78.
6. Anders, *Halleck's War*, 145.
7. Ibid., 175. Halleck's message to Wright on August 25, 1862, stated, "The Government, or rather I should say the President and Secretary of War, is greatly displeased with the slow movements of General Buell. Unless he does something very soon, I think he will be removed. Indeed it would have been done before now if I had not begged to give him a little more time. There must be more energy and activity in Kentucky and Tennessee, and the one who first does something brilliant will get the entire command. I therefore hope to hear very soon of some success in your department."
8. Ibid., 218–219.
9. Noe, *Perryville*, 82–84.
10. Ibid., 84–94, 403.
11. Ibid., 97–98; Sheridan, *Personal Memoirs*, 1: 189–190; Shanks, *Personal Recollections*, 132.
12. Noe, *Perryville*, 98–106, 110–114, 117–122.
13. Ibid., 131–135.
14. Ibid., 135–147; Cozzens, *Stones River*, 7; McCook's Report on Stone's River, http://www.civilwarhome.com/mccookstonesriveror.htm. McCook's account of Stone's River provides an interesting counterpoint to Sheridan's account.
15. Boatner, *Civil War*, 527. McCook was the former law partner of Thomas Ewing and William T. Sherman. Later serving under Sherman, he was killed at Kennesaw Mountain in 1864.
16. Noe, *Perryville*, 147–156.
17. Ibid., 156–161, 164–167.
18. Ibid., 193–198, 214–215.
19. Ibid., 224–233.
20. Ibid., 231–236, 276–294. The quotations regarding Sheridan's plea for assistance and his whipping the enemy are from Noe's *Perryville*, 284, 293.
21. Lytle, *For Honor*, 214.
22. Noe, *Perryville*, 237–241, 263–276, 305–308; Eicher and Eicher, *Civil War*, 358; Cozzens, *Chickamauga*, 357–359, 382–389. Lytle survived Perryville and was exchanged on Feb. 4, 1863, only to be killed at Chickamauga while serving under Philip Sheridan in command of the late Joshua Sill's brigade. Lytle, *For Honor*, 25–29, 140–143, 147–150, 155–160, 167–168, 174–178, 200–224; Tucker, *Chickamauga*, 292–298. It is interesting that Lytle seemingly held no grudge against Sheridan, serving under him amicably until his death. Lytle was a dutiful and yet ambitious man, who resented the delay in his advancement in rank. But in expressing his frustration about promotions, he also demonstrated one of the reasons his men trusted and admired him, for he often bemoaned the fact that the delays in his own advancement (promoted Mar. 17, 1863, to brigadier general, dated to Nov. 29, 1862) were gumming up the works for everyone junior to him.
23. Noe, *Perryville*, 313–322, 328–330, 344; McDonough, *War in Kentucky*, 304–305; Sheridan, *Personal Memoirs*, 1: 199–200. Sheri-

dan, in his memoirs, criticizes Buell for not being on the field at Perryville, and declares that if the unengaged troops of Gilbert's and Crittenden's Corps had been used to assault the Confederate right (not to, you notice, support McCook) things would have been much different.

24. Shanks, *Personal Recollections*, 249–252.
25. Noe, *Perryville*, 333–336.
26. Ibid., 330–341; Marszalek, *Commander*, 151–152; Cozzens, *Stones River*, 12–14; Cooper, *Hazen*, 60, 62.
27. Morris, *Sheridan*, 97.
28. Cozzens, *Stones River*, 16, 22–23; Bobrick, *Master*, 133–135; Woodworth, *Victory*, 224–240, 246–247.
29. Simpson, *Grant*, 151–156.
30. Anders, *Halleck's War*, 237.
31. Marszalek, *Commander*, 153–158.
32. Cooper, *Hazen*, 64.
33. Cozzens, *Stones River*, x–xi, 1–35, 38–39, 44–47, 60–61, 67, 76–77; Spruill, *Winter*, xiv–xv, 108; Cooper, *Hazen*, 64–66, 68–71.
34. Cozzens, *No Better Place to Die*, 30–39.
35. Marszalek, *Commander*, 159–160; Sheridan, *Personal Memoirs*, 1: 239, 246; Spruill, *Winter*, xv, 108, 217, 215–218; McDonough, *Chattanooga*, 32.
36. Bearss, *Receding Tide*, 48.
37. Young, *Around the World*, 304.
38. Marszalek, *Commander*, 161.
39. Woodworth, *Victory*, 248–284.
40. Bearss, *Receding Tide*, 48, 53.
41. Anders, *Halleck's War*, 390.
42. Marszalek, *Commander*, 161–162; Woodworth, *Victory*, 285–292.
43. Marszalek, *Commander*, 134, 162–166.
44. *OR*, Ser. 1, Vol. XX, Pt. 2, 67–68.
45. *OR*, Ser. 2, Vol. V, 671–682; Marszalek, *Commander*, 178, 183.
46. Marszalek, *Commander*, 178.
47. Ibid., 168–173, 192.
48. Woodworth, *Victory*, 286–307.
49. Bearss, *Receding Tide*, 56–57.
50. Woodworth, *Victory*, 300–304; Bearss, *Receding Tide*, 58–59.
51. Woodworth, *Victory*, 304–308; Bearss, *Receding Tide*, 59–65.
52. Woodworth, *Victory*, 308–311; Bearss, *Receding Tide*, 65–71.
53. Woodworth, *Victory*, 300, 306–311; Bearss, *Receding Tide*, 55.
54. Bearss, *Receding Tide*, 78–82.

55. Ibid., 59. I was quite taken aback with Bearss's comments here comparing the reliability of accounts of James Wilson and Joshua Chamberlain. I have to strongly disagree, this once, with Bearss's opinion regarding Chamberlain. After 20 years of research, my consideration and study of Chamberlain has led me to believe that he was an honest and careful historian. Meanwhile, I agree with Bearss that Wilson was a lying scoundrel.
56. Styple, *Generals*, 277; Wilson, *Under*, 1: 132–133, 324.
57. Tucker, *Chickamauga*, 52–53.
58. Woodworth, *Victory*, 252, 317; Dana, *Recollections*, 20–21, 28–30, 40–41, 49; *OR*, Ser. 1, Vol. XXIV, Pt. 1, 80–81, 83.
59. Charles Dana to James Pike, August 18, 1863, University of Maine Special Collections, James S. Pike Collection, Box 273, Folder 172.
60. Wilson, *Dana*, 213.
61. Dana, *Recollections*, 61.
62. Cohen, *Supreme*, 43–47; Wilson, *Dana*, 406–409, 413–439.
63. Woodworth, *Victory*, 315–316; Bearss, *Receding Tide*, 82–83, 90–92; Vicksburg Timeline, http://mobile96.com/cwl/Vicksburg/Vickstimeline.html; Boatner, *Civil War*, 873.
64. Bearss, *Receding Tide*, 82–84, 93–97.
65. Ibid., 139–140; Young, *Around the World*, 623. Grant's version, told many years later, of this gambit to attack Vicksburg rather than assisting Banks at Port Hudson, is of interest. Grant relates that he treated Banks's emissary, a brigadier who had been sent to arrange the joint operations of Grant and Banks, with some derision, telling him that Halleck would hardly expect Grant to back away from the victory he was winning at Vicksburg to go as he had been ordered to Port Hudson.
66. Bearss, *Receding Tide*, 147.
67. Ibid., 147, 154–155, 162–163.
68. Ibid., 155–156, 159.
69. Woodworth, *Victory*, 315–397.
70. Ibid., 387.
71. Boatner, *Civil War*, 873–876; Dana, *Recollections*, 32–33, 50–60, 61–77; *OR*, Ser. 1, Vol. XXXIV, Pt. 1, 80–81, 84, 88–89.
72. *OR*, Ser. 1, Vol. XXIV, Pt. 1, 86–87.
73. Dana, *Recollections*, 56–73.
74. Marszalek, *Commander*, 173–175.
75. Ibid., 179–183.

76. McFeely, *Grant*, 137.
77. *OR*, Ser. 1, Vol. XXIV, Pt. 3, 498; Young, *Around the World*, 615–616.
78. Kiper, *McClernand*, 266–268, 271–272.
79. Simpson, *Grant*, 209–211; Kiper, *McClernand*, 265–266.
80. Ambrose, *Halleck*, 159.
81. McPherson, *This Mighty Scourge*, 199–120.
82. Ambrose, *Halleck*, 159.
83. Marszalek, *Commander*, 184.
84. Ibid., 159–160.
85. Morris, "Bird," 23.
86. Wilson, *General Grant's Letters*, 27–28.
87. Morris, "Bird," 24.
88. Marszalek, *Commander*, 185; Tucker, *Chickamauga*, 85–100; Morris, "Bird," 23–24.
89. Tucker, *Chickamauga*, 140–141.
90. Ibid., 23–30; Cooper, *Hazen*, 75–76; Shanks, *Personal Recollections*, 161.
91. Tucker, *Chickamauga*, 43–45, 62–71, 101–106, 110–112, 118–125, 138–139; Cooper, *Hazen*, 76–78.
92. Tucker, *Chickamauga*, 123, 195–196. For a detailed consideration of the battle on September 19 and 20, 1863, see Glenn Tucker's *Chickamauga*, 126–393.
93. Cozzens, *Chickamauga*, 80; Morris, "Bird," 20–23.
94. Tucker, *Chickamauga*, 292–300, 309–311, 315–316.
95. Cozzens, *Chickamauga*, 479.
96. Tucker, *Chickamauga*, 315–320.
97. Morris, "Bird," 26.
98. Tucker, *Chickamauga*, 315–316; Dana, *Recollections*, 22–25.
99. Tucker, *Chickamauga*, 48–51.
100. Morris, "Bird," 27–29.
101. *OR*, Ser. 1, Vol. XXX, Pt. 1, 201–203.
102. Bob Redman, Sheridan's Ride at Chickamauga, http://www.aotc.net/Sheridan.htm.
103. McDonough, *Chattanooga*, 41–50; Tucker, *Chickamauga*, 370; Cooper, *Hazen*, 88.
104. Cooper, *Hazen*, 88–89. For an analysis of Sheridan's performance at Chickamauga, see Tucker's *Chickamauga*, 299–304, 309–311, 315–316, 370. For Sheridan's version of his actions at Chickamauga, see his report (OR, Ser. 1, Vol. XXX, Pt. 1, 578–582) and his memoirs (Sheridan, 1: 279–288).
105. Marszalek, *Commander*, 186–187; Morris, "Bird," 27–28.

106. McDonough, *Chattanooga*, 20–40, 45–53, 64–68, 96–98; *OR*, Ser. 1, Vol. XXX, Pt. 4, 705, 708; Marszalek, *Commander*, 186–187; Tucker, *Chickamauga*, 75–84, 220–221.
107. Cohen, *Supreme*, 48.
108. Morris, "Bird," 26–27, 29.
109. McDonough, *Chattanooga*, 74, 95–96.
110. Porter, *Campaigning*, 1–2.
111. Wilson, *Dana*, 281.
112. McDonough, *Chattanooga*, 53–60, 98–102. For a detailed description of Smith's audacious and successful plan to open communications to Chattanooga, including the roles of Hazen, Hooker and Howard, Bragg and Longstreet, see McDonough, *Chattanooga*, 76–98. For a summation of Bragg's faulty deployment of his force, see McDonough, 205, 226–229; for maps and description of the action, see Cooper's *Hazen*, 90–93. It is interesting that Baldy Smith chose Hazen and his men to execute his daring plan to outsmart the Rebels.
113. McDonough, *Chattanooga*, 156–157; Lewis, *Sherman*, 321. Historian Lloyd Lewis states that Sherman thought Grant was "daft" when he continued to order Sherman to attack. McDonough cites Sherman's report, 158–159.
114. Bobrick, *Master*, 208–212; Wilson, *Under*, 2: 289–297.
115. Lewis, *Sherman*, 321; McDonough, *Chattanooga*, 161–165; Cooper, *Hazen*, 98–100.
116. Styple, *Generals*, 282; Wilson, *Under*, 2: 289–297.
117. Tucker, "Battles," 32; Young, *Around the World*, 151–152, 305–306.
118. Cooper, *Hazen*, 11–13, 90; Young, *Around the World*, 626–627. Grant later said that Sheridan showed his "military genius" at Missionary Ridge by realizing that "it was necessary to advance beyond the point indicated in his orders. If others had followed his example we should have had Bragg's army."
119. McDonough, *Chattanooga*, 194–195, 199; Tucker, "Battles," 37; Sifakis, 462–463. Brigadier General Wood (USMA, 1845), a native of Munfordville, Kentucky, had a stain on his otherwise unblemished record as his division ascended Missionary Ridge. It was Wood who had received Rosecrans's fatal order at Chickamauga to move his division out of line to fill a gap Wood knew did not exist. He moved, leaving the hole that Longstreet came through, which resulted in the destruction of the Union right. While Wood had received a very public dressing down from Rosecrans the very morning before he received Rosecrans's faulty fatal order, scholars still argue over whether Wood did the right thing by obeying Rosecrans's order quickly or without question, or should Wood have risked delay and further criticism by sending a query to Rosecrans before moving.
120. Holzer, *Hearts*, 747–750.
121. Hutton, *Phil Sheridan*, 149–150.
122. Cooper, *Hazen*, 100–103; McDonough, *Chattanooga*, 176–177.
123. Ibid, 165–195. For Hazen's account of Missionary Ridge, see Hazen, *A Narrative of Military Service* (Boston: Ticknor, 1885), 173–235.
124. Hazen, *Narrative*, 178–180; Cooper, *Hazen*, 104–105; Hutton, *Phil Sheridan*, 148–149, 400n75.
125. Lewis, *Sherman*, 323; McDonough, *Chattanooga*, 163–168, 178–180, 215; *OR*, Ser. 1, Vol. XXXI, Pt. 2, 741–742.
126. Ibid., 102–104. Sherman quotation is cited from McDonough, *Chattanooga*, 162; Grant, *Memoirs*, 1: 389; Hutton, *Phil Sheridan*, 43. For a careful consideration of the battle at Chattanooga, read McDonough's *Chattanooga: A Death Grip on the Confederacy*, 108–230; Young, *Around the World*, 295–296.
127. Joshi and Schultz, *Sole Survivor*, 28–29.
128. McDonough, *Chattanooga*, 104–107.
129. Marszalek, *Commander*, 187–188, 193.
130. Daniel, *Army of the Cumberland*, 378; Wilson, *Under*, 1: 303–307.
131. Marszalek, *Commander*, 187–188.
132. Boatner, *Civil War*, 351–352, 412–414. In April of 1864, when Sherman took command in the West, Granger was replaced with O.O. Howard as commander of the Army of the Cumberland's 4th Corps, the command he had been given following his decisive role at Chickamauga. Granger ended up in the hinterlands, the District of Southern Alabama, Dept. of the Gulf.
133. Cooper, *Hazen*, 108–111.
134. Marszalek, *Commander*, 193–194.
135. Ibid., 184, 193–5; Badeau-Wilson Letters, Princeton University, July 24, Nov. 10, Dec. 2, 1863.
136. Anders, *Halleck's War*, 499; *OR*, Ser. 1, Vol. XXIV, Pt. 3, 498. Halleck also suggested that if Hooker had remained in command of the Army of the Potomac, Hooker "would have lost the army and the capital."
137. Anders, *Halleck's War*, 512–513. Anders suggests that it was Smith's previous outspoken criticism of his commander, Burnside, after Fredericksburg that might have caused the administration to hesitate to consider Smith, and to seek Dana's assurances about his character. Anders attributes Grant's surprising preference to have Smith go to the Army of the Potomac to a realization that Smith, who had previously served with the Army of the Potomac, would be more successful than the westerner Sherman, a perceived outsider. He also speculates that it was already foreseen that when Grant went east, Sherman would take command in the West.
138. Marszalek, *Commander*, 195–196.
139. Ibid., 196–199.
140. Anders, *Halleck's War*, 530–533; Simpson, *Grant*, 298.
141. Marszalek, *Commander*, 195–200.
142. Boatner, *Civil War*, 37; Henry John Steiner, "A Little Pale Blue-eyed Man," http://henrysteiner.com/DIRsteiner/historian.htm.
143. Smith, *American Gothic*, 66–67; Titone, *My Thoughts*, 172–176, 200–201, 225–227; Shattuck, *Hamlet*, 18–50. In fact, Badeau was one of only four people at Edwin Booth's first wedding, and Badeau visited with the newly married couple on their honeymoon.
144. Sifakis, 16; Shattuck, *Hamlet*, 29; Titone, *My Thoughts*, 287, 289, 293–301; Ruggles, *Prince*, 156.
145. Lockridge, *Darling*, 84–85.
146. Shattuck, *Hamlet*, 35; Titone, *My Thoughts*, 273; James Wilson to Adam Badeau, May 12, 1865, Badeau Collection, Rare Books and Special Collections, Princeton University. Badeau wrote a book, *The Vagabond*, published in 1859 by Russ and Carleton of New York. In this book of theatri-cal anecdotes, Badeau wrote the following about a night Edwin Booth and he had spent alone in a country house. Relating that he fell asleep while Edwin

was telling him stories, Badeau commented, "I warrant you, some of his fair admirers would not have slept, so long as he talked, and doubtless they envy me my snooze on his arm. But 'twas dark, and I couldn't see his eyes; besides, I had seen them all day."

147. Shattuck, *Hamlet*, 18–50; Badeau-Wilson Letters, July 28, Aug. 7, Oct. 28, Sept. 20, 1863, and undated.

148. Young, *Around the World*, 464.

149. Marszalek, *Commander*, 200–204; Cooper, *Hazen*, 111–113.

150. For additional reading on the fate of Hazen's brigade, see Cooper, *Hazen*, 112–153.

Chapter Four

1. Meade, *Life and Letters*, 125–157, 168–183; Young, *Around the World*, 300.

2. Taylor, *Warren*, 119–139; Walker, *History*, 331–364.

3. Meade, *Life and Letters*, 125–157.

4. Keneally, *American*, 278–293. Sickles, with other Meade critics, would testify on Feb. 26, 1864, against Meade before the Joint Committee on the Conduct of the War. "Testimony of General Daniel Sickles Before the Joint Committee on the Conduct of the War," Meade Archives, http://adams.patrot.net/~jcampi/sickles.htm.

5. Marszalek, *Commander*, 178–180; Meade, *Life and Letters*, 133–142, 147.

6. Ibid., 142–143, 146–153.

7. McPherson, *Battle Cry*, 671, 675.

8. Graham, *Mine Run*, 1–2. Hill lost 1,400 men, Warren fewer than 600.

9. Ibid., 2.

10. Ibid., 2–7.

11. Meade, *Life and Letters*, 154.

12. Anders, *Halleck's War*, 497–498; Taylor, *Warren*, 146–147.

13. Meade, *Life and Letters*, 153–156; Jordan, *Happiness*, 106–110.

14. Ibid., 111; Sifakis, 183.

15. Taylor, *Warren*, 150–151; Pullen, *Twentieth Maine*, 160.

16. *OR*, Ser. 1, Vol. XXIX, Pt. 2, 361–362; Graham, *Mine Run*, 5.

17. Graham, *Mine Run*, 8–9; Rafuse, *Lee*, 147.

18. Graham, *Mine Run*, 5–31; Pullen, *Twentieth Maine*, 162–164. While the attack near Rappahannock Station was a 6th Corps affair, they received some slight, unauthorized support from the 5th Corps. When the 6th Corps' 6th Maine Regiment was ordered to attack, the nearby 20th Maine of the 5th Corps saw that their fellow Mainers were going into a tight spot, so a number of the skirmishers from the 20th Maine went with them. Though it was a long time coming, in 1898, the leader and instigator of the 20th Maine's participation in this charge, Walter Morrill, was awarded the Medal of Honor for his actions at Rappahannock Station.

19. Graham, *Mine Run*, 20–21.

20. Ibid., 9–10, 28. Gen. William H. French (USMA, 1837), while a successful division commander, had only recently been given command of the 3rd Corps, but was commanding the 2nd and 3rd Corps this day.

21. Ibid., 38–39.

22. Ibid., 31–36. Several of Meade's corps commanders would testify early the following year before the U.S. Congressional Joint Committee on the Conduct of the War, that, in their opinion, an assault should have been made following Rappahannock Station, and could have successfully cut Lee's army in two. While Gen. David B. Birney, a division commander in the 3rd Corps, specifically blamed Meade in his testimony for the failure to make a swift advance, General Warren was more circumspect in just who was at fault for the Federals' "wasted time and uncertain movements."

23. Ibid., 40–45.

24. *OR*, Ser. 1, Vol. XXIX, Pt. 1, 13.

25. Ibid., 13–14; Graham, *Mine Run*, 41–43.

26. Joshi, *Devil's Dictionary*, 686.

27. *OR*, Ser. 1, Vol. XXIX, Pt. 1, 14–16; Graham, *Mine Run*, 44–55.

28. Ibid., 16; Graham, *Mine Run*, 47–59. Over the course of Nov. 27th, the Union 3rd Corps lost 952 men, while the Confederate troops of Edward Johnson, who it could be said had neutralized the entire Federal force, sustained 545 casualties.

29. Graham, *Mine Run*, 59, 69–70; Meade, *Life and Letters*, 156–157; Jordan, *Happiness*, 112–113; Taylor, *Warren*, 158–165.

30. Graham, *Mine Run*, 70–73; Meade, *Life and Letters*, 156–157; Walker, *History*, 365–387.

31. Taylor, *Warren*, 150–152, 157–165; Graham, *Mine Run*, 73–77; Walker, *History*, 382–383.

32. Graham, *Mine Run*, 77.

33. Ibid., 78–79.

34. Ibid., 79; Livermore, *Days*, 304.

35. *OR*, Ser. 1, Vol. XXIX, Pt.1, 13–14.

36. Ibid., 16–20.

37. Ibid., 16–18.

38. Meade, *Life and Letters*, 156–161.

39. Taylor, *Warren*, 163–165; Walker, *History*, 384–385; Meade, *Life and Letters*, 156–164, 201; Gibbon, *Personal Recollections*, 239; Sedgwick, *Correspondence*, 163; Rafuse, *Lee*, 121. While Meade, certain that he would be replaced after Mine Run, waited for news from Washington, idle rumor had it that the president and Secretary Chase wanted Hooker back, while others thought General Thomas might be brought east, and Hooker sent west to command the Army of the Cumberland.

40. Meade, *Life and Letters*, 168–183; Hyde, *Union*, 163–181.

41. Keneally, *American*, 304, 306; Who was Historicus?, www.civilwarhome.com/historicus.htm.

42. Meade, *Life and Letters*, 160.

43. Ibid., 163, 169.

44. Ibid., 166, 168; *OR*, Ser. 1, Vol. XXXIII, 721–723; Taylor, *Warren*, 168–169; Hyde, *Union*, 163–181. Warren biographer Emerson Taylor quotes part of Warren's testimony before the Committee on the Conduct of the War, and while Warren defends Meade, he is very critical of his fellow corps commanders other than Hancock, and recommends the reorganization that was eventually adopted.

45. Wittenberg, *Little Phil*, 17–18, 53; Boatner, *Civil War*, 655–656. Kilpatrick was transferred to Sherman's command, and Pleasonton, who had also had disagreements with Meade, was relieved of command and exiled to the Department of Missouri.

46. Wilson, *Under*, 1: 325–343; Boatner, *Civil War*, 930.

47. Wittenberg, *Little Phil*, 18–19.

48. Agassiz, *Headquarters*, 17.

49. Wittenberg, *Little Phil*, 18–20; Steere, *Wilderness*, 471; Rockwell, *Rambling*, 164. A modern historian has besmirched the sterling reputation of Gen. David Gregg in a recent biography, *General John Buford* by Edward Longacre, p. 141, citing the recollections of Dr. Alonzo Rockwell, who served under David Gregg. Longacre attributes Gregg's 1865

resignation from the army to cowardice, and Dr. Rockwell is no doubt spinning in his grave, for having told of Gregg's marked bravery under fire, it's true that Rockwell related that he had heard the ever-modest Gregg admit at a 1864 Thanksgiving dinner with fellow officers that the fear of violent death in battle was taking a toll on him. But Rockwell also wrote that he thought the real reason for Gregg's resignation was the idea that he would have to serve again under Sheridan, when Sheridan returned to the Army of the Potomac after his stint in the Shenandoah Valley. Rockwell also hypothesized that Gregg was offended by the advancement of younger, flashier men, such as Custer and Kilpatrick, over his head. It's hard to know what prompted Longacre to make such a mean-spirited interpretation of Rockwell's tribute to his former commander. One could also observe that the definition of real courage may well be the ability to be able to overcome real and natural fear and go ahead and get the job done.
50. Grant, *Memoirs*, 2: 129–141.
51. McFeely, *Grant*, 156–157.
52. U.S. Grant, "Preparing for the Campaigns of '64," in Holzer, *Hearts*, 869. Grant commented, "I tried to make General Meade's position as nearly as possible what it would have been if I had been in Washington or any other place away from his command. I therefore gave all orders for the movements of the Army of the Potomac to Meade to have them executed. To avoid the necessity of having to give orders direct, I established my headquarters near his, unless there were reasons for locating them elsewhere. This sometimes happened, and I had on occasions to give orders directly to the troops affected." Grant apologists and Meade detractors often try to make the case that Meade was making the decisions that ended in disaster on the battlefield, but according to Grant, it is apparent that some significant number of the orders for movements during the Overland Campaign were conceived of and given to the Army of the Potomac by Grant through Meade.
53. Grant, *Memoirs*, 2: 216.

Chapter Five

1. Porter, *Campaigning*, 43; Steere, *Wilderness*, 73; Roebling, "Report," 2.
2. Grant, *Papers,* 10: 397; Grant, *Memoirs,* 2: 183, 185. Grant offers Lee's lack of opposition to the Army of the Potomac's crossing of the Rapidan as proof that he surprised Lee.
3. Badeau, *Military,* 96–97; Humphreys, *Virginia,* 21–22, 53–57.
4. Steere, *Wilderness,* 47–48; Roebling, "Report," 1.
5. Roebling, "Letter Book," 505.
6. *OR,* Ser. 1, Vol. XXXVI, Pt. 2, 378; Steere, *Wilderness,* 51, 53, 57–58.
7. Steere, *Wilderness,* 29–40.
8. Ibid., 73–80.
9. Rafuse, *Lee,* 143; Charles S. Venable E-notes, http://www.enotes.com/topic/Charles_S._Venable. Charles S. Venable, educated at the University of Virginia and in Germany, was a professor of mathematics and astronomy before the war. Although he enlisted and fought as a private in the 2nd South Carolina, in the spring of 1962, he joined Lee's staff. After the war he returned to academic pursuits. He is an interesting and astute observer.
10. Steere, *Wilderness,* 73–87; *OR,* Ser. 1, Vol. XXXVI, Pt. 2, 371.
11. Steere, *Wilderness,* 74–83.
12. McFeely, *Grant,* 156–159.
13. Steere, *Wilderness,* 259–280.
14. *OR,* Ser. 1, Vol. XXXVI, Pt. 2, 378; Steere, *Wilderness,* 259–260, 263. Steere considers the possibility that Wilson's reports that night indicated to some extent his intention of withdrawing from the Turnpike, and Steere puzzles over why this made no apparent impression on Sheridan, Meade or Grant.
15. Wilson, *Under,* 1: 378–379.
16. Steere, *Wilderness,* 39–40.
17. Schaff, *Wilderness,* 141; *OR,* Ser. 1, Vol. XXXVI, Pt. 2, 371; Steere, *Wilderness,* 39, 67, 267–268.
18. Steere, *Wilderness,* 262–274.
19. *OR,* Ser. 1, Vol. XXXVI, Pt. 2, 403–404, 413.
20. Steere, *Wilderness,* 120–122.
21. Roebling, "Report," 2–18. Roebling consistently refers to the Chewning Field as the "Tuning Farm." Charles S. Venable, "General Lee in the Wilderness Campaign," in Holzer, *Hearts,* 812.
22. Steere, *Wilderness,* 40.
23. Ibid., 184–242.
24. Steere, *Wilderness,* 123–134, 243–258; Roebling, "Report," 5; Schaff, *Wilderness,* 338. Warren's aide, Morris Schaff (USMA, 1862), wrote in his memoirs that Grant, before leaving the Wilderness, rode out to the gap in the Army of the Potomac's line between Burnside and Warren, and sat upon his horse staring at the Rebel-held Chewning Farm. Unfortunately this personal reconnaissance came way too late.
25. Steere, *Wilderness,* 108–168; *OR,* Ser. 1, Vol. XXXVI, Pt. 1, 539–540.
26. Steere, *Wilderness,* 315.
27. Ibid., 184–196, 285–286; *OR,* Ser. 1, Vol. XXXVI, Pt. 2, 407.
28. Steere, *Wilderness,* 106–114, 122.
29. *OR,* Ser. 1, Vol. XXXVI, Pt. 1, 413, 539.
30. Roebling, "Report," 7; Steere, *Wilderness,* 132–135, 149–183.
31. Roebling, "Letter Book," 509.
32. Steere, *Wilderness,* 86–87.
33. Ibid., 156.
34. Grant *Memoirs,* 2: 194; *OR,* Ser. 1, Vol. XXXVI, Pt. 2, 407, 409, 413.
35. Steere, *Wilderness,* 184–242, 257–258; Roebling, "Report," 7–12.
36. Steere, *Wilderness,* 243–249.
37. Ibid., 294–295.
38. Ibid, 149–156, 192–194, 197–244, 284–287.
39. *OR,* Ser. 1, Vol. XXXVI, Pt. 1, 539–540.
40. The One Hundred Fifty-fifth Pennsylvania Association, 376; Agassiz, *Headquarters,* 91.
41. OR, Ser. 1, Vol. XXXVI, Pt. 2, 439–449; Steere, *Wilderness,* 387–430; Matter, *If It Takes,* 3.
42. Steere, *Wilderness,* 431–453, 455; Wilson, *Under,* 1: 390. It has been said that Grant on the night of May 6th went into his tent, threw himself upon his camp cot, and gave way to the greatest emotion. The only source I was able to find is Wilson's memoirs, but he wasn't there, although he claims he heard it from Grant's aide, Rawlins. Since the author considers Wilson a most unreliable witness, I relegated this to the endnotes.
43. Steere, *Wilderness,* 283–284, 377–388; *OR,* Ser. 1, Vol. XXXVI, Pt. 2, 466–467. For accounts of the second day at the Wilderness, see. Steere, *Wilderness,* 285–450.
44. Steere, *Wilderness,* 390–391; Roebling, "Report," 13–15.
45. Pearson, *Wadsworth,* 268–286; *OR,* Ser. 1, Vol. XXXVI, Pt. 2, 554; Roebling, "Report," 11–13. Warren made a note beside Wadsworth's name here in Roebling's report, writing "a noble spirited brave soldier."

46. *OR*, Ser. 1, Vol. XXXVI, 438–453; Parker, *History*, 378, 411.
47. Gallagher, *Spotsylvania*, 125.
48. Wilson, *Under*, 1: 378–386.
49. Steere, *Wilderness*, 463; Schaff, *Wilderness*, 210.
50. Anders, *Halleck's War*, 560–565.

Chapter Six

1. Steere, *Wilderness*, 450–453, 457.
2. Matter, *If It Takes*, 1.
3. Steere, *Wilderness*, 455–466.
4. Matter, *If It Takes*, 18–19, 25–27.
5. Ibid., 16, 20, 27–28.
6. Ibid., 15.
7. Ibid., 22–23.
8. Robertson, *Back Door*, 246–264.
9. Steere, *Wilderness*, 466; Matter, *If It Takes*, 48; Schaff, *Wilderness*, 344–345.
10. Ford, *Cycle*, 131; Matter, *If It Takes*, 4–5. Rumors circulated that Meade had not agreed with Grant's decision for another attempt to flank Lee after the Wilderness. Meade would later angrily eject a journalist from the army who published a story claiming Meade had wanted to retire back across the Rapidan after the battle.
11. Matter, *If It Takes*, 16, 21, 32, 75. Matter recounts that the 2nd Ohio Cavalry, one of the last Federal units to leave the Wilderness, gathered as many blankets as they could find to leave with the wounded who were left behind. Humphreys, *Virginia*, 57.
12. Matter, *If It Takes*, 14, 52–53.
13. Humphreys, *Virginia*, 57.
14. Matter, *If It Takes*, 29–30.
15. Ibid., 34–41.
16. Ibid., 42–43.
17. Ibid, 42–43.
18. Ibid., 32–33, 52–53.
19. Ibid., 44; Humphreys, *Virginia*, 58. Humphreys defends Warren's commitment to seeing that his men withdrew without a response from the enemy.
20. Grant, *Memoirs*, 2: 210–211; Matter, *If It Takes*, 48.
21. Ibid., 23; Smith, *Petersburg*. Ned Smith, who did the maps for *Chamberlain at Petersburg*, coped with these challenges while using wartime Federal maps, which contained roads that didn't exist, didn't show roads that did exist, and had many examples of roads with two or three names.
22. Humphreys, *Virginia*, 58.
23. Comstock, *Diary*, 265.
24. Matter, *If It Takes*, 50–52, 77–78; *OR*, Ser. 1, Vol. XXXVI, Pt. 2, 552–553.
25. Matter, *If It Takes*, 21.
26. Ibid., 69; *OR*, Ser. 1, Vol. XXXVI, Pt. 1, 878, Pt. 2, 554; McClellan, *Sheridan*, 18–21.
27. Matter, *If It Takes*, 47–48; Humphreys, *Virginia*, 58n2.
28. Humphreys, *Virginia*, 59.
29. Chamberlin, *History*, 224–225; Hopper, "Military Order," 5–6.
30. Matter, *If It Takes*, 54–55; Humphreys, *Virginia*, 59–60; McClellan, *Grant*, 28. An observer would later comment that Warren harbored no hard feelings toward Merritt's troopers, acknowledging the difficulties that the density of the woods presented.
31. Matter, *If It Takes*, 55; Humphreys, *Virginia*, 71.
32. Wyckoff, *History*, 182.
33. Matter, *If It Takes*, 57–59, 69.
34. Comstock, *Diary*, 265. It was Anderson's corps, not Ewell's that confronted Warren, but the point is, Confederate infantry was waiting for Warren. Lee hadn't fallen back as Comstock had recorded the day before in his diary.
35. Matter, *If It Takes*, 342–343.
36. Ibid., 81.
37. Ibid.
38. *OR*, IIIVI, Pt. I, 787–789; Humphreys, *Virginia*, 70. Humphreys witnessed the contents and signing of Meade's orders to Gregg and Merritt, as well as Meade's notification to Sheridan.
39. Matter, *If It Takes*, 367–372; Humphreys, *Virginia*, 68–70.
40. Grant, *Memoirs*, 2: 211–213; Matter, *If It Takes*, 372.
41. Matter, *If It Takes*, 370–372; McClellan, *Grant*, 2, 27–30.
42. McClellan, *Sheridan*, 16–17.

Chapter Seven

1. Boatner, *Civil War*, 704–705. Robinson was an old regular, having served in the Mexican and Seminole Wars; he received the Medal of Honor for this fight at Laurel Hill. On the 100th Anniversary of his birth, a statue of Robinson was dedicated at Gettysburg, where his two 1st Corps brigades held off five Rebel brigades for four hours. There is a Robinson Avenue at Gettysburg.
2. Ibid., 496.
3. Wyckoff, *History*, 182–184; Jones, "Official Diary," 492. Anderson's diary recorded that they repulsed the Federals "with great slaughter."
4. Roebling, "Report," 21–23.
5. Matter, *If It Takes*, 60–62.
6. Ibid., 63–67.
7. Ibid., 68–74, 85; Simon, *Papers*, 10: 411.
8. Matter, *If It Takes*, 80.
9. Ibid., 81–82; *OR*, Ser. 1, Vol. XXXVI, Pt. 2, 552–553; Jordan, *Happiness*, 346.
10. Grant, *Memoirs*, 2: 215–216.
11. Matter, *If It Takes*, 71–73, 81–82; Gallagher, *Spotsylvania*, 33. The five cavalry regiments left with the Army of the Potomac were the 5th New York, 3rd New Jersey, 22nd New York, 2nd Ohio, and 13th Pennsylvania.
12. Matter, *If It Takes*, 84–85.
13. Roebling, "Report," 26–27.
14. Matter, *If It Takes*, 85–93. An ample illustration of the utter confusion of the day is a story which Matter (p. 92) relates of one Rebel captain, who, taken prisoner in the gathering darkness, asked his captors, "Which way is it to the rare [sic]?"
15. Grant, *Memoirs*, 2: 215–216; Simon, *Papers*, 10: 414–415.
16. Wilson, *Under*, 1: 396–397.
17. Matter, *If It Takes*, 109, 390n45. Matter observed that a notation Warren made upon his unsent letter in November of 1864 stated that Warren had had no reason to change the opinions he had expressed therein.
18. Humphreys, *Virginia*, 72n14. The 2nd and 6th Corps experienced casualties of about 150 men each. Matter, *If It Takes*, 108.
19. *OR*, Ser. 1, Vol. XXXVI, Pt. 1, 63–64.
20. Ibid., 64–65.
21. Humphreys, *Virginia*, 71.
22. Matter, *If It Takes*, 128–130, 169.
23. Grant, *Memoirs*, 2: 224–225.
24. Matter, *If It Takes*, 109–148; Humphreys, *Virginia*, 76–81; Walker, *History*, 445–455; Boatner, *Civil War*, 84. Francis Walker, 2nd Corps historian, was an economist and statistician, who after the war became the first president of MIT (Massachusetts Institute of Technology).
25. Matter, *If It Takes*, 134.
26. Comstock, *Diary*, 265–266.
27. Matter, *If It Takes*, 131–148; Humphreys, *Virginia*, 76–81; Walker, *History*, 446–455.

28. *OR*, Ser. 1, Vol. XXXVI, Pt. 1, 65; Humphreys, *Virginia*, 82–83; Walker, *History*, 446–456, 462–463; Gallagher, *Spotsylvania*, 35–36. Matter, as a contributor to Gallagher's consideration of Spotsylvania, specifically attributes the delays and confusion regarding the 2nd Corps' passage to Spotsylvania and their crossing of the Po to the Army of the Potomac's complete lack of cavalry reconnaissance.

29. Humphreys, *Virginia*, 78–83; Walker, *History*, 446–456, 462–463; Simon, *Papers*, 10: 418–419.

30. Gallagher, *Spotsylvania*, 39; *OR*, Ser. 1, Vol. XXXVI, Pt. 2, 596, 600; Simon, *Papers*, 10: 421.

31. Gallagher, *Spotsylvania*, 40.

32. Matter, *If It Takes*, 148–155; Humphreys, *Virginia*, 81–82, 89; Walker, *History*, 456–458; Grant, *Memoirs*, 2: 223–224; Holzer, *Hearts*, 815; Venable, "Address," 6–7.

33. *OR*, Ser. 1, Vol. XXXVI, Pt. 1, 65–66.

34. Warner, *Generals*, 400–401; Jones "Official Diary," 93.

35. *OR*, Ser. 1, Vol. XXXVI, Pt. 1, 66.

36. Grant, *Memoirs*, 2: 222.

37. Matter, *If It Takes*, 158–159; Humphreys, *Virginia*, 84–85.

38. *OR*, Ser. 1, Vol. XXXVI, Pt. 2, 96; Matter, *If It Takes*, 159–160; Humphreys, *Virginia*, 85–87; Walker, *History*, 463.

39. *OR*, Ser. 1, Vol. XXXVI, Pt. 1, 67.

40. Matter, *If It Takes*, 159–160, 167; Gallagher, *Spotsylvania*, 38; Humphreys, *Virginia*, 83, 87.

41. Walker, *History*, 463.

42. Grant, *Memoirs*, 2: 224–225; Smith, *Petersburg*, 70. Upton and Joshua L. Chamberlain were the only battlefield promotions Grant made during the war.

43. Simon, *Papers*, 10: 422–423.

44. Ibid., 423.

45. Gallagher, *Spotsylvania*, 38.

46. Matter, *If It Takes*, 158–159; Grant, *Memoirs*, 2: 224.

47. OR, Ser. 1, Vol. XXXVI, Pt. 1, 67.

48. Humphreys, *Virginia*, 85–87; Matter, *If It Takes*, 158–161; Steere, *Wilderness*, 106–107, 187–188, 199, 207, 212–218. We've seen where all the blame was placed as far as the first attack on the Bloody Angle is concerned, but there were many reasons why Mott failed to support Upton's 6 P.M. attack, and not all of them were attributable Mott. As Matter points out, the plan for a coordinated attack scheduled for 5 P.M. on May 10th on the 5th and 6th Corps' fronts started to come unglued the minute Meade gave Warren orders to attack at around 3:30 instead of 5 P.M. Meade sent orders to Wright to make his attack earlier, but Wright was not ready. In fact, Wright's attack was delayed until 6 P.M., and though some of the force under Wright's command received word of the delay, there is evidence that Mott did not, and Mott attacked on his front, as ordered, at 5 P.M. The distance of Upton's attack from the cover of the woods to the enemy earthworks was about 200 yards. Mott's men, on the other hand, had to advance five times that distance, or about 1,000 yards, the first part of which while confronting Rebel skirmishers in heavy woods. Forming for the assault in plain view of the enemy who prepared to meet him, Mott advanced at 5 P.M., the Rebel skirmishers he drove into the enemy earthworks had plenty of time to alert the defenders to the Federal advance, and the Rebels greeted the advancing Yankees with canister. Mott's assault failed, and Mott's poor performance at the Wilderness made it easy for Wright, who we already know as one who did not accept blame, to let Mott take the fall for the ultimate failure of Upton's assault on the 10th. See Steere for the details of Mott's performance at the Wilderness. Matter, however, also offers (p. 138) that two aides, Meade's staff officer Theodore Lyman and Wright's aide Oliver Wendell Holmes, complained on encounters with Mott at Spotsylvania that the officer appeared "stupid," "listless," and "flustered."

49. Matter, *If It Takes*, 173–183; Humphreys, *Virginia*, 89–90, 94–95; Walker, *History*, 467–472.

50. Matter, *If It Takes*, 170–268; Walker, *History*, 471–476; Humphreys, *Virginia*, 99–100.

51. Sifakis, 160. Lewis Grant was brevetted a major general for several of his 1864 battles, and was eventually awarded the Medal of Honor for his leadership of the Vermonters during the Chancellorsville Campaign. After the war, Lewis Grant served as President Benjamin Harrison's assistant secretary of war.

52. National Park Service, "Battles of the Wilderness and Spotsylvania," http://www.nps.gov/history/history/online_books/civil_war_series/25/sec16.htm.

53. Humphreys, *Virginia*, 104; *OR*, Ser. 1, Vol. XXXVI, Pt. 2, 661.

54. Matter, *If It Takes*, 170, 227; *OR* , Ser. 1, Vol. XXXVI, Pt. 2, 661.

55. *OR*, Ser. 1, Vol. XXXVI, Pt. 2, 662.

56. Matter, *If It Takes*, 227–228.

57. *OR*, Ser. 1, Vol. XXXVI, Pt. 2, 662.

58. Matter, *If It Takes*, 228–229; Roebling, "Report," 35–36.

59. Ibid., 35–36.

60. *OR*, Ser. 1, Vol. XXXVI, Pt. 2, 662–665, 667, 669–670.

61. Matter, *If It Takes*, 229–230; *OR*, Ser. 1, Vol. XXXVI, Pt. 2, 663, 668.

62. Simon, *Papers*, 10: 427.

63. *OR*, Ser. 1, Vol. XXXVI, Pt. 2, 663–665, 671, Pt. 1, 68.

64. Matter, *If It Takes*, 227; Humphreys, *Virginia*, 91–92, 100–101. Humphreys, responding to Badeau's version of this day, politely comments that while he, Humphreys, had been on every part of the Spotsylvania battlefield, Badeau had not, and didn't know what he was talking about. Wyckoff, *History*, 186; Jones, "Official Diary," 493.

65. Taylor, *Warren*, 173–174.

66. *OR*, Ser. 1, Vol. XXXVI, Pt. 2, 654–656, 670.

67. Matter, *If It Takes*, 250–252, 275.

68. Simon, *Papers*, 10: 436, 469–470.

69. Roebling, "Report," 37–38.

70. *OR*, Ser. 1, Vol. XXXVI, Pt. 1, 68.

71. Grant, *Memoirs*, 2: 231–232; OR, Ser. 1, Vol. XXXVI, Pt. 1, 68–69.

72. Walker, *History*, 474.

73. Humphreys, *Virginia*, 93, 96–98, 104; Matter, *If It Takes*, 271.

74. *OR*, Ser. 1, Vol. XXXVI, Pt. 2, 705, 712–718.

75. Meade, *Life and Letters*, 195; Dana, *Recollections*, 199.

76. *OR*, Ser. 1, Vol. XXXVI, Pt. 2, 695; Warner, *Generals*, 315–317; Simon, *Papers*, 10: 471.

77. *OR*, Ser. 1, Vol. XXXVI, Pt. 2, 700.

78. Matter, *If It Takes*, 277–283, 297; Humphreys, *Virginia*, 106–107; *OR*, Ser. 1, Vol. XXXVI, Pt. 2, 746–747, 755–757; Roebling, "Report," 39–40.

79. Matter, *If It Takes*, 283–286; *OR*, Ser. 1, Vol. XXXVI, Pt. 2, 757–763; Roebling, "Report," 41–43; Grant, *Memoirs*, 2: 236. In his memoirs, Grant credited Upton with capturing Myer's Hill, then

losing Myer's Hill, then recapturing Myer's Hill with "Ayers' coming up to his support."
80. Matter, *If It Takes*, 293; *OR*, Ser. 1, Vol. XXXVI, Pt. 2, 760, 788–789.
81. Humphreys, *Virginia*, 109; Roebling, "Report," 43–44; *OR*, Ser. 1, Vol. XXXVI, Pt. 2, 809–810.
82. Grant, *Memoirs*, 2: 236–237; Rafuse, *Lee*, 154.
83. *OR*, Ser. 1, Vol. XXXVI, Pt. 2, 816–817; Roebling, "Report," 44.
84. Meade, *Life and Letters*, 2: 197.
85. Smith, *Petersburg*, 8–10.
86. Humphreys, *Virginia*, 110–111; Matter, *If It Takes*, 306–312.
87. Meade, *Life and Letters*, 197.
88. Humphreys, *Virginia*, 109.
89. Humphreys, *Virginia*, 112–114; Roebling, "Report," 48–52; Matter, *If It Takes*, 317–327.
90. Grant, *Memoirs*, 2: 239–240; Walker, *History*, 488.
91. Grant, *Memoirs*, 2: 240; Humphreys, *Virginia*, 113–115; Badeau, *Military*, 206–208.
92. Walker, *History*, 443–444.
93. Agassiz, *Headquarters*, 106. Theodore Lyman noted that when Rebel and Yankee wounded were placed side by side in field hospitals, they would chatter away together, with the chief topics of conversation being size and quality of rations, marches they had made, and the regiments they had fought against. As Lyman observed, "All sense of personal spite is sunk in the immensity of the contest."
94. *OR*, Ser. 1, Vol. XXXVI, Pt. 3, 52–53.
95. Grant, *Memoirs*, 2: 241–244.
96. *OR*, Ser. 1, Vol. XXXVI, Pt. 3, 52–53.
97. Matter, *If It Takes*, 330, 334–335, 340–341.
98. Alexander, *Military*, 529–530.
99. Humphreys, *Virginia*, 115–118. On pages 114–115 of his history, Humphreys makes a case for the general unreliability of Badeau's accounts.
100. Taylor, *Warren*, 172–175.
101. McFeely, *Grant*, 156–159.
102. Simon, *Papers*, 10: 425–426; Rafuse. *Lee*, 150–151. When Sheridan met Stuart and his force at Yellow Tavern on May 11th, the fight ended with a Union victory and Stuart mortally wounded. Sheridan went on to probe Richmond's outer defenses, found them too strong to attack and hold, and turned his force away toward the Peninsula, making the most of opportunities to destroy Rebel railroads, bridges and supplies.
103. Simon, *Papers*, 10: 491; Holzer, *Hearts*, 817; Venable, "Address," 12; Rafuse, *Lee*, 157.
104. Meade, *Life and Letters*, 198; *OR*, Ser. 1, Vol. XXXVI, Pt. 3, 115.

Chapter Eight

1. Humphreys, *Virginia*, 119.
2. Grant, *Memoirs*, 2: 243; Smith, *Petersburg*, 96n5.
3. Wittenberg, *Little Phil*, 31.
4. Alexander, *Military*, 529–530; Humphreys, *Virginia*, 120, 122.
5. Baltz, *Cold Harbor*, 22–23.
6. Roebling, "Report," 53–55.
7. Simpson, *Grant*, 246, 249–250.
8. Simon, *Papers*, 10: 475.
9. Roebling, "Report," 56–57; Smith, *Petersburg*, 13–14, 96. J. Michael Miller in his book *The North Anna Campaign* implies that the 5th Corps stood idly by and watched the Rebel wagon train pass by, when, according to Roebling, the only ones who had a knowledge of it and a chance to intercept it were this remnant of the Federal cavalry.
10. Humphreys, *Virginia*, 125–126.
11. Simon, *Papers*, 10: 479.
12. *OR*, Ser. 1, Vol. XXXVI, Pt. 3, 90–92; Roebling, "Report," 58–59; Smith, *Petersburg*, 15–17; Humphreys, *Virginia*, 126–127.
13. Roebling "Report," 59–61; *OR*, Ser. 1, Vol. XXXVI, Pt. 3, 116–118, 125. As these communications running back and forth between Hancock and Warren on May 23rd indicate, it was hard to know, given the state of the maps and Torbert's confusion, who had gone wrong, and which way was right.
14. *OR*, Ser. 1, Vol. XXXVI, Pt. 3, 124–127.
15. Smith, "Petersburg," 17–19; Roebling, "Report," 57, 61; Humphreys, *Virginia*, 124; *OR*, Ser. 1, Vol. XXXVI, Pt. 3, 125–128.
16. Roebling, "Report," 62; Smith, *Petersburg*, 8–19; *OR*, Ser. 1, Vol. XXXVI, Pt. 3, 128; Venable "Address," 13; Rafuse, *Lee*, 157.
17. Roebling, "Report," 62; Smith, *Petersburg*, 19–20.
18. *OR*, Ser. 1, Vol. XXXVI, Pt. 1, 76–77; Rafuse, *Lee*, 157–158.
19. *OR*, Ser. 1, Vol. XXXVI, Pt. 3, 128–130, 145, Pt. 1, 77.
20. Simon, *Papers*, 10: 89, 490–491; Smith, *Petersburg*, 20–21; Roebling, "Report," 65.
21. Simon, *Papers*, 10: 486–487.
22. Aggasiz, *Headquarters*, 125–126.
23. Wittenberg, *Little Phil*, 27–28, 137.
24. Humphreys, *Virginia*, 133, 165; Grant, *Memoirs*, 2: 254; Baltz, *Cold Harbor*, 34–35; Rafuse, *Lee*, 159; Roebling, "Report," 66–67.
25. Humphreys, *Virginia*, 160–161, 164–165; The Battle at Cold Harbor: The Cavalry Battle at Haw's Shop, http://www.nps.gov/history/history/online_books/civil_war_series/11/sec6.htm; Smith, *Petersburg*, 24.
26. *OR*, Ser. 1, Vol. XXXVI, Pt. 1, 854.
27. *OR*, Ser. 1, Vol. XXXVI, Pt. 1, 80; Rafuse, *Lee*, 139; Sheridan, *Personal Memoirs*, 1: 401–402; Grant, *Memoirs*, 2: 259; Baltz, *Cold Harbor*, 24–25, 30. To further confuse this tangled tale, Cold Harbor historian Louis Baltz conjectured that Sheridan might have taken it upon himself to order a brigade from Hancock's 2nd Corps to assist him at Haw's Shop. While there are no records of Sheridan's supposed request for infantry support in the *OR*, there is record of Hancock reporting that one of his brigades was at Haw's Shop late on May 28th. Meade was unaware of that 2nd Corps movement, and ordered Hancock to either recall the brigade or maneuver to rejoin the 2nd Corps' flanks with that of the corps on its right and left.
28. Smith, *Petersburg*, 22–23.
29. Roebling, "Report," 68; Baltz, *Cold Harbor*, 24.
30. Baltz, *Cold Harbor*, 23; Agassiz, *Headquarters*, 130; Madison Barracks, http://www.madisonbarracks.com/?page=history; Civil War Surgery Manuals, http://jeffline.jefferson.edu/SML/Archives/Highlights/Manual/.
31. Humphreys, *Virginia*, 166–167; Baltz, *Cold Harbor*, 25, 38–41; Alexander, *Military*, 534.
32. Baltz, *Cold Harbor*, 29.
33. Humphreys, *Virginia*, 166–170; *OR*, Ser. 1, Vol. XXXVI, Pt. 2, 303–304, 336, 341; Roebling, "Report," 69–70; Smith, *Petersburg*, 25–26; Baltz, *Cold Harbor*, 42; *OR*, Ser. 1, Vol. XXXVI, Pt. 3, 336.
34. *OR*, Ser. 1, Vol. XXXVI, Pt. 3, 303.
35. Ibid., 335–336.
36. Baltz, *Cold Harbor*, 42–44,

48, 51; Sifakis, 239; Boatner, *Civil War*, 86. A confounding variable during the initial fighting at Bethesda Church was the presence of the 5th Corps' 2nd Division, commanded by the newly arrived Brigadier General Henry Hayes Lockwood. Lockwood, who had brought out former garrison troops as reinforcements on May 26th, was assigned to command the 5th Corps' newly constituted 4th Division. Not only was Lockwood new to his command, but he would prove to be, in Warren's and Grant's eyes, of no use on the battlefield, and would remain in command of the division for less than a month. Though placed in support of Crawford on the 5th Corps' left, Lockwood was of little assistance on May 30th, other than to distract the attention of one of the three divisions attacking Warren by his position of Crawford's flank. Smith, *Petersburg*, 25–26; Humphreys, *Virginia*, 167–168; Roebling, "Report," 70–71; *OR*, Ser. 1, Vol. XXXVI, Pt. 3, 340–343, Pt. 1, 81.

37. Baltz, *Cold Harbor*, 46–48; Humphreys, *Virginia*, 168; Smith, *Petersburg*, 25–27; Roebling, "Report," 71–72; *OR*, Ser. 1, Vol. XXXVI, Pt. 3, 341–348, 350–351, 361.

38. Baltz, *Cold Harbor*, 46–54; Humphreys, *Virginia*, 168–170.

39. Baltz, *Cold Harbor*, 46–54. Historian Baltz offers that three squadrons of Devin's 17th New York Cavalry were assigned to be on Warren's flank. If they were, they offered no warning of Early's three-division-strong approach and attack. Humphreys, *Virginia*, 168–170; *OR*, Ser. 1, Vol. XXXVI, Pt. 1, 84.

40. Meade, *Life and Letters*, 199.
41. Simon, *Papers*, 10: 490–491.
42. Ibid., 419.
43. Ibid., 429–430, 447, 454, 456, 488, 491–492.
44. *OR*, Ser. 1, Vol. XXXVI, Pt. 3, 389, 39.

Chapter Nine

1. Simon, *Papers*, 1: 475, 477–478, 484, 487–488.
2. Baltz, *Cold Harbor*, 56; Humphreys, *Virginia*, 170. Humphreys mistakenly believed that Lee had not learned of Smith's arrival until June 1st.
3. Baltz, *Cold Harbor*, 62–65; Humphreys, *Virginia*, 172–173.
4. Baltz, *Cold Harbor*, 63–65; *OR*, Ser. 1, Vol. XXXVI, Pt. 3, 361; Humphreys, *Virginia*, 171.
5. Baltz, *Cold Harbor*, 56–57, 63–69, 71; Simon, *Papers*, 10: 496–499; Humphreys, *Virginia*, 169–171.
6. Baltz, *Cold Harbor*, 69–70; Wilson, *Under*, 1: 429–432.
7. Humphreys, *Virginia*, 172.
8. Baltz, *Cold Harbor*, 80–82, 84.
9. *OR*, Ser. 1, Vol. XXXVI, Pt. 2, 85; Grant, *Memoirs*, 2: 264–265; *OR*, Ser. 1, Vol. XXXVI, Pt. 1, 85.
10. Baltz, *Cold Harbor*, 84; *OR*, Ser. 1, Vol. XXXVI, Pt. 3, 454, Pt. 1, 86.
11. *OR*, Ser. 1, Vol. XXXVI, Pt. 1, 83–84.
12. Baltz, *Cold Harbor*, 81–85.
13. *OR*, Ser. 1, Vol. XXXVI, Pt. 3, 452, Pt. 1, 87–88.
14. Baltz, *Cold Harbor*, 85–95; Humphreys, *Virginia*, 174–176.
15. Baltz, *Cold Harbor*, 96; Humphreys, *Virginia*, 170; Roebling, "Report," 74–75.
16. *OR*, Ser. 1, Vol. XXXVI, Pt. 2, 446; Wainwright, *Diary*, 395–398; Smith, *Petersburg*, 28; Roebling, "Report," 74.
17. Baltz, *Cold Harbor*, 96–98, 100–102; *OR*, Ser. 1, Vol. XXXVI, Pt. 3, 447–448, 450; Smith, *Petersburg*, 28; Roebling "Report," 76–77; *OR*, Ser. 1, Vol. XXXVI, Pt. 1, 86.
18. *OR*, Ser. 1, Vol. XXXVI, Pt. 1, 999.
19. *OR*, Ser. 1, Vol. XXXVI, Pt. 3, 452.
20. Grant, *Memoirs*, 2: 265–266; Baltz, *Cold Harbor*, 98–100.
21. *OR*, Ser. 1, Vol. XXXVI, Pt. 1, 85.
22. Baltz, *Cold Harbor*, 101–102; *OR*, Ser. 1, Vol. XXXVI, Pt. 3, 450.
23. Baltz, *Cold Harbor*, 102–103; *OR*, Ser. 1, Vol. XXXVI, Pt. 1, 86.
24. Agassiz, *Headquarters*, 138; *OR*, Ser. 1, Vol. XXXVI, Pt. 1, 1000–1002.
25. Grant, *Memoirs*, 2: 266.
26. OR XXXVI, III, 432–433, 452; Humphreys, *Virginia*, 176; *OR*, Ser. 1, Vol. XXXVI, Pt. 1, 543.
27. Meade, *Life and Letters*, 2: 200.
28. *OR*, Ser. 1, Vol. XXXVI, Pt. 3, 457–458.
29. Baltz, *Cold Harbor*, 117–118; *OR*, Ser. 1, Vol. XXXVI, Pt. 1, 344.
30. *OR*, Ser. 1, Vol. XXXVI, Pt. 1, 1001.
31. *OR*, Ser. 1, Vol. XXXVI, Pt. 3, 482, 484–485, 490, 497.
32. Ibid., 487–489.
33. Humphreys, *Virginia*, 177; *OR*, Ser. 1, Vol. XXXVI, Pt. 3, 486–488, 491, 498–504.
34. Baltz, *Cold Harbor*, 124–125; *OR*, Ser. 1, Vol. XXXVI, Pt. 3, 491.
35. Baltz, *Cold Harbor*, 124–129; *OR*, Ser. 1, Vol. XXXVI, Pt. 3, 491–493; Roebling, "Report," 79–81; Grant, *Memoirs*, 2: 268; Humphreys, *Virginia*, 179–180; Smith, *Petersburg*, 29–30.
36. *OR*, Ser. 1, Vol. XXXVI, Pt. 3, 478, 481.
37. Ibid., 494.
38. Roebling, "Report," 81–82.
39. *OR*, Ser. 1, Vol. XXXVI, Pt. 3, 478–479; Roebling, "Report," 82–83.
40. Baltz, *Cold Harbor*, 133–134.
41. *OR*, Ser. 1, Vol. XXXVI, Pt. 3, 526–527.
42. Comstock, *Diary*, 271–272.
43. Baltz, *Cold Harbor*, 156; *OR*, Ser. 1, Vol. XXXVI, Pt. 3, 524–539.
44. Baltz, *Cold Harbor*, 133.
45. *OR*, Ser. 1, Vol. XXXVI, Pt. 3, 526.
46. Baltz, *Cold Harbor*, 152, 156–159, 161, 231; *OR*, Ser. 1, Vol. XXXVI, Pt. 3, 524; Comstock, *Diary*, 271. Grant's engineer, Cyrus Comstock, recorded in his diary that Federal casualties for June 1st–3rd were 7,000. For a full account of the 2nd, 5th, 6th, 9th and 18th Corps' attacks on June 3rd, a grim, but enlightening look can be found in Louis Baltz, *Cold Harbor*, 133–173. Baltz, quoting Dyer's *Compendium*, lists the total Federal losses throughout their stay at Cold Harbor as 14,931 killed, wounded or captured. Humphreys, *Virginia*, 191, states that the wounded brought to the army's hospitals from the fighting on the 3rd of June alone numbered 4,517, with the number killed estimated at an additional 1,100.
47. Baltz, *Cold Harbor*, 135–137.
48. Ibid., 139–144.
49. Ibid., 145–153.
50. *OR*, Ser. 1, Vol. XXXVI, Pt. 3, 525, 544–545.
51. Baltz, *Cold Harbor*, 154–160.
52. Holzer, *Hearts*, 819.
53. Rafuse, *Lee*, 171–172.
54. Roebling, "Report," 84; *OR*, Ser. 1, Vol. XXXVI, Pt. 2, 538.
55. Humphreys, *Virginia*, 189; *OR*, Ser. 1, Vol. XXXVI, Pt. 1, 88; Roebling, "Report," 84; Boatner, *Civil War*, 348.
56. Humphreys, *Virginia*, 189; *OR*, Ser. 1, Vol. XXXVI, Pt. 1, 88. Actually, Dana *did* mention Warren in his report to Washington that day, but he stated, incorrectly, that,

since Warren's line was so long and thin, he made no effective assaults that day.

57. Baltz, *Cold Harbor*, 161–165, 176; *OR*, Ser. 1, Vol. XXXVI, Pt. 3, 538–543; Humphreys, *Virginia*, 193.

58. Baltz, *Cold Harbor*, 163–165; Roebling, "Report," 83–85; *OR*, Ser. 1, Vol. XXXVI, Pt. 1, 88; Humphreys, *Virginia*, 189.

59. Meade, *Life and Letters*, 200; Grant, *Memoirs*, 2: 276.

60. Baltz, *Cold Harbor*, 166, 197; Boatner, *Civil War*, 418–419. Union general David Hunter (USMA, 1822), having taken command of West Virginia in May of 1864 after Sigel's defeat in the valley, was sent to disrupt Rebel supply lines and communications. Hunter was successful, until routed by Rebel general Jubal Early at Lynchburg. Hunter's retreat into West Virginia left the Shenandoah Valley open for Early's highly disruptive Washington raid later in 1864. *OR*, Ser. 1, Vol. XXXVI, Pt. 3, 526; Comstock, *Diary*, 271; Wilson, *Under*, 1: 445–446.

61. Meade, *Life and Letters*, 200–201; Agassiz, *Headquarters*, 147.

62. Humphreys, *Virginia*, 192–193; Baltz, *Cold Harbor*, 169–170, 177; *OR*, Ser. 1, Vol. XXXVI, Pt. 1, 92–93; Baltz, *Cold Harbor*, 183–193.

63. Roebling, "Report," 85–86; *OR*, Ser. 1, Vol. XXXVI, Pt. 3, 378, 570–571, 576.

64. *OR*, Ser. 1, Vol. XXXVI, Pt. 3, 570–571.

65. Ibid., 609.
66. Ibid., 631.
67. Ibid., 627, 631.
68. Ibid., 610.
69. Ibid., 628.
70. Ibid., 628–629.
71. Roebling, "Report," 87–88.
72. Smith, *Petersburg*, 32.
73. Ibid., 32; Roebling, "Report," 89; Baltz, *Cold Harbor*, 196, 199.
74. Robertson, *Back Door*, 225, 239–240, 254.
75. *OR*, Ser. 1, Vol. XXXVI, Pt. 1, 94.
76. Meade, *Life and Letters*, 202–203.
77. Ibid., 201–202; Baltz, *Cold Harbor*, 197–202.
78. Smith, *Petersburg*, 33.
79. Baltz, *Cold Harbor*, 194, 196, 202.
80. *OR*, Ser. 1, Vol. XV, Pt. 1, 18.
81. Smith, *Petersburg*, 33; Roebling, "Report," 91–92; Jordan, *Happiness*, 165.

82. Wilson, *Memoirs*, 397–401; Robertson, *Back Door*, 40. Military historian William Glenn Robertson observes that Wilson was also one of the chief proponents for Baldy Smith replacing George Meade as commander of Army of the Potomac.

83. Roebling, "Report," 93–95; Battle of Cold Harbor, http://www.nps.gov/history/history/online_books/civil_war_series/11/sec17.htm.

84. Ibid.; Smith, *Petersburg*, 35; Roebling, "Report," 93–95.

85. Venable, "Address," 16; Holzer, *Hearts*, 820.

Chapter Ten

1. Battle of Cold Harbor, http://www.nps.gov/history/history/online_books/civil_war_series/11/sec17.htm.

2. Smith *Petersburg*, 35–36; Roebling, "Report," 95–96; Comstock, *Diary*, 273; Battle of Cold Harbor, http://www.nps.gov/history/history/online_books/civil_war_series/11/sec17.htm.

3. *Richmond Whig*, June 15, 1864.

4. Coffey, *Sheridan's*, 30–35; Comstock, *Diary*, 275; *OR*, Ser. 1, Vol. XV, Pt. 1, 22.

5. *OR*, Ser. 1, Vol. XXXVI, Pt. 1, 95–96.

6. Walker, *History*, 525–527; Roebling, "Report," 96.

7. *OR*, ser. 1, vol. XL, Pt. 2, 72; 12-hour Clock, http://en.wikipedia.org/wiki/12-hour_clock. The older tradition of using "12:00 m" for noon[1] (Latin meridies), and "12:00 mn" for midnight (Latin media nox).

8. Battle of Cold Harbor, http://www.nps.gov/history/history/online_books/civil_war_series/11/sec17.htm.

9. Grant, *Memoirs*, 2: 294–295.

10. Boatner, *Civil War*, 402–403. Gen. Edward Hinks of Maine was in the Regulars, though he did not attend USMA. Boatner, *Civil War*, 448–449. Gen. August Kautz, though born in Germany, graduated from the USMA in 1852.

11. Battle of Cold Harbor, http://www.nps.gov/history/history/online_books/civil_war_series/11/sec17.htm.

12. Walker, *History*, 529.
13. Ibid., 532–534.
14. *OR*, Ser. 1, Vol. XV, Pt. 2, 60–61. See Walker, *History of the 2nd Army Corps*, 530, for a discussion of the disagreements on the time of Hancock's arrival at Petersburg.

15. *OR*, Ser. 1, Vol. XL, Pt. 2, 49, 50.

16. Smith, *Petersburg*, 36–38; Walker, *History*, 531–532; *OR*, Ser. 1, Vol. XV, Pt. 1, 19; Young, *Around the World*, 306.

17. *OR*, Ser. 1, Vol. XL, Pt. 1, 23, Pt. 2, 39. On June 17th, Dana reported to Stanton that Butler had relieved Gillmore from command of the 10th Army Corps, and ordered him to Fortress Monroe to await a court of inquiry concerning, in Dana's words, Gillmore's "disgraceful failure to capture Petersburg after he had volunteered for the duty." However, on hearing Gillmore's side of the story, Grant "modified the order so that Gillmore is relieved at his own request and ordered to Washington to report to the Adjutant-General for orders."

18. McFeely, *Grant*, 174–175; The Battle of Cold Harbor, http://www.nps.gov/history/history/online_books/civil_war_series/11/sec17.htm.

19. Grant, *Memoirs*, 2: 293–294.
20. *OR*, Ser. 1, Vol. XL, Pt. 2, 87, 98.
21. Ibid., 98–100.
22. Grant, *Memoirs*, 2: 248; Smith, *Petersburg*, 36–38; *OR*, Ser. 1, Vol. XL, Pt. 2, 70–72; Roebling, "Report," 93–95.
23. *OR*, Ser. 1, Vol. XL, Pt. 2, 63; Walker, *History*, 529–530.
24. Walker, *History*, 530–531.
25. *OR*, Ser. 1, Vol. XL, Pt. 2, 36–37, 63; Comstock, *Diary*, 273.
26. *OR*, Ser. 1, Vol. XL, Pt. 2, 72–73.
27. Ibid., 98.
28. *OR*, Ser. 1, Vol. XV, Pt. 1, 20–21.
29. *OR*, Ser. 1, Vol. XL, Pt. 2, 86.
30. Ibid., 91; Boatner, *Civil War*, 372.
31. Comstock, *Diary*, 273; Meade, *Life and Letters*, 205; Smith, *Petersburg*, 38.
32. *OR*, Ser. 1, Vol. XV, Pt. 2, 91, 97; Agassiz, *Headquarters*, 63. Meade took only his chief of staff, Humphreys, the aides Sanders and Lyman, and Gen. Ingalls on the boat to City Point.
33. *OR*, Ser. 1, Vol. XL, Pt. 2, 86; Boatner, *Civil War*, 44–45.
34. Smith, *Grant*, 374.
35. *OR*, Ser. 1, Vol. XL, Pt. 2, 79, 91.
36. Smith, *Petersburg*, 40–41.
37. *OR*, Ser. 1, Vol. XL, Pt. 2, 88–89, 97.

38. Walker, *History*, 334–537.
39. Smith, *Petersburg*, 38–39; Roebling, "Report," 97.
40. *OR*, Ser. 1, Vol. XL, Pt. 2, 94–95, 98.
41. Smith, *Petersburg*, 40–41; Agassiz, *Headquarters*, 165–166; Roebling, "Report," 98.
42. Smith, *Petersburg*, 41–42.
43. Ibid., 42–43; Roebling, "Report," 99–101.
44. Roebling, "Report," 101–102; Smith, *Petersburg*, 43. This will not be the last time that Crawford loses all sense of direction, or fails to use common sense, for that matter. See Afterword for Crawford.
45. Meade, *Life and Letters*, 205.
46. Smith, *Petersburg*, 43–45.
47. Ibid., 44–45; Agassiz, *Headquarters*, 167.
48. *OR*, Ser. 1, Vol. XL, Pt. 2, 172.
49. Roebling, "Report," 103–5; *OR*, Ser. 1, Vol. XL, Pt. 2, 173; Agassiz, *Headquarters*, 169.
50. *OR*, Ser. 1, Vol. XL, Pt. 2, 175–176.
51. Roebling, "Report," 105–106; *OR*, Ser. 1, Vol. XL, Pt. 2, 177.
52. Roebling, "Report," 103–106; Smith, *Petersburg*, 45.
53. *OR*, Ser. 1, Vol. XL, Pt. 2, 174.
54. Walker, *History*, 539–540.
55. *OR*, Ser. 1, Vol. XL, Pt. 2, 174, 177, 179; Walker, *History*, 541.
56. Roebling, "Report," 106–107; Agassiz, *Headquarters*, 170. See the author's book *Chamberlain at Petersburg* for an annotated account of Chamberlain's own account of his brigade's fight at Rives Salient, Petersburg.
57. *OR*, Ser. 1, Vol. XL, Pt. 2, 179.
58. OR, Ser. 1, Vol. XV, Pt. 1, 25. There seems to be no question that the attacks of June 17th and 18th were made under Meade's orders. Dana claims that Grant was in command on the 16th, while Meade commanded on the 17th and 18th. Meade actually claims that he was completely in command at Petersburg from the moment he arrived on the 16th.
59. Walker, *History*, 541–542; Shaw, *First Maine*, 121–123.
60. Meade, *Life and Letters*, 206; Roebling, "Report," 108.
61. *OR*, Ser. 1, Vol. XL, Pt. 2, 170; Roebling, "Report," 109–111.
62. *OR*, Ser. 1, Vol. XV, Pt. 1, 25–27.
63. Ibid., 25.
64. Taylor, *Warren*, 182.
65. Ibid.
66. Ibid., 182–183. Meade's enclosed statement to Warren stated, "I have received your note of this date calling my attention to the article in the *Pittsburg Commercial* of the 14th Instant. The statement there made — that I have preferred charges against you for disobedience and tardy execution of orders — is entirely without foundation in fact."
67. *OR*, Ser. 1, Vol. XL, Pt. 1, 28.
68. Jordan, *Happiness*, 173.
69. Ibid., 175.

Appendix

1. Titone, *My Thoughts*, 14.
2. Eicher and Eicher, *Civil War*, 111–112; Adams, *Education*, 222–223. Adams, whom Badeau took to the White House to meet President Grant, gave a scathing appraisal of him, describing Grant as a "man whose energies were the greater, the less they wasted on thought."
3. Anonymously written report in *Literary World* 37 (March 30, 1888): 299, on Badeau suit against Mrs. Grant.
4. Shattuck, *Hamlet*, 30, 26–27.
5. Bierce, *Phantoms*, 326–327.
6. Morris, *Bierce*, 256–268.
7. Sifakis, 57–58.
8. Smith, *Fanny and Joshua*, 152–160, 182–213, 215–303, 349–350.
9. Chamberlain, *Passing*, 87–134; Boatner, *Civil War*, 207–208.
10. Mr. Lincoln and Friends, http://www.mrlincolnandfriends.org/inside.asp?pageID=97&subjectID=9; Wilson, *Dana*, 469.
11. Shanks, *Personal Recollections*, 116; Grant's Home, http://www.granthome.com/; Richardson, *Grant*, 455.
12. Young, *Around the World*, 163–165, 167–169.
13. Richardson, *Grant*, 600–601.
14. Wittenberg, *Little Phil*, 42–46.
15. Longacre, *Buford*, 141.
16. Wittenberg, *Little Phil*, 42–46, 68, 101, 115–116.
17. Smith, *Fanny and Joshua*, 187–188.
18. Marszalek, *Commander*, 201–213; Porter, *Campaigning*, 182.
19. Marszalek, *Commander*, 205–213.
20. *OR*, Ser. 1, Vol. XXXIX, Pt. 2, 503.
21. Marszalek, *Commander*, 214.
22. Anders, *Halleck's War*, 590–692; Warner, *Generals*, 195–197; Marszalek, *Commander*, 227–251.
23. Sifakis, *Who*, 175–176.
24. Cooper, *Hazen*, 12, 206–208.
25. Hutton, *Phil Sheridan*, 19.
26. Styple, *Generals*, 171; Battle of Pickett's Mill, http://ehistory.osu.edu/uscw/features/articles/0006/picketts.cfm; Boatner, *Civil War*, 412–413; Woodworth, *Victory*, 169–171; Jones, *Logan*, 144–145.
27. Shanks, *Personal Recollections*, 126.
28. Jones, *Logan*, 40–41.
29. Boatner, *Civil War*, 525; Warner, *Generals*, 293–294.
30. Meade, *Life and Letters*, 196–197, 199.
31. Boatner, *Civil War*, 609–610. Ord was the commander who had replaced McClernand when Grant removed him from, 387; Warner, *Generals*, 315–317; Boatner, *Civil War*, 539–540; Find a Grave/Meade, http://www.findagrave.com/cgi-bin/fg.cgi?page=gr&GRid=702.
32. Smith, *Grant*, 471; Boatner, *Civil War*, 681–682; Sifakis, 328; Find a Grave/Rawlins, http://www.findagrave.com/cgi-bin/fg.cgi?page=gr&GRid=6521.
33. Rensselaer Alumni Hall of Fame/Roebling, http://www.rpi.edu/about/hof/roebling.html; Smithsonian Civil War Studies/Roebling, http://civilwarstudies.org/articles/vol_3/augustus-roebling.shtm.
34. Roebling, "Letter Book," 413; Dickinson College/Rusling, http://deila.dickinson.edu/theirownwords/author/RuslingJ.htm. Roebling's correspondent was Brevet Brigadier General James Rusling, M.A., LL.D., of New Jersey, who authored *Men and Things I Saw in Civil War Days* in 1899.
35. Marszalek, *Commander*, 239; Bobrick, *Master*, 288–289.
36. Bobrick, *Master*, 327–329; Boatner, *Civil War*, 726–727.
37. Medal of Honor/Schofield, http://www.history.army.mil/html/moh/civwarmz.html. Bobrick, *Master*, 288–289.
38. Boatner, *Civil War*, 525–526; Bobrick, *Master*, 288–289.
39. Young, *Around the World*, 297, 627; Sheridan, *Personal Memoirs*, 1: 11–13; Morris, *Sheridan*, 21–22; Boatner, *Civil War*, 830–831.
40. Young, *Around the World*, 300, 450; Boatner, *Civil War*, 747–748.
41. Hanson, *Unknown*, 7, 360.
42. Arlington Cemetery/Sheridan, http:www.arlingtoncemetery.net/ireneruc.htm.
43. Coffey, *Sheridan's*, xvii, 142; Hutton, *Phil Sheridan*, 125, 129; Find a Grave/Sheridan, http://www.findagrave.com/cgi-bin/fg.cgi?page=gr&GRid=949.

44. Hutton, *Phil Sheridan*, 124–129, Cooper, *Hazen*, 318. For a consideration of Sheridan's postwar military career, the author recommends Paul Hutton's *Phil Sheridan and his Army* (Lincoln: University of Nebraska Press, 1985).
45. Marszalek, *Commander*, 205; *OR*, Ser. 1, Vol. XXXVIII, Pt. 4, 454.
46. Marszalek, *Commander*, 213–215.
47. Goodwin, *Team*, 651–655.
48. Smith, *Grant*, 542–543.
49. U.S. Senate History/Belknap Impeachment, http://www.senate.gov/artandhistory/history/minute/War_Secretarys_Impeachment_Trial.htm.
50. Cooper, *Hazen*, 209–224, 318.
51. Boatner, *Civil War*, 748, 751; Find a Grave/Sherman, http://www.findagrave.com/cgi-bin/fg.cgi?page=gr&GRid=951; Young, *Around the World*, 290–291; Bobrick, *Master*, 339–341–343.
52. Bobrick, *Master*, 260–269.
53. Ibid., 286–289, 291–317.
54. Ibid., 257–309.
55. Young, *Around the World*, 295.
56. Van Horne, *Thomas*, 421.
57. Young, *Around the World*, 295–296.
58. Bobrick, *Master*, 327–329; Tucker, *Chickamauga*, 323.
59. Bobrick, *Master*, 331, 334–337.
60. Young, *Around the World*, 290.
61. Boatner, *Civil War*, 891–892; Jordan, *Happiness*, 309.
62. Smith, *Grant*, 470–471.
63. Wilson, *Under*, 1: 528–530.
64. Sifakis, 458–459; Styple, *Generals*, 271–272, 276.
65. Boatner, *Civil War*, 134; Coffey, *Sheridan's*, 94.

Bibliography

Articles

"Badeau vs. Grant." *Literary World* 37 (March 30, 1888).

Emerson, John W. "Grant's Life in the West and his Mississippi Campaign: Halleck's Plot Against Grant." *Midland Monthly* 9 (1898): 225–232.

Geare, Randolph. "Historic Swords." *Chatauquan* 33 (April–Sept.1901): 629.

Jones, J. William. "Official Diary of First Corps A.N.V. while commanded by Lieutenant-General R.H. Anderson, May 7–31, 1864." *Southern Historical Society Papers* 7 (Jan.–Dec. 1879).

Mahood, Wayne. "The Stuff of Legends: James S. Wadsworth." *North and South* 4, no. 1 (November 2000).

Meagher, Thomas F. "The Last Days of the 69th in Virginia." Pamphlet published by *The Irish American* (1861), copy available at USAMHI, Carlisle Barracks, PA.

Morris, Roy, Jr. "A Bird of Evil Omen: The War Department's Charles Dana." *Civil War Times Illustrated* (January 1987): 20–29.

Morrison, James L., Jr. "Educating the Civil War Generals: West Point, 1833–1861." *Military Affairs* 38, no. 3 (Oct. 1974): v. IV, #1.

Tucker, Glenn. "The Battles for Chattanooga." Eastern Acorn Press, 1981.

Venable, Charles. "Address of Col. C.S. Venable." Richmond, VA: Geo. W. Gary, 1879.

Unpublished Sources

Badeau-Wilson Letters. Princeton University Library, Rare Books and Special Collections, Civil War Letters of Adam Badeau, Princeton, NJ.

Dana-Pike Letters. University of Maine, Special Collections, James S. Pike Collection, Box 273, Orono, ME.

Hopper, George C. "George C. Hopper to the Military Order of the Loyal Legion, Detroit: 'Beverly Ford to Bottom's Bridge: The First Michigan Infantry from May 1st to June 6.'" Bentley Historical Library, University of Michigan, Ann Arbor, MI.

Redman, Bob. "Sheridan's Ride at Chickamauga." http://www.aotc.net/Sheridan.htm.

Roebling, Washington A. "Report, May 4 to Aug 20, 1864." Gouverneur K. Warren Papers, New York State Library, Albany, NY.

———. "Roebling Letter Book." Rutgers University Special Collection, Archibald Alexander Library, New Brunswick, NJ.

Steiner, Henry. "A Litte Pale Blue-Eyed Man." http://HenrySteiner/DIRsteiner/historian.htm

Books

Adams, Henry. *The Education of Henry Adams*. Oxford University Press, 1999.

Agassiz, George R. *Meade's Headquarters, 1863–1865: Letters of Col. Theodore Lyman*. Boston: Atlantic Monthly Press, 1922.

Alexander, Edward Porter. *Military Memoirs of a Confederate*. New York: Charles Scribner's Sons, 1907.

Ambrose, Stephen. *Halleck: Lincoln's Chief of Staff*. Baton Rouge: Louisiana State University Press, 1990.

Anders, Curt. *Henry Halleck's War*. Carmel: Guild Press of Indiana, 1999.

Badeau, Adam. *Military History of Ulysses S. Grant*. New York: D. Appleton, 1885.

Baltz, Louis J., III. *The Battle of Cold Harbor, May 27–June 13, 1864*. Lynchburg, VA.: H.E. Howard, 1994.

Bearss, Edwin. *Receding Tide: Vicksburg and Gettysburg*. Washington, DC: National Geographic, 2010.

Bierce, Ambrose. *Phantoms of a Bloodstained Period*. Edited by Russell Duncan and David Klooster. Amherst: University of Massachusetts Press, 2002.

Boatner, Mark M. *The Civil War Dictionary*. New York, Random House, 1991.

Bobrick, Benson. *Master of War: The Life of General George H. Thomas*. New York: Simon and Schuster, 2009.

Brinton, John. *Personal Memoirs of John H. Brinton:*

Major and Surgeon U.S.V. 1861–1865. New York: Neale Publishing, 1914.

Bundy, Carol. *The Nature of Sacrifice: A Biography of Charles Russell Lowell, Jr.* New York: Farrar, Straus and Giroux, 2005.

Chamberlain, Joshua L. *Passing of the Armies*. New York: Bantam Books, 1993.

Chamberlin, Thomas. *History of the 150th Regiment Pennsylvania Volunteers, Second Regiment, Bucktail Brigade*. Philadelphia: F. McManus, Jr. 1905. Reprinted Baltimore: Butternut and Blue, 1986.

Coffey, David. *Sheridan's Lieutenants*. New York: Rowman and Littlefield, 2005.

Cohen, Eliot A. *Supreme Command: Soldiers, Statesmen and Leadership in Wartime*. New York: Free Press, 2002.

Comstock, Cyrus B. *Diary of Cyrus B. Comstock*. Dayton, OH: Morningside, 1987.

Cooling, Benjamin Franklin. *Forts Henry and Donelson*. Knoxville: University of Tennessee Press, 1987.

Cooper, Edward S. *William Babcock Hazen: The Best Hated Man*. Madison, NJ: Fairleigh Dickinson University Press, 2005.

Cozzens, Peter. *No Better Place to Die : The Battle of Stones River*. Urbana: University of Illinois Press, 1990.

_____. *This Terrible Sound: The Battle of Chickamauga*. Urbana: University of Illinois Press, 1996.

Dana, Charles A. *Recollections of the Civil War*. Lincoln: University of Nebraska Press, 1996.

Daniel, Larry J. *Days of Glory: The Army of the Cumberland, 1861–1865*. Baton Rouge: Louisiana State University Press, 2004.

_____. *Shiloh*. New York: Simon and Schuster, 1997.

Donald, David. *Lincoln*. New York: Touchstone, 1995.

Eicher, John, and David Eicher. *Civil War High Commands*. Stanford, CA: Stanford University Press, 2001.

Engle, Stephen. *Don Carlos Buell: Most Promising of All*. Chapel Hill: University of North Carolina Press, 1999.

Force, M.F. *From Fort Henry to Corinth*. New York: Charles Scribner's Sons, 1881.

Ford, Worthington Chauncey. *A Cycle of Adams Letters*. Boston: Houghton Mifflin, 1920.

Gallagher, Gary W., ed. *The Spotsylvania Campaign*. Chapel Hill: University of North Carolina Press, 1998.

Gibbon, John. *Personal Recollections of the Civil War*. New York: G.P. Putnam's Sons, 1928.

Goodwin, Doris Kearns. *Team of Rivals*. New York: Simon and Schuster, 2005.

Graham, Martin. *Mine Run: A Campaign of Lost Opportunities*. Lynchburg, VA.: H.E. Howard, 1977.

Grant, U.S. *The Papers of Ulysses S. Grant*. Vol. 10. Edited by David Wilson. Carbondale: Southern Illinois University Press, 1982.

_____. *Personal Memoirs of U.S. Grant*. 2 vols. New York: Charles L. Webster, 1886.

Hanson, Neil. *Unknown Soldiers*. New York: Knopf, 2006.

Hayes, Rutherford B., et al. *Life and Reminiscences of General Wm. T. Sherman by Distinguished Men of His Time*. Baltimore: R.H. Woodward, 1891.

Hazen, William B. *A Narrative of Military Service*. Boston: Ticknor, 1885.

Holzer, Harold. *Hearts Touched by Fire: The Best of Battles and Leaders of the Civil War*. New York: Modern Library, Random House, 2011.

Hoppin, James Mason. *Life of Andrew Hull Foote, Rear-Admiral United States Navy*. New York: Harper and Brothers, 1874.

Howe, M.A. DeWolfe. *Home Letters of General Sherman*. New York: Charles Scribner's Sons, 1909.

Hughes, Nathaniel Cheairs, Jr. *The Battle of Belmont*. Chapel Hill: University of North Carolina Press, 1991.

Humphreys, Andrew. *The Virginia Campaign of 1864 & 1865*. New York: Charles Scribner's Sons, 1883.

Hutton, Paul Andrew. *Phil Sheridan and His Army*. Lincoln: University of Nebraska Press, 1985.

Hyde, Bill. *The Union Generals Speak: The Meade Hearings on the Battle of Gettysburg*. Baton Rouge: Louisiana State University Press, 2003.

Jones, James P. *"Black Jack": John A. Logan and Southern Illinois in the Civil War Era*. Tallahassee: Florida State University, 1967.

_____. *"Your Left Arm": James H. Wilson's Letters to Adam Badeau*. Kent, OH: Kent State University Press, 1966.

Jordan, David. *"Happiness Is Not My Companion."* Bloomington: Indiana University Press, 2001.

Joshi, S.T. *Ambrose Bierce: The Devil's Dictionary, Tales & Memoirs*. New York: Library of America, 2011.

_____, and David E. Schultz. *Ambrose Bierce: A Sole Survivor, Bits of Autobiography*. Knoxville: University of Tennessee Press, 1998.

Keneally, Thomas. *American Scoundrel: The Life of the Notorious Civil War General Dan Sickles*. New York: Anchor Books, 2003.

Kennett, Lee. *Sherman: A Soldier's Life*. New York: HarperCollins, 2001.

Kiper, Richard L. *Major General John Alexander McClernand: Politician in Uniform*. Kent, OH: Kent State University Press, 1999.

Lewis, Lloyd. *Sherman: Fighting Prophet*. New York: Harcourt, Brace, l932.

Livermore, Thomas. *Days and Events: 1860–1866*. Boston: Houghton Mifflin, 1920.

Lockridge, Richard. *Darling of Misfortune: Edwin Booth*. New York: B. Blom, 1971.

Longacre, Edward. *General John Buford*. Conshohocken, PA: Combined Books, 1995.

Lytle, William Haines. *For Honor, Glory and Union*. Lexington: University Press of Kentucky, 1999.

Mahan, Dennis Hart. *Advanced-Guard, Out-Post, and Detachment Service of Troops with the Essential Principles of Strategy and Grand Tactics for the Use of Officers of the Militia and Volunteers*. New York: John Wiley, 1870.

Marszalek, John F. *Commander of All Lincoln's Armies: A Life of General Henry W. Halleck*. Cambridge, MA: Belknap Press Of Harvard University Press, 2004.

Matter, William. *If It Takes All Summer*. Chapel Hill: University of North Carolina Press, 1988.

McClellan, Carswell. *Notes on the Personal Memoirs of P.H. Sheridan*. St. Paul, MN: William Banning Jr., 1889.

_____. *The Personal Memoirs & Military History of U.S. Grant Versus the Record of the Army of the Potomac*. Boston: Houghton Mifflin, 1887.

McClellan, George B. *Mexican War Diary and Correspondence of George B. McClellan*. Edited by Thomas W. Cutrer. Baton Rouge: Louisiana State University, 2009.

McDonough, James Lee. *Chattanooga—A Death Grip on the Confederacy*. Knoxville: University of Tennessee Press, 1984.

_____. *Shiloh—In Hell Before Night*. Knoxville: University of Tennessee Press, 1977.

_____. *War in Kentucky: From Shiloh to Perryville*. Knoxville: University of Tennessee Press, 1994.

McFeely, William S. *Grant: A Biography*. New York: W.W. Norton, 1981.

McKinney, Francis F. *Education in Violence: The Life of George H. Thomas and the History of the Army of the Cumberland*. Chicago: Americana House, 1991.

McPherson, James M. *Battle Cry of Freedom*. New York: Ballantine Books, 1988.

_____. *This Mighty Scourge*. Oxford: Oxford University Press, 2007.

Meade, George. *The Life and Letters of George Gordon Meade*. 2 vols. New York: Scribner's Sons, 1913.

Morris, Roy, Jr. *Ambrose Bierce: Alone in Bad Company*. New York: Crown Publishers, 1995.

_____. *Sheridan: The Life and Wars of General Phil Sheridan* New York: Crown, 1992.

Noe, Kenneth W. *Perryville: This Grand Havoc of Battle*. Lexington: University Press of Kentucky, 2001.

155th Pennsylvania Association. *Under the Maltese Cross: Antietam to Appomattox*. Pittsburgh: Warner, 1910.

Parker, John L. *History of the 22nd Massachusetts Infantry, the 2nd Co. Sharpshooter, & the 3rd Light Battery*. Boston: Rand Avery, 1887.

Pearson, Henry G. *James S. Wadsworth of Generseo: Brevet Major General of Volunteers*. New York: Charles Scribner's Sons, 1913.

Pennypacker, Isaac R. *General Meade*. New York: D. Appleton, 1901.

Porter, Horace. *Campaigning with Grant*. Bloomington: Indiana University Press, 1961.

Powell, William H. *The Fifth Army Corps*. New York: G.P. Putnam's Sons, 1896.

Pullen, John. *The Twentieth Maine*. Dayton, OH: Morningside, 1991.

Rafuse, Ethan. *Robert E. Lee and the Fall of the Confederacy*. New York: Rowman and Littlefield, 2008.

Richardson, Albert D. *Personal History of Ulysses S. Grant*. Hartford, CT: M.A. Winter and Hatch, 1885.

Robertson, William Glenn. *Back Door to Richmond*. Baton Rouge: Louisiana State University Press, 1987.

Rockwell, Alonzo P. *Rambling Recollections: An Autobiography*. New York: B. Hoeber, 1920.

Ruggles, Eleanor. *Prince of Players: Edwin Booth*. New York: W.W. Norton, 1953.

Schaff, Morris. *The Battle of the Wilderness*. Boston: Houghton Mifflin, 1910.

Sears, Stephen W. *Controversies and Commanders*. Boston: Houghton Mifflin, 1999.

Sedgwick, John. *Correspondence of John Sedgwick, Major General*. New York: De Vinne Press, 1903.

Shanks, William F.G. *Personal Recollections of Distinguished Generals*. New York: Harper and Brothers, 1866.

Shattuck, Charles H. *The Hamlet of Edwin Booth*. Urbana: University of Illinois Press, 1969.

Shaw, Horace H. *The First Maine Heavy Artillery*. Portland, ME: 1903; reprinted by Higginson Book Company of Salem, MA, 1998.

Sheridan, P.H. *Personal Memoirs of P.H. Sheridan*. 2 vols. New York: Charles L. Webster, 1888.

Sherman, John. *John Sherman's Recollections of Forty Years in the House, Senate and Cabinet*. Vol. 1. New York: Werner, 1895.

Sherman, William T. *Personal Memoirs of General William T. Sherman*. 2 vols. New York: Charles L. Webster, 1891.

Sifakis, Stewart. *Who Was Who in the Union*. New York: Facts on File, 1988.

Simon, John, ed. *Papers of Ulysses S. Grant*. Vols. 4, 5, 10. Carbondale: Southern Illinois University Press, 1972, 1974, 1982.

Simpson, Brooks. *Ulysses S. Grant*. New York: Houghton Mifflin, 2006.

Simpson, Brooks D., Stephen W. Sears, and Aaron Sheehan-Dean, eds. *The Civil War: The First Year Told by Those Who Lived It*. New York: Library of America, 2011.

Slade, A.D. *A.T.A. Torbert: Southern Gentleman in Union Blue*. Dayton, OH: Morningside, 1992.

Smith, Diane Monroe. *Chamberlain at Petersburg: The Charge at Fort Hell*. Gettysburg, PA: Thomas Publications, 2004.

_____. *Fanny & Joshua: The Enigmatic Lives of Frances Caroline Adams & Joshua Lawrence Chamberlain*. Gettysburg, PA: Thomas Publications, 1999.

Smith, Gene. *American Gothic: The Story of America's Legendary Theatrical Family—Junius, Edwin, and John Wilkes Booth* New York: Simon and Schuster, 1992.

Smith, Jean Edward. *Grant*. New York: Simon and Schuster, 2001.

Spruill, Matt, and Lee Spruill. *Winter Lightning: A Guide to the Battle of Stones River* Knoxville: University of Tennessee Press, 2007.

Star, Stephen Z. *The Union Cavalry in the Civil War*. Baton Rouge: Louisiana State University Press, 1981.

Steere, William. *The Wilderness Campaign*. Harrisburg, PA: Stackpole, 1960.

Stickles, Arndt M. *Simon Bolivar Buckner*. Chapel Hill: University of North Carolina Press, 1940.

Styple, William B. *Generals in Bronze*. Kearny, NJ: Belle Grove, 2005.

Tarbell, Ida. *Life of Abraham Lincoln*. New York: Lincoln Memorial Association, Doubleday and McClure, 1900.

Taylor, Emerson Gifford. *Gouverneur Kemble Warren: The Life & Letters of an American Soldier*. Boston: Houghton Mifflin, 1932.

Titone, Nora. *My Thoughts Be Bloody*. New York: Free Press, 2010.

Tucker, Glenn. *Chickamauga: Bloody Battle in the West* Indianapolis, IN: Bobbs-Merrill, 1961.

U.S. War Department. *Atlas to Accompany the Official Records of the Union & Confederate Armies*. Washington, Government Printing Office, 1891–1895.

_____. *The War of the Rebellion: A Compilation of the Official Records of the Union & Confederate Armies*. Washington: Government Printing Office, 1880–1901.

Van Horne, Thomas B. *The Life of Major-General George H. Thomas*. New York: Charles Scribner's Sons, 1882.

Wainwright, Charles. *A Diary of Battle: The Personal Journals of Colonel Charles S. Wainwright*. Edited by Allan Nevins. New York: Harcourt, Brace and World, 1962.

Walker, Francis A. *History of the Second Army Corps*. New York: Charles Scribner's Sons, 1891.

Warner, Ezra. *Generals in Blue*. Baton Rouge: Louisiana State University Press, 1991.

Waugh, John C. *The Class of 1846*. New York: Warner, 1994.

Wilson, James Grant. *General Grant's Letters to a Friend, 1861–1880*. New York: T.Y. Crowell, 1897.

Wilson, James Harrison. *Life of Charles Dana*. New York: Harper and Brothers, 1907.

_____, ed. *Under the Old Flag*. 2 vols. New York: D. Appleton, 1912.

Wittenberg, Erik J. *Little Phil: A Reassessment of the Civil War Leadership of Gen. Philip H. Sheridan*. Washington, DC: Brassey's, 2002.

Woodworth, Steven E. *Nothing but Victory: The Army of the Tennessee, 1861–1865*. New York: Knopf, 2005.

Wyckoff, Mac. *A History of the 3rd South Carolina Infantry*. Fredericksburg, VA: Sgt. Kirkland's Museum, 1995.

Young, John Russell. *Around the World with General Grant*. New York: American News Company, 1879.

Index

Adams, Henry 212, 238*n*2
Alexander, E. Porter 154
Altamont, Tennessee 55
Anderson, Richard H. 120, 121, 123, 124, 125, 129, 131, 133, 136, 141, 142, 144, 154, 165, 169, 170, 182, 191, 204
Anderson, Robert 6, 8
Arkansas Post, Arkansas, Battle of 65, 66
Atlanta, Georgia 88, 147, 215, 219, 220
Averell, William W. 102, 148, 214
Avery House 202
Ayres, Romeyn B. 147, 148, 234*n*79

Babcock, Orville 202
Badeau, Adam 85–88, 101, 103, 126, 127, 135, 136, 151, 180, 212, 230*n*143, 230*n*146, 234*n*64, 235*n*99, 238*n*2, 238*n*3
Banks, Nathaniel P. 63, 71, 89, 229*n*65
Barlow, Francis C. 134–136, 175, 180, 181, 201
Barnard, John G. 200
Bartlett, Joseph J. 142, 149
Bates, William 82
Baxter Road *see* Norfolk Pike
Beauregard, Pierre G. T. 20, 41, 42, 44, 45, 48, 54, 148, 167, 168, 191, 196, 197, 200, 201, 204, 205, 225*n*2, 227*n*126
Belknap, William W. 220
Belmont, Battle of 11, 13–15, 225*n*39
Bermuda Hundred 148, 155, 167, 168, 189, 197, 198, 200, 202
Bethesda Church 164, 166, 169, 171, 174–176, 183, 187, 188, 235*n*36
Bierce, Ambrose 38, 75, 76, 83, 95, 96, 212
Big Black River, Mississippi 72

Birney, David B. 134, 135, 183, 184, 201, 205, 207, 231*n*22
"Bloody Angle" (aka "Mule Shoe") 137–146, 149, 150, 234*n*48
Blunt, James G. 227*n*140, 228*n*140
Booth, Edwin 86, 88, 212, 230*n*143, 230*n*146
Booth, John Wilkes 88, 212
Boutwell, George Sewall 223
Bowers, Theodore S. 168
Bragg, Braxton 42, 54, 55, 56, 58, 59, 61–64, 75, 76, 78–80, 83, 88, 91, 186, 227*n*126, 230*n*112, 230*n*118
Breathed, James 157
Breckinridge, John C. 148, 150, 191
Brinton, Dr. John 46, 227*n*93, 227*n*114
Bristoe Station, Battle of 92, 93
Bruinsburg, Mississippi 71
Buchanan, James 6, 24
Buckner, Simon B. 26–30, 226*c*2*n*45, 226*c*2*n*48
Buell, Don Carlos 6, 9, 10, 15–19, 23, 30–34, 36–39, 41–43, 47, 49, 51, 52, 54–63, 227*n*93, 228*n*7, 228*n*23
Buford, John 69, 100, 101
Burnside, Ambrose 7, 63, 66, 75, 80, 84, 104, 105, 110, 111, 113–115, 117, 119, 130, 133, 134, 139–141, 145, 148, 151, 155, 159, 160, 164, 165, 170, 173, 175–178, 182–186, 188, 190, 197–202, 205, 206, 211, 212, 222, 225*n*8, 230*n*137
Butler, Benjamin 63, 67, 89, 102, 119, 129, 148, 150, 153, 155, 167, 168, 189, 196, 198, 200, 202, 237*n*17
Butterfield, Daniel 99

Cairo, Illinois 11, 13–15, 21, 23, 32, 37

USS *Carondelet* 23, 24, 26
Cedar Creek, Battle of 219, 223
Chamberlain, Joshua L. 149, 206, 212, 213, 215, 229*n*55
Chambliss, John 157
Champion's Hill, Mississippi 72
Chapman, George H. 101
Charles City Court House 192
Chase, Salmon 9, 77, 231*n*39
Chattanooga, Tennessee 17, 32, 51, 54, 55, 64, 75, 77–80, 83, 84, 88, 91, 92, 215
Chewning Farm 104, 109–111, 113, 115, 117, 121, 232*n*21
Chickamauga, Tennessee, Battle of 75–78, 84, 91, 222, 230*n*119, 230*n*132
Chickasaw Bayou, Mississippi 65, 70
City Point, Virginia 155, 188, 192, 194, 195, 199–202, 207, 214, 237*n*32
Clarke, Asia Booth 88
Clark's Mountain, Virginia 103
Cleburne, Patrick 61, 80
Cold Harbor, Battle of 93, 166–191, 195, 235*n*36, 236*c*8*n*36, 236*n*46
Columbus, Kentucky 11, 13, 14, 16, 19, 32, 225*n*28
Committee on the Conduct of the War 7, 34, 63, 99, 231*n*4, 231*n*22, 231*n*44
Comstock, Cyrus 72, 87, 115, 122, 125, 134, 135, 140, 149, 180, 185, 189, 192, 194, 198–201, 207, 208, 233*n*34, 236*n*46
Corbin's Bridge 121, 122
Corinth, Mississippi 37, 38, 39, 41, 44, 48–50, 54, 62, 63, 73, 102
Cox, Jacob 218, 222
Craig's Tavern 108
Crapsey, Edward 189
Crawford, Samuel W. 109–112, 129, 131, 145, 164, 165, 172, 191,

245

202, 203, 207, 208, 213, 236c8n36, 237n44
Crittenden, George 16
Crittenden, Thomas L. 59, 64, 77, 78, 228n23
Crook, George 101, 219
Crump's Landing 43
Cullum, George W. 46, 227n93
Culpeper, Virginia 95, 152
Curtis, Sam 32, 56, 67
Custer, George Armstrong 101, 114, 115, 124, 156, 161, 167, 192, 218, 231–232c4n49
Cutler, Lysander 129, 142, 144, 145, 162, 172, 202

Dahlgren, Ulric 100
Dana, Charles A. 1, 69–73, 75–79, 85, 101, 133, 135, 136, 138, 140, 143, 145–147, 155, 159, 160, 161, 169–174, 182–185, 190, 194, 197, 199, 207–209, 213, 216, 230n137, 236n56, 237n17, 238n58
Danville, Kentucky 62
Davies, Henry E. 100, 101
Davis, President Jefferson 16–18, 41, 72, 223
Davis, Jefferson C. 57
Devin, Thomas C. 101, 115, 124, 236c8n39
Dimmock Line 199, 204, 205
Doubleday, Abner 99
Downer's Bridge 155
Duff, William L. 72

Early, Jubal A. 130, 134, 150, 151, 164, 165, 169, 176, 182, 183, 185, 190, 191, 215, 223, 236c8n39, 237n60
Emancipation Proclamation 64
USS Essex 21, 22
Ewell, Richard S. 112, 113, 115, 131, 142, 146, 150, 151, 154, 164, 182, 190

Ferrero, Edward 114, 120
Field, Charles W. 129, 144
Fisher's Hill, Battle of 219
Five Forks, Battle of 132, 213, 214, 218, 222
Flippo, Doctor 157
Floyd, John B. 6, 24, 26, 28, 29, 31
Foote, Andrew 10, 15, 19–24, 26–28, 32, 36, 226n5
Forrest, Nathan Bedford 28, 29, 45, 54, 64
Forsythe, Joseph 124, 219
Fort Donelson 15, 16, 18, 19–24, 26, 27, 29–37, 39, 41, 45, 49, 72, 226n31, 226c2n44, 226c2n48, 49, 54, 227n87
Fort Foote 22
Fort Heiman 20
Fort Henry 15, 16, 18, 19–24, 26, 35, 36, 41
Fort Powhatan 190

Foster, J.G. 67
Frémont, John 10, 13
French, William 94–98, 231n20

Galena, Illinois 5, 33, 213
Garfield, James 77, 215
Gay, Ebenezer 59
General Order No. 100 66, 67
Getty, George W. 110, 113
Gettysburg, Battle of 73, 74, 90, 91, 99, 102, 218
Gibbon, John 134, 135, 139, 145
Gilbert, Charles C. 56–62, 228n23
Gillmore, Quincy 189, 197, 199, 237n17
Gordon, John B. 117, 165, 173
Grand Gulf, Mississippi 68, 71
Granger, Gordon 77, 82–84, 230n132
Grant, Julia Dent 2, 34–36, 44, 48, 49, 212, 213, 222
Grant, Lewis A. 141, 234n51
"Grant's Men" 1, 2, 3, 21, 49, 86, 90, 132, 155, 173, 211
Greeley, Horace 70, 77
Gregg, David McMurtie 100, 101, 107, 109, 161, 163, 194, 214, 231n49, 231–232c4n49
Gregg, J. Irvin 101, 121, 122, 130, 233n38
Grierson, Benjamin 71
Griffin, Charles 103, 110–112, 114, 115, 123, 129, 142–147, 149, 151, 155, 157, 158, 162, 164, 165, 171, 173, 176, 177, 182, 183, 185, 202, 205–207, 214, 215

Hagood, Johnson 181
Hagood Line 199
Halleck, Henry W. 3, 7, 9, 10, 13, 15, 16, 18–24, 26, 30–40, 43–51, 54–56, 62–68, 71, 73–76, 78–80, 84–86, 88, 91–93, 102, 103, 106, 129, 131, 135, 139, 145, 148, 155, 180, 181, 189, 215, 218–220, 222, 227n87, 227n93, 227n140, 228n174, 228n7, 230n136
Hamburg, Tennessee 41
Hamilton's Crossing 108, 109
Hammond, John 110, 120
Hampton, Wade 126, 132, 154, 161, 168, 182, 190, 192, 194, 214
Hancock, Winfield S. 73, 91, 99, 103, 106, 110–114, 117, 130–135, 140, 141, 144–146, 148, 150, 151, 154–156, 162, 164, 165, 172–175, 177, 180, 182, 186, 195–200, 203, 205, 207, 211, 215, 231n44, 235n13, 235n27, 237n14
Hanover Junction 154, 157, 161
Hardee, William J. 58, 59
Harris Line 202
Harris Store 157
Harrison's Creek 195, 198
Haskell, Frank A. 93

Haw's (Hawe's) Shop 161, 162, 235n27
Hayes, Rutherford, B. 222
Hazen, William B. 64, 77, 78, 82–84, 89, 212, 215, 216, 230n112
Heavy Artillerymen 141, 150, 170, 171, 180, 206
Heth, Henry 135, 176, 182, 183, 185
Hill, A.P. 92, 110, 113–115, 149, 158, 159, 166, 182, 191
Hinks, Edward 189, 196, 198, 237n10
"Historicus" 99
Hitchcock, Ethan 31
Hoke, Robert 150, 168, 169, 170, 191
Holly Spring, Mississippi 65
Holmes, Oliver Wendell 234n48
Hood, John Bell 219–221
Hooker, Joseph 7, 63, 66, 67, 73, 78–82, 91, 92, 106, 230n136, 231n39
Hornet's Nest, Battle of Shiloh 44
Howard, Oliver O. 78–80, 84, 89, 216, 230n132
Humphreys, Andrew A. 96, 103, 104, 119, 123, 126, 133, 135, 136, 138, 140, 143, 144, 150, 152, 167, 168, 183, 187, 188, 233c6n19, 233n38, 234n64, 235n99, 237n32
Hunt, Henry J. 96
Hunter, David 67, 180, 185, 188, 190–192, 194, 195, 214, 236n60
Hurlbut, Stephen 40

USS Indianola 71
Iuka, Mississippi, Battle of 62

James River, Crossing of 179, 189–192, 195–202
Jericho Mills 158
Jerusalem Plank Road (aka Jerusalem Pike) 200–202, 204, 207
Johnson, Andrew 17, 33, 55, 218
Johnson, Bushrod 30, 61
Johnson, Edward 96, 111, 112, 146, 231n28
Johnston, Albert Sidney 16, 17, 23, 26, 30–32, 41, 42, 44
Johnston, Joseph 7, 71, 72, 88, 89, 101, 148, 215, 219, 220

Kautz, August 189, 196, 201, 237n10
Kellogg, Elisha S. 171
Kelly, James E. 69
Kershaw, Joseph B. 128, 144, 169, 204
Kilpatrick, Hugh Judson 100, 231n45, 232c4n49
Knoxville, Tennessee 17, 75, 80, 83

Lacey House 107
Laiboldt, Bernard 59
Laurel Hill 128–147

Law, Evander M. 180, 181
Lee, Fitzhugh 115, 123, 126, 132, 168–170, 190, 194
Lee, Robert E. 3, 7, 73, 79, 90–95, 97–99, 105–107, 109, 111, 114, 115, 117–122, 125, 129, 131, 134, 136, 140, 146, 148, 150–152, 154, 155, 157–162, 164–168, 170, 171, 177, 178, 180, 182, 183, 186, 189, 191, 192, 194, 196–198, 202, 204, 215, 217, 222, 232n2
Lee, William H.F. "Rooney" 132, 182
USS *Lexington* 13
Lincoln, Abraham 1, 6, 7, 14, 17, 19, 23, 30–34, 37, 47, 50–52, 62, 63, 66, 67, 73, 76, 78, 85, 86, 91, 116, 133, 136, 212, 220
Livermore, Thomas 97
Lockwood, Henry H. 172, 173, 235n36, 236c8n36
Logan, John A. 3, 6, 14, 20, 28, 30, 31, 47, 216, 217, 221, 226c2n54
Longstreet, James 75–77, 79, 83, 88, 91, 106, 114, 115, 120
Lookout Mountain, Tennessee, Battle of 80, 82
Louisville, Kentucky 55–58, 215
Lowell, Charles F., Jr. 119
Lyle, Peter 128
Lyman, Theodore 160, 162, 174, 186, 201, 206, 234n48, 235n93, 237n32
Lytle, William 60, 61, 76, 77, 228n22

Mackenzie, Ranald S. 137, 219
Mahan, Dennis Hart 42, 227n124
Mangohick Church 162
Massaponax Church 155, 157
McClellan, Carswell 123, 126, 127
McClellan, George Brinton 3, 6, 7, 8, 10, 16–20, 31, 33–36, 40, 49–52, 54, 55, 63, 67, 220, 227n87, 227n93
McClernand, John A. 6, 13–15, 19–24, 27–31, 33, 36, 40, 41, 44, 48, 65–67, 69–74, 216, 217, 226n31, 238n31
McCook, Alexander 60, 61, 62, 64, 75, 77, 78, 228n14, 228n15, 228n23
McCook, Daniel 59, 60, 62
McIntosh, John B. 101, 198
McMinnville, Tennessee 55
McPherson, James B. 21, 23, 30, 31, 41, 44, 49, 50, 63, 68, 69, 71–74, 86, 88, 89, 216, 227n133
Meade, George G. 66, 69, 73, 74, 85, 90–94, 96–99, 102, 105–115, 117, 119–123, 125–127, 129–136, 138, 141–147, 149, 151–155, 157, 158, 160–162, 164–166, 168, 169, 172–181, 183–189, 194–198, 200–209, 211, 213,

216–218, 220, 223, 231n4, 231n22, 231n39, 231n44, 231n45, 232n52, 233c6n10, 233n38, 234n48, 235n27, 237n82, 237n32, 238n58, 238n66
Memphis, Tennessee 16, 19, 22, 65, 78
Merritt, Wesley 100, 101, 121–124, 130, 219, 223, 233c6n30, 233n38
Miles, Nelson 219
Mill Springs, Battle of (aka Logan Cross Roads) 16, 17
Milliken's Bend, Louisiana 65, 71
Mine Run, Virginia 94–99, 106, 107, 122, 152, 177, 185, 231n39
Missionary Ridge, Tennessee, Battle of 80–84, 215, 230n118, 230n119
Mitchel, O.M. 225n8
Morgan, John Hunt 54
Mott, Gershom 138–140, 234n48
"Mule Shoe" *see* "Bloody Angle"
Munfordville, Kentucky 55, 62, 64
Murfreesboro, Tennessee 32, 63, 65
Myer's Hill 147, 148, 234n79

Nance's Shop *see* St. Mary's Church
Nashville, Tennessee 16, 17, 26–28, 32, 34, 35, 37, 49, 55, 62, 63, 215, 216, 218
Nashville, Tennessee, Battle of 221, 222
Negley, James S. 77
Neill, Thomas H. 131
Nelson, William "Bull" 32, 41, 43, 44, 56, 57
New Castle, Virginia 167, 170
New York Draft Riots 73, 88
Norfolk Pike (aka Sussex Road or Baxter Road) 202
North Anna, Battle of 154–161, 235n9
North Anna River, Virginia 119, 152

Oates, William C. 77
Oglesby, Richard 15
Ord, Edward O.C. 102, 217, 238n31

Paine, William H. 175
Parker, Ely S. 190
Parker's Store, Virginia 95, 106, 109, 110
Pemberton, John C. 65, 71, 72
Perryville, Kentucky, Battle of 49, 58–62, 76, 218, 228n23
Petersburg, Virginia 119
Petersburg, Battle of 189–209, 212, 213, 238n58
Pickett, George 150, 198
Pillow, Gideon 6, 13–14, 24, 26–29, 31, 226c2n48

Pittsburg Landing, Tennessee 37–49
Pleasonton, Alfred 100, 101, 231n45
Polk, Leonidas 6, 13, 14, 19, 58–60, 64, 225n28
Poor Creek (aka Poo Creek) 205
Pope, Edmund M. 155, 156, 158
Pope, John 7, 31, 36, 51, 52
Port Gibson, Mississippi 71
Port Hudson, Louisiana 71, 88, 229n65
Porter, David 65, 66, 68, 71
Porter, Fitz-John 63
Porter, Horace 79
Prentiss, Benjamin M. 44, 45

USS *Queen of the West* 71

Ramseur, Stephen 173
Rappahannock Station, Battle of 93, 94, 231n18, 231n22
Rawlins, John A. 5, 10, 28, 29, 34, 47, 49, 69, 74, 81, 87, 101, 114, 152, 167, 168, 170, 185, 217, 218, 220, 232n42
Resaca, Georgia, Battle of 89
Richardson, Lester I. 164
Richmond, Kentucky 56
Ricketts, Brewerton 170, 171
Rives' Salient 204
Robertson's Tavern, Virginia 95, 96
Robinson, John C. 109, 115, 123, 125, 128, 233n1
Rockwell, Dr. Alonzo 214, 231n49, 232c4n49
Rodes, Robert E. 177
Roebling, Emily 217
Roebling, Washington 3, 97, 98, 103, 109, 110, 112, 128, 130, 131, 141–143, 147, 150, 155, 160, 163, 172, 173, 177, 178, 182, 185, 186, 190–192, 195, 202, 205–207, 217, 218, 232n21, 232n45, 235n9
Rosecrans, William S. 17, 62–67, 75–79, 91, 230n119
Rosser, Thomas L. 109, 115, 157
Rowley, William R. 33, 47
Russell, David A. 94, 151

St. Louis, Missouri 220
St. Mary's Church 191, 194, 198, 214
Samaria Church *see* St. Mary's Church
Sanitary Commission 37, 203
Savannah, Tennessee 37–39, 43
Schaff, Morris 116, 232n24
Schofield, John 67, 84, 88, 215, 216, 218, 221, 222
Scott, Gen. Winfield 7, 8, 10, 31, 225n2
Sedgwick, John 73, 93, 94, 98, 106, 111, 113, 114, 117, 130–133, 211
Seward, William H. 214

Index

Shady Grove 106, 162, 164, 177, 186
Shanks, William 17, 57, 62, 75, 228*n*140
Sheridan, Philip H. 3, 6, 17, 45, 46, 49, 56, 57, 59, 60, 62, 64, 65, 75–78, 82–84, 90, 94, 99–101, 105–107, 109, 110, 113–115, 118, 120–127, 129, 130, 132, 133, 136, 145, 148, 152, 154–156, 160, 161, 163–165, 167–171, 173, 175, 180, 186–190, 192, 194, 211, 213–220, 222, 223, 227*n*140, 228*n*20, 228*n*22, 228*n*23, 230*n*118, 231*n*49, 233*n*38, 235*n*102, 235*n*27
Sherman, John 8, 9, 149
Sherman, Thomas W. 88
Sherman, William T. 2–3, 6, 8, 9, 10, 15, 17, 23, 24, 31, 32, 34, 37, 38, 40–45, 47, 49, 50, 65–71, 73, 74, 78–80, 83–86, 88–91, 100, 101, 106, 147, 148, 152, 153, 160, 215, 216, 218–222, 228*n*15, 230*n*113, 230*n*132, 230*n*137, 231*n*45
Shiloh, Battle of 30, 38–48, 220, 227*n*132, 228*n*143
Sickles, Daniel E. 91, 99, 153, 231*n*4
Sigel, Franz 89, 102, 148, 150, 237*n*60
Sill, Joshua 228*n*22
Smith, Andrew J. 72
Smith, Charles F. 13, 15, 20, 21, 24, 26–31, 34–37, 40, 41, 48, 72, 226*n*31, 226*c*2*n*49
Smith, Giles 72
Smith, Kirby 54–56, 58–62
Smith, William F. "Baldy" 79, 80, 83–85, 152, 155, 161, 167, 170–175, 181–184, 188–190, 192, 196–200, 208, 230*n*112, 230*n*137, 237*n*82
Spotsylvania, Battle of 118–152, 154, 186, 233*n*1, 233*n*14, 233*n*17, 233*n*28, 234*n*48, 234*n*64
Sprague, William 150
Stanley, David 83
Stanton, Edwin 7, 17, 31, 33, 35, 36, 47, 50, 62, 63, 66, 70, 72, 75, 78, 85, 86, 91, 94, 101, 133, 136, 145, 147, 189, 199, 218, 220, 237*n*17
Steele's Bayou Expedition 68
Stone's River, Tennessee, Battle of 63–65, 76
Stuart J.E.B. 118, 120, 121, 123–125, 128, 130, 132, 136, 152, 160, 235*n*102
Sussex Road *see* Norfolk Pike
Swinton, John 182
Sykes, George 92, 95, 96, 99

Terrill, William R. 218
Terry, Alfred H. 202
Thomas, George H. 6, 8, 9, 16, 18, 48, 49, 55, 57, 59–62, 64, 73, 75–80, 82–84, 88, 215, 216, 218, 220–223, 226*c*1*n*57, 231*n*39
Tilghman, Lloyd 21, 22
Todd's Tavern 109, 114, 115, 118–123, 130, 133
Torbert, A.T.A. 100, 101, 107, 109, 110, 154, 158, 187, 194, 214, 235*n*13
Totopotomoy, Battle of 161–166, 170–172
Trevilian Station 192, 194, 214, 223
USS *Tyler* 13
Tyler, Robert O. 150

Upton, Emory 131, 137–140, 147, 170, 234*n*48, 234*n*79

Van Cleve, Horatio P. 77
Vanderbilt, William H. 214
Van Dorn, Earl 63, 65
Venable, Charles S. 106, 182, 232*n*9
Vickburg, Mississippi 49, 52, 65–68, 71–75, 78, 91, 229*n*65
Virginia Central Railroad 151, 154, 158, 160, 162

Wade, Benjamin F. 77
Wadsworth, James S. 109–115, 129, 232*n*45
Wainwright, Charles 171
Walk, Henry 13
Walker, Francis A. 134, 138, 139, 146, 151, 175, 196, 198, 205, 233*n*24
Wallace, Lewis 24, 26, 27, 28–31, 43, 44, 47, 226*n*31
Wallace, W.H.L. 225*n*30
Warren, Gouverneur K. 3, 90–93, 95–99, 102, 107, 109, 111–118, 121, 123, 125, 128–136, 138, 141–152, 155–160, 162–165, 169–178, 182–191, 201–203, 205–209, 211, 214, 217, 222, 223, 231*n*22, 231*n*44, 232*n*45, 233*c*6*n*19, 233*c*6*n*30, 233*n*17, 234*n*48, 235*n*13, 236*n*56, 238*n*66
Washburn, Cadwallader 32, 73
Washburne, Elihu 1, 5, 6, 10, 19, 30, 32–34, 36, 39, 40, 47, 49, 51, 103, 139, 223
Weitzel, Godfrey 202
Wheeler, Joseph 64
White House Landing 167, 170, 175, 181, 188, 194, 214
Wilcox, Cadmus M. 158
Wilcox's Landing 195
Wilder, John T. 77
Wilderness, Virginia 97
Wilderness, Virginia, Battle of 103–120, 122, 128, 129, 160, 189, 233*c*6*n*10, 233 *c*6*n*11, 233 *c*6*n*19
Wilderness Church 107
Wilderness Tavern 103, 106, 107, 120
Wilson, James H. 68–70, 72, 74, 79–81, 84–86, 88, 90, 101, 103, 107–110, 115, 116, 122–126, 129, 132, 136, 152, 155, 161, 162, 168, 171, 173, 175, 182, 183, 185, 187, 188, 190, 191, 194, 198, 212, 213, 223, 229*n*55, 230*n*146, 232*n*14, 232*n*42, 237*n*82
Wood, Thomas J. 82, 83, 230*n*119
Wright, Horatio 56, 57, 59, 66, 94, 110, 111, 113, 114, 129–131, 133, 134, 138–146, 148, 151, 152, 162, 168–170, 173–175, 181, 182, 202, 223, 228*n*7, 234*n*48

Yates, Richard 5
Yazoo Pass, Mississippi 68, 71
Yellow Tavern, Battle of 160, 235*n*102
Young, John Russell 213, 218, 221, 222, 228*n*141

www.ingramcontent.com/pod-product-compliance
Lightning Source LLC
Chambersburg PA
CBHW081549300426
44116CB00015B/2813